ILLINOIS GENEALOGICAL RESEARCH

by

George K. Schweitzer, Ph.D., Sc.D.
407 Ascot Court
Knoxville, TN 37923-5807

Wordprocessing by
Anne M. Smalley

TABLE OF CONTENTS

Chapter 1

ILLINOIS BACKGROUND

1. Geography

The state of Illinois (hereafter IL), which was admitted to the US in 1818 as the 21st state, is located in the central section of the Midwest. The state is in the shape of a rough upright rectangle with the lower left-hand corner cut off appreciably and the lower right-hand corner cut off slightly. There is also a bulge at the center of the left side. IL is about 380 miles tall and about 210 miles wide at its extremes. See Figure 1. IL is bordered on the north by WI, on the east by Lake MI, IN, and the Wabash River (with southern IN just across), on the west by the MS River across which lie IA and MO, and on the south by the OH River, across which rests KY. Its capital city Springfield is centrally located, and has a population of about 106,000 (106 K). The other large cities in the state are Chicago (2784 K) in the northeast, Rockford (140 K) in the north, Peoria (114 K) in the northcentral, Aurora (99K) just west of Chicago, Napierville (86K) just west of Chicago, and Decatur (84K) in the center. The total population of the state is about 11,800K, and the population of the IL portion of the Chicago Metropolitan Area is about 7,600K, so well over half of IL's people live in the Chicago area.

The state of IL has four major land regions, the Lake Plains in the northeast, the Dubuque Hills in the far northwestern corner, the Central Plains in the center, and the Hills and Lowlands in the south. These are depicted in Figure 2. The LAKE PLAINS region is an area of gently-rolling fertile lowlands with many small lakes, low hills, and some marshes. It is made up chiefly of the metropolitan Chicago area. The DUBUQUE HILLS occupy a small triangle in the far northwestern corner of the state. The area is chiefly only one county (Jo Daviess). It is characterized by high hills and deep valleys, the hills being the highest in IL. The HILLS AND LOWLANDS region occupies the very lower tip of IL. Along the banks of the OH River is a narrow lowland area. Behind it to the north are the Shawnee Hills, a band of hills, valleys, and river bluffs varying from 10 miles wide in the west to 40 miles wide on the east. The CENTRAL PLAINS, which make up the remaining 90% of the state's area, are generally fairly flat, and have rich soil. At the time of settlement, they were mainly treeless grassy prairie land with trees in the river valleys and patches or groves of trees spotting the prairie.

Figure 1. IL and Its Neighbors

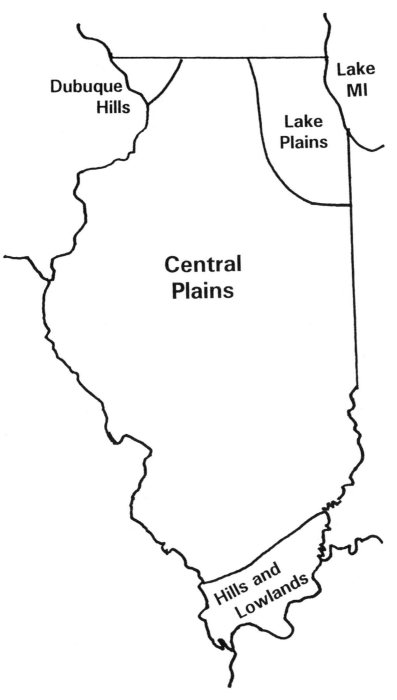

Figure 2. Land Regions of IL

IL is a state whose borders are largely determined by waterways: the MS River on the west, the OH River on the south, the Wabash River on the southeast, and Lake MI in the northeast. See Figure 3. The state thus sits at the focal point of a vast network of water routes, connecting the Rocky Mountains in the west (Platte and MO Rivers into the MS River), MN in the north (MS River), LA and the Gulf in the south (MS River), TN and KY in the southeast (TN, KY, and Cumberland Rivers into the OH River), PA in the east (OH River), northern IN and OH in the northeast (Wabash River), and the Great Lakes (from MN in the west to the St. Lawrence River in the east).

The interior rivers of IL are also of immense importance. Most of the state drains from the northeast to the southwest, with the exception of the southeastern area which drains to the southeast. Now take a look at IL's interior rivers which are shown in Figure 4. The principal internal river of IL is the IL River which flows from the northeast to the southwest. It is made up in the northeast by the confluence of the Des Plaines and the Kankakee Rivers, and as it flows southwestward is fed by the following tributaries: the Fox, Vermilion, Mackinaw, Spoon, and Sangamon Rivers. The IL River then joins the MS River (MS) just north of St. Louis. In northwestern IL, the Rock River enters from WI at the center of the northern border, then flows southwestward to join the MS River. In the southeast the Kaskaskia and the Big Muddy Rivers empty into the MS River. And in the southwest, the Embarrass and the Little Wabash Rivers flow into the Wabash River. It is important that you understand this river geography of IL since the rivers of IL were its early transportation and communication routes and thereby influenced its pioneer settlement and development. An important portage in northeastern IL is the very short one between Lake MI and the Des Plaines River. This occurs at the site of present-day Chicago. Such a portage gave early travelers access to the interior of IL as well as a route from the Great Lakes waterway network to the MS River waterway network.

2. The French period

As of about 1600, the area now defined by IL was inhabited by a loose confederation of Indian tribes, chief of which were the Illini. About this time, three European nations were beginning to become active in North America: Spain, France, and England. In 1565, the Spanish had placed outposts in the FL area, and soon thereafter in GA country. Then, in

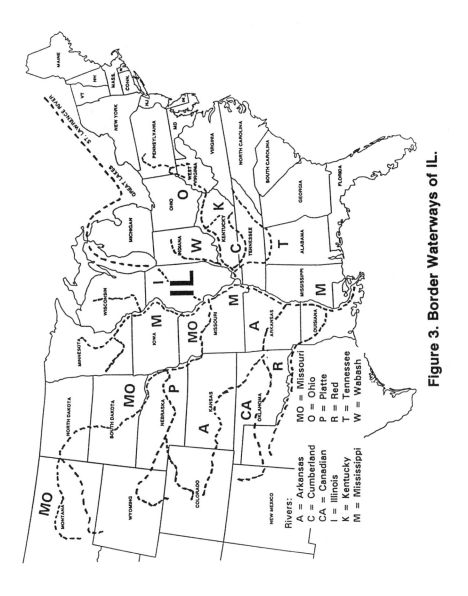

Figure 3. Border Waterways of IL.

10

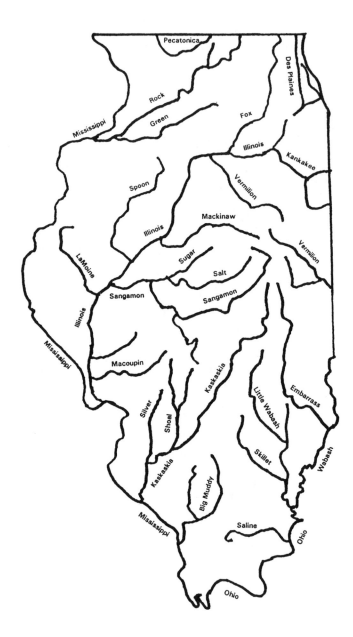

Figure 4. Interior Waterways of IL.

1598, they had begun operations in what is now NM. In 1604, the French founded Port Royal (now in Nova Scotia), then in 1608 settled Quebec to establish New France. They began to explore the interior, and to engage in fur trading and missionary activities, as they moved progressively southwest and west from Quebec. About the same time, in 1607, the English planted a colony at Jamestown in VA, and settlements began to spread north, south, and west of that center. The second Charter of VA, framed in 1609, gave the Northwest Country, including the IL area, to the colony of VA. By the 1660s, a few French trappers, traders, and missionaries had penetrated into the western Great Lakes area and soon were to move into the upper MS Valley. Some of these were probably working in what is now IL.

In 1673, the French explorer Jolliet and the French missionary priest Marquette came into Lake MI, crossed what is now central WI, found the WI River, at the mouth of the WI River entered the MS River, and travelled down it to the AR River. There they turned back, came up the MS River, entered the IL River, took it to the Des Plaines River, portaged to Lake MI, and went back to their base at St. Ignace which was located at the northern end of Lake MI. In 1675, Marquette returned and formed the Mission of the Immaculate Conception on the IL River near Starved Rock, which is just west of present Ottawa. In 1680, LaSalle and his Italian lieutenant Tonti came south on Lake MI, joined the Kankakee River in northwestern IN, and came down it to the IL River. At a site just opposite present-day Peoria, he built Ft. Crevecoeur (Heartbreak) and left a contingent there to begin to secure the area for the French Empire. When he returned a few months later, he found that the men had mutinied, stolen the supplies, wrecked the fort, and deserted. After leading an expedition in 1681 to the mouth of the MS River, claiming all the lands he had traversed for Spain, and naming them Louisiana, LaSalle returned to IL country and built Ft. St. Louis on Starved Rock on the IL River (just west of where Ottawa is today). He put Tonti in charge, some French settled nearby, and land patents were issued. The structure at Starved Rock was abandoned in 1691, and a new Ft. St. Louis (Ft. Pimitoui) was built downstream at the site of Peoria. Very quickly a mission and a village grew up around it, thus it became the first European settlement in IL. In 1696, the Mission of the Guardian Angel was established on the site of Chicago, but it was short-lived because of Indian hostility.

Meanwhile, Louisiana began to be settled, Mobile and Biloxi in 1699, and later, Natchitoches in 1714, and New Orleans in 1718. Four years after, New Orleans was made the capital. In 1699, priests of the Seminary of Foreign Missions at Quebec established the Mission of the Holy Family at Cahokia (just south of the site of East St. Louis). Cahokia stood at the north of a very fertile MS River flood plain which ran southward along the river for over 70 miles. Very soon a village grew up around the mission, and settlers began to farm the rich lands. In 1703, Jesuit priests reactivated the Mission of the Immaculate Conception at a site about 60 miles south of Cahokia near the mouth of the Kaskaskia River. The settlement was called Kaskaskia, and in addition to the fertile land, there were salt deposits close by. It, too, grew, and the region rapidly became the food source for the French in the MS Valley. Its importance to Louisiana was recognized in 1717 when the area was taken from Canadian governance and made a district under the French province of Louisiana. In 1720, slaves were introduced to work the farms, and Ft. de Chartres, a district capital, was completed about 15 miles north of Kaskaskia. This stronghold served as the governmental and military seat of the villages in the region. Other villages were soon settled, including Prairie du Rocher, one around Fort de Chartres, and St. Phillippe. A settlement was also made across the MS River at Ste. Genevieve (MO). As of 1723, there were about 200 European residents in Kaskaskia, 130 in Prairie du Rocher, 15 in Cahokia, and perhaps 40 more in other nearby locations. The area's prosperity soared as New Orleans became more important. By 1732, the non-native population totalled over 600, about 170 being black slaves. The non-native population grew to about 2000 in 1753, approximately 500 being slaves.

The French Empire in North America seemed quite secure and prosperous as of 1749. It extended from northeastern Canada to the Great Lakes to New Orleans with forts and stations all along the way. However, English fur traders, chiefly from VA and PA, continued to push down the OH River and toward IL. They were paying more for the furs, and were giving the Indians better trading goods at lower prices, so the Indians were slowly abandoning the French market for the English. In order to redress this trend, the French destroyed an English trading post in OH in 1752, and began building a series of forts between themselves and the English. The most strategically-located of these forts was Fort Duquesne which was set up in 1754 at the present-day site of Pittsburgh. In the IL country, they added Ft. Ascension (Massac) at the southern tip of IL on the OH River.

In this same year of 1754, the French and Indian War broke out in North America. This conflict was an extension of French-British warfare in Europe. The major actions of the War took place to the east of the IL country, with many Indians siding with the French and the Iroquois fighting on the British side. At first the French prevailed, but soon the British took the upper hand, and in 1758, the major French bulwark in PA, Fort Duquesne, fell to the British forces. It was renamed Fort Pitt. In the succeeding year, 1789, Quebec fell to the British, and then in 1760, Montreal was conquered. These major British victories forced France to relinquish the Northwest area including IL. In 1763, the Treaty of Paris formally ended the French and Indian War, and resulted in the transfer of almost everything east of the MS River to Britain. The British also received Florida from Spain, and Spain received New Orleans and the French lands west of the MS River. To avoid British rule, many of the French in the IL country crossed over to the new village of St. Louis (MO), which was set up in 1764.

3. The British period

No sooner had the French and Indian War ended than the Indians were stirred up by a leader called the Prophet. He encouraged them to rise up and retake the lands that the English had now received from the French. The challenge was taken up by the Ottawa Indian chief Pontiac, who united several tribes, then put Detroit under siege. Many Indians of the IL-IN country joined the effort and soon captured Forts Miami (Fort Wayne) and Quiatenon (Lafayette). Other forts fell, so that by the middle of 1763 nine British outposts had fallen to the Indians, and Fort Pitt was also under siege. As winter came on, and supplies became scarce, Pontiac's forces dwindled, the captured forts were abandoned, and the sieges were lifted. To placate the Indians, the British issued the Proclamation of 1763, which forbid colonists to settle west of the Appalachian Mountains, the area being reserved for Indians and fur traders. A British agent Croghan was dispatched to the northwest area to make peace with the Indians for the British occupation.

In 1765, the British occupied Ft. de Chartres, renaming it Ft. Cavendish. A census showed about 1050 French in the district, with about 600 of them in Kaskakia, 130 in Prairie du Rocher, 60 in Cahokia, 15 at Chartes Village, and 15 at St. Phillippe, a total of about 1100. The French were permitted to stay, to practice their Catholic religion, to keep their slaves, and peace was made with the Indians. The Proclamation of 1763 was not effective in keeping land speculators and settlers back in the east. In the 1760s they flooded into western PA, and in the 1770s, they surged into KY. Some American settlers, however, came as far as IL.

They asked for self-government in 1771, but were refused. In 1772, the British abandoned Ft. de Chartres, and left a small garrison at Kaskaskia. From then on, the IL country was treated to neglect, civil chaos prevailed, and the population diminished. The British finally put a Frenchman in charge and left the region. In order to attempt to forestall the occupation of the northwest country by people violating the Proclamation of 1763, the British attached the area (everything south to the OH River and west to the MS River) to Quebec in 1774.

In 1775, the American Revolution broke out between the thirteen colonies along the eastern coast and the mother country. The fundamental issue was the denial to the colonials of their rights and freedoms as British citizens. In the west, the British set up military headquarters at Detroit, and from there, they supported Indian raids into western PA and KY. A fort on the IL border at Vincennes (IN) was strengthened and the Indians in that area were armed. George Rogers Clark of KY (a VA county) was commissioned to suppress the Indian raids and to take the British forts in the area northwest of the OH River. In 1778, Clark took the British outpost at Kaskaskia in southwestern IL, then he marched eastward to Vincennes and took over that fortress also. Upon receiving word of the loss of Vincennes, a British force was dispatched from Detroit. They attacked Vincennes and regained it, but a second expedition from Kaskasia under Clark retook the fort in early 1779. On the basis of this victory, VA organized the area into Illinois County, VA, with the county seat at Kaskaskia. A county official was sent there, civil and criminal court jurisdiction was organized, and a court at Vincennes granted land. The year 1779 saw the establishment of the first entirely-English settlement in IL. Near the site of present-day Waterloo, settlers from VA and MD set up Bellefontaine. In 1783, peace was signed between Britain and the new United States in Paris, and the entire northwestern country was given over to the US. However, the British delayed abandoning several of their forts up near the Canadian border, including Fort Miami(Fort Wayne) and Ouiatenon (Lafayette) in the IN country. Late in the year, the state of VA conveyed all of these northwestern lands over to the US, except for a small tract in IN (the Clark tract) and a large area in OH called the VA Military Tract. The IL country was left without a governmental structure, and several years of lawlessness set in.

4. The Northwest Territory period

KY was a major destination of settlers after the Revolutionary War, and the population there was to rise to over 70,000 in the next seven years. As KY filled, some frontiersmen began to settle on the north side of the OH River, particularly in southern OH and southern IN. The US, apprehensive that hordes of settlers were about to stream into the area northwest of the OH River, in 1785 enacted a Land Ordinance which provided for the survey of the region into square townships six miles on a side. Each township was then subdivided into 36 numbered square-mile sections. This would allow every bit of land to be identified for purposes of sale. The new ordinance provided for land to be sold at auctions held in the East, and the minimum purchase was set at 640 acres. This arrangement was not satisfactory for many would-be settlers and they protested vigorously. The US Army was stationed along the OH River to protect surveyors, and two companies of troops occupied a fort just opposite Louisville. In 1787, about 100 soldiers were stationed at Vincennes, which had grown to have 900 French and 400 American inhabitants. At this time, about 65 Americans were living in the Cahokia-Kaskaskia region (Bellefontaine, New Design, Kaskaskia), a few of them having come as early as 1779.

In 1787, the US Congress passed the Northwest Ordinance which set up the Northwest Territory and provided for its government. The territory included all of what is now OH, IN, IL, MI, WI, and part of MN. The act provided for a governor, a court of three judges, and a secretary. It provided for an elected legislature when the population reached 5000 voters, and for statehood when the population reached 60,000. The capital was established at Marietta (now in OH). In the year following, about 20,000 pioneers entered the Northwest Territory, most coming across from KY or down the OH River. The majority of these people were of Scots-Irish extraction. In 1790, the governor of the Territory visited the settlements at Kaskaskia and Cahokia, and found only about 750 people in the Cahokia-Kaskaskia region. The period of lawlessness had taken its toll on the population. Shortly thereafter the governor made Kaskaskia, Cahokia, and Prairie du Rocher joint county seats of St. Clair County, a county set up for the southwestern part of the IL country. Almost all of the eastern half of the IL country was included in Knox County, which also contained part of OH, all of IN, and parts of MI and WI. Its county seat was Vincennes. In order to stem the French exodus from IL, as of 1791, 400 acres was granted to any family who had been there before 1783.

In 1794, several of the most powerful Indian tribes were defeated at the Battle of Fallen Timbers (in northwestern OH near the IN border).

In the year after, in the Treaty of Greenville large tracts of land were ceded to the US. Included were several important areas in the IL country: land at the mouth of the Chicago River, all lands occupied by white settlers, land at and around Peoria, land at the mouth of the IL River, and land at Fort Massac on the southern tip of IL. The next year, 1795, saw the southern part of St. Clair County split off as Randolph County with the county seat at Kaskaskia. The county seat of St. Clair County now became Cahokia. In 1797, about 150 VA Baptists came to the Cahokia-Kaskaskia area to the village of New Design.

5. The IN Territorial period

By 1798, the Northwest Territory qualified to enter the second stage of its government. A lower legislative house was elected, and an upper house was appointed. In May of 1800, most of the land west of the present IN-OH line was split off from the Northwest Territory. It was constituted as a new territory, the IN Territory, with Vincennes as its capital. There were about 5600 people in the entire IN Territorial area, about 3100 being in what is present-day IN, and about 2500 in the IL country. In the old French villages, there were about 720 people at Cahokia, 470 at Kaskaskia, 210 at Prairie du Rocher, and 100 at Peoria. In the newer American settlements, there were about 290 at Bellefontaine, 250 in southern St. Clair County, 90 at Ft. Massac, and 340 scattered at various small places in between Cahokia and Kaskaskia. Not too many settlers were coming into IL because of Indian raids, problems with the French, lack of effective government, and failure to open the land for sale. The old arrangement for land sales was amended in 1800 to make it easier for settlers to obtain land in the territories. This new Land Act of 1800 reduced the minimum purchase to 320 acres, began to set up land offices near the land, and permitted sales on credit. The liberalized regulations eventually led to a flood of migration into the new territory.

The new IN Territory received a governor, a secretary, and a court with three judges. Harrison, the new governor, immediately began negotiations with the Indians, and a number of treaties followed in the next decade and a half. Among the things that this permitted was the re-establishment of a fort at the site of Chicago, Ft. Dearborn being constructed in 1803. The slave holders in the Cahokia-Kaskaskia region were not satisfied with the anti-slavery provision of the 1787 Northwest Ordinance, and fearful that it would be enforced, petitioned for help. The governor placated them by enacting a law which permitted long-term indentures. In 1804, US land offices were opened at Vincennes and Kaskaskia. However, there were no land sales at Kaskaskia for about 10 years, because the officials were busy settling claims for lands granted during the French and British periods. Even so, there was considerable migration into IL, such that by 1809, the population was about 12,000.

During the period when IL was part of the IN Territory (1800-09), an important set of events involving the lands west of IL took place. In 1801, Napoleon obtained from Spain a vast territory west of the MS River up to the Rocky Mountains, hoping to re-establish a French presence in North America. His plans did not materialize following the failure of an diversionary expedition to quell a rebellion in Santo Domingo. So Napoleon sold the area, Louisiana, to the US in 1803. This act moved the western frontier from IL much farther west and completely opened the MS River and New Orleans to US trade. IL became the central focus of the nation with water transportation routes in all directions. And, interestingly, this occurred on the eve of the coming of the steamboat, which occurred in 1811.

6. The IL Territorial period

In 1809, the IL Territory (IL, WI, part of MN) was split from the IN Territory, with its capital at Kaskaskia. Two counties made up the Territory, Randolph covering the lower fourth of the area, and St. Clair all the rest. During the IL territorial period (1809-18), 13 more counties would be created, almost all in the south, where settlement was occurring. The English speaking settlers who had already started coming in 1779 would increase greatly and rapidly. These people were mostly of southern upland stock, chiefly Scots-Irish, England-Scotland border people, and German. Their forefathers had come from the British Isles and Germany to the back country of PA, MD, VA, and the Carolinas, then had spread into KY and TN. From all these places, they had come down the OH River or crossed through KY to settle in southern IN and southern IL. Surveyors began marking IL in 1810 and in 1814 land was offered for sale. The Kaskaskia land office had opened in 1804 (for claims at first), Shawneetown would open in 1812, and Edwardsville in 1816. The numerous people who had simply squatted on the land prior to 1814 petitioned successfully for preemption laws. These laws gave them first chance at buying the land they occupied.

The year 1812 saw the breaking out of the War of 1812, with the northern Indians siding with the British against the US. The British quickly took Ft. Mackinac at the upper end of Lake MI, and Ft. Dearborn was ordered to be abandoned. There were about 60 troops and 40 civilians at the site. As they left the fort and began marching toward Ft. Wayne, they were attacked and massacred by Indian allies of the British, 60 men, 2 women, and 12 children being killed. This signalled a series of Indian attacks on the IL settlements along the frontier. Blockhouse forts were built on the frontier, military forces were raised, and counterattacks on Indian villages were mounted. Some settlers moved back from the frontier, immigration dropped to almost nil, and land sales were few. Gradually, the Indians were suppressed, a large confederacy of them was defeated at the Battle of the Thames in Canada near Detroit, they slowly abandoned the British, and raids on the settlers ended. The major conflicts of the War occurred back in the east and at New Orleans, with a peace being signed in Europe late in 1814, and word of it reaching the US in 1815. Shortly thereafter, the IL frontier was again rapidly being settled and moved northward. Its position at the end of the War was just north of the interface between southern and central IL. Ft. Dearborn at the site of Chicago was rebuilt in 1816, and trade and settlement around it resumed.

The US set aside the large triangle of IL land between the IL and MS Rivers for the awarding of 160-acres of bounty land to veterans of the War of 1812. In late 1817 the land was made available and within four months, over 18,000 land patents were issued. Most of these were sold by veterans or their widows to land speculators. Land at the land offices was selling on credit for about $2.00 an acre with a minimum purchase of 160 acres, which was reduced to 80 acres in 1817. The price was reduced to $1.25 per acre in 1820. Several Indian treaties negotiated during the time of the IL Territory put the US Government in possession of most of IL by 1818. In that year, IL applied for statehood, and even though its population was falsified as 40,258 (40,000 being required), IL was admitted in 1818. The actual population was nearer 35,000. Part of the approval for admission provided for the movement of the northern boundary of IL 41 miles north of the tip of Lake MI. This gave IL coastline on Lake MI and also the land that would later be the sites of Chicago and Rockford.

---

7. Early IL statehood

The capital of the new state of IL was located at Kaskaskia. No sooner had IL entered the Union in 1818 than a national depression set in, and westward migration was slowed. Recovery began soon, and once again settlers began coming in. The first settlements had been along the rivers in southern IL, but now pioneers began coming into the lands between the rivers and moving northward into the upper three fifths of the state. The major centers of trade were Kaskaskia in the southwest and Shawneetown, a new port on the OH River in the southeast. Land offices were located in both these towns, as well as at Edwardsville in west central IL. Near Edwardsville was the new town of Alton, a rapidly developing port on the MS River. As mentioned before, steamboat travel on the rivers increased, but steamboat travel on Lake MI did not become prevalent until 1832. Shawneetown became the port of entry for many immigrants. Unsurveyed land in the state was free, no one collected any taxes on such land, the right of preemption gave security, and often the improved land could be sold at a profit to a second settler. The original owner then moved west or north where more unsurveyed land was available.

In the year of 1820, the population had risen to a little over 55,000 and there were 19 counties functioning. The state capital was moved to Vandalia to try to keep pace with the direction of settlement. In 1823, many people went to Galena in northwestern corner of IL to work in the lead mines and smelter which were beginning large scale production. In IL at this time, there were holders of slaves and holders of indentured blacks plus a large number of people who desired IL to be a slave state. They launched a campaign to call a convention to amend the state constitution to permit slavery. An election of 1824 ended in the people voting against such a convention. IL, however, continued to have covert slavery in the form of indentures.

The Erie Canal in NY state opened in 1825. This new commercial waterway effected a direct connection between New England and NY and IL. The route ran north up the Hudson River, then west on the Mohawk River, joining the Erie Canal to arrive at Buffalo. From Buffalo, on Lake Erie to Detroit. Then overland across southern MI to northern IL. Or, from Detroit on Lake Huron to Lake MI to Chicago. By this time NY City had become the most used immigration port of the US, so foreigners as well as New Englanders and New Yorkers had a clear route to northern IL. And so, they came: New Yorkers, New Englanders, Irish, Germans, and later Italians, Swedes, Poles, and Russians. And they kept coming through the 1830s and 1840s.

By 1830, the IL population had risen to 157,000, and the state had 50 counties. IL Congressmen were pushing the federal government for lower land prices, better preemption rights for squatters, more land offices, more postal roads, and grants for transportation improvements. IL settlers about this time began to discover that the previously-avoided treeless prairies actually had richer soil than the timbered river valleys which had first been occupied. And so, cultivation of the prairies began. As newcomers moved into the north, they threatened the lands of the remaining Indians in northwest IL. The Sauk and Fox tribes were induced to go into IA in 1831, but the year following, a group of them returned. They initially defeated an IL militia force, but a reinforced militia drove them into WI and defeated them there. Shortly thereafter all other Indian tribes in IL ceded their lands and left the state.

The northern immigration resulted in the rapid growth of Chicago at its favored site on Lake MI. The Village of Chicago was incorporated in 1833 with 150 people. A land office was opened there in the following year. A new harbor was completed and steamboats began replacing the sailing vessels on the Great Lakes. The year 1836 was another formative year for Chicago, because in 1836 construction on the IL and MI Canal began. This canal was to connect Lake MI at Chicago with the IL River in north central IL, thus actually connecting Lake MI and the MS River. The canal was not finished until 1848, but it provided IL with the central position on a trade route that connected the East Coast with the Gulf of Mexico and served all the land along the way. The year 1837 saw Chicago made a city with a population of about 4000. Realizing the problems that prairie farmers were having with the old inadequate iron plow, Deere in 1837 invented the steel, self-cleaning plow. This remarkable improvement increased the productivity of the farmers greatly, and made of IL one of the leading agricultural areas of the US. The year 1838 saw the completion of the National Road from Cumberland, MD, to the IL border just west of Terre Haute, IN. The road provided another feeder route for the coming of immigrants to IL from the middle Atlantic states.

The state capital was moved to the centrally-located Springfield in 1839. In that year, Mormons fleeing from persecution in MO established the town of Nauvoo in Hancock County in west central IL. By 1842, there were over 16,000 Mormons in or near Nauvoo, and by 1845, it was the largest city in IL. Resentment and fear of the Mormon religion caused civil war to break out between the non-Mormons of the county and the Mormons. After two years of sporadic hostilities including the murder of the two Mormon leaders, the Mormons left in 1847. They went to UT and there founded Salt Lake City. IL in 1840 had a population of about 476,000, only approximately 10,000 of the people living in urban areas. The Mexican War was fought during 1846-48. IL with its many southern sympathizers saw the war as leading to statehood for TX, a slave state, so many favored it. When three regiments were called for, far more volunteers came forward than were needed. Six regiments were finally raised, two fighting at Buena Vista, two fighting at Cerro Gordo, and two did not engage in any battlefield action. In 1847, McCormick built a factory in Chicago to produce his new mechanical reaper. Other plants for the manufacture of further new mechanized farm machinery were to follow soon. They marked IL as becoming a pre-dominant agricultural state as well as the farm equipment center of the US.

Now, several genealogically-pertinent trends which occurred during this early period need to be recognized. The first of these is that the state was settled from the south to the north, the major reasons being the positions of the Indians and the locations of the transportation routes. This is readily seen by the opening dates for sales by the land offices: (1) in the south, Vincennes in 1804, Kaskaskia in 1809, Shawneetown in 1814, Edwardsville in 1816, Vandalia in 1821, (2) in the center, Springfield in 1823, Quincy in 1831, Danville in 1831, and (3) in the north, Galena in 1835, Chicago in 1835, and Dixon in 1840. Another way of viewing this is in terms of county formation. As of 1800, the number of counties with their southern borders in the south was 2, in the center 0, in the north 0. In 1810 the numbers were: south 2, center 0, north 0. In 1820, the numbers were: south 19, center 0, north 0. In 1830 the numbers were: south 28, center 19, north 4. In 1840, the numbers were: south 34, center 32, north 21.

The second item that is of import is the people who settled IL. The first immigrants who came into the southern portion were people of Ulster-Scot derivation (with some Scots, Germans and English) who came from KY, TN, western VA, western NC, northwestern SC, and western PA. The main routes their ancestors and they used were (1) from PA to western VA to western NC (or SC) to TN to KY to IL, (2) from PA to western VA to KY to IL, (3) from PA to western VA to TN to KY to IL, (4) from VA to western VA down the Kanawha River then down the OH River to IL, (5) from PA to western PA down the OH River to IL. The next immigrants who settled the central portion of the state were also from the southeastern state uplands (as above), from southern IL, and people from the mid-Atlantic states east of IL (PA, MD, DE, NJ, OH). Most of this last group came down the OH River or through the state of OH. The last section to be settled was north IL, and those settlers came from the mid-Atlantic states, from central IL, but chiefly from northeastern states (NY, NJ, New England). Many of the last group came into IL across the northern lakeshore routes, west on the Erie Canal, and on the Great Lakes. Not too many foreign-born immigrants came into IL early, but in the 1830s, Germans and Irish were coming in goodly numbers.

The third facet of IL's pioneer history that is genealogically relevant is its economy and transportation. The first residents were subsistence farmers, who quickly developed a surplus of produce, especially corn, wheat, cattle, and hogs. That surplus could be turned into prosperity only by developing good transportation to and from the farms. The earliest farmers had only horrible roads and the rivers, plus the blockage to the east of the Appalachian Mountains and the westward flow of the rivers. In order to reach eastern markets, IL produce had to go down the OH River to the MS River to New Orleans, then by sailboat to the Atlantic ports. The demand for improvements grew more pressing year by year. After the War of 1812, steamboat traffic reversed the flow of goods on the OH River, and improved canals and roads fed products from non-River farms to the OH River. Then, by the 1830s, steamboat operation on the Great Lakes to Chicago was well under way. This steamboat operation opened a shorter route to the east. And by 1838, the National Road had reached the state. The IL and MI Canal was about to be finished as of 1848, and railroads would soon be built.

The fourth aspect of the early statehood of IL is its religious situation. As you will recall, the pre-territorial period of the IL country was Catholic by virtue of the French control of the area. However, much of this was lost when the British took over, the main Catholic remnants being in the Cahokia-Kaskaskia region. When settlement by Americans began in the late 1700s, the predominant type of early religion was an evangelical Protestantism. This was due to the predominance of people from the upcountry of VA, NC, SC, TN, and KY during the territorial and early state years. Baptists came first in the 1787, followed by Methodists in late 1793. Baptist ministers were usually unpaid and uneducated farmer-preachers, who farmed six days a week and preached most of the day Sunday and on Wednesday evening. They conducted marriages and funerals, held emotionally-laden meetings, and kept church members under strict moral regulation. Methodist ministers were usually circuit riders (horseback travellers), who moved from one group to another for preaching services, established new congregations, and ministered to the spiritual needs of the people. They were not as emotionally oriented as the Baptists, but they also could get a good rousing revival going. Gradually, the congregations of these groups grew and began to build churches, the Methodists hiring permanent pastors. It is not to be inferred that all early settlers were church goers. To the contrary, many, if not most, were not actively concerned with organized religion.

Adherents of other denominations also came early as is indicated by the Presbyterians in 1802, the Congregationalists in 1809, and later the Episcopalians and the Lutherans. The Presbyterians differed considerably from the Baptists and Methodists in that they had a paid educated clergy, and therefore attracted people who were socially different. Their growth was thereby somewhat slower. As IL was being settled in the early 1800s, the people were participating in what came to be known as the Second Great Awakening. Sweeping the country were emotional revivals and camp meetings which were adding large numbers to the churches, including many of the unchurched of IL. The churches were providing important elements to IL's social structure: spiritual needs, moral stability, recreation, community, and emotional release. In 1832, a new religious group was organized in an attempt to do away with denominations. They believed that there were no denominations, there were only individuals who could be simply called Disciples or Christians. The movement, which began in KY and PA, quickly spread into IN and IL, and many people rapidly embraced it. The result, as one might suspect, was the development of a new denomination, one called the Disciples of Christ. Catholic regrowth was sufficient by 1834 that a Catholic bishop was seated at Vincennes, and in 1843 a new diocese was established in Chicago. By the end of the pioneer period (1848), the leading IL churches in order of their numbers were Methodist, Baptist, Presbyterian, Disciples of Christ, Roman Catholic, Lutheran, Congregationalists, and Episcopalians. Smaller-numbered groups were the Quakers, United Brethren, Mennonites, German Amish, Dunkards, and Moravians.

8. The Civil War era

The next period of IL's history is termed the Civil War era, which dates from 1848 to 1865. This name was chosen because the issues involved in the War were those that increasingly affected the national agenda during these years. The northern states and the southern states had been in controversy over slave-holding, slave law enforcement, tariffs, and admissions of new states for a sizable number of years. However, the differences had been settled by compromise and trade-offs. In the 1850s, the differences became more extreme, and there was a growing sense that peaceful resolution might not continue to work. The two opposite forces were strongly at work in IL, with people supporting and implementing the Underground Railroad and many people expressing strong sympathies toward the southern positions. This latter was largely due to the fact that many IL citizens had their origins in slave states.

In 1848, the IL and MI Canal was finished, this waterway altering the trade measurably, particularly by making the route to the eastern states much shorter and easier. Such great changes had occurred in the state that the people saw fit to frame a revised constitution, this task being accomplished in 1848. By 1850, the population of IL had grown to about 851K, with 67K having been born in NY, 64K in OH, 50K in KY, 38K in PA, 38K in Germany, and 32K in TN. In the early 1850s, many veterans of the Mexican and Indian Wars were granted 160 acres of land in IL in between the MS and IL Rivers. Most of them sold their holdings to speculators who fostered the rapid settlement of this area. The major event of the 1850s for the US was the growing animosity between the states. For IL, however, the major event of the 1850s was the coming of the railroads, centering in the granting of a charter for the construction of the IL Central Railroad in 1851, the construction from 1851-56, and its completion in 1856.

IL was granted 2,595,000 acres of land by the US government in 1851 to build a south-to-north railroad. The contract was won by an eastern group who took the name of the IL Central Railroad Company. They planned a Y-shaped rail line from Cairo north to a new town Centralia, then branching northeast to Chicago, and northwest to Galena. Much of the line ran through rich prairie land which had not been settled very much. The railroad was given every other section (each one mile square) for five miles on each side of the tracks. The IL Central recruited laborers to build the line and settlers to take up the land along the tracks in IL, the eastern states, and in Europe, especially Ireland and Germany. A few years before construction was started and continuing during construction, other railroads were being built from east to west across the state. These intersected the IL Central lines and formed a network with broad IL coverage. The MI Central and MI Southern lines reached Chicago in 1852, and tracks were extended northwest, west, and southwest from Chicago. This gave Chicago a pivotal position for trade in the midwest, it being the terminus of the IL and MI Canal, the center of lines from the east and extending westward, the major port of Lake MI, and the northern terminus of the IL Central Railroad, which connected to every portion of the state, and beyond. Chicago thus had transportation routes in every direction; north, east, west, and south. New York was the major trade and immigration center of the US, and Chicago forged contracts with her merchants to make Chicago New York City's western trade partner.

Development of the lands along the IL Central and its tributaries' tracks added to IL's growing production of wheat, corn, cattle, and hogs. And Chicago became the grain and meat-packing center of the entire area. And so, IL's economy grew in the 1850s, as farming prospered, manufacturing industries made several notable starts, transportation (canals, roads, railroads) expanded, more markets called for the state's produce, quarries and mines opened, the mines producing the coal needed by the railroads. The increased trade with the north and the east led to a weakening of the ties of IL with the south. The towns began to increase in size, and professionals and skilled laborers began to practice in them. The railroads began taking the traffic away from canals, which started to decline. German and Irish immigration increased, many of the Germans and most of the Irish being Catholic.

The population stood at about 1712K in 1860, the numbers having more than doubled in 10 years. Urbanization had begun with the largest cities now being Chicago (112K), Peoria (14K), Quincy (14K), Springfield (9K), and Galena (8K). Of the 1712K population, 131K had been born in OH, 310K in Germany, 121K in NY, 88K in Ireland, and 83K in PA. Most families who came from the south were now in their second generation.

The Douglas-Lincoln debates of 1858 placed Lincoln in the national spotlight as a worthy opponent of the famed Douglas, and gave a national audience to Lincoln's appeal that the nation not be divided regarding slavery. This led to Lincoln's election as US president in 1860. In early 1861, southern states challenged the Union by bombarding and capturing the Federal Fort Sumter in Charleston, SC. This marked the outbreak of the Civil War, with IL facing the conflict divided by sympathy for the south and loyalty to the north. When Lincoln called for troops, however, IL, both north and south, met its quota with far more than the number called for. The town of Cairo, projecting as an arrow into the south, became the military staging place and supply depot for the War in the west. As the War wore on, more and more wounded and dead shocked IL into the realization that it would be a long, hard struggle. Popularity for the Union declined, there rose organizations advocating letting the southern states go, the draft was viewed unfavorably by some, desertions increased, attempts were made to remake the constitution to make slavery legal, and the political split between the peace-promoting-Democrats and Republicans grew. In spite of all this, Lincoln had a great reservoir of grass-roots support and was re-elected in 1864. By this time, the last Confederate victory was long in the past. Soon Lee surrendered to Grant and Johnston surrendered to Sherman, effectively ending the war. However, before Lincoln could put his forgiving and redemptive programs for the south into effect, he was assassinated.

IL had fielded over 259,000 men, about 35,000 of them dying while in service. Deaths from disease made up about 23,000 of these, battle deaths about 6000, deaths from wounds in battle about 4000, and approximately 2000 from other causes. The fighting men of IL made up 150 infantry regiments, 17 cavalry regiments, two light artillery regiments, eight military batteries, some special units, and over 2000 sailors and marines. IL soldiers fought chiefly in the western arena of the war, but quite a number also participated in battles in the eastern theater. To support the war effort, IL's agriculture operated at full strength, factories multiplied, and more mines and smelters were developed,

Despite some opposition, IL voters were ready to accept the 13th, 14th, and 15th amendments to the US Constitution (slavery abolished, rights of citizenship not to be limited, vote not to be denied on basis of race), and ratified them all. During Reconstruction, IL harbored both a demand for punishment of the south and a demand for leniency and forgiveness, but the former attitude prevailed both in the state and nationally. This attitude gradually faded, and by the early 1870s, its strength was largely dissipated. In spite of the turbulence of the War, German and Irish immigrants kept coming in larger numbers to IL during 1840-70.

9. The Post-Civil War era

During the War Between the States, IL's farming, mining, forestry, and industry had developed to support the military effort. These trends continued at an ever accelerating pace after the conflict. Large-scale mechanized agriculture increased as agricultural implements, machinery, techniques, and fertilizers were improved. The increased profits from the increased produce were mainly put back into land development which greatly increased the land under cultivation. To protect their interests, IL farmers organized as the Grange in the 1870s. They protested the high rates that the railroads and the warehouses were charging them. In 1871, they were able to get the legislature to put into effect laws regulating these charges, further such laws being passed in succeeding years.

In 1871, a fire started in Chicago and was rapidly spread into the city business district by strong winds. The dry wooden buildings of the district were ignited and the fire grew in intensity. By the next day the uncontrollable conflagration had moved in a northerly direction. By the time a rainstorm extinguished the flames, over 2100 acres had been consumed. About 300 people died and over 18,000 buildings valued at $200 million dollars were lost. The city's recovery was remarkable, both in its extent and in its rate, and a era of phenomenal prosperity was inaugurated. Chicago became a center for meat packing, metal product manufacturing, farm machinery, grain milling, rail and water transportation, and wholesale and retail trade. This prosperity also started to develop in other IL cities as mills and factories were set up there. New settlers continued to arrive in IL, and coal mining in the south developed markedly. As of 1870, the population in IL stood at 2,540K people with about 600K of them in urban areas.

Not only did farmers organize in the 1870s to improve their lot, so did laboring men, especially factory workers, miners, and railroad workers. There were bitter disputes between labor and management during the 1870s and 1880s. The issues which the labor unions were interested in were wages, hours, child labor, and working conditions. Union activities resulted in a number of work stoppages and strikes, some of them bloody. There were also several riots, one of the most violent being the Haymarket Riot in Chicago in 1886. Slowly, wages were raised, the workday was shortened, child labor was regulated, and safer working conditions were provided. The labor unrest continued into the 1890s and up to World War I. In 1892, a laborer-farmer coalition elected Altgeld governor, and under him the state government became an active agent of reform in workmen's compensation, safety practice, factory inspection, and civil service practices. The population of IL in 1880 was about 3,100K with 940K being urban dwellers. In 1890 the figures showed a population of 3,800K with 1,700K being city people. In this year (1890),

IL had become the third largest state and Chicago the second largest city in the US.

In 1893, IL participated in the national economic panic of the country. This resulted in factory closures, bank failures, labor unrest, and hard times for much of the population. Recovery was fairly rapid, and was well underway when the US fought the Spanish-American War of 1898. Only a few IL men participated. German and Irish immigrations continued, and these newcomers were joined by people from east central Europe. Then with the development of more large industries, especially in northeastern IL, people from southeastern Europe began to come. By 1900, there was an urban population of 2,600K in a total state population of 4,800K, which meant that over half the state's people were urbanites. Chicago alone had 1,700K. And by 1910, Germans were most numerous among the foreign-born in IL (28%), Austrians and Hungarians next (16%), Scandanavians (12%), Russians (12%), Irish (8%), and Italians (6%). These peoples settled largely in the north of the state, the cities of Chicago, Joliet, and Rockford having half of their population foreign-born.

In 1900, a canal connecting Lake MI with the Des Plaines River at Chicago was completed. This development reversed the flow of water and sent Chicago's sewage downstate rather than into Lake MI. The IL government brought in numerous reforms in the 1900s and 1910s, including suffrage, welfare programs, election improvements, educational promotion, a civil service code, mine and factory safety laws, workmen's compensation, and anti-monopoly measures. Chicago and other IL cities made further progressive moves in the arts (museums, libraries, theater, music, galleries, architecture), building on foundations laid in the previous century. During these years many blacks entered the state, the large majority of them settling in Chicago. Although there were some black-white conflicts, slow progress was made in racial relations.

The industrial and agricultural growth of IL was further stimulated by the needs of the US in World War I (1917-18). IL provided over 314K troops for this War, and its citizens bought large quantities of war bonds. The 1920s in IL were characterized by governmental corruption at the state and local levels, and after prohibition began in 1920, by years of crime, violence, and gangsterism in Chicago. In other parts of the state violence erupted between bootleggers and the law, and bootleggers fought among themselves. During the 1920s, factory production continued to increase, railways were expanded, hard-surfaced roads were built, and the cities grew greatly. There were over 1,600K automobiles licensed in IL in 1929. A general depression began in the US in 1929, and in the early 1930s, IL suffered failed banks, farm mortgage foreclosures, industrial bankruptcies, and widespread unemployment. Government programs were put in place to assist the people and provide jobs, but a general degree of economic depression persisted. In the midst of this, oil fields were discovered in southeastern IL, and an oil boom ensued. The outbreak of World War II (1939-45) ended the depression, with industry and agriculture operating at full capacity to support the military action. Over 928K men and women from IL served in the armed forces. Of these, about 19K died. The economy of the state showed good strength after the War, with most people well off and many prospering. There have been several periods of slack economy since that time, several pollution crises, the Korean War, the Vietnam War, and the collapse of Communism. IL, the Prairie State, remains a land of promise for many people, with its notable agricultural, industrial, technological, and educational enterprises being among the best.

10. Illinois counties

Figure 5 presents the 102 counties of the State of IL as they have been since 1859 (except for some very small alterations in the border between Rock Island and Whiteside Counties). The IL counties arose in the following order. The counties which represent land in the present State of IL and which were set up by the Northwest Territory are: (1790) Knox, St. Clair, (1795) Randolph. Those established by the IL Territory are: (1809) Knox eliminated, area reassigned to St. Clair and Randolph, (1812) Madison, Gallatin, Johnson, (1814) Edwards, (1815) White, (1816) Jackson, Pope, Monroe, Crawford, (1817) Bond, (1818) Franklin, Union, Washington, (1819) Alexander, Clark, Jefferson, Wayne, (1821) Lawrence, Greene, Sangamon, Pike, Hamilton, Montgomery, Fayette, (1823) Edgar, Marion, Fulton, Morgan, (1824) Clay, Clinton, Wabash, (1825) Calhoun, Adams, Hancock, Henry, Knox, Mercer, Peoria, Putnam, Schuyler, Warren, (1826) Vermilion, McDonough, (1827) Shelby, Perry, Tazewell, Jo Daviess, (1829) Macoupin, Macon, (1830) Coles, McLean, (1831) Cook, LaSalle, Rock Island, Effingham, Jasper, (1833) Champaign, Iroquois, (1836) Will, Kane, McHenry, Ogle, Whiteside, Winnebago, (1837) Livingston, Bureau, Cass, Boone, DeKalb, Stephenson, (1839) Marshall, Brown, DuPage, Dane [Christian], Logan, Menard, Scott, Carroll, Lee, Jersey, Warren, DeWitt, Lake, Hardin, Stark, (1841) Henderson, Mason, Piatt, Grundy, Kendall, Richland, Woodford, (1843) Massac, Moultrie,

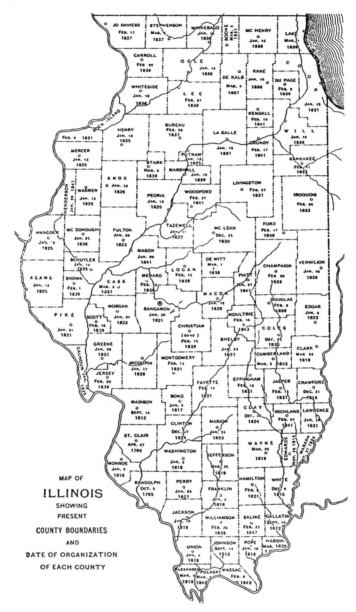

Figure 5. IL Counties since 1859. Map reproduced by permission of the Office of IL Secretary of State George H. Ryan.

Cumberland, Pulaski, (1847) Saline, (1853) Kankakee, (1859) Douglas, Ford.

As noted above, Figure 5 depicts the IL counties as they were in 1859 and as they continue to be. Figures 6 through 27, which appear at the end of this chapter, show the counties in the land area that is now the State of IL as they were in 1790, 1795, 1801, 1803, 1809, 1812, 1813, 1815, 1816, 1817, 1818, 1819, 1821, 1823, 1824, 1825, 1826, 1827, 1831, 1835, 1836, and 1839. These maps have been reproduced with the permission of the Office of IL Secretary of State George H. Ryan as they appear in the book listed below. Notice that the county formation proceeds from south to north, reflecting the settlement pattern of IL. For considerable detail on the formation of IL counties and the consequent boundary changes, see:

___ G. H. Ryan, ORIGIN AND EVOLUTION OF IL COUNTIES, IL Secretary of State, Springfield, IL, 1993.

___ J. H. Long and S. L. Hansen, HISTORICAL ATLAS AND CHRONOLOGY OF COUNTY BOUNDARIES, 1788-1980, G. K. Hall, Boston, MA, 1984, volume 2.

11. Recommended readings

A knowledge of the history, geography, government, and laws of IL and its local regions is of extreme importance for tracing the genealogies of its former inhabitants. This chapter has been a brief treatment of some of these. Your next step should be the reading of two of the following relatively short one-volumed works:

___ L. A. Carrier, IL, CROSSROADS OF A CONTINENT, University of IL Press, Urbana, IL, 1993.

___ R. P. Howard, IL, A HISTORY OF THE PRAIRIE STATE, Eerdmans Publishing Co., Grand Rapids, MI, 1972.

___ D. Buisseret, HISTORIC IL FROM THE AIR, University of Chicago Press, Chicago, IL, 1990.

___ R. J. Jensen, IL, A BICENTENNIAL HISTORY, Norton, New York, NY, 1978.

___ T. C. Pease and M. J. Pease, THE STORY OF IL, University of Chicago Press, Chicago, IL, 1965.

A six-volume set of books giving the history of IL in considerable detail was published by the IL Centennial Commission in 1917-20. The first four volumes of this set are generally accepted as excellent works, but the last two deal largely with the economics and politics of IL, ignoring much of the other material. Hence, the IL Sesquicentennial Commission sponsored replacements for the 5th and 6th volumes. The four volumes from 1917-20 and the two replacements published in 1977 and 1980 are:

___C. W. Alvord, THE IL COUNTRY, 1673-1818, IL Centennial Commission, Springfield, IL, 1920.

___S. J. Buck, IL IN 1818, IL Centennial Commission, Springfield, IL, 1918.

___T. C. Pease, THE FRONTIER STATE, 1818-48, IL Centennial Commission, Springfield, IL, 1922.

___A. C. Cole, THE ERA OF THE CIVIL WAR, 1848-70, IL Centennial Commission, Springfield, IL, 1922.

___J. H. Keiser, BUILDING FOR THE CENTURIES, IL 1865-98, University of IL Press, Urbana, IL, 1977.

___D. F. Tingley, THE STRUCTURING OF A STATE, IL 1899-1928, University of IL Press, Urbana, IL, 1980.

Two other multi-volumed histories of IL are:

___G. W. Smith, A HISTORY OF IL AND HER PEOPLE, American Historical Society, Chicago, IL, 1927, 6 volumes, last 3 volumes biography.

___E. F. Dunne, IL, HEART OF THE NATION, Lewis Publishing Co., Chicago, IL, 1933, 5 volumes, last 3 volumes biography.

Some specialized volumes of particular interest include:

___R. E. Banta, THE OH [RIVER], Rinehart, New York, NY, 1949.

___A. C. Boggess, THE SETTLEMENT OF IL, 1778-1830, Chicago Historical Society, Chicago, IL, 1908.

___P. W. Gates, THE IL CENTRAL AND ITS COLONIZATION WORK, Harvard University Press, Cambridge, MA, 1934.

___J. Gray, THE IL [RIVER], Rinehart, New York, NY, 1940.

___W. V. Pooley, THE SETTLEMENT OF IL FROM 1830-50, University of WI, Madison, WI, 1908.

___M. M. Quaife, LAKE MI, Bobbs-Merrill, New York, NY, 1944.

___M. Wyman, IMMIGRANTS IN THE VALLEY: IRISH, GERMAN, AND AMERICANS IN THE UPPER MS COUNTRY, Nelson-Hall, Chicago, IL, 1984.

For detailed listings of many works dealing with many aspects of the history of IL, the standard reference work is:

___J. Hoffmann, A GUIDE TO THE HISTORY OF IL, Greenwood Press, Westport, CT, 1991.

Definitely not to be overlooked is the major historical periodical dealing with IL. This journal is a gold mine of historical information, much of which is pertinent to IL genealogical research.

___IL HISTORICAL JOURNAL (until 1984 the JOURNAL OF THE IL STATE HISTORICAL SOCIETY), quarterly, IL State Historical Library, Springfield, IL, 1908-present. With three collective indexes covering 1908-33, 1934-57, and 1958-67.

Further historical materials in the publications of the IL State Historical Society are indexed in:

___J. N. Adams, INDEX TO THE TRANSACTIONS OF THE ISHS AND OTHER PUBLICATIONS OF THE ISHL, ISHL, Springfield, IL, 1953, 2 volumes. Also see [NEW] TRANSACTIONS OF THE ISHS, ISHL, Springfield, IL, 1984-85, in the back is a cumulative index to the 1980-85 volumes.

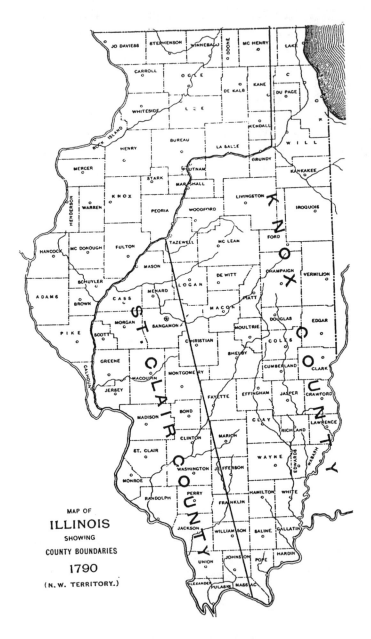

Figure 6. IL Counties in the NW Territory as of 1790. Map reproduced by permission of the Office of IL Secretary of State George H. Ryan.

35

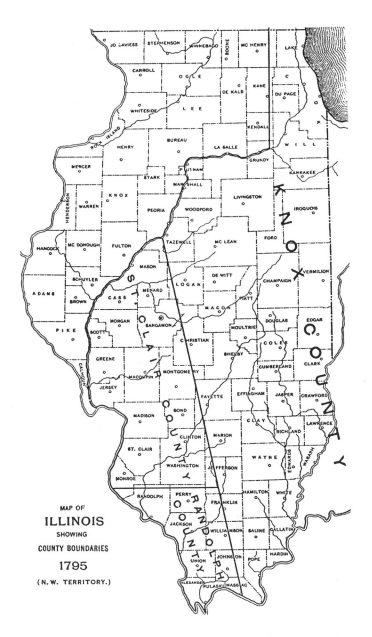

**Figure 7. IL Counties in the NW Territory as of 1795.
Map reproduced by permission of the Office of IL
Secretary of State George H. Ryan.**

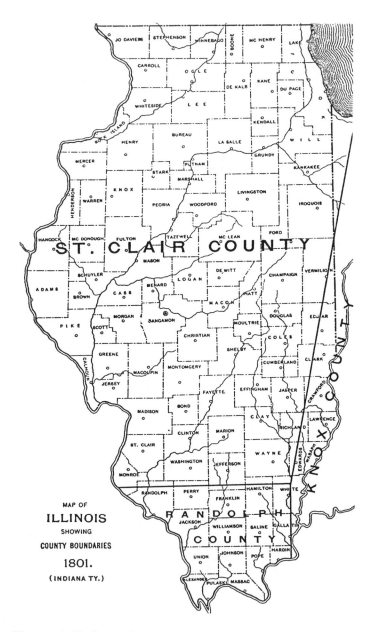

Figure 8. IL Counties in the IN Territory as of 1801. Map reproduced by permission of the Office of IL Secretary of State George H. Ryan.

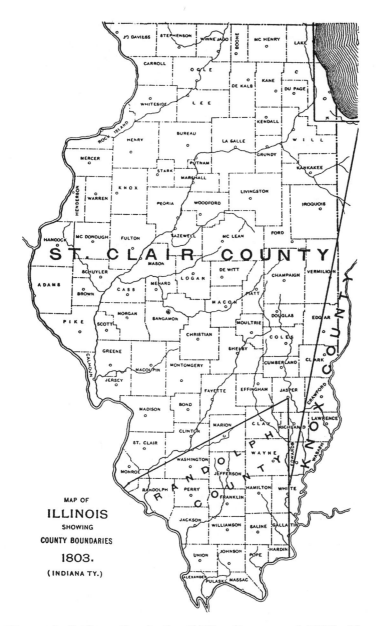

MAP OF
ILLINOIS
SHOWING
COUNTY BOUNDARIES
1803.
(INDIANA TY.)

Figure 9. IL Counties in the IN Territory as of 1803. Map reproduced by permission of the Office of IL Secretary of State George H. Ryan.

MAP OF
ILLINOIS
SHOWING
COUNTY BOUNDARIES
1809.
(ILLINOIS TY.)

Figure 10. IL Counties in the IL Territory as of 1809. Map reproduced by permission of the Office of IL Secretary of State George H. Ryan.

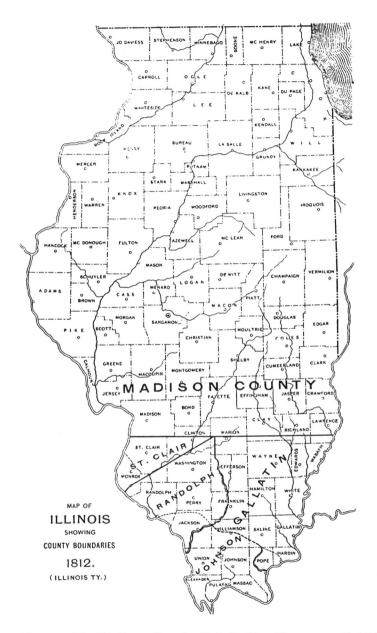

MAP OF
ILLINOIS
SHOWING
COUNTY BOUNDARIES
1812.
(ILLINOIS TY.)

Figure 11. IL Counties in the IL Territory as of 1812.
Map reproduced by permission of the Office of IL
Secretary of State George H. Ryan.

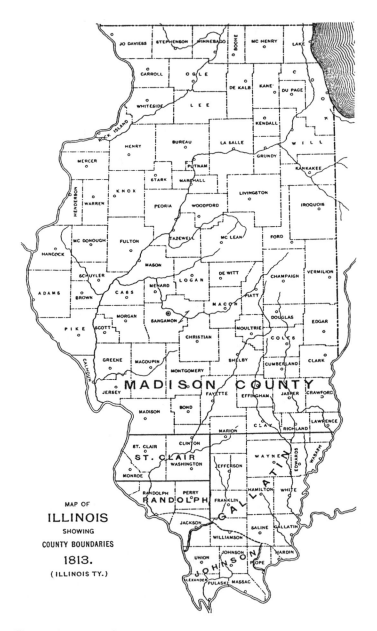

**Figure 12. IL Counties in the IL Territory as of 1813.
Map reproduced by permission of the Office of IL
Secretary of State George H. Ryan.**

41

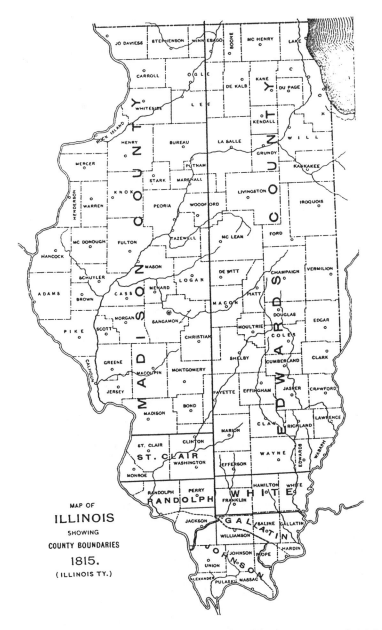

MAP OF
ILLINOIS
SHOWING
COUNTY BOUNDARIES
1815.
(ILLINOIS TY.)

Figure 13. IL Counties in the IL Territory as of 1815. Map reproduced by permission of the Office of IL Secretary of State George H. Ryan.

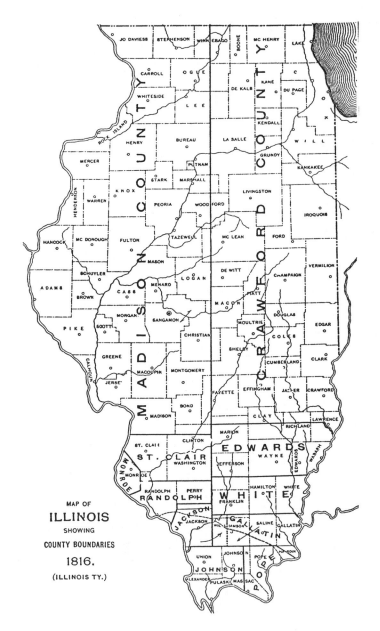

MAP OF
ILLINOIS
SHOWING
COUNTY BOUNDARIES
1816.
(ILLINOIS TY.)

Figure 14. IL Counties in the IL Territory as of 1816. Map reproduced by permission of the Office of IL Secretary of State George H. Ryan.

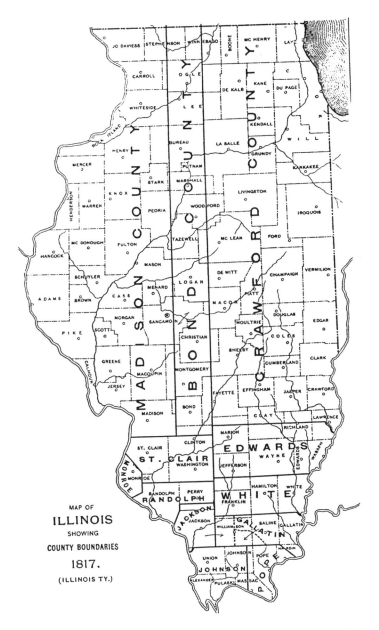

MAP OF
ILLINOIS
SHOWING
COUNTY BOUNDARIES
1817.
(ILLINOIS TY.)

Figure 15. IL Counties in the IL Territory as of 1817. Map reproduced by permission of the Office of IL Secretary of State George H. Ryan.

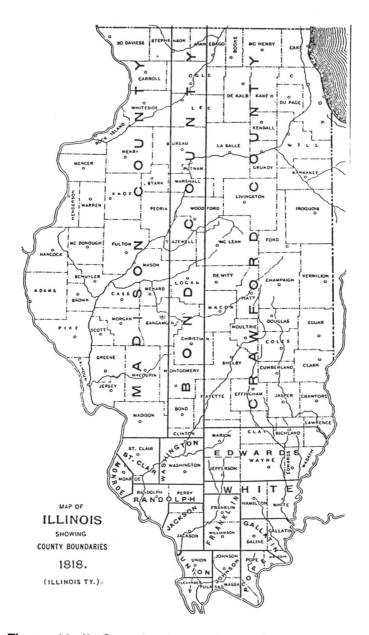

Figure 16. IL Counties in the IL Territory as of 1818. Map reproduced by permission of the Office of IL Secretary of State George H. Ryan.

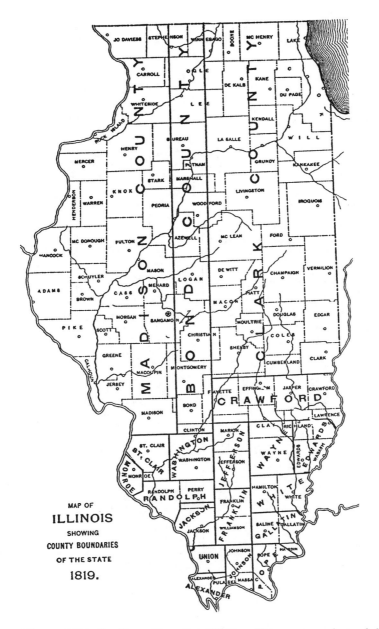

Figure 17. IL Counties in 1819. Map reproduced by permission of the Office of IL Secretary of State George H. Ryan.

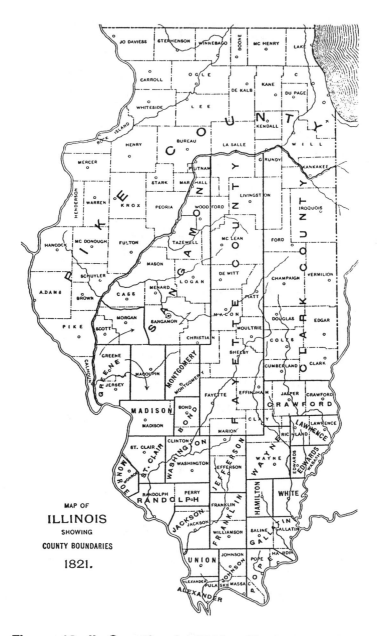

Figure 18. IL Counties in 1821. Map reproduced by permission of the Office of IL Secretary of State George H. Ryan.

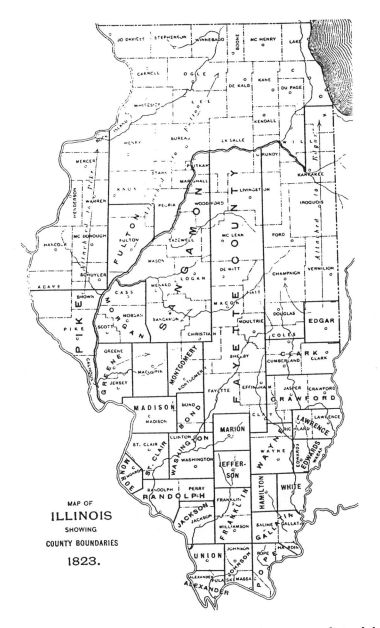

MAP OF
ILLINOIS
SHOWING
COUNTY BOUNDARIES
1823.

Figure 19. IL Counties in 1823. Map reproduced by permission of the Office of IL Secretary of State George H. Ryan.

48

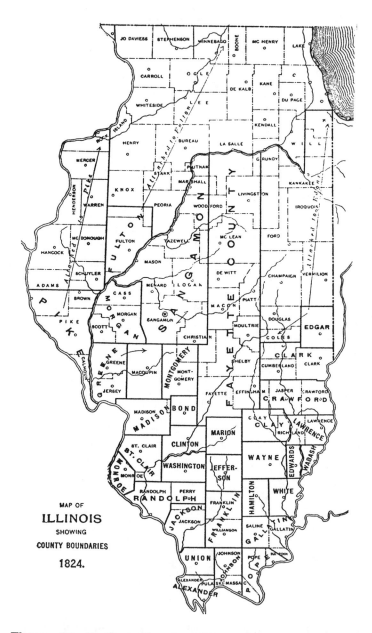

MAP OF
ILLINOIS
SHOWING
COUNTY BOUNDARIES
1824.

Figure 20. IL Counties in 1824. Map reproduced by permission of the Office of IL Secretary of State George H. Ryan.

Figure 21. IL Counties in 1825. Map reproduced by permission of the Office of IL Secretary of State George H. Ryan.

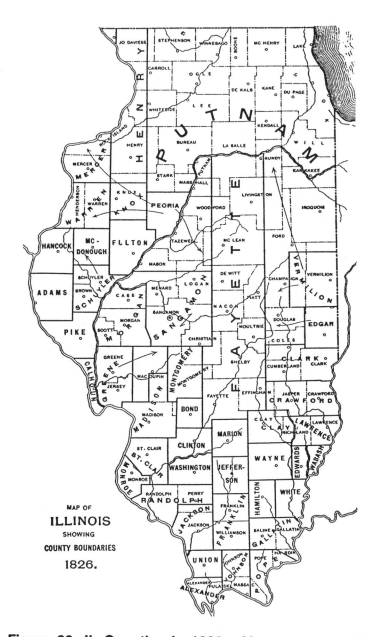

Figure 22. IL Counties in 1826. Map reproduced by permission of the Office of IL Secretary of State George H. Ryan.

MAP OF
ILLINOIS
SHOWING
COUNTY BOUNDARIES
1827.

Figure 23. IL Counties in 1827. Map reproduced by
permission of the Office of IL Secretary of State
George H. Ryan.

MAP OF
ILLINOIS
SHOWING
COUNTY BOUNDARIES
1831.

Figure 24. IL Counties in 1831. Map reproduced by permission of the Office of IL Secretary of State George H. Ryan.

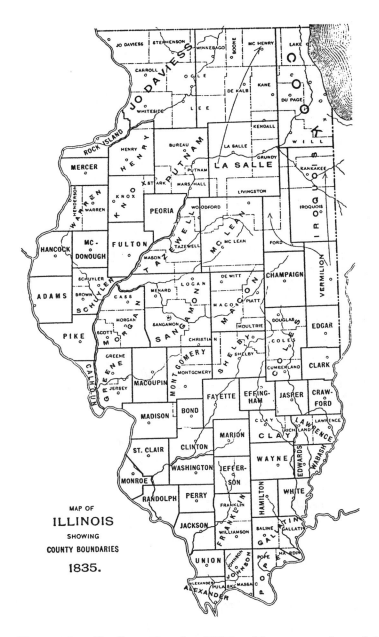

Figure 25. IL Counties in 1835. Map reproduced by permission of the Office of IL Secretary of State George H. Ryan.

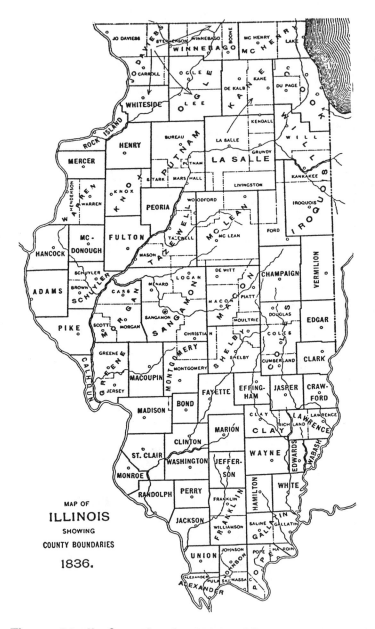

Figure 26. IL Counties in 1836. Map reproduced by permission of the Office of IL Secretary of State George H. Ryan.

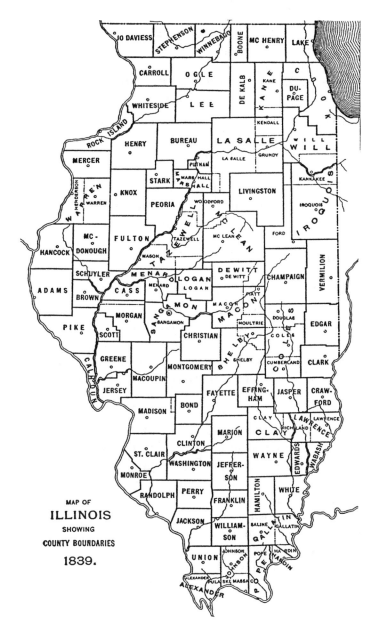

Figure 27. IL Counties in 1839. Map reproduced by permission of the Office of IL Secretary of State George H. Ryan.

List of Abbreviations

CCB	=	Cook County Building, Chicago
CCH	=	Chicago City Hall
CH	=	Court House(s)
CHSL	=	Chicago Historical Society Library
CJCLDS	=	Church of Jesus Christ of Latter Day Saints
CPL	=	Chicago Public Library
D	=	Federal mortality censuses
DC	=	Daley Center, Chicago
E	=	Early inhabitant lists
F	=	Federal Farm and Ranch censuses
FHC	=	Family History Center(s), branches of FHL
FHL	=	Family History Library, Salt Lake City, UT
IL	=	Illinois
IRAD	=	IL Regional Archives Repository(ies)
IRAD-EIU	=	IRAD at Eastern IL University, Charleston
IRAD-ISU	=	IRAD at IL State University, Normal
IRAD-NIU	=	IRAD at Northern IL University, DeKalb
IRAD-SIU	=	IRAD at Southern IL University, Carbondale
IRAD-SSU	=	IRAD at Sangamon State University, Springfield
IRAD-UNI	=	IRAD at Northeastern IL University, Chicago
IRAD-WIU	=	IRAD at Western IL University, Macomb
ISA	=	IL State Archives, Springfield
ISGS	=	IL State Genealogical Society, Springfield
ISGSQ	=	IL State Genealogical Society Quarterly
ISHL	=	IL State Historical Library, Springfield
ISHS	=	IL State Historical Society, Springfield
ISL	=	IL State Library, Springfield
LL	=	Local Library(ies)
LR	=	Local Repositories
M	=	Federal Manufactures censuses
NA	=	National Archives, Washington, DC
NAGL	=	National Archives - Great Lakes Region, Chicago
NARC	=	National Archives Regional Centers
NL	=	Newberry Library, Chicago
P	=	1840 Revolutionary War pension census
R	=	Regular federal censuses
RL	=	Regional Library(ies)
S	=	IL State censuses
T	=	IN and IL Territorial censuses

Chapter 2

TYPES OF RECORDS

━━━━━━━━━━━━

1. Introduction

━━━━━━━━━━━━

The state of IL is relatively rich in genealogical source materials, although there are some gaps in the early years and there are some problems with the loss of records in court house (CH) fires, which were fairly common in the 19th century. A great deal of work has been done in accumulating, preserving, photocopying, transcribing, and indexing records, and therefore many are readily available. The best overall collections of IL materials are to be found in the following repositories:

___(ISA) IL State Archives, Spring and Edwards Streets, Springfield, IL 62756.

___(ISHL) IL State Historical Library, Old State Capitol, Springfield, IL, 62701.

___(ISL) IL State Library, Second and Capitol Streets, Springfield, IL, 62756.

___(IRAD) IL Regional Archives Depositories, IRAD Coordinator, IL State Archives, Spring and Edwards Streets, Springfield, IL 62756. Consists of 7 regional archives containing records deposited by counties in the region. Located in DeKalb, Macomb, Normal, Springfield, Charleston, Carbondale, and Chicago.

___(FHL) Family History Library, Genealogical Library of the Church of Jesus Christ of Latter-day Saints, 35 North West Temple, Salt Lake City, UT 84150.

___(FHC) Family History Center(s), over 1700 of them, located all over the world. They are local branch affiliates of the Family History Library (FHL). They can be found in most major US cities, including 9 in IL: Champaign, Chicago Heights, Fairview Heights, Napierville, Nauvoo, Peoria, Rockford, Schaumburg, Wilmette.

___(NL) Newberry Library, 60 West Walton St., Chicago, IL 60610. This library holds a very large collection of published (print and microform) IL genealogical materials. Included are local histories, family histories, church records, vital record transcriptions, cemetery readings, censuses, maps, Civil War regimental histories, and county records. Accompanying these are many large indexes and other IL ancestor finding aids.

Two major repositories for IL genealogical materials are clustered together in Springfield: the IL State Archives (ISA), and the IL State

Historical Library (ISHL). There is also the IL State Library, which holds some records of genealogical value. Further, one of the IL Regional Archives Depositories (IRAD-SSU) is also located in Springfield. Together they constitute the best place in the world to do IL genealogical research. In addition, there are two remarkable sources for IL research in Chicago: the National Archives-Great Lakes Region (NAGL) which houses a number of federal records relating to IL, and the Newberry Library (NL). And, as you might imagine, Chicago and Cook County research must be supplemented with materials found in Chicago in the Chicago Public Library (CPL), Chicago Historical Society Library (CHSL), the Chacago-area Regional Archives Depository (IRAD-UNI), the Daley Center (DC), the Cook County Building CCB), and the Chicago City Hall (CCH).

The IL State Archives (ISA), is the official repository for state records. Its chief genealogically-related materials include state and federal census records for 1810-1920, census indexes, 1850-80 census mortality and agriculture records, bounty land records, military records, veterans' burial records, federal land grant records, Civil War enrollments, county histories, some microfilmed records for some counties (mostly those in southern IL), a computer index to IL marriages, and some published transcribed governmental records.

The IL State Historical Library (ISHS) is a state organization with its offices and library in the Old State Capitol. Its collection is made up of manuscripts, county histories, atlases, genealogy reference works, genealogical record compilations (DAR, cemetery, birth, death, probate, land, marriage), church records, plat books, census indexes, biographical volumes, city directories, military reports (Indian, Black Hawk, Mexican, Civil, Spanish-American wars), family files, genealogical periodicals, fraternal organization records, newspapers, rare books, maps, business records, journals, pamphlets, and historical materials relating to IL's history, but especially the early state days.

The IL State Library (ISL) has as its major responsibility the collection and maintenance of all printed records produced by the IL government. The ISL does not maintain a genealogy collection, but it does have some materials which genealogists will find of value. These include federal and state censuses, a very large microfilm name index to early IL records, IL Adjutant Generals' reports, IL [Court] Reports, IL Veterans' Commision reports, land tract record index, county histories, county atlases, regimental histories, city directories, territorial papers for the Northwest, IN, and IL

Territories, and American State Papers (especially those related to public lands and claims).

The collections in Springfield and Chicago are somewhat matched by that of the FHL (Family History Library) of Salt Lake City, UT. They have by far the largest collection of IL genealogical materials outside of IL. The FHL has microfilmed a number of IL documents, which they make available through their numerous branch libraries (called Family History Centers, FHC), located all over the US and in many overseas countries. All these materials can be readily located in the catalogs and indexes of the FHL, which are available at every FHC.

Finally, it should not be overlooked that there are some fairly well-stocked regional libraries (RL) in the state of IL. These are generally smaller than the large libraries noted above, but considerably larger than most town and county libraries. Of course, local libraries (LL), that is, county, city, town, and private libraries are sources which are very important to the family history researcher.

The above repositories and their collections and other sources will be treated in detail in Chapters 3 and 4. In this chapter the many types of records which are available for IL genealogical research are discussed. Those records which are essentially national or state-wide in scope will be treated in detail. Records which are basically county or city records will be discussed only generally, but a detailed listing of them will be delayed to Chapters 4 and 5, where the local records available for each of the 102 IL counties will be given.

2. Genealogical evidence

When you do your genealogy, it is of ultimate importance for you to substantiate the data by finding, examining, and referencing the most reliable sources possible. One way of treating the reliability of sources is to classify them as primary and secondary. The events in people's lives are the occasions which permit family history research to be done. These events include such things as birth, church affiliation, marriage, purchase of land, voting, being sued, joining an organization, death, and burial. A primary source is a document which has been recorded by a reliable person shortly after the event on the basis of personal eye-witness participation or the report of one or more trustworthy eye-witnesses to the event. The most reliable recorders are usually deemed to be governmental or church officials. And the most reliable reporters are generally deemed to be persons who are capable of making a true report and who would suffer consequences as a result of a false report. A secondary source, which is less reliable, is a report of an event by someone who is not an eye-witness or by someone who has not recorded the testimony of an eye-witness shortly after the event. Secondary sources are therefore those based on what someone has read or has heard from a non-eye-witness.

In this chapter, numerous sources will be discussed. Examples of those which are likely to be primary, that is, based on eye-witness testimony, are:
___PRIMARY SOURCES: birth(governmental or church), church, court, death (governmental or church), divorce, land, marriage (governmental or church), military, naturalization, probate, tax, territorial, voter, will. Note that these are often records taken under governmental supervision. Microform copies of these records are often as good, but sometimes they are less than perfect.
Examples of those which are usually secondary, that is, not based on eye-witness testimony, are:
___SECONDARY SOURCES: abstracted records, biography, city directory, extracted records, histories, genealogical compilations, indexes, newspaper, pedigrees, periodicals, published genealogies, transcribed records.
Examples of records that can be either primary or secondary are as follows. Which category they fit depends upon whether an eye-witness account is the basis for the record.
___EITHER PRIMARY OR SECONDARY SOURCES: Bible, cemetery, census, organizational records, emigration, manuscripts, mortuary.

Taking the above distinctions into account and applying some other probabilities, a chart can be derived which approximates the trust-worthiness and the utility of sources with regard to connecting the generations. Such a chart is presented below. The list shows the major types of genealogical source materials that are used. After each are indications of its trustworthiness and of whether it names the parents or connects the generations. It is to be recognized that these indications are statistical only, which means that they will not apply to every instance, only to most instances. In other words, there will be exceptions.

Record Type	Trustworthiness?	Name Parents?
Bible records	Fair-Good	Usually
Biographies	Fair-Good	Usually
Birth Records, Church	Good-Excellent	Usually
Birth Records. Government	Good-Excellent	Usually
Cemetery Markers	Fair-Good	Sometimes
Cemetery Records	Fair-Good	Sometimes
Census Records 1790-1840	Fair-Good	Rarely
Census Records 1850-1870	Good	Possibly
Census Records after 1880	Good	Often
Church Records	Fair-Good	Sometimes
City Directories	Fair-Good	Rarely
City/county Histories	Poor-Good	Sometimes
Court Records	Good-Excellent	Sometimes
Death Records, Church	Good-Excellent	Rarely
Death Records, Government	Good-Excellent	Often
Divorce Records	Good-Excellent	Rarely
Emigration Records	Good	Rarely
Family Tradition	Poor	Often
Genealogies, Documented	Good	For most
Genealogies, Undocumented	Poor	For most
Immigration Records	Good	Rarely
Indexes, Printed	Fair-Good	Rarely
Land Records	Good-Excellent	Rarely
Manuscripts	Fair-Good	Sometimes
Marriage Records, Church	Good-Excellent	Usually
Marriage Records, Governm'l	Good-Excellent	Sometimes
Military Records	Good	Rarely
Mortuary Records	Fair-Good	Sometimes
Naturalization Records	Good-Excellent	Rarely
Newspaper Articles	Fair-Good	Sometimes
Probate Records	Good-Excellent	Often name children
Record Abstracts & Extracts	Poor-Good	Sometimes
Record Compilations	Poor-Good	Sometimes
Record Transcripts	Poor-Good	Sometimes
Tax Records	Good-Excellent	Rarely
Will Records	Good-Excellent	Often name children

In all considerations of source reliability, careful thought must be given to how the record was generated, who generated it, when it was generated, where it was generated, why it was generated, and what circumstances might cause it to be false. Further, the good researcher will consider whether the data fit with the current historical situation. In all presentations of genealogical data, it is mandatory that the researcher carefully reference exactly where the data were obtained so that others can readily locate the sources. In ambiguous situations, which crop up increasingly as the line is developed farther back, it is also important to state exactly how your conclusions were reached, so that others can follow your line of reasoning. This lets your reader know precisely what the situation is in case she/he wants to continue the investigation.

3. Bible records

During the past 200 years it was customary for families with religious affiliations to keep vital statistics on their members in the family Bible. These records vary widely, but among the items that may be found are names, dates, and places of birth, christening, baptism, marriage, death, and sometimes military service. Although most Bibles containing recorded information probably still remain in private hands, some of the information has been submitted for publication and some has been filed in libraries and archives. Bible records may be found in libraries and archives throughout IL. You should inquire about such records at every possible library and archives in and near your ancestor's county or district, especially the regional libraries (RL) and the local libraries (LL). Sometimes there will be indexes or the records will be arranged alphabetically. RL will be listed in Chapter 3, and LL will be listed under the counties in Chapters 4 and 5. You should not overlook the possibility that Bible records may be listed in indexes or in files labelled something other than Bible records. The most likely ones are family records, genealogies, manuscripts, names, surnames. Also do not fail to look in the major card index of each library for the names you are seeking.

There are many published compilations of IL Bible records. Among those you should examine are:
__DAR Chapters in IL, THE BLUE BOOKS [TRANSCRIPTS OF IL GENEALOGICAL RECORDS], and the GRANDPARENT PAPERS, various sub-titles, various DAR Chapters, various cities, various dates. These many volumes include Bible, cemetery, church, marriage, death, and will records.
These and other Bible record compilations for IL are listed in:
__FHL, FAMILY HISTORY LIBRARY CATALOG, LOCALITY SECTION, Salt Lake City, UT, latest microfiche and/or computer edition. Look under IL and then under the county of interest.

___E. K. Kirkham, AN INDEX TO SOME OF THE BIBLE AND FAMILY RECORDS OF THE US, Everton Publishers, Logan, UT, 1980/4, volume 2.

___National Society, DAR, DAR LIBRARY CATALOG, VOLUME 2: STATE AND LOCAL HISTORIES AND RECORDS, The Society, Washington, DC, 1986.

___CARD AND COMPUTER CATALOGS in ISHL, FHL(FHC), NL, RL, and LL.

The Bible record compilations referred to above should be sought in the ISHL, FHL(FHC), NL, RL, and LL, and in the DAR Library in Washington, DC. Do not fail to look for vertical files of Bible records in these repositories. Bible records also appear in genealogical periodical articles and in published family genealogies. These two types of records, as well as details on manuscript sources will be discussed in sections 16, 19, and 22 of this chapter.

4. Biographies

There are several major national biographical works which contain sketches on nationally-prominent IL personages. There are also numerous good biographical compilations for the state of IL or for sections of it. These volumes list persons who have attained some prominence in the fields of law, agriculture, business, politics, medicine, engineering, science, military, teaching, public service, or philanthropy. There are also many local (county, township, city, town) biographical works, and numerous regional and county histories also contain biographies of leading citizens. In addition, some professional organizations have compiled biographical information on their members. All of these can be of considerable use to genealogical researchers, because they usually carry birth, marriage, and death data, as well as details on children, parents, grandparents, and other ancestors.

Over 500 national biographical compilations have been indexed in a large microfilm/computer set which contains over 6 million entries. This set is available in large libraries, and is added to annually:

___BIOBASE, Gale Research Co., Detroit, MI, latest edition. This database is the successor to M. C. Herbert and B. McNeil, BIOGRAPHY AND GENEALOGY MASTER INDEX, Gale Research Co., Detroit, MI, various dates.

Several of the larger repositories in IL have indexes to biographies in local histories, atlases, and/or biographical compilations. Notable among these are:

___ISA, INDEX TO BIOGRAPHIES FOUND IN LOCAL HISTORIES, ISA, Springfield, IL.

___NL, CARD INDEX TO SELECTED CHICAGO, COOK COUNTY, AND IL COLLECTIVE BIOGRAPHIES AND MUG BOOKS PUBLISHED PRIOR TO 1930, NL, Chicago, IL.

The NL has also published an index to over 500,000 names taken from genealogy and local history books in its collection. Many of the references are to biographical material. The index includes materials published up to about 1918.

___NL, THE GENEALOGICAL INDEX OF THE NL, G. K. Hall, Boston, MA, 1960, 4 volumes.

Over the years, many regional and state biographical compilations have been published for IL or sections of it. Among the most useful of these for your investigations are:

___B. Alderson, WOMEN OF THE PRAIRIE STATE HISTORY, The Author, Springfield, IL, 1977.

___American Medical Association, AMERICAN MEDICAL DIRECTORY, The Association, Chicago, IL, 1906.

___N. Bateman, and others, HISTORICAL ENCYCLOPEDIA OF IL AND BIOGRAPHICAL MEMOIRS, Munsell, Chicago, IL, numerous editions from 1896 forward. State volume combined with county volume for several counties. Counties: Carroll, Cass, Champaign, Christian, Coles, Cook, DuPage, Fayette, Fulton, Hancock, Henderson, Kane, Kankakee, Knox, Lake, Lee, McLean, Montgomery, Ogle, Peoria, Rock Island, Sangamon, Schuyler, Shelby, Winnebago,

___F. O. Bennett, POLITICS AND POLITICIANS OF CHICAGO, COOK COUNTY, AND IL, 1787-1887, Blakely Printing Co., Chicago, IL, 1886.

___B. Blenz, ENCYCLOPEDIA OF IL, Somerset Publ. Co., St. Clair Shores, MI, 1980.

___H. J. Boswell AMERICAN BLUE BOOK, IL ATTORNEYS, Farnham Printing, Minneaspolis, MN, 1927.

___S. J. Buck, TRAVEL AND DESCRIPTION [OF IL], 1765-1865, ISHL, Springfield, IL, 1914.

___J. D. Caton, EARLY BENCH AND BAR OF IL, Legal News Co., Chicago, IL, 1922.

___F. B. Crossley, COURTS AND LAWYERS OF IL, American Historical Society, Chicago, IL, 1916.

___J. S. Currey, THE MAKERS OF IL, Clarke Publ. Co., Chicago, IL, 1915.

___E. F. Dunne, IL, THE HEART OF THE NATION, Lewis Publ. Co., Chicago, IL, 1933, 5 volumes.

___J. Gillespie, RECOLLECTIONS OF EARLY IL AND HER NOTED MEN, Fergus Printing Co., Chicago, IL, 1880.

___A. G. Gilman and G. M. Gilman, WHO'S WHO IN IL, WOMEN, MAKERS OF HISTORY, Eclectic Publishers, Chicago, IL, 1927.

___HISTORICAL AND DESCRIPTIVE REVIEW OF IL, SOUTHERN SECTION, Lethem, Chicago, IL, 1894.

___THE HISTORY OF IL CENTENNIAL FARMS, Curtis Media, Dallas, TX, 1986.

___IL BIOGRAPHICAL DICTIONARY, Somerset, New York, NY, 1993.

___IL: BLUE BOOK OF BIOGRAPHY, IL Blue Book Co., Chicago, IL, 1916.

___IL POLITICAL DIRECTORY, Bodine, Chicago, IL, 1898, 2 volumes.

___IL THROUGH 245 YEARS, 1673-1918, Chicago Historical Society, Chicago, IL, 1918.

___IL Women's Press Assn., PROMINENT WOMEN OF IL, 1885-1932, The Assn., Chicago, IL, 1932.

___IN MEMORIAM, FOUNDERS AND MAKERS OF IL, Clarke Publ. Co, Chicago, IL, 1931.

___U. F. Linder, REMINISCENCES OF THE EARLY BENCH AND BAR OF IL, Chicago Legal News, Chicago, IL, 1879.

___E. G. Mason, EARLY CHICAGO AND IL, Fergus Print. Co., Chicago, IL, 1890.

___N. Matson, PIONEERS OF IL, Knight and Leonard, Chicago, IL, 1919.

___H. McCormick, THE WOMEN OF IL, Pantagraph Printing, Bloomington, IL, 1913.

___H. McGrath, ENCYCLOPEDIA OF BIOGRAPHY OF IL, Century Publishing and Engraving Co., Chicago, Il, 1892-1902, 3 volumes.

___MEN OF IL, Chicago Historical Society, Witherspoon, Chicago, IL, 1902.

___Moss, J., BIOGRAPHICAL DICTIONARY AND PORTRAIT GALLERY OF THE REPRESENTATIVE MEN OF THE US, IL EDITION, Lewis Publishing Co., Chicago, IL, 1896.

___NOTABLE MEN OF IL AND THEIR STATE, Chicago Daily Journal, Chicago, IL, 1912.

___J. M. Palmer, THE BENCH AND BAR OF IL, Lewis Publ. Co., Chicago, IL, 1899.

___E. R. Pritchard, IL OF TODAY, The Author, Chicago, IL, 1897.
___PROMINENT DEMOCRATS OF IL, Democrat Publ., Co., Chicago, IL, 1899.
___G. B. Raum, HISTORY OF IL REPUBLICANISM, Rollins Publ. Co, Chicago, IL, 1900.
___REPUBLICANS OF IL, Lewis Publ. Co., Chicago, IL, 1905.
___J. Reynolds, PIONEER HISTORY OF IL, Fergus Printing Co., Chicago, IL, 1887.
___C. Robson, BIOGRAPHICAL ENCYCLOPEDIA OF IL OF THE 19TH CENTURY, Galaxy Publ. Co., Philadelphia, PA, 1875.
___H. L. Ross, THE EARLY PIONEERS AND PIONEER EVENTS OF THE STATE OF IL, Eastman Brothers, Chicago, IL, 1899.
___G. W. Smith, A HISTORY OF IL AND HER PEOPLE, American Historical Society, Chicago, IL, 1927, 6 volumes.
___W. A. Townsend, IL DEMOCRACY, A HISTORY OF THE PARTY, Democratic Historical Association, Springfield, Il, 1935, 4 volumes.
___US BIOGRAPHICAL DICTIONARY AND PORTRAIT GALLERY OF EMINENT AND SELF-MADE MEN, IL VOLUME, American Biographical Publishing C., Chicago, IL, 1876, 2 volumes.
___C. C. Walton, IL LIVES, THE PRAIRIE STATE BIOGRAPHICAL RECORD, Historical Record Assn., Hopkinsville, KY, 1969.
___WHO'S WHO IN CHICAGO AND IL, Marquis, Chicago, IL, 1945.
___D. W. Wood, HISTORY OF THE REPUBLICAN PARTY, Lincoln Publ. Co., Chicago, IL, 1895.
Most of these volumes will be found in ISHL, NL, and FHL(FHC). Those pertinent to various regions will usually be found in RL and larger LL in the area.

In addition to the above national, state, and regional biographical works, there are many local (county, township, district, city, and town) biographical volumes. Further, biographical sketches are more often than not included in county histories. Listings of many of the biographical volumes and county histories are provided in:
___FAMILY HISTORY LIBRARY CATALOG, LOCALITY SECTION, on microfiche and computer, FHL, Salt Lake City, UT, and at every FHC.
___M. J. Kaminkow, US LOCAL HISTORIES IN THE LIBRARY OF CONGRESS, Magna Carta Book Co., Baltimore, MD, 1975, 5 volumes, with SUPPLEMENTS.
___P. W. Filby, A BIBLIOGRAPHY OF AMERICAN COUNTY HISTORIES, Genealogical Publishing Co., Baltimore, MD, 1985.

When volumes containing biographical information are available in the various IL counties, this fact will be noted under the county listings in Chapters 4 and 5. Such volumes will be found in ISHL, NL, and FHL(FHC). Those pertinent to various counties will be found in RL and LL in the counties. There are also some special biographical collections and some unpublished compilations in several IL libraries. Do not fail to inquire in libraries near your ancestor's homeplace. Care should be exercised in taking the data in biographical sketches too literally. Remember that your ancestor or some family member supplied the information, quite often from memory and/or family tradition, and sometimes from an inventive imagination.

5. Birth records

Prior to 1877, a few IL counties kept a few birth records. A law was passed in 1877 requiring counties to record births, but compliance was not good and enforcement was non-existent, most counties doing nothing. Even in those counties in which there was some record-keeping, the records are very incomplete. Counties which kept at least some birth records before 1877 include Cass, Hardin, Lake, Macon, Madison, Massac, McLean, Moultrie, Ogle, Pulaski, Scott, Shelby, Stark, Union, Vermilion, Warren, White, Williamson, and Woodford. The major exception to this poor recording is Chicago, for which fairly complete birth records are available from 1871. In 1916, it was mandated by the state that birth records be kept and that copies be sent to the state capital. Again, enforcement and compliance were not complete at first, and it was 1920 or 1921 before the records began to approach being complete. By about 1922, compliance was almost complete. The birth records available for each IL county are indicated in the separate county listings in Chapters 4 and 5.

Birth records prior to 1916, are available in the counties and some are on microfilm at the FHL(FHC). Birth records from 1916 onwards are held by county clerks and:
___Office of Vital Records, IL State Department of Public Health, 605 West Jefferson St., Springfield, IL 62761.
IL state law permits the issuing of birth records only after they are more than 74 years old. If such is the case, you may obtain them from the above sources. These records usually contain name of child, place and date of birth, sex, race; name, age, birthplace, nationality, occupation and residence of father; maiden name, age, birthplace, nationality, and residence of mother; number of children of mother; name and address of medical attendant; and the date on which the birth was registered. In

many counties, there were delayed and amended birth registrations, so be sure and seek them out, if you do not find what you want in the regular records.

Prior to the time when IL birth reports come to be almost complete (1922), other records may yield dates and places of birth: biographical, cemetery, census, church, death, divorce, marriage, military, mortuary, newspaper, pension, and published. These are all discussed in other sections of this chapter. The finding of birth record articles in genealogical periodicals is also described separately in this chapter.

6. Cemetery records

If you know or suspect that your ancestor was buried in a certain cemetery, the best thing to do is to write to the caretaker of the cemetery, enclose an SASE and $5, and ask if the records show your ancestor. If this fails, other cemeteries in the region can be investigated. Very convenient listings of many IL cemeteries are provided in:
___Beckstead, G., and M. L. Kozub, SEARCHING IN IL, A REFERENCE GUIDE TO PUBLIC AND PRIVATE RECORDS, ISC Publications, Costa Mesa, CA, 1984. Listing of many cemeteries in IL.
___IL Cemetery Project, CARD FILE OF CEMETERY LOCATIONS IN IL, ISHL, Springfield, IL; also see lists of cemeteries published in the IL State Genealogical Society Quarterly (1972-).

Should this prove unsuccessful, then the next step is to look into cemetery record collections for your ancestor's county. These have been made by the DAR, local genealogical and historical societies, and individuals. Much work has been done, and at least some cemeteries in every county have been read and the data published. Listings of many of the available records will be found in:
___FAMILY HISTORY LIBRARY CATALOG, LOCALITY SECTION, FHL, Salt Lake City, UT, latest edition, on both microfiche and computer. Look under IL and its counties.
___National Society, DAR, DAR LIBRARY CATALOG, VOLUME TWO: STATE AND LOCAL HISTORIES AND RECORDS, The Society, Washington, DC, 1986.
When you consult these, you will find that the main sources of IL cemetery records are the ISHL, NL, and FHL(FHC). In addition, local libraries (LL) in the IL counties often have records of their own

cemeteries. IL regional libraries (RL) and large genealogical libraries (LGL) outside of IL may also have records.

Several of the larger genealogical periodicals published in IL contain cemetery listings quite frequently (especially IL State Genealogical Society Quarterly, Central IL Genealogical Quarterly, Chicago Genealogist, Circuit Rider, Saga of Southern IL, Prairie Roots, Where the Trails Cross, Searching IL Ancestors, Tri-state Packet, and Twigs and Branches). In addition, many of the local genealogical publications carry cemetery records from time to time. A useful index which covers numerous periodicals and which will locate many of these articles for you is:

___Allen County Public Library, PERIODICAL SOURCE INDEX, The Library Staff, Fort Wayne, IN, many volumes, 1985-.

There are also some cemetery record compilations which could be of value to you:

___DAR Chapters in IL, THE BLUE BOOKS [TRANSCRIPTS OF IL GENEALOGICAL RECORDS], and the GRANDPARENT PAPERS, various sub-titles, various DAR Chapters, various cities, various dates. These many volumes include Bible, cemetery, church, marriage, death, and will records.

___CEMETERY RECORDS OF IL, Genealogical Society of UT, Salt Lake City, UT, 1960-66, 13 volumes.

___IL Adjutant General, RECORD OF BURIAL PLACES OF SOLDIERS, SAILORS, MARINES, AND ARMY NURSES OF ALL WARS OF THE US BURIED IN IL, State of IL, Springfield, IL, 1929, 2 volumes.

___H. J. Walker, REVOLUTIONARY SOLDIERS BURIED IN IL, Genealogical Publishing Co., Baltimore, MD, 1967.

___St. Louis Genealogical Society, CEMETERY RELOCATION BY THE US ARMY CORPS OF ENGINEERS IN IL, IA, MO, AND AR, The Society, St. Louis, MO, 1977.

In Chapters 4 and 5, those counties for which extensive cemetery records exist in printed or microfilmed form are indicated. Instructions regarding locating the above reference volumes and the records themselves will be presented in Chapter 3. More detailed instructions regarding the finding of cemetery records in genealogical periodical articles are given in a section of this chapter devoted to such periodicals.

7. Census records

Excellent ancestor information is available in seven types of census reports which have been accumulated for IL: Early inhabitant lists (E),

IN and IL Territorial Censuses (T), IL state censuses (S), the regular federal censuses (R), the federal farm and ranch censuses (F), the federal manufactures censuses (M), the federal mortality censuses (D for death), and the special 1840 Revolutionary War Pension Census (P).

Some very early inhabitant lists (E) for French settlements during and after the French period are available. Three good sources for these are as follows:

___N. M. Belting, EXTRACTS FROM PARISH REGISTERS [1723-63] and NOTES ON THE CENSUS OF 1752, in KASKASKIA UNDER THE FRENCH REGIME, IL Studies in the Social Sciences 29(3), University of IL Press, Urbana, IL, 1948.

___C. V. Alvord, KASKASKIA RECORDS, 1778-90, Collections of the IL State Historical Library, Springfield, IL, 1909.

___C. V. Alvord, CAHOKIA RECORDS, 1778-90, Collections of the IL State Historical Library, Springfield, IL, 1907.

In 1807/10 a Census of the IN Territory (T) was taken. The territory included what is now IL. The census was meant to list every free white male over 21, but in some cases only the head of the household is given. Only the Randolph County information has survived. The information is published in:

___R. Fraustein, CENSUS OF IN TERRITORY FOR 1807/10, IHS, Indianapolis, IN, 1980.

___R. V. Jackson, EARLY IL, 1787-1819, Accelerated Indexing Systems, Bountiful, UT, 1980. Includes 1810 IN territorial census for Randolph County.

___Norton, M. C., IL CENSUS RETURNS, 1810, 1818, 1820, Genealogical Publishing Co., Baltimore, MD, 1969.

In addition, there was a census for IL Territory in 1818:

___Norton, M. C., IL CENSUS RETURNS, 1810, 1818, 1820, Genealogical Publishing Co., Baltimore, MD, 1969.

___R. V. Jackson, IL 1818 CENSUS INDEX, Accelerated Indexing Systems, Bountiful, UT, 1987.

Also useful are several compiled volumes:

___C. M. Franklin, IN TERRITORIAL PIONEER RECORDS, 1801-15, Heritage House, Indianapolis, IN, 1983. Includes early IL country people.

___C. E. Carter, TERRITORIAL PAPERS OF THE US, THE TERRITORY OF IL, 1809-18, USGPO, 1948-50, Washington, DC, 2 volumes. Also see C. E. Carter, THE TERRITORY NORTHWEST OF THE RIVER OHIO, 1787-1803, 2 volumes, and THE

TERRITORY OF IN, 1800-1810, USGPO, Washington, DC, 1934-50. Also available as National Archives, TERRITORIAL PAPERS OF THE US, Microfilm M721, The Archives, Washington, DC.

___E. James, THE TERRITORIAL RECORDS OF IL, 1809-18, ISHL, Springfield, IL, 1901.

___R. Hammes, IL MILITIAMEN, 1790, AND SQUATTERS IN TERRITORIAL IL, 1807 AND 1813, IL Libraries 59:5 (May 1977).

Another set of records which has some use is:

___National Archives, TERRITORIAL PAPERS OF THE US SENATE, 1789-1873, Microfilm M200, The Archives, Washington, DC.

A number of state (S) censuses for IL were taken, and sizable portions of some of them survive. These include state censuses for 1820, 1825, 1830, 1840, 1845, 1855, and 1865. They are available as:

___R. V. Jackson, IL 1820 STATE CENSUS INDEX, Accelerated Indexing Systems, Bountiful, UT, 1987. Complete for all counties except Edwards.

___R. V. Jackson, IL 1825 STATE CENSUS INDEX, Accelerated Indexing Systems, Bountiful, UT, 1984. Only for Edwards, Fulton, and Randolph Counties.

___R. V. Jackson, IL 1830 STATE CENSUS INDEX, Accelerated Indexing Systems, Bountiful, UT, 1984. Only for Morgan County.

___R. V. Jackson, IL 1835 STATE CENSUS INDEX, Accelerated Indexing Systems, Bountiful, UT, 1984. Only for Fulton, Jasper, and Morgan Counties.

___R. V. Jackson, IL 1840 STATE CENSUS INDEX, Accelerated Indexing Systems, Bountiful, UT, 1984. No heads of household named for Alexander, Brown, Carroll, Clay, DeKalb, DeWitt, Greene, Hancock, Henry, Iroquois, Jefferson, Jersey, Lee, Scott, Shelby, Tazewell, Wabash, Warren, Washington, Wayne, Will, and Winnebago Counties.

___CENSUSES OF 1835, 1840, AND 1845, IL, KTO Microform, Millwood, NJ, 1974, microfiche. The 1845 records are for only Cass, Madison, Putnam, and Tazewell Counties.

___IL Secretary of State, 1855 STATE CENSUS OF IL, ISA, Springfield, IL. Originals in ISA, microfilms in FHL(FHC). Missing counties are Carroll, Champaign, Franklin, Gallatin, Henry, Jefferson, Jo Daviess, Lake, Stark, Will, and Woodford.

___IL Secretary of State, 1865 STATE CENSUS OF IL, ISA, Springfield, IL. Originals in ISA, microfilms in FHL(FHC). Missing counties are Gallatin, Mason, Monroe, and Elm Grove Township in Tazewell.

These are indexed in a very good overall index in the ISA:

___NAME INDEX TO EARLY IL RECORDS, INCLUDING 1810-65 TERRITORIAL, STATE, AND FEDERAL CENSUSES, ISA, Springfield, IL. Incomplete, but being added to constantly. Also at FHL for 1810-55.

There is a pseudo-census of members of the IL militia (men 18 to 45) taken in 1862-63. It can often be helpful during the turbulent period of the Civil War.

___IL Assessors, IL MILITIA ROLLS, 1862-63, ISA, Springfield, IL. Originals in ISA, microfilms in FHL(FHC).

Regular federal census records (R) are available for almost all IL counties in 1820, 1830, 1840, 1850, 1860, 1870, 1880, 1900, 1910, and 1920. Please note that the only records of the 1890 census that survived were those for Mound Township in McDonough County. The 1840 census and all before it listed the head of the household plus a breakdown of the number of persons in the household according to age and sex brackets. Beginning in 1850 the names of all persons were recorded along with age, sex, real estate, marital, and other information, including the state of birth. With the 1880 census and thereafter, the birthplaces of the mother and father of each person are also shown. Chapters 4 and 5 list the regular census records (R) available for each of the 102 IL counties.

State-wide indexes have been compiled and most have been printed or computerized for the 1820, 1830, 1840, 1850, 1860, and 1880 IL regular census records. These volumes and CD-ROMs are:

___Bohannan, L. C., FOURTH CENSUS OF THE US, 1820, IL POPULATION SCHEDULES, Century Enterprises, Huntsville, AR, 1968.
___R. V. Jackson, IL 1820 CENSUS INDEX, Accelerated Indexing Systems, Bountiful, UT, 1977.
___L. M. Volkel and J. V. Gill, 1820 FEDERAL CENSUS OF IL, Heritage House, Thomson, IL, 1966.
___Family Archives, US CENSUS INDEX, 1820, CD-ROM CD-0314, The Archives, AGLL, Bountiful, UT, 1996. Includes IL.
___Gill, J. V., and M. R. Gill, INDEX TO THE 1830 CENSUS OF IL, Heritage House, Thomson, IL, 1968-70, 4 volumes.
___R. V. Jackson, IL 1830 CENSUS INDEX, Accelerated Indexing Systems, Bountiful, UT, 1976.
___Family Archives, US CENSUS INDEX, 1830, CD-ROM CD-0315, The Archives, AGLL, Bountiful, UT, 1996. Includes IL.
___R. V. Jackson, IL 1840 CENSUS INDEX, Accelerated Indexing Systems, Bountiful, UT, 1977.

___M. E. Wormer, IL 1840 CENSUS INDEX, Heritage House, Thomson, IL, 1973-77, 5 volumes.

___Family Archives, US CENSUS INDEX, 1840, CD-ROM CD-0316, The Archives, AGLL, Bountiful, UT, 1996. Includes IL.

___R. V. Jackson, IL 1850 CENSUS INDEX, Accelerated Indexing Systems, Bountiful, UT, 1976.

___IL 1850 CENSUS INDEX, Bloomington-Normal Genealogical Society, Normal, IL, 1978.

___Family Archives, US CENSUS INDEX, 1850, CD-ROM CD-0317, The Archives, AGLL, Bountiful, UT, 1996. Includes IL.

___R. V. Jackson, IL 1860 CENSUS INDEX, NORTH, Accelerated Indexing Systems, North Salt Lake City, UT, 1987.

___R. V. Jackson, IL 1860 CENSUS INDEX, SOUTH, Accelerated Indexing Systems, North Salt Lake City, UT, 1986.

___Family Archives, US CENSUS INDEX, 1860, CD-ROM CD-0318, The Archives, AGLL, Bountiful, UT, 1996. Includes IL.

___Precision Indexing, CHICAGO AND COOK COUNTY 1870 CENSUS INDEX, CD K3C-IL1, AGLL, Bountiful, UT, 1990. No index available for the rest of IL.

___Family Archives, US CENSUS INDEX FOR CHICAGO AND COOK COUNTY, 1880, CD-ROM CD-0320, The Archives, AGLL, Bountiful, UT, 1996. See below for a partial index to the rest of IL.

Do not fail to remember the very useful integrated index which was mentioned above:

___NAME INDEX TO EARLY IL RECORDS, INCLUDING 1810-65 TERRITORIAL, STATE, AND FEDERAL CENSUSES, ISA, Springfield, IL. Incomplete, but being added to constantly. Also at FHL for 1810-55.

No state-wide index is available for the 1870 IL Census, but a number of county-wide and city-wide indexes are in print. An overall state-wide index is in preparation.

In addition to the above indexes, there is a National Archives microfilm index which contains only families with a child 10 or under in the 1880 census. There are also complete National Archives microfilm indexes to the 1900, 1910, and 1920 IL censuses. These four indexes are arranged by Soundex or Miracode. Librarians or archivists can show you how to use them. The microfilm indexes are:

___US Bureau of the Census, INDEX (SOUNDEX) TO THE 1880 POPULATION SCHEDULES, IL, Microfilm T746, Rolls 1-143, National Archives, Washington, DC.

US Bureau of the Census, INDEX (SOUNDEX) TO THE 1900 POPULATION SCHEDULES, IL, Microfilm T1043, Rolls 1-479, National Archives, Washington, DC.

US Bureau of the Census, INDEX (MIRACODE) TO THE 1910 POPULATION SCHEDULES, IL, Microfilm T1264, Rolls 1-491, National Archives, Washington, DC.

US Bureau of the Census, INDEX (SOUNDEX) TO THE 1920 POPULATION SCHEDULES, IL, Microfilm M1559, Rolls 1-509, National Archives, Washington, DC.

The Soundex listings for O-200 through O-240 from the above film are missing, so a supplement has been published:

Frederick, N. G., THE 1880 IL CENSUS INDEX, SOUNDEX CODE O-200 through O-240, THE CODE THAT WAS NOT FILMED, The Author, Evanston, IL, 1981.

Once you have located an ancestor in the indexes, you can then go directly to the reference in the census microfilms and read the entry. When complete indexes are not available (1870, 1880), it may be necessary for you to go through the census listings entry-by-entry. This can be essentially prohibitive for the entire state, so it is helpful to know the county in order to limit your search. The census record microfilms are as follows:

US Bureau of the Census, FOURTH CENSUS OF THE US, 1820, IL, Microfilm M33, Rolls 11-12, National Archives, Washington, DC.

US Bureau of the Census, FIFTH CENSUS OF THE US, 1830, IL, Microfilm M19, Rolls 22-25, National Archives, Washington, DC.

US Bureau of the Census, SIXTH CENSUS OF THE US, 1840, IL, Microfilm M704, Rolls 54-73, National Archives, Washington, DC.

US Bureau of the Census, SEVENTH CENSUS OF THE US, 1850, IL, Microfilm M432, Rolls 97-134, National Archives, Washington, DC.

US Bureau of the Census, EIGHTH CENSUS OF THE US, 1860, IL, Microfilm M653, Rolls 154-241, National Archives, Washington, DC.

US Bureau of the Census, NINTH CENSUS OF THE US, 1870, IL, Microfilm M593, Rolls 186-295, National Archives, Washington, DC.

US Bureau of the Census, TENTH CENSUS OF THE US, 1880, IL, Microfilm T9, Rolls 174-262, National Archives, Washington, DC.

US Bureau of the Census, TWELFTH CENSUS OF THE US, 1900, IL, Microfilm T623, Rolls 235-356, National Archives, Washington, DC.

___US Bureau of the Census, THIRTEENTH CENSUS OF THE US, 1910, IL, Microfilm T624, Rolls 229-337, National Archives, Washington, DC.

___US Bureau of the Census, FOURTEENTH CENSUS OF THE US, 1920, IL, Microfilm T625, Rolls 296-419, National Archives, Washington, DC.

Both the census indexes and the census films are available in NA, NARC, ISHL, ISA, NL, FHL(FHC), and some RL, LGL, and LL. Other LL have the printed or microfiche or computer disk indexes, but not the microfilmed indexes or censuses. In such cases, LL can borrow the microfilm indexes and/or censuses on interlibrary loan from:

___American Genealogical Lending Library, PO Box 329, Bountiful, UT 84011.

Farm and ranch census records (F), also known as agricultural census records, are available for 1850, 1860, 1870, and 1880 for IL. These records list the name of the owner or tenant or agent, size of the farm or ranch, value of the property, and other details. If your ancestor was a farmer (many were), it will be worthwhile to seek him in these records. No indexes are available, so it helps to know the county. The records or microfilm copies are available at ISA, FHL(FHC), NA, NARC, and NL. The records appear in:

___ISA, AGRICULTURAL (FARM AND RANCH) CENSUS SCHEDULES FOR IL, 1850-80, originals and on microfilm, ISA, Springfield, IL. Microfilms are NA Microfilm T1133.

These schedules can be very useful because in several census years, particularly 1850, many rural families were omitted in the regular census, but may be found in the farm and ranch scdedules.

Manufactures census records (M), also known as industry census records, are available for 1850, 1860, 1870, and 1880. The records list manufacturing firms which produced articles having an annual value of $500 or more. Given in these records are the name of the firm, the owner, the product, the machinery used, and the number of employees. No indexes are available, so a knowledge of the county is helpful. The records or microfilmed copies are at ISA, NA, NARC, and FHL(FHC). The records appear in:

___ISA, MANUFACTURES CENSUS SCHEDULES FOR IL, 1850-80, on microfilm, ISA, Springfield, IL. Microfilms are NA Microfilm T1133.

Mortality census records (D for death) are available for the periods June 01-May 31, 1850, 1860, 1870, and 1880. The records for 1870 are incomplete in that all counties beginning with A through Ka are lost. These records give information on persons who died in the year preceding the 1st of June of each of the above census dates (1850, 1860, 1870, 1880). They are very useful, but are only 60-70% complete. The data contained in the compilations include name, age, sex, occupation, place of birth and other such information. The ISL holds the original schedules along with a card index, and the schedules have been microfilmed. The indexed schedules for 1850-60-70 have been published as:

___L. M. Volkel, IL MORTALITY SCHEDULE, 1850, Heritage House, Indianapolis, IN, 1972, 3 volumes.

___L. M. Volkel, IL MORTALITY SCHEDULE, 1860, Heritage House, Indianapolis, IN, 1979, 5 volumes.

___L. M. Volkel, IL MORTALITY SCHEDULE, 1870, Heritage House, Indianapolis, IN, 1985, 2 volumes.

The mortality censuses for 1850-60-70-80 are also recorded and indexed on a CDROM:

___Automated Archives, MORTALITY RECORDS, CDROM 164, AGLL, Bountiful, UT, 1995.

The unindexed original or microfilmed schedules may be found at the ISA, FHL(FHC), NA, NARC, and NL.

___US Bureau of the Census, NON-POPULATION SCHEDULES, 1850-80, IL, Microfilm T1133, National Archives, Washington, DC.

In 1840 a special census of Revolutionary War Pensioners (P) was taken. This compilation was an attempt to list all pension holders, however, there are some omissions and some false entries. The list and an index have been published:

___CENSUS OF PENSIONERS, A GENERAL INDEX FOR REVO-LUTIONARY OR MILITARY SERVICE (1840), Genealogical Publishing Co., Baltimore, MD, 1965.

This volume may be found at ISHL, FHL(FHC), AND NL, and in some RL and LL.

8. Church records

Many early IL families were affiliated with a church. In 1834/35, estimated numbers of organized congregations were: Methodist (220), Baptist (200), Presbyterian (50), Christian or Disciples (20), Cumberland Presbyterian (15), Dunker (5), Lutheran (3), Quaker (2), United Brethren (1), Mormon (1). By 1850, many denominations were represented in IL's

1200 churches: Amish, Baptist, Catholic, Christian (Disciples), Episcopal, Friends (Quakers), German Baptist (Dunkers), Jewish, Lutheran, Mennonite, Methodist, Presbyterian, and United Brethren. As of 1855, the major groups in order of decreasing size were Methodist, Baptist, Presbyterian, Christian (Disciples), Catholic, Lutheran, Congregational, and Episcopal. By 1860, there were 2500 churches in the state. An important volume and two articles regarding the denominations in IL are:

___J. F. Moeller, GENEALOGY COLLECTIONS III, in IL Libraries, 74[5], (Sep 1992) 453-80. Fifteeen excellent articles on church repositories for IL churches.

___Historical Records Survey, GUIDE TO CHURCH VITAL STATISTICS RECORDS IN IL, WPA, Chicago, IL, 1942.

___H. T. Stock, PROTESTANTISM IN IL BEFORE 1835, Journal of the ISHS 12 (1919/20) 1-31.

It is well to recognize however, that most early IL settlers had no church affiliation. Some were outright irreligious, and other were religious, but were indifferent to religious organizations.

The records of the churches often prove to be very valuable since they frequently contain information on births, baptisms, marriages, deaths, admissions, dismissals, and reprimands. The data are particularly important for the years before county or state vital records were kept. Unfortunately, records of evangelical Protestant churches tend not to contain birth and death references. Many church records have been copied into books or microfilmed, some have been sent to denominational archives, but many still remain in the individual churches. Several major works and collections list sizable numbers of available church records:

___Historical Records Survey, GUIDE TO CHURCH VITAL STATISTICS RECORDS IN IL, WPA, Chicago, IL, 1942. Data for about 1000 churches as of 1942.

___J. Hoffmann, A GUIDE TO THE HISTORY OF IL, Greenwood Press, New York, NY, 1991. See names of the denominations in the index (pages 311-49) for historical volumes and archival collections.

___FAMILY HISTORY LIBRARY CATALOG, LOCALITY SECTION, FHL, Salt Lake City, UT, latest edition. Look under IL and its counties.

___MANUSCRIPT AND LOCALITY CARD AND COMPUTER CATALOGS, at ISA, ISHL, NL, and RL.

___Historical Records Survey, UNPUBLISHED INVENTORIES OF CHURCH RECORDS, WPA, Chicago, IL, 1936-42. Stored in the ISA. For these Denominations: Adventist, Assembly of God, Baptist, Brethren, Christian Union, Church of Christ-Scientist, Church of God,

Church of the Living God, Church of the Nazarene, Congregational, Disciples of Christ, Evangelical, Evangelical and Reformed, Holiness, Jewish, Latter-Day Saints, Lutheran, Methodist, Moravian, Non-Denominational, Pentecostal, Presbyterian, Protestant Episcopal, Quakers, Roman Catholic, Salvation Army, and Universalist.
___EARLY GERMAN CHURCHES OF IL, IL Palatines to America, Quincy, IL, 1989.

Use of the above works will convince you that the major sources of church records are the individual churches, ISA, ISHL, NL, FHL(FHC), RL, and special denominational archives. If you have the good fortune to know your ancestor's church, then you can write directly to the proper church official, enclosing a $5 donation and an SASE, and requesting a search of the records. If you don't know the church and therefore need to look at records of several churches in the county, the above-mentioned books and the collections at the aforementioned repositories should be consulted. LL may have some local records, as is the case for LGL. The RL usually have some records for the area. In Chapters 4 and 5, counties which have church records in published or microfilmed form are indicated. Instructions regarding the above referenced volumes and locating the records will be given in Chapter 3. Church records are often published in genealogical periodicals, so instructions for finding these will be given in a section to follow.

If, as is often the case, after exploring the resources mentioned above, you have not located your ancestor's church, you will need to dig deeper. This further searching should involve writing letters (with an SASE) to the LL, the local genealogical society, and/or the local historical society. Names and addresses of these organizations are given under the various counties in Chapters 4 and 5. If these procedures still do not yield data, then it might be well for you to contact the headquarters of the denomination you think your ancestor may have belonged to. It is well to remember that English immigrants were usually Episcopalian, Methodist, Quaker, or Congregational, Germans and Swiss were usually Lutheran or Reformed or German Methodist (although those from southern Germany were often Catholic), the Scots-Irish were generally Presbyterian or Quaker, the Dutch were Reformed, the Swedes Lutheran, and the Irish ordinarily Roman Catholic. The denominational headquarters can usually give you a list of the churches of their denomination in a given county, and the dates of their origin. Often they can also direct you to collections of church records.

Some of the major denominations of IL are listed below along with brief historical notes, their denominational and/or historical headquarters, and books which deal with their histories and/or genealogical records. There is also an indication of the genealogical value (Genealogical Value) that the records of each group usually have: good, fair, or poor. Good records means that vital statistics are usually to be found, fair records means that some vital statistics are sometimes found, and poor records means that vital statistics are seldom found (except some in obituaries in denominational periodicals).

___(Amish) Genealogical Value = poor. Broke away from Swiss Mennonites in 1693 under leadership of Jakob Ammann. First came to America in 1727, settling in PA. They began coming into central IL in 1829. Contact: Archives of the Mennonite Church, 1700 South Main St., Goshen, IN 46526. Books: J. A. Hostetler, AMISH SOCIETY, Johns Hopkins Press, Baltimore, MD, 1980; J. A. Hostetler, ANNOTATED BIBLIOGRAPHY OF THE AMISH, Mennonite Publishing House, Scottsdale, PA, 1951; C. Browning, THE AMISH IN IL, Author, Decatur, IL, 1971; H. F. Weber, CENTENNIAL HISTORY OF THE MENNONITES OF IL, 1829-1929, Mennonite Historical Society, Goshen, IN, 1931; W. H. Smith, MENNONITES IN IL, Mennonite Publishing House, Scottsdale, PA, 1983: D. P. Miller, THE IL AMISH, Pequea Publ., Gordonsville, PA, 1980.

___(Baptist) Genealogical Value = poor. Originated under leadership of John Smyth, who organized a Baptist Church among English exiles in Holland about 1607. Some of these exiles returned to England and started a Baptist Church there in 1611. The first Baptist Church in the American colonies was formed in Providence, RI, by Roger Williams in 1639. Itinerant Baptist ministers were active in IL as early as 1787, with the first Baptist Church in IL being organized in 1797 at New Design. There are four major Baptist groups today: American Baptist Churches, Southern Baptist Convention (separated in 1845), National Baptist Convention USA, and National Baptist Convention of America (separated in 1880), the latter two being predominantly black. Contacts: The Baptist Record Collections at ISHL in Springfield, IL; American Baptist Churches, PO Box 851, Valley Forge, PA 19482; American Baptist Historical Society, 1100 South Goodman Street, Rochester, NY 14620; Southern Baptist Historical Commission, 901 Commerce Street, Nashville, TN 37203; National Baptist Convention USA Headquarters, 1620 Whites Creek Pike, Nashville, TN 37207. Books: R. L. Webb, WALK ABOUT

ZION, A HISTORY OF THE PRIMITIVE BAPTISTS OF IL, 1796-1976, The Author, Burlington, IA, 1976; A. Coffey, A BRIEF HISTORY OF REGULAR BAPTISTS, PRINCIPALLY OF SOUTHERN IL, Martin and Co., Paducah, KY, 1877; W. P. Throgmorton, HISTORY OF THE FRANKLIN ASSOCIATION OF UNITED BAPTISTS, Baptist Banner Print, Benton, IL, 1880; S. M. Eltscher, THE RECORDS OF AMERICAN BAPTISTS IN IL, American Baptist Historical Society, Rochester, NY, 1982; W. W. Sweet, RELIGION ON THE AMERICAN FRONTIER, VOL. 1, BAPTISTS, Harper, New York, NY, 1931; R. G. Torbet, A HISTORY OF THE BAPTISTS, Judson Press, Valley Forge, PA, 1973; H. L. McBeth, THE BAPTIST HERITAGE, Broadman Press, Nashville, TN, 1983; ENCYCLOPEDIA OF SOUTHERN BAPTISTS, Broadman Press, Nashville, TN, 1958, 3 volumes; C. S. Hayne, THEY WHO MADE THE WAY, American Baptist Publishing Society, Philadelphia, PA, 1934.

___(Brethren or Dunkers) Genealogical Value = poor. A German pietistic Anabaptist sect founded in 1709 by Alexander Mack in Schwarzenau, Germany. First came to American colonies in 1719, settling at Germantown, PA. The first IL Brethren came from PA, OH, NC, and KY. Headquarters: Brethren Historical Library and Archives, Church of the Brethren, 1451 Dundee Avenue, Elgin, IL 60120; also contact Fellowship of Brethren Genealogists at the same address; Library, Manchester College, College Avenue, North Manchester, IN 46962. Books: H. Holsinger, HISTORY OF THE TUNKERS AND THE BRETHREN CHURCH, Pacific Press, Lathrop, CA, 1901; M. G. Brumbaugh, A HISTORY OF THE GERMAN BAPTIST BRETHREN IN EUROPE AND AMERICA, AMS Press, New York, NY, 1909; THE BRETHREN ENCYCLOPEDIA, Brethren Encyclopedia, Inc., Philadelphia, PA, 1983-4, 3 volumes; L. Eby, EVERY NAME INDEX, BRETHREN IN NORTHERN IL AND WI, Heckman and Miller, Mill Valley, CA, 1941; M. S. Buckingham, CHURCH OF THE BRETHREN IN SOUTHERN IL, Brethren Publ. House, Elgin, IL, 1950; NEWSLETTER OF THE FELLOWSHIP OF BRETHREN GENEALOGISTS, The Fellowship, Elgin, IL, 1969-.

___(Christian Church-Disciples of Christ) Genealogical Value = poor. Established largely from a melding of movements started by three Presbyterians, Barton W. Stone (1804) in KY and Thomas and Alexander Campbell (1809) in PA. The first Christian Churches were organized in 1819 north of Mt. Carmel and near the site of Cantrell. More Christian Churches and like-minded Disciple Churches followed rapidly. The two groups united in IL in 1832. Contact: Disciples of Christ Historical Society, 1101 Nineteenth Avenue, Nashville, TN 37212; Christian Theological Seminary, 1000 West 42nd St., Indianapolis, IN 46208; Booke: W. E. Garrison and A. T. DeGroot, THE DISCIPLES OF CHRIST, A HISTORY, Bethany Press, St. Louis, MO, 1948; N. S. Haynes, HISTORY OF THE DISCIPLES OF CHRIST IN IL, 1819-1914, Standard Publ. Co., Cincinnati, OH, 1915.

___(Churches of Christ) Genealogical Value = poor. Individual churches began to split off from the Christian Church (Disciples) after the 1860s, the movement being essentially complete by about 1900. The Christian Church had been established from a melding of movements started by Barton W. Stone (1804) of KY and by Thomas and Alexander Campbell (1809) of PA. Contact: Harding Graduate School of Religion Library, 1000 Cherry Road, Memphis, TN 38117. Books: W. E. Garrison and A. T. DeGroot, THE DISCIPLES OF CHRIST, A HISTORY, Bethany Press, St. Louis, MO, 1948; A. T. DeGroot, THE GROUNDS OF DIVISIONS AMONG THE DISCIPLES OF CHRIST, The Author, St. Louis, MO, 1940.

___(Congregationalists) Genealogical Value = good-fair. Started in England in the early 1600s as a branch of Puritanism, called Separatists. First settled in the colonies in MA in 1620, where they merged with non-Separatist Puritan settlers to form the Congregational Church. Congregational missionaries were in IL fairly early, but they became ministers of Presbyterian churches. The first Congregational churches appeared in 1833, three being organized at Mendon, Napierville, and Jacksonville, and a Presbyterian church at Quincy changing over. In 1931, the denomination merged with other groups to form the Congregational Christian Churches. This group, in turn, merged with the Evangelical and Reformed Church in 1957 to form the United Church of Christ. Contact: Congregational Library, 14 Beacon Street, Boston, MA 02108. Books: M. Spinka, A HISTORY OF IL CONGREGATIONAL AND CHRISTIAN CHURCHES, Congregational and Christian Conference of IL, Chicago, IL, 1944; IL Society of Church History, Congregational, HISTORICAL STATEMENT AND PAPERS, The Society, Chicago, IL, 1895; W. W. Sweet, RELIGION ON THE AMERICAN FRONTIER, VOL. 3, THE CONGREGATIONALISTS, Harper, New York, NY, 1939-40; G. G. Atkins and F. L. Fagley, HISTORY OF AMERICAN CONGRE-GATIONALISM, Pilgrim Press, Boston, MA, 1942; W. Walker, THE HISTORY OF THE CONGREGATIONAL CHURCHES IN THE US, American Congregational Historical Society, New York, NY, 1894.

___(Episcopal Church) Genealogical Value = good. Developed from the Church of England which split from the Roman Catholic Church in 1534. First brought to the American colonies by English settlers of VA in 1607. There was little Episcopal activity early in central and southern IL, but a church was organized in Chicago in 1824. Contact: Historiographer's Office, Episcopal Diocesan Center, 821 South Second St., Springfield, IL 62704; Archives of the Episcopal Church, 815 Second Avenue, New York, NY 10017; Library and Archives of the Church Historical Society, 606 Rathervue Place, Austin, TX 78767. Books: P. L. Shutt, 3653 IL NAMES, Episcopal Diocese of Springfield, Springfield, IL, 1978; THE EPISCOPAL CHURCH ANNUAL, Morehouse, Wilton, CT, latest issue; W. S. Perry, HISTORY OF THE AMERICAN EPISCOPAL CHURCH, 1587-1883, Osgood, Boston, MA, 1885, 2 volumes; R. W. Albright, A HISTORY OF THE PROTESTANT EPISCOPAL CHURCH, Macmillan, New York, NY, 1964; P. V. Norwood, THE PRIMARY CONVENTION OF THE [EPISCOPAL] DIOCESE OF IL, Historical Magazine of the Protestant Episcopal Church 24 (Sep 1955).

___(German Methodists) Genealogical Value = fair-poor. There were two predominant groups of German people who adopted Methodist polity. The first was the United Brethren established by Philip W. Otterbein and Martin Boehm in PA in 1800, an IL congregation being organized in 1830. The second was the Evangelical Church formed by Jacob Albright in PA in 1803. These two united in 1946 to form the Evangelical United Brethren which in turn, united with the Methodist Church in 1968 to form the United Methodist Church. Contact: Center for Evangelical United Brethren Studies, 1810 Harvard Boulevard, Dayton, OH 45406; Archives and Library, Huntington College, Huntington, IN 46750; Books: J. M. Overton, MINISTERS AND CHURCHES OF THE CENTRAL GERMAN (METHODIST) CONFERENCE, 1835-1907, Heritage House, Thomson, IL, 1975; P. F. Douglass, THE STORY OF GERMAN METHODISM, Methodist Book Concern, New York, NY, 1939; L. W. Turner, THE UNITED BRETHREN CHURCH IN IL, in PAPERS IN IL HISTORY AND TRANSACTIONS FOR 1939, ISHL, Springfield, IL, 1939; J. G. Schwab, HISTORY OF THE IL CONFERENCE OF THE EVANGELICAL CHURCH, 1837-1937, The Evangelical Church, Harrisburg, PA, 1937.

___(Jewish) Genealogical Value = good-fair. Jewish congregations stem back to the Old Testament patriarch Abraham at about 1900 BC. The first established religious community was formed in 1654 in New York, NY. The first IL Jewish congregation was established in 1847 in Chicago.

Contact: American Jewish Archives, 3101 Clifton Avenue, Cincinnati, OH 45220; American Jewish Historical Society, 2 Thornton Road, Waltham, MA 02154; Jewish Genealogical Society of IL, PO Box 515, Northbrook, IL 60065; Silber Library, Hebrew Theological College, 7135 North Carpenter Road, Skokie, IL 60077. Books: M. A. Gutstein, A PRICELESS HERITAGE: THE EPIC GROWTH OF 19TH CENTURY CHICAGO JEWRY, Bloch Publishing Co., New York, NY, 1953; JEWISH ENCYCLOPEDIA, Funk and Wagnalls, New York, NY, 1901-6, 12 volumes; D. Rottenberg, FINDING YOUR FATHERS, Random House, New York, NY, 1977; M. H. Stern, FIRST AMERICAN JEWISH FAMILIES, American Jewish Archives, Cincinnati, OH, 1991.

___(Lutheran) Genealogical Value = good. Lutheran church bodies derive from the controversy of Martin Luther with the Roman Catholic Church in the Germanic area in 1521. A Dutch Lutheran Church was formed in New Amsterdam (New York, NY) in the middle 1600s, but most of the early Lutherans came from Germanic areas into Philadelphia and New York, and then moved north, west, and south. Today there are several Lutheran groups, so it may be necessary to contact several agencies. Contact: Lutheran Church MO Synod Archives and Library, 801 De Mun Avenue, St. Louis, MO 63105; Archives of the Lutheran Church in America, 333 Wartburg Place, Dubuque, IA 52001; Lutheran Archives Center, 7301 Germantown Avenue, Philadelphia, PA 19119; Archives of Cooperative Lutheranism, Evangelical Lutheran Church in America, 8765 West Higgins Road, Chicago, IL 60631; ELCA Archives, 8765 West Higgins Road, Chicago, IL 60631; Books: J. Bodensieck, THE ENCYCLOPEDIA OF THE LUTHERAN CHURCH, Augsburg Publishing House, Minneapolis, MN, 1965; E. L. Luecker, LUTHERAN CYCLOPEDIA, Concordia Press, St. Louis, MO, 1975; L. M. Heilman, HISTORICAL SKETCH OF THE EVANGELICAL LUTHERAN SYNOD OF NORTHERN IL, Lutheran Publication Society, Philadelphia, PA, 1892; M. L. Wagner, THE CHICAGO SYNOD AND ITS ANTECEDENTS, Wartburg Publishing House, Waverly, IA, 1909; PROGRESS OF A CENTURY: A HISTORY OF THE IL SYNOD OF THE UNITED LUTHERAN CHURCH IN AMERICA, 1851-1951, The Synod, Chicago, IL, 1951.

___(Mennonite) Genealogical Value = poor. This denomination originated in Switzerland under the leadership of Conrad Grebel and Georg Blaurock in 1525. They were originally known as Anabaptists, but took the name Mennonites after their leader Menno Simons who joined them in 1536. Their first settlement in the American colonies was at

Germantown, PA, in 1683. Contact: IL Mennonite Historical and Genealogical Society Library, PO Box 819, Metamora, IL 61548; Mennonite Historical Committee, 1700 South Main, Goshen IN 46526; Mennonite General Office, 421 South Second Street, Elkhart, IN 46516. Books: H. F. Weber, CENTENNIAL HISTORY OF THE MENNONITES OF IL, 1829-1929, Mennonite Historical Society, Goshen, IN, 1931; W. H. Smith, MENNONITES IN IL, Mennonite Publishing House, Scottsdale, PA, 1983; H. S. Bender and C. H. Smith, THE MENNONITE ENCYCLOPEDIA, Mennonite Brethren Publishing House, Hillsboro, KS, 1955-9, 4 volumes; C. J. Dyck, AN INTRODUCTION TO MENNONITE HISTORY, Herald Press, Scottsdale, PA, 1967.

___(Methodist) Genealogical Value = fair-poor. The Methodist movement began in the Church of England in the late 1720s under the leadership of John Wesley. In 1784, the group formally separated from the Church of England. The first Methodist minister came to IL in 1793, two more arriving in 1796. In 1803, the first circuit rider began his rounds. Congregations were rapidly established, the first being at Sharon in 1805. Contact: Central IL Methodist Conference Historical Society, 1211 North Park St., Bloomington, IL 61701; Garrett Theological Seminary, 2121 Sheridan Road, Evanston, IL 60201; IL Wesleyan University Library, Bloomington, IL 61702; McKendree College Library, Lebanon, IL 62254; General Commission on Archives and History, The United Methodist Church, P.O. Box 127, Madison, NJ 07940; Historical Archives of the Free Methodist Church, 901 College, Winona Lake, IN 46590; Wesleyan Methodist Church Archives, PO Box 2000, Marion, IN 46952. Books: J. G. Melton, LOG CABINS TO STEEPLES, THE COMPLETE STORY OF THE UNITED METHODIST WAY IN IL, 1824-1974, Parthenon, Nashville, TN, 1974; A. M. Pennewell, THE METHODIST MOVEMENT IN NORTHERN IL, Sycamore Tribune, Sycamore, IL, 1942; A. D. Field, MEMORIALS OF METHODISM IN THE BOUNDS OF THE ROCK RIVER CONFERENCE, Cranston and Stowe, Cincinnati, OH, 1880; W. J. Walls, AFRICAN METHODIST EPISCOPAL ZION CHURCH, REALITY OF THE BLACK CHURCH, Zion A. M. E. Publishing House, Charlotte, NC, 1974; H. C. Luccock, THE STORY OF METHODISM, Abingdon Press, New York NY, 1949; W. W. Sweet, RELIGION ON THE AMERICAN FRONTIER, VOL. 4, THE METHODISTS, Harper, New York, NY, 1946; B. R. Little, METHODIST UNION CATALOG OF HISTORY, BIOGRAPHY, DISCIPLINES, AND HYMNALS, Association of Methodist Historical Societies, Lake Junaluska, NC, 1967; J. B. Finley, SKETCHES OF WESTERN METHODISM, Arno Press, New York, NY, 1969.

___(Moravian) Genealogical Value = good. Moravians had their origins as a community of followers of the Reformer John Hus about 1410 in Bohemia (now the Czech Republic). The faith spread into neighboring Moravia (now the western section of the Slovak Republic), but the members were almost annihilated in the Thirty Years War (1618-48). They first came to the American colonies in 1735, settling in GA, then moving to PA in 1740. Contact: Archives of the Moravian Church, 41 West Locust Street, Bethlehem, PA 18018; Moravian Historical Society, 214 East Center St., Nazareth, PA 18064. Books: J. E. Hutton, HISTORY OF THE MORAVIAN CHURCH, Moravian Publication Office, London, England, 1909; E. Langton, HISTORY OF THE MORAVIAN CHURCH, Allen and Unwin, London, England, 1955.

___(Mormon or Church of Jesus Christ of Latter-day Saints) Genealogical Value = good. Organized in 1830 at Fayette, NY, by Joseph Smith. Mormons came to IL in sizable numbers in 1839, set up Nauvoo, and within three years numbered 16,000. In 1847, they left for UT because of continuing hostilities with non-Mormons in the area. Contact: Library and Historical Department, CJCLDS, both at 50 East North Temple, Salt Lake City, UT 84150. Books: S. B. Kimball, SOURCES OF MORMON HISTORY IN IL, 1839-48, AT SOUTHERN IL UNIVERSITY, The University, Carbondale, IL, 1966.L. J. Arrington and D. Bitton, THE MORMON EXPERIENCE, A HISTORY OF THE LATTER DAY-SAINTS, Random House, New York, NY, 1979; T. F. O'Dea, THE MORMONS, University of Chicago Press, Chicago, IL, 1957; J. Shipps, MORMONISM, THE STORY OF A NEW RELIGIOUS TRADITION, Harper, New York, NY, 1985.

___(Presbyterian) Genealogical Value = good-fair. The churches of the Presbyterian or Reformed tradition (as they were and are called in Europe) are Protestant churches governed by boards of ministers and lay persons called elders (presbyters). These churches had their origin by John Calvin in Zurich, Switzerland, during the Reformation in the year 1523. The doctrines and church organization were introduced into Scotland in 1557-60 by John Knox. Although there were some similar churches before, the first clearly Presbyterian congregation in the colonies was probably the one on the Elizabeth River near Norfolk, VA, about 1675. A church was definitely formed at Rehoboth, MD, in 1683, and the first presbytery (association) dates back to 1706 in Philadelphia. Presbyterians came to IL only in small numbers prior to about 1815, establishing their first church at Sharon in 1816. They cooperated closely with Congregationalists in IL mission work, some of their earlier churches being served by Congregationalist ministers. Contact: Library, Hanover College, PO Box 287, Hanover, IN 47243; American Home Missionary Society, Amistad Research Center, Tilton Hall, Tulane University, 6823 St. Charles Avenue, New Orleans, LA 70118; Presbyterian Historical Association, Presbyterian Church USA, 425 Lombard Street, Philadelphia, PA 19147; Historical Center, Presbyterian Church in America, 12330 Conway Road, St. Louis, MO 63141. Books: J. B. Logan, HISTORY OF THE CUMBERLAND PRESBYTERIAN CHURCH IN IL, Perrin and Smith, Alton, Il, 1878; A. T. Norton, HISTORY OF THE PRESBYTERIAN CHURCH IN THE STATE OF IL, Bryan, St. Louis, MO, 1879; Historical Records Survey, INVENTORY OF THE CHURCH ARCHIVES OF IL, WPA, Chicago, IL, 1941-42, 3 volumes, only the Cairo, Springfield, and Cumberland Presbyteries; W. W. Sweet, RELIGION ON THE AMERICAN FRONTIER, VOL. 2, THE PRESBYTERIANS, Harper, New York, NY, 1936; L. A. Loetscher, A BRIEF HISTORY OF THE PRESBYTERIANS, Westminster Press, Philadelphia, PA, 1978; W. L. Lingle, PRESBYTERIANS, THEIR HISTORY AND BELIEFS, John Knox Press, Richmond, VA, 1960; UNION CATALOG OF PRESBYTERIAN MANUSCRIPTS, Presbyterian Library Association, Philadelphia, PA, 1964.

___(Quakers or Religious Society of Friends) Genealogical Value = good. These people trace their origin back to George Fox who began making converts in 1647 in the midlands of England. Quakers soon began showing up in the American colonies. The first Quaker yearly meeting in the colonies was organized in 1661 in Newport, RI, by the many Friends who had come to RI. The first Monthly Quaker meeting in IL came together in Putnam County in 1841. Contact: Lilly Library, Earlham College Archives, Richmond, IN 47374. Books: ABSTRACTS OF THE RECORDS OF THE SOCIETY OF FRIENDS OF THE VERMILION QUARTERLY MEETING, Illiana Genealogical Society, Danville, IL, 1970; E. T. Elliott, QUAKERS IN THE AMERICAN FRONTIER, Friends United Press, Richmond, IN, 1969.

___(Roman Catholic) Genealogical Value = good. The Roman Catholic Church traces its origins back to Peter, an apostle of Jesus and traditionally the first Bishop of Rome, approximately 55-64 AD. The first coming of Catholics to the American English colonies was to St. Marys, MD, in 1634. The Catholic presence in IL dates from 1675 with the establishment of the Mission of the Immaculate Conception on the IL River near Starved Rock. Following the British victory in the French and Indian War, the Catholic population diminished, and dropped almost to zero after the American Revolution. The church was slowly reestablished with the coming of Catholics from the East beginning about 1805. Growth was so rapid that the See for all of IL was set up in Chicago in 1843. After checking the individual parish, contact the Archdiocese of Chicago (Archives and Records Center, 5150 Northwest Hwy., Chicago, IL 60630), or one of the other dioceses of IL: Belleville, Joliet, Peoria, Rockford, and Springfield. Addresses in the telephone books. Books: H. C. Koenig, A HISTORY OF THE ARCHDIOCESE OF CHICAGO, Chicago, IL, The Archdiocese, 1980; A. O'Rourke, THE GOOD WORK BEGUN, CENTENNIAL HISTORY OF PEORIA DIOCESE, Donnelley and Sons, Peoria, IL, 1977; R. R. Miller, THAT ALL MAY BE ONE, A HISTORY OF THE ROCKFORD DIOCESE, The Diocese, Rockford, IL, 1976; CENTENNIAL EDITION OF THE MESSENGER OF THE CATHOLIC DIOCESE OF BELLEVILLE, The Diocese, Belleville, IL, 1988; H. J. Alerding, A HISTORY OF THE CATHOLIC CHURCH IN THE DIOCESE OF VINCENNES, Carlon and Hollenbeck, Indianapolis, IN, 1883; J. P. Dolan, THE AMERICAN CATHOLIC EXPERIENCE, A HISTORY FROM COLONIAL TIMES TO THE PRESENT, Double-day, New York, NY, 1985; THE NEW CATHOLIC ENCYCLOPEDIA, McGraw-Hill, New York, NY, 1967, 15 volumes, with supplementary volumes published after.

___(Shakers) Genealogical Value = fair. This fellowship, more correctly the United Society of Believers in Christ's second coming, was founded in 1772 in Manchester, England, by Ann Lee. She and some of her followers came to Watervliet, NY, in 1776. Contact: Western Reserve Historical Society Library, 10825 East Boulevard, Cleveland, OH 44106; Shaker Historical Society, 16740 South Park Blvd., Shaker Heights, OH 44120. Books: E. A. Andrews, THE PEOPLE CALLED SHAKERS, Dover Publications, New York, NY, 1953; M. F. Melcher, THE SHAKER ADVENTURE, Oxford University Press, London, England, 1960.

___(Unitarian-Universalist) Genealogical Value = poor. In 1779, John Murray became the pastor of the first Universalist Church in the US at Gloucester, MA. Many other churches in New England and PA soon joined them. The first Unitarian Church in the US was established by Joseph Priestly in 1796 in Philadelphia. By the early 1800s, many Congregational churches were joining the movement, and in 1825 a separate denomination was formed. In 1961, the Unitarians and the Universalists united to form the Unitarian-Universalist Association. Contact: Archives of the Unitarian-Universalist Association, 25 Beacon Street, Boston, MA 02108. Books: C. L. Scott, THE UNIVERSALIST

CHURCH OF AMERICA, A SHORT HISTORY, Universalist Historical Society, Boston, MA, 1957; G. W. Cooke, UNITARIANISM IN AMERICA, American Unitarian Association, Boston, MA, 1906.

Many IL city and county histories contain histories of churches. These city and county histories are discussed in section 9 of this chapter. Numerous church records have also been published in genealogical periodicals. Indexes are generally available for these periodicals, which makes searching them for church records very convenient. The periodicals and their indexes will be treated in a later section. The books referred to above can be located at ISHL and NL, with some being available at FHL(FHC) and in some RL and LL. Look up the county, the church name, and the denominational name in the card and/or computer catalogs in these repositories.

---

9. City directories

During the 19th century many larger cities in the US began publishing city directories. These volumes usually appeared erratically at first, but then began to come out annually a little later on. They list heads of households and workers plus their addresses and occupations. In addition, there will usually be city officials, church addresses, assoications, hospitals, banks, libraries, cemeteries, clubs, unions, schools, and other such helpful data.

The earliest dates of city/town directories in IL (starting before 1899, and with some county directories appended) are:

Adrian 1867-	Jacksonville 1890-	Rockford 1857-
Alton 1858-	Joliet 1861-	Rock Island 1855-
Belleville 1860-	Kankakee 1896-	Springfield 1855-
Bloomington 1870-	Keywest 1887-	Sterling 1890-
Cairo 1864-	Lake 1885-	Streator 1898-
Canton 1893-	LaSalle 1891-	Waukegan 1895-
Chicago 1839-	Lincoln 1889-	Bureau Co 1858-
Danville 1889-	Lockport 1866-	Coles Co 1894-
Decatur 1889-	Maywood 1896-	Livingston Co 1898-
Evanston 1887-	Moline 1860-	McLean Co 1887-
Freeport 1896-	Oak Park 1887-	Randolph Co 1859-
Galena 1847-	Ottawa 1888-	Sangamon Co 1866-
Harlem 1896-	Pekin 1870-	Will Co 1859-
Hyde Park 1883-	Peoria 1844-	Northern IL 1855-
Irving Park 1899-	Quincy 1848-	

After about 1865, many of these towns and cities published a city directory each year. In general, the smaller cities and towns of IL did not begin regular publication until later in the 19th or in the 20th century. Many of the directories are available in ISHL, NL, and FHL(FHC). RL and LL also usually have collections pertaining to their own cities.

The telephone was invented in 1876-7, underwent rapid development, and became widespread fairly quickly. By the late years of the century telephone directories were coming into existence. Older issues can often be found in LL, and as the years go on, they have proved to be ever more valuable genealogical sources.

10. City and county histories

Histories for many IL counties and numerous cities have been published. These volumes usually contain biographical data on leading citizens, details about early settlers, histories of organizations, businesses, trades, and churches, and often list clergymen, lawyers, physicians, teachers, governmental officials, farmers, military men, and other groups. Several works which list many of these histories are:

___M. J. Kaminkow, US LOCAL HISTORIES IN THE LIBRARY OF CONGRESS, Magna Carta, Baltimore, MD, 1975, 5 volumes, index in the 5th volume.

___P. W. Filby, A BIBLIOGRAPHY OF COUNTY HISTORIES IN 50 STATES, Genealogical Publishing Co., Baltimore, MD, 1985.

___FAMILY HISTORY LIBRARY CATALOG, LOCALITY SECTION, in either microform or computer, FHL, Salt Lake City, UT, latest edition. Look under state, then under county, then city or town. Also at every FHC.

___COUNTY AND REGIONAL HISTORIES OF THE OLD NORTHWEST [INCLUDING IL], Research Publns., New Haven, CT, 1975, 96 microfilm rolls.

___S. J. Buck, TRAVEL AND DESCRIPTION [OF IL], 1765-1865, ISHL, Springfield, IL, 1914. Contains list of county histories and atlases available then.

___R. H. Kaige and E. L. Vaughan, IL COUNTY HISTORIES, A CHECK LIST OF IL COUNTY HISTORIES IN THE ISL, IL Libraries 50 (Sep 1968).

Most of the IL volumes in these bibliographies can be found in ISL, ISHL, and NL. Many are available at FHL or through FHC, and some are usually in LGL. RL and LL are likely to have those relating to their particular areas.

A useful index to 68 of the county histories of IL is available. It is at the Winnetka Public Library and at ISA. The index was compiled as part of the IL Bicentennial Project of the IL State Genealogical Society and the Winnetka Public Library Genealogy Committee.

__INDEX TO COUNTY HISTORIES OF IL, Genealogy Projects Committee, Winnetka Public Library, Winnetka, IL, 1976. Also available at ISA.

In Chapters 4 and 5 you will find listed under the counties various recommended county histories. Also there will be an indication under each county for which city histories are available.

---

11. Court records

Among the most unexplored genealogical source materials are the court records of the state of IL and of the IL counties. They are often exceptionally valuable, giving information that is obtainable no where else. It is, therefore, of great importance that you carefully examine court documents, especially for difficult searches. Several good treatments of the court system of IL are available:

__D. F. Rolewick, A SHORT HISTORY OF THE IL JUDICIAL SYSTEMS, Administrative Office of the IL Courts, Springfield, IL, 1971.

__G. Fiedler, THE IL LAW COURTS IN THREE CENTURIES, 1673-1973, Physicians Record Co., Berwyn, IL, 1973.

__F. B. Crossley, COURTS AND LAWYERS OF IL, American Historical Society, Chicago, IL, 1916.

There are some difficulties that need to be recognized if you are not to miss court data. The first is that there were several types of courts, some no longer exist, some replaced others, some had their names changed, often their jurisdictions overlapped, and further, the exact court situation sometimes varies from county to county. In addition, the court systems during 1693-1787 were beset with neglect and controversy between French and English systems and settlers. The court systems during the earlier years of statehood were plagued by the fact that the constitutions gave the legislature so much power over the judiciary that it was manipulated, perverted, and continually altered. The most important courts whose records you might seek will now be listed. Notes are added regarding the main types of cases they handled. The courts during the French regime (1673-1765) were:

___Commandant Court (1717-22)

___Provincial Council (1722-26)

___Court of Royal Justice (1726-65)

___Commanders Courts in the Settlements (1722-65) minor cases

When IL was under the British (1765-78), these were the important courts:

___Court of Justice (1768-78)

___Court of Inquiry (1770-78) civil cases

And under the Commonwealth of VA (1778-87) and for a while thereafter, the IL County courts were:

___Court of Kaskaskia (1779-90)

___Court of Cahokia (1779-90)

___Court of Vincennes (1779-90)

___Justice of the Peace Courts (1779-90) minor cases

Under the Northwest Territory, the IL country (1787-1800) was served by these courts:

___Territorial General Court (1788-1800) civil, criminal, and appeals, judges also rode circuit

___County Courts of General Quarter Sessions (1788-1800) civil, criminal, administrative, and probate matters

___County Courts of Common Pleas (1790-1800) civil

___County Probate or Orphans Court (1788-1805); guardianships, probates [activated in St. Clair County in 1790, in Randolph County 1795]

___Justice of the Peace Courts (1788-1800) minor cases, not courts of record

When the IL country came under the IN Territory (1800-09), the important courts were:

___Territorial General Court (1801-09) civil, criminal, appeals

___Circuit Courts (1801-09) civil, criminal

___County Courts of General Quarter Sessions (1801-05) criminal, administrative, jurisdictions transferred to the County Courts of Common Pleas in 1805

___County Probate Courts (1801-05) probate, jurisdictions transferred to the County Courts of Common Pleas in 1805

___County Courts of Common Pleas (1801-09) civil, then after 1805 criminal, administrative, probate

___Justice of the Peace Courts (1801-09) minor cases, not courts of record

Establishment of the IL Terrritory (1809-18) gave these important courts:

___Territorial General Court (1809-14) civil, criminal, appeals, replaced
by Territorial Supreme Court in 1814
___Territorial Supreme Court (1814-18) civil, criminal, appeals
___Circuit Courts (1809-18) civil, criminal
___Territorial Court of Appeals (1815-18) appeals
___County Courts of Common Pleas (1809-14) civil, criminal, probate,
administrative, replaced by County Courts in 1814
___County Courts (1814-18) civil, criminal, probate, administrative
___Justice of the Peace Courts (1809-18) minor cases, not courts of record

When IL became a state in 1818, its court system was defined by its
first constitution and laws enacted implementing the constitution. The
courts were:
___Supreme Court (1818-48) appeals
___Circuit Courts (1818-48) civil, criminal
___County Commissioners (1818-48) administrative, and probate during
1818-21, after which Probate Courts were set up
___Probate Courts (1821-48) probate
___Justice of the Peace Courts (1818-48) minor cases, not courts of record
___Municipal Courts of Chicago and Alton (1837-39) civil, criminal
___Cook County and Jo Daviess County Courts (1845-48)
A new constitution was framed in 1848, and it gave rise to the following
judiciary organizations:
___Supreme Court (1848-70) appeals
___Circuit Courts (1848-70) civil, criminal
___County Courts (1848-70) civil, criminal, probate; except for Cook
County 1849-70
___Cook County Court (1848-49) civil, criminal, probate
___Cook County Court of Common Pleas (1849-59), civil, criminal,
probate, formerly Cook County Court
___County Boards of Supervisors (1848-70) administrative
___Recorders Court of Chicago (1853-74) civil, criminal
___Court of Common Pleas at Cairo (1855-69) civil, criminal
___Recorders Courts at LaSalle and Peru (1857-70) civil, criminal
___Courts of Common Pleas at Aurora and Elgin (1857-70) civil, criminal
___Superior Court of Chicago (1859-70) civil and criminal, formerly Cook
County Court of Common Pleas
___City Court at Alton (1859-74) civil, criminal
___Recorders Court at Peoria (1861-63) civil, criminal
___Courts of Common Pleas at Amboy, Mattoon, and Sparta (1869-70)
civil, criminal

___Justice of the Peace Courts (1848-70) minor cases, not a court of record

The third constitution for IL was put in place in 1870. The courts that it and legislation based on it provided were:
___Supreme Court (1870-1964) appeals
___Appellate Courts (1877-1964) appeals
___Court of Claims (1903-64) claims
___Circuit Courts (1870-1964) civil, criminal
___County Courts (1870-1964) probate, administration, civil, criminal
___Justice of the Peace Courts (1870-1964) minor cases
___Police Magistrate Courts (1870-1964) minor cases
___City Courts (1901-64) civil, criminal
___Superior Court of Cook County (1874-1964) civil, criminal, formerly the Superior Court of Chicago
___Probate Courts [in larger counties] (1877-1964) probate, replaced the probate actions of County Courts in larger counties
___Criminal Court of Cook County (1874-1964) criminal, formerly the Recorders Court of Chicago
___Municipal Court of Chicago (1905-64) civil, criminal, had numerous specialized branch courts
In 1964, a remarkable simplification of the IL court system occurred. Only three courts were designated:
___Supreme Court (1964-) appeals
___Courts of Appeal (1964-) appeals
___Circuit Courts (1964-) all cases
Because of the very large population of Cook County, the Circuit Court of Cook County was sub-divided into two departments: the Municipal and the County. The Municipal Department was then further sub-divided into six geographical districts, each having a criminal and a civil section. The County Department was divided into several specialized divisions: Law (large recovery of damage suits), Probate (wills, estates, minors, incompetents), Family (dependent and neglected children, delinquency), Divorce (divorce, annulment, separate maintenance), Criminal (felony cases), County (adoption, tax, municipal organizations, elections, mental health), and Chancery (injunctions, will and trust arrangements, foreclosures). The federal courts serving the state of IL are:
___US Federal District Courts (approximately 1819-present)
___US Federal Circuit Courts (approximately 1819-1911)

A second difficulty with IL court records is that the records of the different courts appear in record books, file cabinets, and filing boxes with various titles and labels. These titles and labels do not always describe everything in the volumes, and records of various types may be mixed up or they may all appear in a single set of books. This latter is especially true in earlier years. Fortunately, there is a simple rule that avoids all these difficulties: look for your ancestor in all available court records that have alphabetical finding aids, regardless of what the labellings on the books, cabinets, files, and boxes happen to be. In cases in which you may be having difficulty in locating information on your ancestor, you may need to extend your investigation to unindexed records.

In certain kinds of court matters (such as trials, estates, wills, and others), the record books will refer to folders which contain detailed documents concerning the matters. The folders are usually filed in the court house (CH) and must not be overlooked because they are often gold mines of information. In the county of your interest, you may find records dealing with proceedings of the various courts (records, minutes, dockets, enrollments, registers, orders), with land (deeds, entries, land grants, mortgages, trust deeds, surveys, ranges, plats, roads), with probate matters (wills, estate, administrators, executors, inventories, settlements, sales, guardians, orphans, insolvent estates, bastardy, apprentices, insanity), with vital records (birth, death, marriage, divorce), and with taxation (tax, bonds, appropriations, delinquent taxes). In most cases there will not be records with all these titles, but several of these items will appear in one type of book, cabinet, file, or box. If all of this seems complicated, do not worry. All you need to do is to remember the rules: examine all court records which have alphabetical finding aids, be on the lookout for references to folders, ask about them and then examine them also. Then, if needed, proceed to the unindexed records.

First, we will discuss the county records. The original record books, boxes, cabinets, files, and folders are in the county court houses (CH) and/or in the IL Regional Archives Depository (IRAD) for the area. Microfilms and transcripts (published and manuscript) of many of the books have been made, but only a very few of the boxes, files, folders, and cabinet contents have been copied. Many of the microfilmed and transcribed records are available at ISHL and NL. Many are in FHL and are available through FHC. Some of the transcribed materials are to be found in RL but only a few of the microfilms. A few LGL have some of the transcribed records. LL may have transcribed records for the local area. Listings of many of the microfilms available at ISHL, NL, and/or FHL(FHC) are shown in:

___FAMILY HISTORY LIBRARY CATALOG, LOCALITY SECTION, FHL, Salt Lake City, UT, latest microfiche and computer editions. Look under IL and its counties.

Chapter 3 discusses the process of obtaining these records, and Chapters 4 and 5 list those available for each of the 102 IL counties.

Not only were there county-based courts, there were ones with regional and state-wide jurisdiction. The records of many of these are available in original, microfilm, or published form. Included among the most promising of these sources for genealogists are:

___State Supreme Court (1817-present): appeals. See inventories, indexes, and microfilms in ISA.

___State Court of Appeals (1877-present): appeals. See inventories, indexes, and microfilms in ISA.

Further, there is a name index to cases which were appealed from a lower IL court to a higher one:

___IL DIGEST, West Publ. Co., St. Paul, MN, 1939-, many volumes.

Finally, the federal and territorial court records must not be overlooked. Many of the records of the US Federal District and Circuit Courts for IL (approximately 1819-1982) are available in Record Group 21 at the Chicago Branch of the National Archives, 7358 South Pulaski Road, Chicago, IL 60629 [Phone 1-(312)-581-7816]. Northwest Territorial records (for 1787-1801), IN Territorial records (for 1804-16), and IL Territorial records (for 1809-18), including some court records, are available at the National Archives in Washington, DC in Record Group 59.

12. DAR records

The Daughters of the American Revolution (DAR), in their quest for the lines linking them to their Revolutionary War ancestors, have gathered and published many volumes of records of genealogical pertinence. The IL chapters of the organization have provided many volumes of county records (chiefly court, deed, marriage, probate, tax, will), Bible records, cemetery records, and family records.

___DAR Chapters in IL, THE BLUE BOOKS [TRANSCRIPTS OF IL GENEALOGICAL RECORDS], and the GRANDPARENT PAPERS, various sub-titles, various DAR Chapters, various cities, various dates. These many volumes include Bible, cemetery, church, marriage, death, obituary, and will records.

Copies of most of the books or microfilms of most of them are available at the DAR Library in Washington, ISHL, NL, FHL, and through FHC. Copies of some are in RL and LGL, and materials of local interest will often be found in LL. Chapter 3 tells you how to locate these records, and in Chapters 4 and 5, these records are included in the listings for the various IL counties.

There are several excellent catalog volumes to the many records that the DAR members have compiled:
__National Society, DAR, DAR LIBRARY CATALOG, VOLUME 1: FAMILY HISTORIES AND GENEALOGIES, VOLUME 2: STATE AND LOCAL HISTORIES AND RECORDS, The Society, Washington, DC, 1982/6.
Those counties for which there are DAR compilations will be so indicated in Chapters 4 and 5. Look into these DAR volumes for materials on your IL ancestor(s).

13. Death records

Prior to 1877, a few IL counties kept a few death records. Counties which kept at least some death records before 1877 include Cass, Hardin, Lake, Macon, Madison, Massac, McLean, Moultrie, Ogle, Pulaski, Scott, Shelby, Stark, Union, Vermilion, Warren, White, Williamson, and Woodford. A law was passed in 1877 requiring counties to record deaths, but compliance was not good and enforcement was non-existent, most counties doing nothing. Even in those counties in which there was some record-keeping, the records are very incomplete. The major exception to this poor recording is Chicago, for which fairly complete death records are available from 1871. In 1916, it was mandated by the state that death records be kept and that copies be sent to the state capital. By about 1919, compliance was over 95% complete. The death records available for each IL county are indicated in the separate county listings in Chapters 4 and 5.

Death records prior to 1916, are available in the counties and some are on microfilm at the FHL(FHC). Death records from 1916 onwards are held by county clerks and:
__Office of Vital Records, IL State Department of Public Health, 605 West Jefferson St., Springfield, IL 62761. Office has a State-wide index. State-wide index for 1916-43 available at ISA and FHL(FHC).
Only death records older than 20 years are available for genealogical purposes. These records usually contain name, sex, whether married or

not, date of death, occupation, cause of death, address, place of birth, date of burial, name of undertaker, length of residence in IL. After 1909, the names and birth places of the parents were included.

Prior to the time when IL death reports come to be almost complete (1919), other records may yield dates and places of death: Bible, biographical, cemetery, census, church, estate, manuscript, military, mortuary, newspaper, pension, and published genealogy. These are all discussed in other sections of this chapter. The finding of death record articles in genealogical periodicals is also described separately in this chapter.

14. Divorce records

From 1795-1800 divorces in the area which is now IL are by the General Court and the Circuit Court of the Northwest Territory. The General Court and the Circuit Courts of the IN Territory granted divorces from 1800-1809, except for one divorce that was given by the Legislature in 1808. In the IL Territory 1809-18, a similar arrangement adhered. From 1818, IL divorces were taken care of by the Circuit Court. In some instances divorce was granted by the Legislature. Compilations of the divorces granted by the General Assembly have been published:
___DIVORCE DOCUMENTS IN THE IL GENERAL ASSEMBLY FILES AND JOURNALS, IL State Genealogical Society Quarterly, Volume 17, pages 65, 136, and 223.
Even though divorces were handled in each county by the Circuit Court, other county courts were sometimes active in this capacity. Even so, the records are usually found in the office of the Clerk of the Circuit Court, where indexes are often to be found.

15. Emigration and immigration

Early settlement in IL (1673-1763) involved the French under whose government the area was. However, very few moved into IL during the ensuing British period and during the American Revolution. Following the War, Scots-Irish and some Scottish left from KY and TN and the back country of VA, NC, and PA, and came to the area which is now southern IL. They settled along the OH River and near the MS River sites where the French has first come. During the 1800-20s, more people from these same areas arrived and began moving toward the center of the state. The southern part of IL was thus settled chiefly from the upland southeast of the US. Beginning about 1825, New Englanders and people from NY, NJ,

PA, and northern OH entered the northern section of the state. Several surges of overseas Germans came into IL during the time frame of 1836-60, most of them coming directly from their landings in New York, New Orleans, Philadelphia, and Baltimore. They were in a large measure escaping the military turbulence of the times. The several Irish famines during 1830-60, coupled with the need for labor on the roads, canals, and railroads brought many Irish to IL during these times. After about 1870, the above foreign immigrants to IL were joined by Italians, Slavs, Jews, Polish, Ukrainians, and Slovaks, who usually settled in the northern part of the state. After the turn of the century, more of all the above plus many more ethnic groups were attracted to the industries of northern IL.

The movement of population into IL can be readily seen by examination of the statistics provided by the censuses of the latter half of the 19th century. Numbers of people are expressed in thousands (K). The birth places of IL people who had been born outside of IL were as follows:

___In 1850: 67K(NY), 64K(OH), 50K(KY), 38K(Germany), 38K(PA), 32K(TN)
___In 1860: 131K(OH), 130K(Germany), 121K(NY), 88K(Ireland), 83K(PA)
___In 1870: 203K(Germany), 192K(Irish-British), 163K(OH), 133K(NY), 98K(PA)
___In 1880: 236K(Germany), 136K(OH), 119K(NY), 117K(Ireland), 90K(IN)
___In 1890: 338K(Gemany), 126K(OH), 124K(Ireland), 110K(NY), 96K(IN)
___In 1900: 332K(Germany), 137K(OH), 128(IN), 114K(Ireland), 111K(NY)

Now, let us turn to view those living in other states which were born in IL. This will show you the pattern of migration out of IL:

___In 1850: 7K(IA), 1K(UT)
___In 1860: 14K(IA), 9K(KS), 4K(OR), 2K(UT)
___In 1870: 72K(MO), 65K(IA), 35K(KS), 10K(NE), 5K(OR), 2K(UT)
___In 1880: 107K(KS), 103K(IA), 103K(MO), 45K(NE), 8K(OR), 3K(WA), 2K(IL)
___In 1890: 138K(KS), 136K(MO), 114K(IA), 107K(NE), 18K(WA), 14K(OR), 5K(OK), 3K(UT), 3K(WY), 2K(NM)
___In 1900: 179K(MO), 142K(IA), 114K(KS), 86K(NE), 27K(IL), 22K(WA), 18K(SD), 17K(OR), 5K(WY), 4K(UT), 3K(NM)

In addition to IL histories which have been previously mentioned, there are several other items which will give you information on the above topics:

__M. Rubincam, MIGRATIONS TO IL, 1673-1860, IL State Genealogical Quarterly 4:3 (Oct 1972) 127-34.

__E. P. White, IL SETTLERS AND THEIR ORIGINS, National Genealogical Society Quarterly 74:1 (Mar 1986) 7-17.

__S. S. Sprague, KENTUCKIANS IN IL, Genealogical Publishing Co., Baltimore, MD, 1987.

__H. E. Freund, EMIGRATION RECORDS FROM THE GERMAN EIFEL REGION, 1834-1911, McHenry County Genealogical Society, Crystal Lake, IL, 1991. Contains many who came to IL.

__RECORDS OF THE RUSSIAN CONSULAR OFFICE IN THE US [INCLUDING CHICAGO], 1862-1928, FHL, Salt Lake City, UT, microfilmed records. Available through FHC.

__M. Wyman, IMMIGRANTS IN THE VALLEY, IRISH, GERMANS, AND AMERICANS IN THE UPPER MS COUNTRY, 1830-60, Nelson-Hall, Chicago, IL, 1984.

__M. Wyman, IMMIGRATION HISTORY AND ETHNICITY IN IL, ISHS, Springfield, IL, 19--.

__A. C. Boggess, THE SETTLEMENT OF IL, 1778-1830, Chicago Historical Society, Chicago, IL, 1908.

__W. V. Pooley, THE SETTLEMENT OF IL FROM 1830 TO 1850, University of WI, Madison, WI, 1908.

16. Ethnic records

The various ethnic groups of IL tended to each be largely affiliated with a particular religious persuasion. The English tended to be Congregational, Episcopalian, and Quaker. Many of these turned Methodist or Baptist or Christian later. Blacks tended to be Baptist or Methodist. Early Germans were Lutheran, Brethren, Mennonite, Moravian, and Reformed, with many later Germans being Catholic. The Scots-Irish and the Scots were chiefly Presbyterian, and the Irish were usually Catholic. The immigrants from eastern and southern Europe tended to be Catholic if they were from the western parts of these areas and Orthodox if they were from the eastern parts. Hence, for many of these groups, ethic information and connections are closely allied with their religious affiliations. Therefore, for all but the blacks and Indians, please see the previous section on church records.

Black slavery began in the IL country in 1720 when slaves were first brought in. Even though slavery was prohibited by the Northwest

Ordinance of 1787, this was overlooked, and the IN territorial government (1800-16) got around the law by allowing slaves to be held in permanent indenture. When IL became a separate territory in 1809, the same device was introduced. The first IL state constitution forbid new slaves to be brought in, but nothing was done about those that were in place. IL over the following years passed laws forbidding slaves to be brought into IL to be freed and forbidding free blacks from settling in the state. After the Civil War, blacks came into IL, but were discriminated against. In the 1940s, many blacks migrated from the south into northern IL, where they took up work in the industrial cities.

Among the historical, reference, and source materials for blacks in IL are the following volumes which will get you started if you have interest in this ethnic group.
__Harris, N. D., THE HISTORY OF NEGRO SERVITUDE IN IL, Haskell House, New York, NY, 1904.
__Hodges, C. G., IL NEGRO HISTORYMAKERS, IL Emancipation Centennial Commission, Chicago, IL, 1964.
__Tregellis, H. C., RIVER ROADS TO FREEDOM, FUGITIVE SLAVE NOTICES AND SHERIFF NOTICES FOUND IN IL SOURCES, Heritage Books, Bowie, MD, 1988.

The Black Hawk War essentially marked the end of the presence of Native American people in IL. For investigations of the many Native American groups of IL, a beginning can be made by the use of the following volumes and resources:
__S. Rafert, AMERICAN INDIAN GENEALOGICAL RESEARCH IN THE MIDWEST, RESOURCES AND PERSPECTIVES, National Genealogical Society Quarterly 76 (1988) 212.
__Tregellis, H. C., THE INDIANS OF IL, A HISTORY AND GENEALOGY, Anundsen Publishing Co., Decorah, IA, 1983.
__ISA, NATIVE AMERICAN RECORDS IN THE ISA, Record Groups 100, 103.62, 952.19, 953.14, and 953.18, ISA, Springfield, IL.
__H. W. Beckwith, THE IL AND IN INDIANS, Fergus Printing Co., Chicago, IL, 1884.
__L. S. Watson, INDIAN REMOVAL DOCUMENTS, SENATE DOCUMENT NO. 512, 23RD CONGRESS, 1ST SESSION, Histree, Laguna Hills, CA, 1988, 5 volumes.
__C. C. Royce, INDIAN LAND CESSIONS IN THE US, Bureau of American Ethnology, Washington, DC, 1899.

17. Gazetteers, atlases, and maps

A gazetteer is a volume which lists geographical names (towns, settlements, rivers, streams, hills, mountains, crossroads, villages, districts), locates them, and sometimes gives a few details concerning them. Several such volumes or similar volumes which list IL place names which could be of help to you include:

___L. C. Beck, A GAZETTEER OF THE STATES OF IL AND MO, Webster, Albany, NY, 1823.

___J. M. Peck, A GAZETTEER OF IL, Grigg and Elliot, Philadelphia, PA, 1837.

___J. N. Adams, IL PLACE NAMES, ISHL, Springfield, IL, 1968. Also see L. M. Volkel, ADDENDUM TO IL PLACE NAMES, ISHL, Springfield, IL, 1989.

___IL STATE GAZETTEER AND BUSINESS DIRECTORY, 1864-5, Bailey, Chicago, IL, 1865.

___L. A. Wilson, WILSON'S HISTORY AND DIRECTORY FOR SOUTHEASTERN MO AND SOUTHERN IL, Cape Girardeau, MO, 1875-76.

___IL STATE GAZETTEER AND BUSINESS DIRECTORY, 1858-59, Scripps, Gross, and Spears, Chicago, IL, 1858.

___IL STATE GAZETTEER AND BUSINESS DIRECTORY, 1882, Polk and Co., Chicago, Il 1882.

___F. R. Abate, editor, OMNI GAZETTEER OF THE USA, Omnigraphics, Detroit, MI, 1991, see IL listings.

___US Geological Survey, IL GEOGRAPHIC NAMES, The Survey, Washington, DC, 1981.

Numerous early atlases (collections of maps) are available for IL, for its counties, and for some of its larger cities. Many of these are listed in:

___C. E. LeGear, US ATLASES, Library of Congress, Washington, DC, 1950-3, 2 volumes.

___M. P. Conzen, J. R. Akerman, and D. T. Thackery, IL COUNTY LANDOWNERSHIP MAP AND ATLAS BIBLIOGRAPHY, IL Board of Higher Education, Springfield, IL, 1991.

___A. Sherwood, ISL'S COMPLETE HOLDING OF IL COUNTY LAND OWNERSHIP MAPS AND ATLASES, IL Libraries 66 (Sep 1984).

Among the state volumes and the county/state compilations are:

___L. A. Brown, EARLY MAPS OF THE OH VALLEY, 1673-1783, University of Pittsburgh Press, Pittsburgh, PA, 1959.

___J. H. Long and S. L. Hansen, HISTORICAL ATLAS AND CHRONOLOGY OF COUNTY BOUNDARIES, 1788-1980, Newberry Library, Chicago, IL, 1984, Volume 2.

___W. Thorndale and W. Dollarhide, MAP GUIDE TO THE US FEDERAL CENSUSES, IL, 1790-1920, Bellingham, WA, 1984.

___W. R. Wood, AN ATLAS OF EARLY MAPS OF THE AMERICAN MIDWEST, IL State Museum, Springfield, IL, 1983.

___Warner and Beers, ATLAS OF THE STATE OF IL, Union Atlas Co., Chicago, IL, 1876. Landowner names are indexed in J. R. Felldin and C. M. Tucker, LANDOWNERS OF IL, 1876, Genealogical Publications, Tomball, TX, 1976.

___Office of the IL Secretary of State, COUNTIES OF IL, THEIR ORIGIN AND EVOLUTION, The Secretary, Springfield, IL, latest edition. With county development maps.

___IL TOWNSHIPS, THEIR COUNTIES, AND BOUNDARY COORDINATES, 1849-1910, Office of the Secretary of State, Springfield, IL, 1982, 2 manuscript volumes. On microfilm at FHL(FHC).

___J. H. Long and S. L. Hansen, HISTORICAL ATLAS AND CHRONOLOGY OF COUNTY BOUNDARIES, 1788-1980, Hall, Boston, MA, 1984, volume 2.

Those counties for which atlases are available are indicated in Chapters 4 and 5. There are some incomplete compiled indexes to selected county histories, which often contain maps:

___BIOGRAPHY INDEX TO COUNTY HISTORIES, ISHL, Springfield, IL.

___INDEX TO SOME COUNTY HISTORIES, ISA, Springfield, IL.

ISHL, ISL, NL, and FHL(FHC) have many of the above materials. Some RL have some of them, and LL are likely to have those of the counties in which they are located. The best collections of IL maps are to be found in the libraries of The University of IL (Urbana), Southern IL University (Carbondale), and the University of Chicago (Chicago). The special indexes in each of these places should be consulted. These collections contain state maps, county maps for practically every county (some quite early), considerable numbers of city maps, and some for towns. Not to be overlooked is a good listing of IL maps:

___R. W. Karrow, Jr., CHECKLIST OF PRINTED MAPS OF THE MIDDLE WEST TO 1900, Hall, Boston, MA, 1981, Volume 4 IL. Indexed in Volume 14.

Especially valuable are landowner maps, also known as county plat maps. These are maps which show the lands of a county with the names of the owners written on them. Most of these maps date between 1860-1900 and are available for many IL counties. Such maps are listed in:

___R. W. Stephenson, LAND OWNERSHIP MAPS, Library of Congress, Washington, DC, 1967. [35 IL counties have such maps.] Available at Library of Congress and on microfiche at ACPL.

___A. Sherwood, ISL'S COMPLETE HOLDING OF IL COUNTY LAND OWNERSHIP MAPS AND ATLASES, IL Libraries 66 (Sep 1984).

___M. P. Conzen, J. R. Akerman, and D. T. Thackery, IL COUNTY LANDOWNERSHIP MAP AND ATLAS BIBLIOGRAPHY, IL Board of Higher Education, Springfield, IL, 1991.

Very good detail maps of IL are available at reasonable prices from the US Geological Survey. Each of these maps displays only a portion of a county and therefore a great deal of detail can be shown. Write to the address below and request the Index to Topographic Maps of IL. Or call the indicated number. Then order the maps pertaining to your ancestor's area. These maps show roads, streams, cemeteries, settlements, and churches. Such maps will aid you greatly if your ancestor lived in a rural area and you desire to visit the property and the surrounding region.

___US Geological Survey, Information Service, PO Box 25286, Denver, CO 80225. Call 1-800-USA-MAPS for the IL Index to Topographic Maps. Or call up http://www-nmd.usgs.govl.

Another source of detailed county maps is the IL Department of Transportation. They can provide you with individual maps of the IL counties showing roads, cities, streams, railroads, and other features. Order' them from:

___Map Sales, IL Department of Transportation, 2300 South Dirksen Parkway, Springfield, IL 62764.

18. Genealogical compilations and indexes

For the state of IL there are a number of books and manuscripts which are essentially compilations and/or indexes of state-wide or regional genealogical information. Some of the volumes are mentioned under other headings in this chapter: Biographies, County histories, DAR records, Regional publications. Others of this general sort which can possibly be useful to you include:

___J. N. Adams, INDEX TO THE TRANSACTIONS AND OTHER PUBLICATIONS OF THE IL STATE HISTORICAL LIBRARY, ISHL, Springfield, IL, 1953, 2 volumes.

___L. M. Volkel, ILLIANA ANCESTORS, Heritage House, Thomson, IL, 1967-69, 3 volumes.

___Mrs. O. B. Lunde, IL STATE GENEALOGICAL SOCIETY, 1981 SURNAME INDEX, The Society, Decatur, IL, 1982.

___H. L. Ross, AN INDEX TO THE EARLY PIONEERS AND PIONEER EVENTS OF THE STATE OF IL, McHarry, Havana, IL, 1899.

___GENEALOGICAL INDEX OF THE NEWBERRY LIBRARY, G. K. Hall, Boston, MA, 1960. A 1915 surname index to local histories and some periodicals in the Newberry Library.

___J. F. Moeller, and L. M. Volkel, GENEALOGICAL COLLECTIONS IN IL, IL Libraries 68:4 (Apr 1986) 244-284, 70:7 (Sep 1988) 480-536, and 74:5 (Nov 1992) 393-480.

___Society of Mayflower Descendants, DESCENDANTS IN THE STATE OF IL, The Society, Chicago, IL, 1962.

___ISGS, INDEX TO PRAIRIE PIONEERS OF IL, The Society, Springfield, IL, 1994.

___ISGS, IL STATE GENEALOGICAL QUARTERLY, 25-YEAR INDEX, VOLUMES 1-25, The Society, Springfield, IL, 1995.

___Central IL Genealogical Society, CENTRAL IL GENEALOGICAL QUARTERLY, INDEX TO VOLUMES 1-24, The Society, Decatur, IL, 1989.

___ISGS FAMILY BIBLE RECORDS, The Society, Springfield, IL, 1991-forward.

___APPLICATIONS FOR IL PRAIRIE PIONEER CERTIFICATES, ISGS, Springfield, IL. Also on microfilm at FHL(FHC).

___DAR Chapters in IL, THE BLUE BOOKS [TRANSCRIPTS OF IL GENEALOGICAL RECORDS], and the GRANDPARENT PAPERS, various sub-titles, various DAR Chapters, various cities, various dates. These many volumes include Bible, cemetery, church, marriage, death, obituary, and will records.

___B. Rochefort, PRAIRIE PIONEERS OF IL, ISGS, Lincoln, IL, 1986.

___J. G. Sager, GENERAL INDEX TO COLLECTIONS, JOURNALS, AND PUBLICATIONS OF THE ISHL, 1899-1928, Royal Print, Quincy, IL, 1930.

___V. Hart and others, ISGS ANCESTOR CHARTS OF MEMBERS, ISGS, Springfield, IL, 1988-, numerous volumes.

___J. N. Perrin, J. NICK PERRIN COLLECTION, ISA, Springfield, IL. Over 4900 documents regarding Cahokia, Belleville, and St. Clair

County, 1737-1850. Include materials from the French, British, and American periods. Include vital, land, petition, and tax records.
___KASKASKIA MANUSCRIPT COLLECTION, ISA, Springfield, IL. Date from 1708, include marriages and land records.

19. Genealogical periodicals

Many genealogical periodicals have been or are being published in IL. These journals or newsletters contain genealogies, local histories, genealogical records, family queries and answers, book reviews, and other pertinent local information. If you had an IL ancestor, you will find it of great value to subscribe to one or more of the state-wide periodicals, as well as to any periodicals published in the region or county where he/she lived. Among the more important previous or present IL statewide and regional periodicals are:
___CENTRAL IL GENEALOGICAL QUARTERLY, Decatur Genealogical Society, Decatur, IL, 1965-.
___CHICAGO GENEALOGIST, Chicago Genealogical Society, Chicago, IL, 1969-.
___THE CIRCUIT RIDER, Sangamon County Genealogical Society, Springfield, IL, 1969-.
___GLEANINGS FROM THE HEART OF THE CORNBELT, Bloomington-Normal Genealogical Society, Normal, IL, 1967-.
___THE ILLIANA GENEALOGIST, Illiana Genealogical Society, Danville, IL, 1965-.
___IL MENNONITE HERITAGE NEWSLETTER, IL Mennonite Historical and Genealogical Society, Benson, IL, 1964-.
___IL STATE GENEALOGICAL SOCIETY QUARTERLY, The Society, Springfield, IL, 1969-. With 25-year index.
___MENNONITE HERITAGE, IL Mennonite Historical and Genealogical Society, Normal, IL, 1974-.
___NEWS FROM THE NORTHWEST, Northwest Suburban Council of Genealogists, Mt. Prospect, IL, 1977-.
___NEWSLETTER OF THE FELLOWSHIP OF BRETHREN GENEALOGISTS, The Fellowship, Elgin, IL, 1969-.
___POLISH GENEALOGICAL SOCIETY OF IL NEWSLETTER, The Society, Chicago, IL, 1979-.
___PRAIRIE ROOTS, Peoria Genealogical Society, Peoria, IL, 1973-.
___SAGA OF SOUTHERN IL, Genealogical Society of Southern IL, Cartersville, IL, 1974-.
___SEARCH, IL Jewish Genealogical Society, Normal, IL, 1981-.

___SEARCHING IL ANCESTORS (formerly CENTRAL IL CHRONICLES), H. C. Tregellis, Shelbyville, IL, 1984-.
___TRI-STATE PACKET, Tri-State Genealogical Society, Evansville, IN, 1977-.
___TWIGS AND BRANCHES, North Central IL Genealogical Society, Rockford, IL.
___WHERE THE TRAILS CROSS, South Suburban Genealogical and Historical Society, South Holland, IL, 1970-.

In addition to the above statewide and regional periodicals, many county, and some city and private historical and genealogical organizations publish periodicals (newsletters, quarterlies, monthlies, journals, yearbooks) which can be of exceptional value to you if you are forebear hunting in their areas. Those societies which issue periodicals and/or record compilations are indicated in the county listings of Chapters 4 and 5. Most of these publications are in the ISHL, and at NL. Many are available at FHL(FHC) and RL, some are in LGL, and those of various local regions are likely to be found in LL.

Not only do articles pertaining to IL genealogy appear in these IL publications, they also are printed in other genealogical periodicals. Fortunately, indexes to the major genealogical periodicals (including those from IL) are available:
___For periodicals published 1847-1985, then annually 1986-present, consult Allen County Public Library Foundation, PERIODICAL SOURCE INDEX, The Foundation, Fort Wayne, IN, 1986-.
These index volumes will be found in ISHL, NL, and FHL(FHC), most RL, most LGL, and a few LL. In them you should consult all IL listings under the county names which concern you and all listings under the family names you are seeking.

20. Genealogical and historical societies

In the state of IL various societies for the study of genealogy, the accumulation of data, and the publication of the materials have been organized. These societies are listed in Chapters 4 and 5 under the names of the IL counties in which they have their headquarters. Many of them publish regular journals and/or newsletters containing the data which they have gathered, queries from their members, and book reviews. They are indicated in Chapters 4 and 5. The local members of such societies are generally well informed about the genealogical resources of their regions, and often can offer considerable help to non-residents who had ancestors in the area. It is thus advisable for you to join the societies in your ancestor's county as well as the IL State Genealogical Society (PO Box 10195, Springfield, IL 62791). All correspondence with societies should be accompanied by an SASE. Detailed listings of them are provided by

___E. P. Bentley, THE GENEALOGIST'S ADDRESS BOOK, Genealogical Publishing Co., Baltimore, MD, latest edition.

Historical societies are often also of interest to genealogists. In addition to the IL State Historical Society, there are many city, county, and regional historical societies in IL. These organizations along with their addresses are listed in the reference volumes named below. Some of these societies have strong genealogical interests, some deal with genealogical interests in addition to their historical pursuits, and some have essentially no interest in genealogy. Even if they do not carry out much genealogy as such, their work will be of considerable interest to you since it deals with the historical circumstances through which your ancestor lived. It is often well for you to dispatch an SASE and an inquiry to one or more asking about membership, genealogical interest, and publications. Most of these valuable organizations are named in these very detailed compilations:

___DIRECTORY OF HISTORICAL SOCIETIES AND AGENCIES IN THE US AND CANADA, American Association for State and Local History, Nashville, TN, latest edition.

___E. P. Bentley, THE GENEALOGIST'S ADDRESS BOOK, Genealogical Publishing Co., Baltimore, MD, latest edition.

___Association of IL Museums and Historical Societies, HISTORICAL AND CULTURAL AGENCIES AND MUSEUMS IN IL, The Association, Phillips, Springfield, IL, 1993.

21. Land records

One of the most important types of genealogical records are those which deal with land. This is because IL in its earlier years was predominantly an agricultural state. In addition, land was up until the 20th century (the 1900s) widely available and quite inexpensive. These factors meant that the vast majority of early IL people owned land, and therefore their names appear in land records. The land was first granted by the government to private individuals or groups, and thereafter the land records were locally kept. These latter records (deed, entry, mortgage, settler, survey, tax) for the 102 IL counties are indicated in Chapters 4 and 5 along with the dates of availability. In most cases, the originals are in the CH, but transcripts and/or microfilm copies of many of them are to be found in ISHL, NL, and FHL, and are available through FHC. Some transcribed land records are available in RL and LGL, and transcribed copies and some microfilms for individual counties are often available in the LL of the counties.

In addition to the county records, there were a large number of early land grants made to the first settlers in various areas of the state. To understand the granting of lands by the government to its first owners, it is necessary to recognize that the area which makes up IL was divided into 7 major regions for the original granting of land. These regions are centered around land offices which began to operate at the following dates in the following regions:

1805   Kaskaskia settled early French, British, and US claims
1814   Kaskaskia began selling land in far southwestern IL
1814   Shawneetown began land sales in far southeastern IL
1816   Edwardsville began selling land in southwestern IL 1821
          Palestine began selling land in southeastern IL
1821   Vandalia began selling land in south central IL
1823   Springfield began selling land in central IL
1831   Danville began selling land in east central IL
1831   Quincy began selling land in west central IL
1833   Chicago began selling land in northeastern IL
1833   Galena began selling land in northwestern IL
1840   Dixon takes over the Galena area

Please note that one of the land offices was transferred from Galena to Dixon in 1840. In 1855, all offices except the one at Springfield were closed. Springfield continued to sell land throughout the state until 1876.

Remember that land grants are for the first disposition of the land from the federal government to an individual owner. Thereafter the county records (see above paragraph) must be consulted for changes in land ownership. The ISA has put together a computer index to the federal land grants in IL:

___PUBLIC DOMAIN LAND SALES RECORD LISTING, alphabetically arranged, ISA, Springfield, IL, 1984, on computer and on 144 microfiche. Very important. Over 530,000 entries. Also at FHL(FHC) and on the Internet.

This index leads to numerous records relating to the land grants. You should send the information from this index and request records from the ISA (tract books, plats), Bureau of Land Management-Eastern Division (tract books, plats, patents), the National Archives Branch in Chicago (applications and registers), and the National Archives (case files). You should also check the book by McMullen which is indicated below. The original land grant records for IL are widely dispersed and are available as follows:

___Original land-entry case files, NA, Washington, DC.

___Original federal land record books, tract books, plats, and registers, 1807-76, ISA, Springfield, IL. Not all are indexed.

___Original patents, tract books, and plats, Bureau of Land Management, Springfield, VA.

___Original applications to purchase and registers of cash certificates and sales, 1814-85, National Archives-Great Lakes Region, Chicago, IL. Arranged chronologically by land office. Not indexed.

A number of volumes. microfilms, and manuscripts which present some of the land grant records are available.

___R. H. Hammes, RAYMOND H. HAMMES COLLECTION, ISGS, Springfield, IL, 20 manuscript volumes of abstracts dating 1678-1814, some published by the IL Research Center for Colonial and Territorial Studies, Springfield, IL. Includes Squatters (1807), Preemptions (1813), Kaskaskia Land District correspondence, Kaskasia land record books (1804-14), Randolph County land records (1768-1815), Cahokia and St. Clair County land records (1800-20), Cahokia historical material (1671-1819), militia bounty lands, miscellaneous land records (1722-1812). Most volumes have indexes, Volume 1 is a consolidated Index, but it is incomplete and often confused. Collection also available at FHL(FHC) on microfilm. Original records on 155 reels of microfilm at ISA.

___R. H. Hammes, IL MILITIAMEN, 1790, AND SQUATTERS IN TERRITORIAL IL, 1807 AND 1813, IL Libraries 59:5 (May, 1977).

___R. H. Hammes, IL LAND TRANSACTION PRINTOUTS AND TYPESCRIPTS, 1720-1866, ISGS, Springfield, IL. Also available at FHL(FHC) on microfilm.

___L. M. Volkel, SHAWNEETOWN LAND DISTRICT RECORDS, 1814-20, Heritage Press, Indianapolis, IN, 1979.

___US General Land Office, TRACT BOOKS OF IL, 1826-73, Office of the IL Secretary of State, Springfield, IL, 1966, 19 microfilm reels. Includes these land offices: Kaskasia (1832-61), Shawneetown (1836-73), Palestine (1836-53), Vandalia (1836-73), Danville (1827-64), Chicago (1835-55), Edwardsville (1828-55), Springfield (1829-60), Quincy (1830-61), and Dixon (1830-54).

___US General Land Office, FIELD NOTES FROM SELECTED TOWNSHIP SURVEYS, Microfilm T1240, National Archives, Washington, DC. Contains 200 volumes of IL field notes.

___Bureau of Land Management, FEDERAL LAND RECORDS IN THE BLM FOR IL, and/or GLO AUTOMATED RECORDS AND INDEX TO PATENTS, GRANTS, AND WARRANTS IN ILLINOIS, The Bureau, 7450 Boston Blvd., Springfield, VA 22153. Almost 247,000 documents. On CDROM or write to have the index searched.

___IL Auditor's Office, EARLY IL LAND RECORDS, 1829-65, Office of the Secretary of State, Springfield, IL, 1960, microfilm. Also available at FHL(FHC).

___B. Rochefort, PRAIRIE PIONEERS OF IL, ISGS, Lincoln, IL, 1986.

___Felldin, J. R., and C. M. Tucker, LAND OWNERS OF IL, 1876, Genealogical Publications, Tomball, TX, 1978.

___IL State Canal Commissioner's Office, LAND SALES RECORDS, 1830-84, Office of the Secretary of State, Springfield, IL, microfilm. Also available at FHL(FHC).

___D. and R. T. Taylor, THE HISTORY OF IL CENTENNIAL FARMS, Curtis Media, Dallas, TX, 1986.

___AMERICAN STATE PAPERS, PUBLIC LANDS, Gales and Seaton, Washington, DC, 1832-61, 7 volumes; indexed in P. W. McMullen, GRASSROOTS OF AMERICA, Gendex Corporation, Salt Lake City, UT, 1972.

___C. N. Smith, FEDERAL LAND SERIES, American Library Association, Chicago, IL, 1972/73/80/82, 4 volumes.

___F. C. Ainsworth, PRIVATE LAND CLAIMS, IL, IN, MI, AND WI, The Author, Natchitoches, LA, 1981.

___L. M. Volkel, WAR OF 1812 BOUNTY LAND PATENTS IN IL, Heritage House, Thomson, IL, 1977.

___G. C. Bestor, INDEX OF THE IL MILITARY PATENT BOOK, US General Land Office, Peoria, IL, 1853, with E. S. Green and S. P. Kirkbridge, CORRECTED INDEX OF THE IL MILITARY PATENT BOOK, US General Land Office, Bridgeton, PA, 1855.

The books mentioned in this section on land records are available in ISHL, NL, FHL, and are obtainable through FHC. They are also to be found, or at least some of them, in RL and LGL. In addition a few of the larger LL have them.

Following the first granting of land to the original purchaser by the US government, subsequent land transfers and other land-related records are kept in the counties. Included are deeds, mortgages, tax records, civil land cases, and indexes. Listings of those available for the 102 IL counties will be given in Chapters 4 and 5. In most counties, there are also some records relating to the original US grants to the first owners.

Some of these county-based records are available on microfilm and/or in books at ISHL, NL, and FHL (FHC).

22. Manuscripts

The most valuable sources of genealogically-oriented manuscripts for the state of IL are the ISHL and the ISA in Springfield. There are also moderately-useful collections at The University of IL (Urbana), Southern IL University (Carbondale), RL, LL, local museums, and local historical societies. In addition, there are good collections for Chicago in Chicago. The holdings of these repositories can include records of religious, educational, patriotic, business, social, civil, professional, governmental, and political organizations; documents, letters, memoirs, notes, and papers of early settlers, politicians, ministers, business men, educators, physicians, dentists, lawyers, judges, and farmers; records of churches, cemeteries, mortuaries, schools, corporations, and industries; works of artists, musicians, writers, sculptors, photographers, and architects; and records, papers, letters, and reminiscences of participants in the various wars, as well as records of various military organizations and campaigns.

Many of these repositories are listed in the following volumes, some of which give brief descriptions of their holdings:

___ US Library of Congress, THE NATIONAL UNION CATALOG OF MANUSCRIPT COLLECTIONS, The Library, Washington, DC, issued annually 1959-. Both cumulative indexes and annual indexes. Check your ancestor's county, and then under the heading Genealogy.

___ E. Altman and others, INDEX TO PERSONAL NAMES IN THE NATIONAL UNION CATALOG OF MANUSCRIPT COLLECTIONS, 1959-84, Chadwyck-Healey, Arlington, VA, 1988, 2 volumes. Check your ancestor's name.

___ E. Altman and others, INDEX TO SUBJECTS AND FIRMS IN THE NATIONAL UNION CATALOG OF MANUSCRIPT COLLECTIONS, 1959-84, Chadwyck-Healey, Arlington, VA, 1995, 3 volumes. Check your ancestor's locality.

___ US National Historical Publications and Records Commission, DIRECTORY OF ARCHIVES AND MANUSCRIPT REPOSITORIES IN THE US, The Commission, Oryx Press, New York, NY, 1988.

___ ARCHIVAL AND MANUSCRIPT COLLECTIONS, in J. Hoffmann, A GUIDE TO THE HISTORY OF IL, Greenwood Press, New York, NY, 1991.

___ P. M. Quinn, ARCHIVAL REPOSITORIES IN IL, IL Libraries 69:8 (Oct 1987) 566-606.

___Historical Records Survey, PRELIMINARY GUIDE TO DEPOSI-
TORIES OF MANUSCRIPT COLLECTIONS IN IL, WPA, Chicago,
IL, 1940.

There are also some special volumes which describe and/or catalog the IL
manuscript holdings in various important repositories.

___V. Irons and P. C. Brennan, Office of the IL Secretary of State,
DESCRIPTIVE INVENTORY OF THE ARCHIVES OF THE
STATE OF IL, The Secretary, Springfield, IL, 1976.

___R. E. Bailey, INDEX TO THE DESCRIPTIVE INVENTORY OF
THE ARCHIVES OF THE STATE OF IL, ISA, Springfield, IL,
1993, 34 microfiche.

___T. J. Cassady, GUIDE TO RECORDS HOLDINGS OF THE ISA,
ISA, Springfield, IL, 1978.

___R. E. Bailey, A SUMMARY GUIDE TO LOCAL GOVERNMEN-
TAL RECORDS IN THE IL REGIONAL ARCHIVES, ISA,
Springfield, IL, 1992.

___T. C. Pease, THE COUNTY ARCHIVES OF THE STATE OF IL,
ISHL, Springfield, IL, 1915.

___M. J. Brichford, GUIDE TO THE UNIVERSITY OF IL
ARCHIVES, The University, Urbana, IL, 1986, 7 microfiche.

___J. L. Harper, A GUIDE TO THE DRAPER MANUSCRIPTS, WI
State Historical Society, Madison, WI, 1982. See IL references.

___J. G. Sager, GENERAL INDEX TO COLLECTIONS, JOURNALS,
AND PUBLICATIONS OF THE ISHL, 1899-1928, Royal Print,
Quincy, IL, 1930.

Numerous other manuscripts are listed in the manuscript catalogs and
in special indexes provided at ISHL, ISA, NL, and other archives,
libraries, and museums in IL. There are also good manuscript collections
in some RL and in some of the college and other university libraries of
IL. In the county listings in Chapters 4 and 5, the important manuscript
repositories will be noted.

23. Marriage records

From its beginning, each IL county has kept marriage records. However, marriage licenses were not required until 1877. Since 1962, copies of these marriage records have been filed in Springfield on a statewide basis. The ISA has an index which covers many pre-1900 marriages from over 80 counties. The index is being continually added to and should be complete for all counties soon. As yet, the most populous county, Cook County, has not been done. Please recognize that the index

is incomplete, not only overall, but for many of the counties represented in it.
___COMPUTER INDEX TO PRE-1900 MARRIAGE RECORDS OF IL, ISA, Springfield, IL. Current copy available on microfiche.

Prior to 1962 marriage records were collected by the counties, where the originals remain in the County Clerk's Office (or in the office of the clerk of the court where the ceremony was performed) or in the regional IRAD. Most are indexed or partially indexed. Microfilm copies of the pre-1920 records for about 50 counties will be found at the ISA and FHL(FHC). The early licenses show only the names of the bride and groom, their towns of residence, the date of the return, and the officiating person. The registers are generally incomplete, and some contain errors, especially spelling errors. In some cases, the marriage license applications will reveal more data than the registers.

A number of aids are available for searching out IL marriage records:
___COMPUTER INDEX TO PRE-1900 MARRIAGE RECORDS OF IL, ISA, Springfield, IL. Current copy also available on microfiche. Incomplete.
___Family History Library, INTERNATIONAL GENEALOGICAL INDEX, IL SECTION, FHL, Salt Lake City, UT. Available on microfiche and/or computer at every FHC, and at several LGL. Lists many marriages.
___FAMILY ARCHIVES MARRIAGE INDEX, IL, IN, KY, OH, AND TN, 1720-1926, CD-0002, AGLL, Bountiful, UT, 1995. Includes 18 IL counties.
___FAMILY ARCHIVES MARRIAGE INDEX, IL AND IN, 1790-1850, CD-0228, AGLL, Bountiful, UT, 1995. Includes 82 counties, but not Cook County.
___IL MARRIAGES, EARLY TO 1825, Computer Disk K3M-IL1, Liahona Research, AGLL, Bountiful, UT, 1990.
___IL MARRIAGES, 1826-1850, Computer Disk K3M-IL2, Liahona Research, AGLL, Bountiful, UT, 1990.
___DAR Chapters in IL, THE BLUE BOOKS [TRANSCRIPTS OF IL GENEALOGICAL RECORDS], and the GRANDPARENT PAPERS, various sub-titles, various DAR Chapters, various cities, various dates. These many volumes include Bible, cemetery, church, marriage, death, obituary, and will records.
___Dodd, J. R., IL MARRIAGES, EARLY TO 1825, Precision Indexing, Bountiful, UT, 1990.

___Sanders, W. R., MARRIAGES FROM IL COUNTIES 1812-50, The Author, Litchfield, IL, 1976, several volumes. Not statewide, only selected counties.

___Historical Records Survey, GUIDE TO PUBLIC VITAL STATISTICS RECORDS IN IL, WPA, Chicago, IL, 1941.

The marriage records that are available for the various IL counties will be listed under the counties in Chapters 4 and 5. Instructions for locating the records and microfilms of them will be given in Chapter 3.

Other records which often yield marriage dates and places include biographical, cemetery, church, mortuary, newspaper, obituary, pension, and published. All of these are discussed in other sections of this chapter. In addition, the location of marriage data in genealogical periodicals has been described in section 19.

24. Military records: Revolutionary War

The Revolutionary War was fought before IL became a state, that is, in the years 1775-83. Since the area was quite sparsely populated during these years, very few, if any, Illinoisians actually fought in the Revolution. After the War, however, many veterans came into the IL country as part of a general westward migration. There are three sets of records relating to this War in which data on your ancestor could appear: service records, pension records, and bounty land records. To search out all these records, write the following address and request copies of NATF Form 80:

___Military Service records (NNCC), Washington, DC 20408.

When the forms come, fill them out with as much information on your ancestor as you know, check the record request box on one for military service, the pension box on another, and the bounty land record box on another, attach a note asking for all records, and mail the forms off. The Military Service Records staff will examine their indexes to Revolutionary War soldiers and naval personnel, will try to find your ancestor, then, if they do, will copy and send you a notice, along with a bill for their services. Upon receipt of payment, they will mail you the records. If you live in certain areas of the US, there are quicker alternatives than this route to the military records. The next paragraph will detail these.

Microfilms of the Revolutionary War indexes (M860, 58 rolls, M879, 1 roll), microfilms of Revolutionary War records (M881, 1097 rolls, M880, 4 rolls), and microfilms of pension and bounty land applications (M804, 2670 rolls) are available at the National Archives (Washington, DC), Regional Branches of the National Archives (Waltham, MA; New York, NY; Philadelphia, PA; East Point, GA; Chicago, IL; Kansas City, MO; Ft. Worth, TX; Denver, CO; San Bruno, CA; Laguna Niguel, CA; Seattle, WA), ACPL, and FHL (Salt Lake City, UT). You may look at the indexes in these locations and also read the records. The indexes and the record microfilms may also be ordered through FHC and by your local library from AGLL (PO Box 329, Bountiful, UT 84011).

There are also several printed national sources which you should consult regarding your Revolutionary War ancestor:

___F. J. Metcalf et al., INDEX TO REVOLUTIONARY WAR PENSION [AND BOUNTY LAND] APPLICATIONS, National Genealogical Society, Washington, DC, 1966.

___National Society of the DAR, DAR PATRIOT INDEX, The Society, Washington, DC, latest edition.

___War Department, REVOLUTIONARY WAR PENSIONERS OF 1818, Genealogical Publishing Co., Baltimore, MD, 1959.

___War Department, PENSION ROLL OF 1835, Genealogical Publishing Co., Baltimore, MD, 1968, 4 volumes.

___US Department of State, A CENSUS OF PENSIONERS FOR REVOLUTIONARY OR MILITARY SERVICE TAKEN IN 1840, Genealogical Publishing Co., Baltimore, MD, 1974.

___National Society of the DAR, INDEX TO THE ROLLS OF HONOR, (ANCESTOR'S INDEX) IN THE LINEAGE BOOKS, Genealogical Publishing Co., Baltimore, MD, 1972, 2 volumes.

___J. Pierce, REGISTER OF CERTIFICATES TO US OFFICERS AND SOLDIERS OF THE CONTINENTAL ARMY UNDER THE ACT OF 1783, Genealogical Publishing Co., Baltimore, MD, 1973.

___F. Rider, AMERICAN GENEALOGICAL INDEX, Godfrey Memorial Library, Middletown, CT, 1942-52, 43 volumes, and AMERICAN GENEALOGICAL-BIOGRAPHICAL INDEX, Godfrey Memorial Library, Middletown, CT, 1952-, in process, over 190 volumes so far.

In addition, several printed IL sources for your search are in existence. Among the better ones are:

___G. G. Clift, LIST OF OFFICERS OF THE IL REGIMENT AND OF CROCKETT'S REGIMENT WHO HAVE RECEIVED LAND FOR

THEIR SERVICES, Sons of the American Revolution, Frankfort, IL, 1962.
___V. M. Meyer, DAR of IL, ROSTER OF REVOLUTIONARY WAR SOLDIERS AND WIDOWS WHO LIVED IN IL COUNTIES, The DAR, Chicago, IL, 1962.
___M. S. Devanny and R. B. Hamon, SOLDIERS OF THE AMERICAN REVOLUTION BURIED IN IL, ISGS, Springfield, IL, 1975.
___H. J. Walker, REVOLUTIONARY SOLDIERS BURIED IN IL, Genealogical Publishing Co., Baltimore, MD, 1967. With biographical sketches.
___D. E. Gradeless, REVOLUTIONARY LINEAGES, EVERYNAME INDEX TO THE REGISTRAR'S RECORDS, Sons of the American Revolution in the State of IL, The Author, Springfield, IL, 1986.
___Mrs. M. C. Chatten, ROLL OF REVOLUTIONARY ANCESTORS, STATE OF IL, 3 volumes, typescript. Microfilm copy at FHL(FHC).
Also do not fail to examine:
___ROLL OF HONOR, RECORD OF BURIAL PLACES OF SOLDIERS, SAILORS, MARINES, AND ARMY NURSES OF ALL WARS OF THE US BURIED IN IL, State of IL, Springfield, IL, 1929. At ISA, on microfilm at FHL.
Most of the reference works listed above are in ISHL, NL, and FHL(FHC). Some of them are in RL and LGL.

Numerous other Revolutionary War records sources are listed in the following work which goes into considerable detail and is recommended to all researchers who had Revolutionary War ancestors:
___George K. Schweitzer, REVOLUTIONARY WAR GENEALOGY, The Author, 407 Ascot Court, Knoxville, TN 37923, 1996.

Several sources are available for IL militia which served between the Revolutionary period and the War of 1812:
___R. Hammes, IL MILITIAMEN, 1790, AND SQUATTERS IN TERRITORIAL IL, 1807 AND 1813, IL Libraries 59:5 (May, 1977).
___IL Military and Naval Department, ROSTER OF THE ADJUTANT GENERAL OF THE STATE OF IL, APPENDIX: MILITIA, RANGERS, AND RIFLEMEN, 1810-13, The Department, Springfield, IL, 1882, revised, 1900-02, 9 volumes.
___National Archives, INDEX TO COMPILED SERVICE RECORDS OF VOLUNTEER SOLDIERS WHO SERVED FROM 1784 TO 1811, Microfilm M694, The Archives, Washington, DC, leads to National Archives, COMPILED SERVICE RECORDS OF

VOLUNTEER SOLDIERS WHO SERVED FROM 1784 TO 1811, Microfilm M905, The Archives, Washington, DC, 32 rolls, with Roll 23 giving IL militia.

___C. E. Carter, TERRITORIAL PAPERS OF THE US, VOLUMES 16-17, IL TERRITORY, AMS Press, New York, NY, 1973. Also available as National Archives, TERRITORIAL PAPERS OF THE US, Microfilm M721, The Archives, Washington, DC. Some lists of militiamen.

25. Military records: 1812-48

A number of soldiers from IL Territory saw active service in the War of 1812, which was fought 1812-5. As was the case with the Revolutionary War, three types of records should be sought: military service, pension, and bounty land. The National Archives has original service records, pension records, and bounty land records, plus indexes of all three. These indexes are as follows:

___US Department of War, INDEX TO COMPILED SERVICE RECORDS OF VOLUNTEER SOLDIERS WHO SERVED DURING THE WAR OF 1812, National Archives, Washington, DC, Microfilm M602, 234 rolls.

___US Veterans Administration, INDEX TO WAR OF 1812 PENSION APPLICATION FILES, National Archives, Washington, DC, Microfilm M313, 102 rolls.

___US Bureau of Land Management, WAR OF 1812 MILITARY BOUNTY LAND WARRANTS; National Archives, Washington, DC, Microfilm M848, 14 rolls, with indexes on the first roll.

You can either have the National Archives look into the indexes, or if they are easily available, you can do it. They are located at NA, NARC, FHL(FHC), and some LGL. If you find your ancestor, or if you want the NA to look for him, write the following and request several copies of NATF Form 80:

___Military Service Records (NNCC), Washington, DC 20408.

Upon receiving them, fill three out, giving your ancestor's name and state, as much other pertinent data as you can, check the request box for military service on one, the pension box on another, and the bounty land record box on the third, attach a note asking for all records, then mail them back. There are also several nationally-applicable books which could be of assistance to you:

___F. I. Ordway, Jr., REGISTER OF THE GENERAL SOCIETY OF THE WAR OF 1812, The Society, Washington, DC, 1972.

___E. S. Galvin, 1812 ANCESTOR INDEX, National Society of US Daughters of 1812, Washington, DC, 1970.

___C. S. Peterson, KNOWN MILITARY DEAD DURING THE WAR OF 1812, The Author, Baltimore, MD, 1955.

In addition, there are materials relating specifically to IL. The following can be quite helpful:

___W. R. Matheny, IL INDEX, SOLDIERS OF THE WAR OF 1812, typescript by Author, Springfield, IL, 1967.

___ISA, MUSTER ROLLS OF IL UNITS IN THE INDIAN WARS OF THE WAR OF 1812, The Archives, Springfield, IL. Usually list only names.

___H. A. Walker, IL PENSIONERS LIST OF THE REVOLUTION, WAR OF 1812, AND INDIAN WARS, The Author, Washington, DC, 1955.

___L. M. Volkel, WAR OF 1812 BOUNTY LAND PATENTS IN IL, Heritage House, Thomson, IL, 1977.

___IL Adjutant General's Office, RECORD OF THE BURIAL PLACES OF SOLDIERS, SAILORS, MARINES, AND ARMY NURSES OF ALL WARS OF THE US BURIED IN IL, The Office, Springfield, IL, 1929, 2 volumes.

ISHL, NL, and FHL(FHC) have many of the above books (both the national and IL), and those held by FHL can be borrowed through FHC. The nationally-oriented books are likely to be found in many LGL, and some of the national and IL volumes will be found in RL. Finally, do not overlook records that might be in the counties, most notably discharge and grave records.

Many other War of 1812 record sources are given in the following work which goes into considerable detail for tracing your ancestors who served in this war:

___George K. Schweitzer, WAR OF 1812 GENEALOGY, The Author, 407 Ascot Court, Knoxville, TN 37923, 1995.

During the <u>Indian Wars</u> period (1817-98), IL personnel were involved in several conflicts. National Archives again has military records, pension records, and bounty land records, plus indexes to all three. NATF Form 80 should be used in accordance with the above instructions to obtain records. Also some IL counties have records on the Wars. These are indicated under the counties in Chapter 4 and 5. The Black Hawk War of 1832 was notable in Illinois because it was fought in the northwestern part of the state. Records for the various IL companies that were involved have been published in:

___IL Military and Naval Department, ROSTER OF THE ADJUTANT GENERAL OF THE STATE OF IL, VOLUME 9, RECORD OF SERVICES OF SOLDIERS IN THE BLACK HAWK WAR, 1831-32, AND IN THE MEXICAN WAR, 1846-48, The Department, Springfield, IL, 1882, revised 1900-02.

___P. A. Armstrong, THE SAUKS AND THE BLACK HAWK WAR, with MUSTER ROLL OF IL VOLUNTEERS, BLACK HAWK WAR, 1831-32, Rokker, Springfield, IL, 1887, 2 volumes.

___Whitney, E. M., THE BLACK HAWK WAR, 1831-34, ISHL, Springfield, IL, 1970-78, 2 volumes.

___ISA, MUSTER ROLLS OF IL UNITS IN THE BLACK HAWK WAR, The Archives, Springfield, IL. Give names, residences, and sometimes remarks.

___Coltrin, G. E., BLACK HAWK WAR VETERANS BURIED IN THE STATE OF IL, The Author, Peoria, IL, 1979.

The Mexican War was fought 1846-8, with over 3700 IL soldiers and navy personnel participating. NATF Form 80 should be employed to obtain military service, pension, and bounty land records from the National Archives. Published sources include:

___US Adjutant General's Office, INDEX TO COMPILED SERVICE RECORDS OF VOLUNTEER SOLDIERS WHO SERVED DURING THE MEXICAN WAR, Microfilm M616, 41 rolls, National Archives, Washington, DC. Leads to the records in the NA.

___IL Military and Naval Department, ROSTER OF THE ADJUTANT GENERAL OF THE STATE OF IL, VOLUME 9, RECORD OF SERVICES OF SOLDIERS IN THE BLACK HAWK WAR, 1831-32, AND IN THE MEXICAN WAR, 1846-48, The Department, Springfield, IL, 1882, revised 1900-02.

___ISA, MUSTER ROLLS OF IL UNITS IN THE MEXICAN WAR, The Archives, Springfield, IL. Give names, residences, and sometimes remarks.

___W. H. Robarts, MEXICAN WAR VETERANS: A COMPLETE ROSTER, 1846-8, Washington, DC, 1887.

___C. S. Peterson, KNOWN MILITARY DEAD DURING THE MEXICAN WAR, The Author, Baltimore, MD, 1957.

These source materials should be sought in places such as ISHL, ISA, NL, FHL, LGL, and may be borrowed through FHC.

26. Military records: Civil War

Almost 260,000 men fought for IL in the Civil War, about 35,000 of them dying during the conflict. There are several major keys to the many Civil War participants of the state of IL:

___ REPORT OF THE ADJUTANT GENERAL OF THE STATE OF IL, 1861-66, The Office of the Adjutant General, Springfield, IL, 1900-02, 9 volumes. Index at ISA and on microfilm at FHL.

___INDEX TO COMPILED SERVICE RECORDS OF VOLUNTEER UNION SOLDIERS WHO SERVED IN ORGANIZATIONS FROM THE STATE OF IL, National Archives Microfilm M539, Washington, DC, 101 rolls of microfilm.

The indexes should be looked into for your ancestor's name. Upon finding him, you will discover listed alongside his name his regiment, battalion, or ship, as well as his company. This information is what is needed to locate the detailed records. The above indexes should be sought at ISHL, ISA, NL, and FHL. They are available through FHC or the microfilms may be borrowed on interlibrary loan from:

___American Genealogical Lending Library, PO Box 244, Bountiful, UT 84010.

Once you know your ancestor's military unit, you can write the following address for several copies of NATF Form 80:

___Military Service Records (NNCC), Washington, DC 20408.

When your forms come, fill them out, giving as much data as you can, especially all the information from the above indexes. Then check the military service box on one form and the pension record box on another, ask for all records, and mail the forms back. In a few weeks you will receive a notice of military record data and/or pension data along with a bill.

In addition, there are several other state sources which will be useful to investigate:

___IL Adjutant General's Office, RECORD OF THE BURIAL PLACES OF SOLDIERS, SAILORS, MARINES, AND ARMY NURSES OF ALL WARS OF THE US BURIED IN IL, The Office, Springfield, IL, 1929, 2 volumes.

___THE UNION ARMY, Volume 3, Madison, WI, 1908, pp. 244-368. Histories of IL Union regiments.

___F. H. Dyer, A COMPENDIUM OF THE WAR OF THE REBEL-
LION, National Historical Society, Dayton, OH, 1979, pp. 117-31,
1021-1103. IL Union regimental histories.
___ISA, CIVIL WAR RECORDS: SERVICE RECORDS (89 volumes),
MUSTER ROLLS, REGIMENTAL RECORDS (29 volumes), and
ROSTER OF MEN (9 volumes), The Archives, Springfield, IL.
___ISA, CIVIL WAR MILITARY ENROLLMENT LISTS, 1862, The
Archives, Springfield, IL. Lists of all able-bodied men between the
ages of 18 and 45, by county. Not all counties represented.
The books listed above and several other similar books are available at
ISHL, ISA, NL, and FHL(FHC).

If you care to go into considerable detail in researching your IL Civil
War ancestor, this book will be of considerable help:
___George K. Schweitzer, CIVIL WAR GENEALOGY, The Author, 407
Ascot Court, Knoxville, TN 37923, 1996.
This work treats local, state, and national records, service and pension
records, regimental and naval histories, enlistment rosters, hospital records, court-martial reports, burial registers, national cemeteries,
gravestone allotments, amnesties, pardons, state militias, discharge papers,
officer biographies, prisons, prisoners, battle sites, maps, relics, weapons,
museums, monuments, memorials, deserters, black soldiers, Indian
soldiers, and many other topics.

Some national guard records for the period 1868-1910 are available in
ISA:
___ISA, IL NATIONAL GUARD RECORDS, 1868-1910, The Archives,
Springfield, IL, 18 volumes.

There is in the National Archives an index to the service records of
the Spanish-American War. This index is also available at NARC. Again
a properly filled out and submitted NATF Form 80 will bring you both
military service and pension records. It is also possible that you will find
the following materials useful:
___ISA, IL MUSTER-IN AND MUSTER-OUT ROLLS FOR THE
SPANISH-AMERICAN WAR, 1898-99, The Archives, Springfield,
IL, 13 volumes.
Some records for World War I and subsequent wars may be obtained
from:

___National Personnel Records Center, GSA (Military Records), 9700
Page Blvd., St. Louis, MO 63132.
There are also some records of the IL Service Recognition Board:
___ISA, WORLD WAR I BONUS CLAIMS, RECORDS, AND IN-
DEXES, The Archives, Springfield, IL.

---

27. Mortuary records

Very few IL mortuary records have been transcribed or microfilmed. This means that you must write directly to the mortuaries which you know or suspect were involved in burying your ancestor. Sometimes the death certificate will name the mortuary; sometimes it is the only one nearby; sometimes you will have to write several in order to ascertain which one might have done the funeral arrangements. Mortuaries for IL with their addresses are listed in the following volume:
___C. O. Kates, editor, THE AMERICAN BLUE BOOK OF FUNER-
AL DIRECTORS, Kates-Boylston Publications, New York, NY, latest
issue.
This reference book will usually be found in the offices of most mortuaries. In all correspondence with mortuaries be sure to enclose an SASE.

---

28. Naturalization records

Before IL became a state (1818), it was part of the IL Territory (1809-18), part of the IN Territory (1800-09), and before that part of the Northwest Territory (1787-1800).
During 1776-1789, the original states instituted naturalization regulations and/or procedures applying to their own areas. These requirements usually specified a period of residence, an oath of allegiance, and sometimes a confession of Protestant religion, all to be taken in a court of law. In 1790, the US Congress passed a naturalization act, followed in 1802 by a more comprehensive act. Although there were many modifying laws, the basic citizenship requirement until 1906 was that an alien to become a citizen, must live in the US 5 years, must file a declaration of intent, must wait two years, must then petition for naturalization, and finally take an oath of loyalty before a circuit or district court of the US, a supreme or district court of a territory, or any court of record of a state. The declaration of intent and the petition and oath-taking could occur in different courts. Following June 1906, about the same procedure was em-

ployed, but records and court actions were centralized by the US government. For this post-1906 period, write to the following address for a Form G-641, which you can use to request records:

___Immigration and Naturalization Service, 425 I St., Washington, DC 20536.

Prior to June 1906, the naturalization process could have taken place in a US, state, or local court. This often makes locating the records a fairly difficult process. What it means is that all possible court records must be gone through in the quest. Fortunately, a very useful index for a portion of IL exists:

___National Archives-Great Lakes Region, SOUNDEX INDEX TO NATURALIZATION PETITIONS FOR THE US DISTRICT AND CIRCUIT COURTS OF THE NORTHERN DISTRICT OF IL AND THE IMMIGRATION AND NATURALIZATION DISTRICT NUMBER 9, 1840-1950, The Regional Archives, Chicago, IL. An index to names recorded in naturalization indexes of many courts: federal, state, county, and municipal. Area includes northern IL. Also on microfilm at FHL.

Please be careful to note that this compilation by no means contains all the naturalizations for this time period, but it does contain the majority. The most likely IL courts for naturalizations are the county, circuit, US circuit, and US district courts. However, other courts must not be overlooked. The records are generally filed under headings such as declaration of intent, first papers, second papers, petitions, naturalization records, court journal, and court minutes. From 1790, children under 21 years were automatically naturalized with the parent. And until 1922, a wife was automatically naturalized along with the husband. During and after the Civil War, foreigners who had served in the military could become citizens simply by petition.

Naturalization records for many IL counties are on microfilm at ISL and FHL(FHC). Most of these are noted under the pertinent counties in Chapters 4 and 5. Others need to be sought in the counties. County naturalization records are also to be found in genealogical journals. Many of these articles are indexed in the following publication:

___For periodicals published 1847-1985, then annually 1986-present, consult Allen County Public Library Foundation, PERIODICAL SOURCE INDEX, The Foundation, Fort Wayne, In, 1986-.

Numerous records of the US Federal District and Circuit Courts for IL (approximately 1819-1982) are available at the Chicago Branch of the

National Archives, 7358 South Pulaski Road, Chicago, IL 60629 [Phone 1-(312)-581-7816].

___US Circuit and District Courts, IL Northern District, Chicago, OATHS OF ALLEGIANCE, NATURALIZATION PETITIONS, DECLARATIONS OF INTENTION, and other NATURALIZATION RECORDS 1872-1982, National Archives-Great Lakes Region, Chicago, IL. Also on microfilm at FHL(FHC).

___US Circuit and District Courts, IL Southern District, Springfield and Peoria, OATHS OF ALLEGIANCE, NATURALIZATION PETITIONS, DECLARATIONS OF INTENTION, and other NATURALIZATON RECORDS, 1856-1959, National Archives-Great Lakes Region, Chicago, IL. Also on microfilm at FHL(FHC).

Northwest Territorial records (for 1787-1801), IN Territorial records (for 1804-16), and IL Territorial records (for 1809-18), including some court records, are available at the National Archives in Washington, DC in Record Group 59.

29. Newspaper records

Newspaper publication began in the Northwest Territory with the appearance of the CENTINEL OF THE NORTH-WESTERN TERRITORY in Cincinnati in 1793. The first newspaper published in the IN Territory was the IN GAZETTE which originated in Vincennes in 1804. And the first newspaper published in IL Territory was the IL HERALD, which appeared in Kaskaskia in 1814. A number of original and microfilmed newspapers are available for towns, cities, and counties of IL. These records are likely to contain information on births, deaths, marriages, anniversaries, divorces, family reunions, land sales, legal notices, ads of professionals and businesses, and local news. The largest IL collections are to be found in ISHL and at The University of IL in Urbana, both originals and microfilms being included. Available IL newspapers and their locations will be found listed in:

___C. S. Brigham, HISTORY AND BIBLIOGRAPHY OF AMERICAN NEWSPAPERS, 1690-1820, American Antiquarian Society, Worcester, MA, 1947, 1961, 2 volumes.

___W. Gregory, AMERICAN NEWSPAPERS, 1821-1936, H. W. Wilson Co., New York, NY, 1937.

___Library of Congress, NEWSPAPERS IN MICROFILM, US Library of Congress, Washington, DC, 1973; Supplements, 1978, 1979, etc.

___US NEWSPAPER PROGRAM NATIONAL UNION LIST, OCLC, Dublin, OH, latest version.

___Stark, S. M., NEWSPAPERS IN THE ISHL, IL Libraries 70:3-4 (Mar-Apr, 1988) and 73:4 (Apr 1991), with update every third year thereafter.

___C. Pence, NEWSPAPERS IN THE ISHL, ISHL Special Report Series 1:1, IL Secretary of State, Springfield, IL, 1994.

FHL, FHC, and RL have some IL newspapers. A few IL newspapers have been indexed or abstracts from them have been published. Some LL have newspaper indexes, so it is always important to inquire.

Not to be overlooked are the newsletters and denominational newspapers of the various religious groups in IL. Many were published over considerable periods of time. Of special importance in these periodicals are the obituaries. These publications may be located in ISHL and The University of IL Library. Newspaper abstracts also appear in genealogical journals. The periodical indexes mentioned in the previous section should be used to locate these useful materials.

30. Published genealogies

There are a large number of index volumes and microfilm indexes which list published genealogies at the national level. Among the larger ones which you might examine are:

___FHL and FHC, FAMILY HISTORY LIBRARY CATALOG, Surname index.

___F. Rider, AMERICAN GENEALOGICAL INDEX, Godfrey Memorial Library, Middletown, CT, 1942-52, 48 volumes (millions of references).

___F. Rider, AMERICAN GENEALOGICAL AND BIOGRAPHICAL INDEX, Godfrey Memorial Library, Middletown, CT, 1952-, over 190 volumes (millions of references).

___The Newberry Library, THE GENEALOGICAL INDEX OF THE NEWBERRY LIBRARY, G. K. Hall, Boston, MA, 1960, 4 volumes (500,000 names).

___The New York Public Library, DICTIONARY CATALOG OF THE LOCAL HISTORY AND GENEALOGY DIVISION OF THE NEW YORK PUBLIC LIBRARY, G. K. Hall, Boston, MA, 1974, 20 volumes (318,000 entries).

___M. J. Kaminkow, GENEALOGIES IN THE LIBRARY OF CONGRESS, Magna Carta, Baltimore, MD, 1976-86. (25,000 references). Also see GENEALOGIES CATALOGED BY THE LIBRARY OF CONGRESS SINCE 1986, Library of Congress, Washington, DC, 1991.

__M. J. Kaminkow, COMPLEMENT TO GENEALOGIES IN THE LIBRARY OF CONGRESS, Magna Carta, Baltimore, MD, 1981.

__J. Munsell's Sons, INDEX TO AMERICAN GENEALOGIES, 1771-1908, reprint, Genealogical Publishing Co., Baltimore, MD, 1967 (60,000 references).

The first index is available at FHL and all FHC. At least some of the rest are held by ISHL, NL, FHL, FHC, many RL, and some LGL.

For the state of IL, the above volumes are likely to be of time-saving help. Other major sources of published genealogies of Illinoisians are the catalogs, the special indexes, and the special alphabetical files in ISHL and NL. Surname listings in card catalogs, special surname indexes, and family record files in RL and LL should not be overlooked.

31. Regional publications

In addition to national, state, and local publications, there are also numerous regional publications which should not be overlooked by any IL researcher. For the most part, these are volumes which are basically historical in character, but are likely to carry much genealogical information, sometimes incidentally, sometimes as addenda. They vary greatly in accuracy and coverage, so it is well the treat the data cautiously. In general, they cover specific regions which are made up of many or a few IL counties. In deciding which ones of these books to search for your forebears, you will need to make good use of the historical detail and the maps of Chapter 1.

The following works are ones which should prove useful to you if one or more deal with geographical areas of concern to you:

__H. W. Beckwith, HISTORY OF THE WABASH VALLEY IN INDIANA AND IL, Hill and Iddings, Chicago, IL, 1880.

__M. Butler, VALLEY OF THE OH, KY Historical Society, Frankfort, KY, 1971.

__J. L. Conger, HISTORY OF THE IL RIVER VALLEY, Clarke Publ. Co., Chicago, IL, 1932, 3 volumes.

__M. Custer, CENTRAL IL OBITUARIES, 1848-80, Bloomington-Normal Genealogical Society, Bloomington, IL, 1985-88, 2 volumes.

__M. Custer, PIONEER PORTRAITS OF CENTRAL IL, The Author, Bloomington, IL, 1923.

__FUNERAL NOTICES OF SOUTHERN IL, Cook-McDowell, Owensboro, KY, 1980.

___Gill, J. V., ILLIANA RESEARCH REPORTS, Heritage House, Thomson, IL, 1966.

___IDOLS OF EGYPT (SOUTHERN IL), Egypt Book House, Carbondale, IL, 1947.

___McDermott, J. F., OLD CAHOKIA, THE FIRST CENTURY OF ITS HISTORY, Polyanthos, New Orleans, LA, 1978. Early families.

___THE NORTHERN COUNTIES GAZETTEER AND DIRECTORY, R. Fergus, Chicago,IL, 1855-56.

___Smith, G. W., A HISTORY OF SOUTHERN IL, Lewis Publishing Co., Chicago, IL, 1912, 3 volumes.

___Way, R. B. THE ROCK RIVER VALLEY, Clarke Publ. Co., Chicago, IL, 1912, 3 volumes.

Most of these volumes will be found in ISHL, NL, and FHL(FHC). Those pertinent to various regions will usually be found in RL and larger LL in the area.

32. Tax lists

From its beginnings in 1818, the state of IL has collected taxes. The counties were the collecting agents, and they shared the revenues with the state. Many assessment and tax lists have survived, including ones dealing with taxes of several sorts: land, slaves, indentured servants, bank stock, poor, road, and railroad. The records are located in the CH, the IRADs, and some are on microfilm at the FHL (FHC). The tax lists available for the 102 IL counties are listed in Chapters 4 and 5. These are extremely valuable records, because when the tax records exist for long periods of time (as sometimes they do), you can have a year-by-year accounting of your ancestor. The tax records often give indirect indications of death of a landowner, death of his widow, and distribution of the land to sons and daughters.

There are quite a number of tax lists which have been published in genealogical journals. They may be located by looking in the following genealogical periodical indexes:

___For periodicals published 1847-1985, then annually 1986-present, consult Allen County Public Library Foundation, PERIODICAL SOURCE INDEX, The Foundation, Fort Wayne, In, 1986-.

During and shortly after the Civil War, there were federal tax assessments on IL people. Some of these records are available on microfilm:

___Bureau of Internal Revenue, INTERNAL REVENUE ASSESSMENT LISTS FOR IL, 1862-66, Microfilm M764, National Archives, Washington, DC.

33. Territorial records

As you will recall, before IL became a state (1818), it was part of the IL Territory (1809-18), part of the IN Territory (1800-09), and before that part of the Northwest Territory (1787-1800). Some of the more important references and record collections for these periods are as follows:

___C. E. Carter, TERRITORIAL PAPERS OF THE US THE TERRITORY OF IL, 1809-18, US Government Printing Office, 1948-50, Washington, DC, 2 volumes; THE TERRITORY NORTHWEST OF THE RIVER OHIO, US Government Printing Office, Washington, DC, 1787-1803, 2 volumes, and THE TERRITORY OF IN, 1800-1810, US Government Printing Office, Washington, DC, 1934-50.

___E. James, THE TERRITORIAL RECORDS OF IL, 1809-18, ISHL, Springfield, IL, 1901.

___F. S. Philbrick, THE LAWS OF IL TERRITORY, 1809-18, ISHL, Springfield, IL, 1908.   Also see T. C. Pease, THE LAWS OF THE NORTHWEST TERRITORY, 1788-1800, ISHL, Springfield, IL, 1925, and F. S. Philbrick, THE LAWS OF THE IN TERRITORY, 1801-1809, ISHL, Springfield, IL, 1930.

___C. W. Alvord, CAHOKIA RECORDS, 1778-90, ISHL, Springfield, IL, 1907.

___C. W. Alvord, KASKASKIA RECORDS, 1778-90, ISHL, Springfield, IL, 1909.

___C. M. Franklin, IN TERRITORIAL PIONEER RECORDS, 1801-1815, Heritage House, Indianapolis, IN, 1983.

___R. Hammes, IL MILITIAMEN, 1790, AND SQUATTERS IN TERRITORIAL IL, 1807 AND 1813, IL Libraries 59:5 (May 1977).

___NA, RECORDS RELATING TO THE AFFAIRS IN US TERRITORIES, NORTHWEST (1787-1801), INDIANA (1804-16), IL (1809-18), Record Group 59 of the Department of State, The Archives, Washington, DC.

___National Archives, TERRITORIAL PAPERS OF THE US SENATE, 1789-1873, Microfilm M200, The Archives, Washington, DC.

___Also see the Early and Territorial census records in the Census Section of this Chapter.

34. Wills and probate records

When a person died leaving any property (an estate), it was necessary for the authorities in the county of residence to see that this property was properly distributed. If a will had been written (testate), its wishes were carried out; if no will was left (intestate), the law indicated to whom distribution had to be made. Throughout the distribution process, many records had to be kept. From 1819-21, probate matters were managed by the Clerk of the Commissioners Court, from 1821-48 by the Probate Court, from 1848-70 by the County Court, from 1870-1964 by the County Court in smaller counties, from 1870-1964 by the Probate Court in larger counties, and from 1964-onward by the Circuit Court. This is an oversimplified scheme, because in a number of counties the transfer from County Court jurisdiction to Probate Court jurisdiction occurred between 1870 and 1964 as the populations changed. At the present, the probate records can usually be found in the records of the Circuit Court or in the IRAD for the county.

Many sorts of records may be found in probate proceedings: accounts, administrator, appearance, appraisal, bonds, claims and allowances, executor, estate, fees, final records, guardian, inventories, letters testamentary, orders, partitions, sales, will, and perhaps others. In addition to the books containing the above sorts of records, there were usually estate papers in which the numerous detailed loose records pertaining to the estates were filed. The books carry references to the papers so that they can be found in the boxes or cabinets where they are filed. All of these records are quite valuable genealogically, because they generally mention the heirs, the wife or husband, the children, and the spouses of the children. They may also mention the exact date of death, but if not, they indicate the approximate date. The records thereby serve, as very few others do, to solidly connect the generations.

The original books and estate papers (loose records) are in the CH and/or the pertinent IRAD, usually with some accompanying indexes. FHL(FHC) has microfilm copies of many of the books. And ISHL and NL have transcripts of a number of the books. A few transcripts are also available in RL, LGL, and LL. Very few of the loose records have been microfilmed or transcribed. Listed in Chapters 4 and 5 are the will and probate records available in the IL counties. In seeking records of this type, you need to realize that all books with any of the key words (accounts, administrator, appearance, appraisal, bonds, claims and allowances, executor, estate, fees, final records, guardian, inventories, letters testamentary, orders, partitions, sales, will) need to be examined. Remember that quite often, especially in earlier years, estate records are mixed in with the regular court records. Further, the titles on books may not be precise. For example, a book labelled simply Wills may also contain settlements, inventories, and sales. Or a book labelled Settlements may contain wills, executors, administrators, and inventories. Records of other courts should also be investigated because disputes over inherited land may appear there.

Some useful collections of IL wills are in:
___DAR Chapters in IL, THE BLUE BOOKS [TRANSCRIPTS OF IL GENEALOGICAL RECORDS], and the GRANDPARENT PAPERS, various sub-titles, various DAR Chapters, various cities, various dates. These many volumes include Bible, cemetery, church, marriage, death, obituary, and will records.
Please be careful to note that will records do not list estates of intestates (persons who did not make wills).

---

35. WPA works

The Works Progress Administration (WPA) of the federal government established the IL Historical Records Survey in 1936. The purpose of the IL Survey was to inventory state, county, municipal, and church records of historical importance. In 1939, supervision of the project was taken over by the ISL, with the University of IL at Urbana joining them in 1940. The Survey ended in 1942, and most of the unpublished inventories were deposited in the ISA, but a few materials remained in the University of IL Library. The holdings of the ISA are inventoried in:
___V. Irons, P. C. Brennan, and J. Daly, DESCRIPTIVE INVENTORY OF THE ARCHIVES OF THE STATE OF IL, ISA, Secretary of State, Springfield, IL, 1978.
The data which the WPA Historical Records Survey accumulated are often very useful to genealogists because they indicate where many records were located in the period 1936-42. They, therefore, can alert you to what was available, and can give you clues as to where to start in your search for them. Remember that many of the items to which these works refer remain where they were in 1936-42, but some have been moved to other depositories.

Among the published materials which could be of assistance to you are the following. Many of them are incomplete and there are errors in them, some worse than others:
___Historical Records Survey, GUIDE TO CHURCH VITAL STATISTICS RECORDS IN IL, WPA, Chicago, IL, 1942.
___Historical Records Survey, GUIDE TO PUBLIC VITAL STATISTICS RECORDS IN IL, WPA, Chicago, IL, 1941.

___Historical Records Survey, INVENTORY OF THE CHURCH ARCHIVES OF IL, WPA, Chicago, IL, 1941-42, 3 volumes. Only the Cairo, Springfield, and Cumberland Presbyteries.

___Historical Records Survey, INVENTORY OF THE COUNTY ARCHIVES OF IL, WPA Chicago, IL, 1939-42, 32 volumes. Printed for only 32 counties: Adams, Brown, Carroll, Champaign, Clark, Cumberland, DeWitt, Douglas, Effingham, Fayette, Franklin, Jackson, Jo Daviess, Knox, Macoupin, Menard, Montgomery, Morgan, Moultrie, Ogle, Peoria, Piatt, Pike, Rock Island, Saline, Sangamon, Scott, Shelby, St. Clair, Stephenson, Vermilion. Unpublished volumes are in ISA.

Among the unpublished Historical Records Survey materials which are stored in the ISA are the following:

___State Appellate Court Records
___State Court of Claims Records
___Secretary of State Records
___Supreme Court Records
___State Treasurer Records
___Inventories of County Records for 67 Counties (Cook included)
___Inventories of Municipal Records for 224 Municipalities (Chicago included)
___Inventories of Church Records for these Denominations: Adventist, Assembly of God, Baptist, Brethren, Christian Union, Church of Christ-Scientist, Church of God, Church of the Living God, Church of the Nazarene, Congregational, Disciples of Christ, Evangelical, Evangelical and Reformed, Holiness, Jewish, Latter-Day Saints, Lutheran, Methodist, Moravian, Non-Denominational, Pentecostal, Presbyterian, Protestant Episcopal, Quakers, Roman Catholic, Salvation Army, and Universalist.
___Transcriptions of County Board Minutes for 99 Counties (Cook excluded)

List of Abbreviations

CCB	=	Cook County Building, Chicago
CCH	=	Chicago City Hall
CH	=	Court House(s)
CHSL	=	Chicago Historical Society Library
CJCLDS	=	Church of Jesus Christ of Latter Day Saints
CPL	=	Chicago Public Library
D	=	Federal mortality censuses
DC	=	Daley Center, Chicago
E	=	Early inhabitant lists
F	=	Federal Farm and Ranch censuses
FHC	=	Family History Center(s), branches of FHL
FHL	=	Family History Library, Salt Lake City, UT
IL	=	Illinois
IRAD	=	IL Regional Archives Repository(ies)
IRAD-EIU	=	IRAD at Eastern IL University, Charleston
IRAD-ISU	=	IRAD at IL State University, Normal
IRAD-NIU	=	IRAD at Northern IL University, DeKalb
IRAD-SIU	=	IRAD at Southern IL University, Carbondale
IRAD-SSU	=	IRAD at Sangamon State University, Springfield
IRAD-UNI	=	IRAD at Northeastern IL University, Chicago
IRAD-WIU	=	IRAD at Western IL University, Macomb
ISA	=	IL State Archives, Springfield
ISGS	=	IL State Genealogical Society, Springfield
ISGSQ	=	IL State Genealogical Society Quarterly
ISHL	=	IL State Historical Library, Springfield
ISHS	=	IL State Historical Society, Springfield
ISL	=	IL State Library, Springfield
LL	=	Local Library(ies)
LR	=	Local Repositories
M	=	Federal Manufactures censuses
NA	=	National Archives, Washington, DC
NAGL	=	National Archives - Great Lakes Region, Chicago
NARC	=	National Archives Regional Centers
NL	=	Newberry Library, Chicago
P	=	1840 Revolutionary War pension census
R	=	Regular federal censuses
RL	=	Regional Library(ies)
S	=	IL State censuses
T	=	IN and IL Territorial censuses

Chapter 3

RECORD LOCATIONS

1. Introduction	The purpose of this chapter is to describe for you the major genealogical record repositories for IL records. These repositories are of two major types, libraries and archives.

In general, libraries hold materials which have been published in printed, typescript, photocopied, computerized, and microfilm (microcard, microfiche) forms. Archives, on the other hand, are repositories for original records, largely in manuscript (hand-written) form, but also often as microfilm copies. Usually, libraries will have some original materials, and archives will have some published materials, but the predominant character of each is as indicated. When visiting and making use of the materials of repositories, there are several rules which almost all of them have. (1) You are required to check all overcoats, brief cases, and packages. (2) You are required to present some identification and to sign a register or fill out a form. (3) There is to be no smoking, no eating, no loud talk, and the use of pencils only. (4) All materials are to be handled with extreme care, with no injury to or defacing of any of them. (5) Materials are usually not to be returned to the stacks or drawers from which they came, but are to be returned to designated carts, tables, or shelves. (6) Upon leaving you should submit all materials for inspection and/or pass through security devices.

Libraries and archives have finding aids to facilitate locating the records which they hold. These aids are usually alphabetically arranged lists or indexes according to names or locations or subjects or authors or titles, or combinations of these, or they may be by dates. They consist of computer catalogs, card catalogs, microform catalogs, printed catalogs, typed catalogs and lists, various indexes, inventories, calendars, and tables of contents. In using these aids, especially computer, card, and microform catalogs, they must be searched in as many ways as possible to ensure that you extract everything from them. These ways are by name, by location, by subject, by author, by title, and sometimes by date. Sometimes certain catalogs are arranged by only one or two of these categories, but otherwise be sure and search them for all that are applicable. To help you to recall these categories, remember the word SLANT, with S standing for subject, L for location, A for author, N for name, and T for title. This is not, however, the order in which they should be searched for the maximum efficiency. They should be searched N-L-S-A-T. First, search the catalog for N(name), that is, for the surnames of all your IL forebears. Second, search the catalog for L(location), that is, look under all places where your ancestor lived (Northwest Territory, IN Territory, IL Territory, state of IL, region, county, city, town, village), but especially the county, city, and town. Examine every entry in order to make sure you miss nothing. Third, look under appropriate S(subject) headings, such as the titles related to the sections in Chapter 2 [Bible, biography, birth, cemetery, census, church denomination, church name, court, Daughters of the American Revolution, death, divorce, emigration, ethnic group name (such as Germans, Huguenots, Irish), genealogy, historical records, immigration, marriage, US-history-Revolutionary War, US-history-War of 1812, US-history-Civil War, naturalization, newspaper, pensions, tax, will], but never neglecting these [biography, deeds, epitaphs, family records, genealogy, registers of births etc., wills]. Then finally, look under A(author) and/or T(title) for books mentioned in the sections of Chapter 2 which you need to examine.

When you locate references in finding aids to materials you need to examine, you will usually find that a numbered or alphabetized or combined code accompanies the listing. This is the access code which you should copy down, since it tells you where the material is located. For books it will usually be a code which refers to shelf positions. For microfilms, it usually refers to drawers and reel numbers. For manuscripts, it usually refers to folders, files, or boxes. In some repositories, the materials will be out on shelves or in cabinets to which you have access. In other repositories you will need to give the librarian or archivist a call slip on which you have written the title and code for the material so that it can be retrieved for you. In the microfilm (microfiche) areas of repositories you will find microfilm (microfiche) readers which attendants can help you with, if necessary.

Never leave a library or archives without discussing your research with a librarian or archivist. These people are trained specialists who know their collections and the ways for getting into them. And they can often suggest innovative approaches to locating data relating to your progenitors. They also can usually guide you to other finding aids. When you do discuss your work with librarians and archivists, please remember that they are busy people with considerable demands on their time. So be brief, get to the point, and don't bore them with irrelevant detail. They will appreciate this, and you and others will get more and better service from them.

In general, you cannot expect to do much of your genealogy by corresponding with libraries and archives. The reason is that the hard-working professionals who run these repositories have little time to give to answering mail. This is because of the heavy demands of serving the institutions which employ them, of maintaining the collection, and of taking care of patrons who visit them. Some simply cannot reply to mail requests. Others will answer one brief question which can be quickly looked up in a finding aid, but none of them can do even brief research for you. If you do write them, make your letter very brief, get right to the point, enclose an SASE, and be prepared to wait. Repositories will generally not recommend researchers you can hire, but they will sometimes provide you with a list of researchers. Such a list will bear no warranty from the repository, and they in no way have any responsibility toward either you or the researcher, because they are not in the business of certifying searchers.

As mentioned at the beginning of Chapter 2, there are several record repositories in IL which will be of immense value in your genealogical research. The best collections of IL materials are to be found in the following repositories:

___(ISHL) IL State Historical Library, Old State Capitol, Springfield, IL, 62701. The largest collection of published (print and microform) IL genealogical and historical materials. Also large collections of IL maps, manuscripts, and newspapers

___(ISA) IL State Archives, Spring and Edwards Streets, Springfield, IL 62756. Originals and microform copies of federal, IL, and IL county documents. Also many published records, reference sources, histories, and biographical volumes.

___(NL) Newberry Library, 60 West Walton St., Chicago, IL 60610. This library holds a very large collection of published (print and microform) IL genealogical materials. Included are local histories, family histories, church records, vital record transcriptions, cemetery readings, censuses, maps, Civil War regimental histories, and county records. Accompanying these are many large indexes and other IL ancestor finding aids.

___(FHL) Family History Library, Genealogical Library of the Church of Jesus Christ of Latter-day Saints, 35 North West Temple, Salt Lake City, UT 84150. Microfilmed and published national, state, county, municipal, and private records.

___(FHC) Family History Center(s), over 1700 of them, located all over the world. They are local branch affiliates of the Family History Library (FHL). They can be found in most major US cities, including

9 in IL (Champaign, Chicago Heights, Fairview Heights, Napierville, Nauvoo, Peoria, Rockford, Schaumburg, Wilmette). Most of the microfilmed national, state, county, municipal, and private records held by the FHL can be borrowed through the FHC.

___(NA and NARC) National Archives, Seventh and Pennsylvania Avenue, Washington, DC 20408, and National Archives-Regional Centers (NARC), especially the National Archives-Great Lakes Region (NAGL), 7358 South Pulaski Road, Chicago, IL 60629. Other Regional Centers in Anchorage, AK, Boston, Denver, East Point, GA (suburban Atlanta), Fort Worth, Kansas City, MO, Laguna Niguel, CA (near Los Angeles), New York City, Philadelphia, San Bruno, CA (suburban San Francisco), and Seattle.

___(IRAD) IL Regional Archives Depositories, IRAD Coordinator, IL State Archives, Spring and Edwards Streets, Springfield, IL 62756. Consists of 7 regional archives containing records deposited by counties in the region. Located in DeKalb (north), Macomb, Normal, Springfield, Charleston, Carbondale, and Chicago.

___(RL) Regional Libraries in IL which hold larger genealogical collections than are usually held by most local libraries. Published and some microfilmed national, state, regional, county, and local private records.

___(LL) Local Libraries in the cities and towns of the IL counties. These include county, city, town, and private libraries. Published county, city, and local private records, and sometimes some microfilms.

___(LR) Local Repositories which have special types of records in counties, cities, and towns : historical societies, genealogical societies, record archives and institutes, museums, cemetery offices, organizations, mortuaries, and newspaper offices.

___(CH) County Court Houses in the county seats of the 102 IL counties. Original and microfilmed county records.

Records which are national (federal) and those which are state-wide in scope have been treated in detail in Chapter 2. The locations of the records have also been given. Records which are basically county-wide in scope were treated only generally in Chapter 2, but detailed listings of those available will be given in Chapters 4 and 5.

Most of the original county records referred to in Chapter 2 and partially listed under the counties in Chapters 4 and 5 are stored in the court houses and/or in the appropriate IRAD. The court houses are located in the county seats which are listed along with their zip codes in Chapters 4 and 5. And the IRADs, which are noted above, will be discussed in detail below. The original records ordinarily consist of variously-labelled books (usually handwritten), files with file folders in them, and boxes with large envelopes or file folders in them. The records are generally stored in the offices of various county officials, or in the case of older records they may be found in special storage vaults. In many instances, they are readily accessible. In a few cases, they are put away so that they are very difficult to get out and use. The records which will most likely be found in the county court houses and IRADs include the following, these categories being taken largely from the WPA inventories and the listing by Pease:

___County Board (sometimes called Commissioners or Supervisors): county government, tax regulations, roads, appropriations, pensions, relief

___County Clerk (other titles sometimes): records on tax, valuations, collections, vital statistics (births, marriages, deaths), licenses, elections, bonds of officers, militia, estrays, brands and marks, indentures, maps, plats

___Recorder: deeds, mortgages, soldiers, veterans' burials, name changes, land patents, leases, bonds of officers, corporations, plats, maps, surveys

___County Court (and predecessors): civil, criminal, naturalizations, adoptions, insanity, sometimes probate

___Probate Court: probates, wills, estates, guardians

___Circuit Court: civil, criminal, chancery, naturalization, appeals

___Coroner: inquests

___Sheriff: arrests, jail records, warrants, executions (doing tasks assigned by the court), property sales, tax collection

___Surveyor: surveys, maps, plats

___Treasurer: finances, receipts, disbursements

___State's attorney: indictments, grand juries, imprisonments

___County home: inmates, admissions, dismissals, finances

___Superintendant of schools: finances, teachers, pupils

The precise responsibilities of each of the above offices depend on the size of the county. In some cases, some of the offices do not exist and the tasks are carried out by other officials.

Once you have located the county in which your ancestor lived, it is usually not a good idea to go there first. It is best to explore the microfilmed, transcribed, and published copies of the records at some central repository such as ISHL-ISA, NL, FHL(FHC), and IRAD. (ISHL-ISA are hyphenated to remind you that both may be visited together since both are in Springfield.) This is because it is the business of these repositories to make the records available to you, but the primary task of the county officials and employees at the court houses is to conduct the record keeping task as an aid to regulating the society and keeping the law. Therefore, it is best not to encroach upon their time and their good graces until you have done as much work elsewhere as possible. Many of the major record books have been microfilmed or transcribed so you can go through them nicely at ISHL-ISA, NL, FHL(FHC), and IRAD. Or you can hire a researcher to do the investigating for you if a trip is not workable or would be too expensive. Most of the contents of the case files, however, have not been copied. Hence, after doing work at ISHL-ISA, NL, FHL(FHC), and IRAD you then need to make a trip to the county (LL, LR, CH), or hire a researcher to do so for you. In general, you will find the people there very helpful and cooperative, and often they will make photocopies for you or will give you access to a copying machine. It is usually best to visit the LL before going to the CH, and do not forget the many other possible LR in the counties.

Now, you will be reminded of something very important. Your ultimate goal in searching through all the above materials is to see and copy the original documents (or microfilms of them) which substantiate your family information. Transcripts, compiled lists, family histories, directories, biographies, newspapers, and the like, are highly subject to error, and are not considered as substantiation. This means that many of the sources of Chapter 2 are to be used mainly as aids to assist you in finding the original documents (or microfilm copies).

Researchers who are near ISHS-ISA, NL, FHL, FHC, IRAD, or the CH in the various counties will be listed in:
___G. B. Everton, Jr., editor, GENEALOGICAL HELPER, Everton Publishers, Logan, UT, latest Jul-Aug issue.
In addition, staff members at ISHS-ISA, NL, FHC, and the LL in the various counties will often send you a list of researchers if you will dispatch a request and an SASE to them. Do not write the officials in the CH for researcher recommendations since they generally deem this a matter to be handled by the LL and therefore are ordinarily unable to help you.

2. The IL State Historical Library (ISHL)

The IL State Historical Library (IS-HL) is located in the Old State Capitol, Sixth and Adams Streets, in the midst of downtown Springfield, IL

62701. The telephone number is 1-217-524-7216, and its open hours are 8:30 am to 5:00 pm Monday through Friday. It is important that you recognize that the opening times may change, so do not fail to call before you go. Several convenient, but a bit expensive, parking lots are nearby. There are a number of hotels within walking distance of the ISHL. Included are the following:

___Best Western Lincoln Plaza Hotel, 101 East Adams Street, Springfield, IL 62701. Telephone 1-217-523-5661.

___Renaissance Springfield Hotel, 701 East Adams Street, Springfield, IL 62701. 1-217-544-8800.

___Springfield Hilton Hotel, 700 East Adams Street, Springfield, IL, Telephone 1-217-789-1530.

When you enter the Old State Capitol Building by the main entrance, you will be on the 4th floor. Tell the attendant at the door that you wish to use the ISHL, then turn right to the elevators. Go down to the 2nd floor, get off the elevator, turn right, and proceed straight ahead to the entrance door of the ISHL. Pass through the security gate, register at the Service Desk, remember the basic rules for use of a library, then stand at the door and look around. You will be viewing a repository that manages more than 170,000 books, over 3000 maps, over 1200 periodical series, 4700 newspaper titles, and more than 9,700,000 manuscript items. Off on your far left you will see two very large card catalog cabinets. These house the main card catalog and several smaller card catalogs:

___(Main) Main Card Catalog, search by name, locality (IL, region, county, city, town, township), subject, author, title. Remember SLANT.

___(DAR-1) DAR Family Name Catalog, search by name.

___(DAR-2) DAR Genealogical Index, search under Bible Records by name, then search these sections by location: Birth, Cemetery, Church, Death, Land, Local History, Marriage, Wills.

___(Cem-1) Cemetery Survey Index 1, search by location.

___(Cem-2) Cemetery Survey Index 2, search by cemetery name, card includes reference to cemetery recordings, if available.

___(News-1) Newspaper Index, search by location.

Just to your right beyond the Service Desk is another large card catalog. This is:

___(Sur) Surname Index, made up of names taken from selected IL county histories and biographies, search by name.

Now step over to the Surname Index, face it, and look way off to your left, viewing all the way along the wall, then through the book stacks.

You will see a doorway, beyond which is the Manuscript Room which contains:

___(Man-1) Manuscript Card Catalog, search by name, location, organization, subject, title.

On top or adjacent to the Manuscript Card Catalog you will find several looseleaf notebooks which serve as further finding and information aids for the manuscript collection:

___(Man-2) Loose-leaf Notebook of Subject Bibliographies in the Manuscript Collection. Some of the subjects are Afro-Americans, Churches, Civil War, Immigrants, Indians, Land, Mexican War, Women.

___Three Loose-leaf Notebooks of Small Collection Descriptions.

___Numerous Loose-leaf Notebooks describing many of the collections. If you find materials of interest in the Manuscript Area, you will need to make an appointment to examine them. The telephone number in the Manuscript Area is 1-(217)-785-7942.

Now return to the entrance door, leave the room, and then turn left almost immediately. Down the hall you will see a door leading into the Microfilm Room. In this room, you will see the following finding aids:

___(News-2) Newspaper Index, search by city. Largest newspaper collection in IL.

___(Obit) Obituary Index, search by name.

___(Oth) Other newspaper finding aids available at the desk.

And in the room, you will find microfilm readers.

Go back into the main library area, and observe the shelves along the wall opposite you and the book stacks off on your far right. Beginning at your left and continuing to the right and then into the stacks, you will find the following types of volumes: general reference, national biography, American history, IL history (state and regional), IL State Historical Society publications, IL county biographies, histories, and published records, history reference volumes, DAR collections, immigration works, Rider's index, society lineage books, and IL DAR grandparent records. These books are indexed in the Main Card Catalog, along with many others which must be requested at the Service Desk.

Remember that libraries and archives can be searched by recalling SLANT (S for subject, L for locality, A for author, N for name, and T for title). The best order is N (name) first, the L (locality) second, and then S (subject), A (author), and T (title). So, you should _first_ examine those finding aids which can be examined by _name_. These are: Main, DAR-1, Sur, Man-1, and Obit. _Then_, you should examine those finding aids which will lead you to other available records which might contain data on your ancestor. These will be chiefly finding aids which list records under your ancestor's locality (county, city, IL). The proper ones are: Main, DAR-2, Cem-1, Cem-2, News-1, Man-1, News-2, Oth. Now, carry out the third and fourth steps. The third step is to check the appropriate items for any specialized subjects under which you think you might find information on your forebear. The headings of sections in Chapter 2 will suggest some of these subjects (atlas, Bible, biography, birth, cemetery, church, city directory, city history, county history, court, DAR, death, deed, divorce, ethnic, family history, gazetteer, genealogical periodical, genealogy, map, land, marriage, military, mortuary, naturalization, newspaper abstracts, probate, regional histories, registers of births, tax, and will). Examples of others might be millwrights, Germans, Methodist Episcopal Church, epitaphs, War of 1812, underground railroad. Such items are to be sought in Main, Man-1, and Man-2.

Fourth, do the author and title checking. Look carefully at the large number of books and other items that are listed in the many sections of Chapter 2. As you find books and other items which you have not seen, locate them in the Main and Man-1 by author and/or title.

Do not fail to discuss your research with one of the competent staff of the ISHL, especially those in the Genealogy Section. Be brief, because their time is valuable. You will find that they will be able to save you much time and considerable effort. Remember, however, that they cannot do your work for you, they can only give you guidance. The ISHL will fill requests for specific information from the collections. A fee is requested for non-IL residents. Write them for details.

The IL State Library is another sizable reference library in Springfield (300 South 2nd St., Springfield, IL 62701). This repository does not specialize in genealogy, but is a resource library for the IL state government. Most of its genealogically-pertinent holdings are available elsewhere in Springfield at the ISHS and/or the ISA. It does, however, provide interlibrary loan service for IL county histories, biographies, and atlases, state and federal censuses, some military indexes, and a combined 1810-55 overall census index. Your local library must make requests for these items.

3. The IL State Archives (ISA)

The IL State Archives (ISA) is located in the Archives Building of the Capitol Complex in downtown Springfield, IL 62701. Nearby hotels and parking facilities are the same as for the ISHS. The times for the ISA are 8:30am - 5:00pm, Monday through Friday, and 8:00am - 3:30pm Saturday (except holiday weekends). But times can change, so be sure to check by calling them at 1-217-782-4682 or 1-217-782-3556.

The ISA has an unbelievably large volume of records. Much of this is inventoried in finding aids, and some of it is indexed. Before you go to the ISA, you should order the following volumes from them and make good use of their contents:

___V. Irons and P. C. Brennan, DESCRIPTIVE INVENTORY OF THE ARCHIVES OF THE STATE OF IL, ISA, Springfield, IL, 1978, with SUPPLEMENTS, to date. Consult the various Record Series (RS). Revised edition due out soon.

___R. E. Bailey and E. S. Evans, INDEX TO THE DESCRIPTIVE INVENTORY OF THE ARCHIVES OF THE STATE OF IL, ISA, Springfield, IL, 1990.

These volumes constitute two of the major finding aids to the materials in the ISA. Some of the earlier important genealogical sources listed in these volumes and therefore available at ISA are (RS means Record Series):

___RS100.8 IL Territorial Census 1818. See name index by Norton in Reference Room.

___RS 103.2-103.10 IL State Censuses 1820-65. See published and card name indexes in Reference Room.

___RS 103.31 Deeds to State-Owned Land 1865-1964. Name card index in Reference Room.

___RS 103.75-103.77 Registers of County Officials 1809-1964. Indexes available.

___RS 103.96-103.103 Convict Records 1835-1973. Some indexed.

___RS 105.69 Record of State Land Sales 1843-65. No index.

___RS 208.8 Register of Licensed Dentists 1881-86, 1903-51. No index.

___RS 208.18 Register of Licensed Midwives 1877-1930. Indexed.

___RS 208.28 Register of Licensed Physicians 1877-1952. Index up to 1907.

___RS 251.4 Register of Pupils of Asylum for the Deaf and Dumb 1845-1931. Indexed.

___RS 252.2 Case Records of State Hospital for the Insane 1854-1907, partly restricted. Indexed.

___RS 254.4 Admission Applications for Institution for Feeble-Minded Children 1865-1906, partly restricted. Index up to 1887.

___RS 259.1-259.10 Records of IL Soldiers' and Sailors' Home 1885-1967. Index for 1887-1908 in Reference Room.

___RS 260.1-260.6 Records of IL Soldiers' Widows' Home 1895-1963, RG 260.1 arranged alphabetically by name. Index for 1960-63 only.

___RS 301.7 Black Hawk War Records 1832-91. See Index compiled by Whitney.

___RS 301.8 Mexican War Records 1846-90. See Index compiled by Elliott.

___RS 301.18-301.22 Civil War Records 1861-1903. Name indexes in Reference Room.

___RS 301.29 Civil War Military Censuses 1861-63. Arranged by county, then by township. No name index.

___RS 301.87-301.98 Muster Rolls, Spanish-American War 1898-99. Name index in Reference Room.

___RS 901.1 IL Supreme Court Case Files 1820-1970. Indexed.

___RS 951.1-951.23, 951.27-951.28 Federal Censuses for IL 1820-1920. Indexes in Reference Room.

___RS 952.1-952.79 Kaskaskia Land District Records 1783-1956. Name index.

___RS 952.80-952.135 Shawneetown Land District Records 1812-1956. Name index.

___RS 952.136-952.180 Edwardsville Land District Records 1816-1956. Name index.

___RS 952.181-952.209 Vandalia Land District Records 1820-1956. Name index.

___RS 952.210-952.228 Palestine Land District Records 1821-1956. Name index.

___RS 952.229-952.250 Springfield Land District Records 1823-1956. Name index.

___RS 952.251-952.279 Quincy Land District Records 1831-1956. Name index.

___RS 952.280-952.313 Danville Land District Records 1831-1957. Name index.

___RS 952.314-952.314-952.336 Northeastern Land District Records 1834-1956. Name index.

___RS 952.337-952.363 Northwestern Land District Records 1828-62. Name index.

___RS 953.1-953.19 US Surveyor General's IL Records 1804-1970. Some records indexed.

___RS 954.3 Historical Records Survey Inventory of State Archives 1936-41.

___RS 954.6 Historical Records Survey Transcripts of County Board Minutes (1802-1941), compiled 1938-42.

___RS 954.7 Historical Records Survey Inventory of County Archives 1936-42 (for almost all counties for which the inventories have not been published).

___RS 954.8 Historical Records Survey Historical Sketches of Counties 1936-42.

___RS 954.11 Historical Records Survey Inventory of Municipal Archives 1936-41.

___RS 954.12 Historical Records Survey Inventory of Church Archives 1941-42 (for 27 different denominations and several non-denominational groups).

___RS 954.13 Historical Records Survey Inventory of Manuscript Collections and Depositories 1936-41.

___RS 956.1 World War One Draft Registration Cards 1917-19, by county, then by draft board, then alphabetically by name.

When you enter the ISA Building, turn right, proceed through the first room into the second room, which is the Archives Reference Room. Sign in, place all non-research materials in the provided lockers (hats, coats, parcels, large purses, briefcases, umbrellas, books), and remind yourself of the basic rules for conduct in a repository. Now, stand at the entrance door, and survey the room. Straight ahead of you is a Finding Aids Desk with several loose-leaf binders on it. To your left is the Reference Desk. Just in front of the Reference Desk, a left turn will put you in a long hall with card catalogs on both sides, the Card Catalog Hall. On the far wall, you will see bookshelves. These contain various genealogical reference and record books with heavy concentration on IL, especially IL county histories. In the far right corner, there is a low file cabinet, and just back from it is a door into the Microfilm Room.

The major finding aids for the ISA will now be located and discussed. First, remember

___The published DESCRIPTIVE INVENTORY and the INDEX to it which have been described above.

In the low file cabinet is a valuable reference set of microfilms which contain good materials on the very early IL country.

___Hammes Collection of land transfers 1678-1814, on 157 microfilm reels. Notebook inventory located on the top of the cabinet. Index on the first two microfilm reels.

Down the long Card Catalog Hall, you will find the following card catalogs:

___Name Index to Early IL Records, censuses and other materials, over 500K cards, search by name.

___Index to the 1860 Federal IL Census, search by name.

___Index to the 1865 IL State Census, search by name.

___County History Index No. 1, search by name.

___County History Index No. 2, search by name.

___County History Index No. 3 (further down the hall), search by name.

___Indian Wars Index 1810-13, search by name.

___Mexican War Index, search by name.

___IL Soldiers' and Sailors' Home Index 1887-1908, search by name.

___Danville National Home Index, search by name.

___Mormon War Index, search by name.

___Civil War Index, search by name.

___Spanish-American War Index, search by name.

___State Deeds Index, search by name.

Once a name is located in these files, the information on the card will lead you to the records.

On the Finding Aids Desk, these loose-leaf notebooks and some lists are available for your use:

___IL State Archives Microfilm Collection, including sections on Local Government Records (county and city microfilms, including those from the FHL), and National Archives Records (censuses, naturalizations, military), search by location and type of record.

___IRAD Records Listing, search by county and thereunder by title.

___ISGS Microfilm Collection (includes FHL microfilms), search by IL or by county, and then by type of record.

___ISGS-ISA, IL Cemetery Locations, index in progress, search by county.

___Published County Records, search by county.

Among other larger indexes that you must not miss in the ISA are the following:

___Archives Public Domain Land Records Index, 1814-76, on 144 microfiche, computer, and internet, search by name (or by county, then by name).

___Alphabetical List of Cook County Purchasers of Public Domain Land, search by name.

___Honor Roll of Veterans Buried in IL, 1774-1955, published by the General Assembly, search by county, then by cemetery, then alphabetical by name. Or use the Index for the period 1774-1898.

___Index to Roll of Honor, Cook County, IL, Markham, Salt Lake City, UT, search by name.
___Index to IL Marriage Records up to 1900, on computer, in process, search by name.
___Index to IL Death Records 1916-42, on microfiche, search by name.
___Soundex Index to Nturalization Petitions for the US District and Circuit Courts, Northern District of IL, 1840-1950. Indexed by name.

Using the listings in Chapters 2, 4, and 5, ascertain the records that you wish to use in the ISA. Then employ the above finding aids as follows:
___Look your ancestor up in the finding aids which have a name index.
___Look up your ancestor's county in finding aids which are arranged by county, decide if there are records which might list your ancestor, then locate and use them.
Do not fail to consult an archivist about your investigation. These knowledgeable people can suggest other records which might be of value to you.

4. The Newberry Library (NL)

The Newberry Library (NL) has one of the largest genealogical collections in the US. This library is located at 60 West Walton Street, Chicago, IL 60610. The telephone number is 1-312-943-9090, and the hours are 10:00 am - 6:00 pm Tuesday-Thursday, and 9:00 am - 5:00 pm Friday and Saturday. Hours are subject to change, so if you are planning to go, telephone and inquire about the times. Hotels in the region include:
___Guest Quarters Suite Hotel, 198 East Delaware Place, Chicago, IL 60611. Telephone 1-312-280-8800.
___The Drake Hotel, 140 East Walton Place, Chicago, IL 60611. Telephone 1-312-787-2200.
___The Westin Hotel, 909 North Michigan Avenue, Chicago, IL 60611. Telephone 1-312-943-7200.
___The Raphael Hotel, 201 East Delaware Place, Chicago, IL 60611. Telephone 1-312-943-5000.
___The Seneca Hotel, 200 East Chestnut Street, Chicago, IL 60611. Telephone 1-312-787-8900.
___The Tremont Hotel, 100 East Chestnut Street, Chicago, IL 60611. Telephone 1-312-751-1900.

___Le Meridien Hotel, 21 East Belleview Place, Chicago, IL 60611.
Telephone 1-312-266-2100.

The holdings of the NL include over 1,500,000 printed works, over
220,000 rolls of microfilm or packs of microfiche, and over 5,000,000
manuscripts. These represent genealogical indexes, family histories,
federal and state censuses, city directories, biographies, passenger lists,
federal and state military records, local histories, major genealogical
reference works, patriotic and hereditary society publications, state and
private collections of microfilmed records, manuscript collections, atlases,
maps, gazetteers, native American records, African-American records,
Canadian records, British records, German records, periodicals, computer
data bases, FHL indexes and catalogs, and a comprehensive index to the
most important genealogical periodicals. Their IL collection is very
strong. Many of the materials mentioned in Chapter 2 will be found in
NL. It will be of considerable assistance to you if you will use the
following book before visiting the library:
___P. T. Sinko, GUIDE TO LOCAL AND FAMILY HISTORY AT
THE NEWBERRY LIBRARY, Ancestry Publishing, Salt Lake City,
UT, 1987, especially pages 1-75, 125-130.

After entering the library, leave items not essential to your research
in the lockers on the first floor (hats, coats, parcels, large purses, briefcases, umbrellas, books), then register at the Registration Desk. Proceed
to the third floor where you will be issued a Reader's Card and where you
will have an opportunity to make a donation. Please do this since the NL
is a private institution and needs the help of its patrons to maintain its
excellent collection. You will be in the very large Reference Room of the
NL.

The third floor Reference Room houses the major finding aids in the
NL. The second floor Reading Room is the main place where many
genealogical materials are on open shelves and where even more may be
requested. On some occasions, you may need to go to the Special
Collections Room on the fourth floor for certain items. The major
genealogical finding aids which you will need are located on the third
floor. These are:
___Main Card Catalog, for materials cataloged before 1978, search by
name, location (IL, region of IL, county, city, town), subject, author,
title.

___On-line Computer Catalog, for materials cataloged after 1977, search by name, location (IL, region of IL, county, city, town), subject, author, title, keyword, Boolean combinations (two or more words)
___Map Card Catalog by Areas, search by location and subject
___Map Card Catalog by Titles, search by location
___Map Card Catalog by Cartographers and Publishers
___Manuscript Catalog, search by name, catalog is supplemented by Modern Manuscript Binders on shelves above a table labelled Newberry Library Checklists
___Chronological Card File by Date (incomplete)
___Place Card File by Location (incomplete)
___Serials Card File, search by name of publication
___City Directory Card File, search by city
___Card Catalog of Family History Vertical File, search by name
___Card Catalog of Local History Vertical File, search by county and city
___Chicago and Cook County Biography and Industry Card File, search by name and by organization
___Heraldry Card File, search by name

All these catalogs are in a very large set of card catalog cabinets which occupy most of the Reference Room. The computers which access the On-line Computer Catalog are on separate tables.

The catalogs should be searched by remembering SLANT, that is, by doing NAME first, then LOCATION, then SUBJECT, then AUTHOR, and finally TITLE. When you locate materials of interest, copy down the call numbers from the card or the computer screen.

___If the catalog entry contains any of these designations in the call number (Ayer, Blatchford, Bon. Coll., Broadside, Case, Case Wing, Cather, F.R.C., Graff, Greenlee, INC, INC-fac, Map, Mss, Muir, Museum, Railroads, Ricketts, Sack, Thomas, Wing ZP, Wing ZW, Zabel), the item must be requested on the 4th floor.
___If the catalog entry contains the designation (Ref.) in the call number, the item is on the open shelves on the 3rd floor.
___If the catalog entry contains the designation (Local History) in the call number, the item is on the open shelves on the 2nd floor.
___If the catalog entry contains any other or none of the above designations in the call number, the item is in the stacks and must be requested on the 2nd floor.

All requests are to be made on the 2nd or 4th floor using special request slips which you will find near the catalogs.

The second floor Reading Room is where you will do most of your genealogical work after having employed the finding aids on the third floor. In the Reading Room, you will find many major genealogical reference and record works on the open shelves. In special open shelf areas you will find census indexes, military materials, and immigration works. In addition to the Request Desk, there is a Local and Family History Desk on the second floor. At this desk you will find genealogical consultants and the following:

___Loose-leaf Binders of Federal Census Holdings

Near the desk you will see a computer with the following programs:

___FHL Family Search Program, an extensive genealogical reference and record program, also available at every FHC. A detailed description of the program and instructions for its use will be given in the second section following this one.

___A small collection of genealogical records on CD-ROMs, including the 1880 Census Index for Chicago.

5. The Internet

There are two very significant IL genealogical research sites on the Internet. They will prove to be exceedingly useful to you, since they furnish much data on the state and its counties, and since they are being constantly added to. The first of these is:

___ILLINOIS GATEWAY, a site provided by the IL Secretary of State (accessed at http://www.sos.state.il.us:80/home.html).

Its most valuable genealogical aspects are arranged below in hierarchial order (as they are accessed):

■ Departments
  □ SOS (Secretary of State) departments
    > IL State Library
      * ILLINET (catalog to about 800 IL libraries)
    > IL State Archives
      * Services
        -- Genealogical research: state and federal governmental records holdings
        -- Genealogical research: local governmental records holdings
      * Databases
        -- Public domain land sales (federal)
        -- State governmental records holdings
        -- Local governmental records holdings
        -- Chicago City Council proceedings 1833-71

■ IL libraries
    □ ILLINET (catalog to about 800 IL libraries)
    □ IL State Library

The second of these internet sites is:
__GENEALOGY-FAMILY HISTORY RESEARCH IN ILLINOIS
(accessed at http://www.outfitters.com/illinois/history/family/
illinois2.html‡‡lib).
Its most valuable genealogical aspects are arranged below in hierarchial
order (as they are accessed):
■ Families with IL connections
    □ IL Ancestor Exchange: Database of persons researching various IL
      surnames.
■ References
    □ IL counties, dates of formation, and county seats
      > Details on several IL counties
    □ Addresses of county courthuses
    □ Maps
      > IL county map
      > Rivers of IL
      > Military bounty land tract of IL (War of 1812)
      > Principal meridians and baselines used in IL surveys
      > IRAD regions
      > County outlines
        * Counties of IL
    □ LDS (FHL) research outline for IL (very useful)
    □ IL genealogical and historical societies
    □ IL timeline (detailed historical chronology)
    □ City-county search (enter city, program will tell you what county it
      is located in)
■ Libraries and archives
    □ Genealogical research in Springfield
      > IL State Archives
      > IL State Library
      > IL State Historical Library
      > Sangamon Valley Collection (Lincoln Public Library)
      > Family History Center
      > IRAD-SSU at Sangamon State University
      > Downtown Springfield map
      > Springfield area map
    □ Libraries for research
      >Libraries in IL

* ILLINET (catalog to about 800 IL libraries)
* References to IL libraries
* Libraries within IL
    -- Newberry Library
    -- National Archives, Great Lakes Region
    -- IRADs
>LDS (FHL) Family History Centers
> IL State Archives
    * IRADs
> IL State Historical Society
■ Special topics
□ Military tract in IL (War of 1812)
□ IL and the Civil War
□ Quakers in IL
□ Land sales in IL (federal sales)

---

6. The Family History Library and its Branch Family History Centers (FHL/FHC)

The largest genealogical library in the world is the Family History Library of the Genealogical Society of UT (FHL). This library, which holds almost two million rolls of microfilm, almost 400,000 microfiche, plus a vast number of books, is located at 50 East North Temple St., Salt Lake City, UT 84150. The basic keys to the library are composed of six indexes. (1) The International Genealogical Index, (2) The Surname Index in the FHL Catalog, (3) Listings of the Indexes to the Family Group Records Collection, (4) The Ancestral File, (5) The Social Security Death Index, and (6) The Locality Index in the FHL Catalog. In addition to the main library, the Society maintains a large number of Branches called Family History Centers (FHC) all over the US. Each of these branches has microfiche and computer copies of the International Genealogical Index, the Surname Index, the Index to the Family Group Records Collection, the Ancestral File, the Social Security Death Index, and the Locality Index. In addition each FHC has a supply of forms for borrowing microfilm copies of the records from the main library. This means that the astonishingly large holdings of the FHL are available through each of its numerous FHC branches.

The FHC in or near IL are as follows:
___Cape Girardeau, Missouri FHC, 1048 West Cape Rock Drive.

___Champaign FHC, 604 West Windsor Road.
___Chicago Heights FHC, 402 Longwood Drive.
___Davenport, Iowa FHC, 4929 Wisconsin Avenue.
___Evansville, IN FHC, 519 East Olmstead Avenue.
___Frontenac (St. Louis, Missouri) FHC, 10445 Clayton Road.
___Fairview Heights FHC, 9827 Bunkum Road.
___Hazelwood (St. Louis, Missouri) FHC, 6386 Howdershell Road.
___Napierville FHC, 25 West 341 Ridgeland Road.
___Nauvoo FHC, Durphy Street.
___Peoria FHC, 3700 West Reservoir Boulevard.
___Rockford FHC, 620 North Alpine Road.
___Schaumburg FHC, 1320 West Schaumburg Road.
___Terre Haute, Indiana FHC, 1845 North Center.
___Wilmette FHC, 2801 Lake Avenue.

Other FHC are to be found in the cities listed below. They may be located by looking in the local telephone directory under the listing CHURCH OF JESUS CHRIST OF LATTER-DAY SAINTS-GENEALOGY LIBRARY or in the Yellow Pages under CHURCHES-LATTER-DAY SAINTS.

___In AL: Bessemer, Birmingham, Dothan, Huntsville, Mobile, Montgomery, Tuscaloosa, in AK: Anchorage, Fairbanks, Juneau, Ketchikan, Kotzebue, Sitka, Sodotna, Wasilla, in AZ: Benson, Buckeye, Camp Verde, Casa Grande, Cottonwood, Eagar, Flagstaff, Glendale, Globe, Holbrook, Kingman, Mesa, Nogales, Page, Payson, Peoria, Phoenix, Prescott, Safford, Scottsdale, Show Low, Sierra Vista, Snowflake, St. David, St. Johns, Tucson, Winslow, Yuma, in AR: Fort Smith, Jacksonville, Little Rock, Rogers,

___In CA (Bay Area): Antioch, Concord, Fairfield, Los Altos, Menlo Park, Napa, Oakland, San Bruno, San Jose, Santa Clara, Santa Cruz, Santa Rosa, In CA (Central): Auburn, Clovis, Davis (Woodland), El Dorado (Placerville), Fresno, Hanford, Merced, Modesto, Monterey (Seaside), Placerville, Sacramento, Seaside, Stockton, Turlock, Visalia, Woodland, In CA (Los Angeles County): Burbank, Canoga Park, Carson, Cerritos, Chatsworth (North Ridge), Covina, Glendale, Granada Hills, Hacienda Heights, Huntington Park, La Crescenta, Lancaster, Long Beach (Los Alamitos), Los Angeles, Monterey Park, Northridge, Norwalk, Palmdale, Palos Verdes (Rancho Palos Verdes), Pasadena, Torrance (Carson), Valencia, Van Nuys, Whittier, In CA (Northern): Anderson, Chico, Eureka, Grass Valley, Gridley, Mt. Shasta, Quincy, Redding, Susanville, Ukiah, Yuba City, In CA (Southern, except Los Angeles): Alpine, Anaheim, Bakersfield,

Barstow, Blythe, Buena Park, Camarillo, Carlsbad, Corona, Cypress (Buena Park), El Cajon (Alpine), Escondido, Fontana, Garden Grove (Westminster), Hemet, Huntington Beach, Jurupa (Riverside), Los Alamitos, Mission Viejo, Moorpark, Moreno Valley, Needles, Newbury Park, Orange, Palm Desert, Palm Springs (Palm Desert), Poway (San Diego), Redlands, Ridgecrest, Riverside, San Bernardino, San Diego, San Luis Obispo, Santa Barbara, Santa Maria, Simi Valley, Thousand Oaks (Moorpark), Upland, Ventura, Victorville, Vista, Westminster,

In CO: Alamosa, Arvada, Aurora, Boulder, Colorado Springs, Columbine, Cortez, Craig, Denver, Durango, Fort Collins, Frisco, Grand Junction, Greeley, La Jara, Littleton, Louisville, Manassa, Meeker, Montrose, Longmont, Northglenn, Paonia, Pueblo, in CT: Bloomfield, Hartford, Madison, New Canaan, New Haven, Waterford, Woodbridge, in DC: Kensington, MD, in DE: Newark, Wilmington, in FL: Boca Raton, Cocoa, Ft. Lauderdale, Ft. Myers, Gainesville, Hialeah, Homestead, Jacksonville, Lake City, Lake Mary, Lakeland, Miami, Orange Park, Orlando, Palm City, Panama City, Pensacola, Plantation, Rockledge, St. Petersburg, Tallahassee, Tampa, West Palm Beach, Winterhaven, in GA: Atlanta, Augusta, Brunswick, Columbus, Douglas, Gainesville, Jonesboro, Macon, Marietta, Powder Springs, Roswell, Savannah, Tucker, in HI: Hilo, Honolulu, Kaneohe, Kauai, Kona, Laie, Lihue, Miliani, Waipahu,

In ID: Basalt, Blackfoot, Boise, Burley, Caldwell, Carey, Coeur D'Alene, Driggs, Emmett, Firth, Hailey, Idaho Falls, Iona, Lewiston, McCammon, Malad, Meridian, Montpelier, Moore, Mountain Home, Nampa, Pocatello, Paris, Preston, Rexburg, Rigby, Salmon, Sandpoint, Shelley, Soda Springs, Twin Falls, Weiser, in IL: Champaign, Chicago Heights, Fairview Heights, Nauvoo, Peoria, Rockford, Schaumburg, Wilmette, in IN: Bloomington, Evansville, Fort Wayne, Indianapolis, New Albany, Noblesville, South Bend, Terre Haute, West Lafayette, in IA: Ames, Cedar Rapids, Davenport, Sioux City, West Des Moines, in KS: Dodge City, Olathe, Salina, Topeka, Wichita, in KY: Hopkinsville, Lexington, Louisville, Martin, Paducah, in LA: Alexandria, Baton Rouge, Denham Springs, Monroe, Metairie, New Orleans, Shreveport, Slidell,

In ME: Augusta, Bangor, Cape Elizabeth, Caribou, Farmingdale, Portland, in MD: Annapolis, Baltimore, Ellicott City, Frederick, Kensington, Lutherville, in MA: Boston, Foxboro, Tyngsboro, Weston, Worcester, in MI: Ann Arbor, Bloomfield Hills, East Lansing, Escanaba, Grand Blanc, Grand Rapids, Hastings, Kalamazoo, Lansing, Ludington, Marquette, Midland, Muskegon, Traverse City,

Westland, in MN: Anoka, Duluth, Minneapolis, Rochester, St. Paul, in MS: Clinton, Columbus, Gulfport, Hattiesburg, in MO: Cape Girardeau, Columbia, Farmington, Frontenac, Hazelwood, Independence, Joplin, Kansas City, Liberty, Springfield, St. Joseph, St. Louis, in MT: Billings, Bozeman, Butte, Glasgow, Glendive, Great Falls, Havre, Helena, Kalispell, Missoula, Stevensville, in NE: Grand Island, Lincoln, Omaha, Papillion,

In NV: Elko, Ely, Henderson, LaHonton Valley, Las Vegas, Logandale, Mesquite, Reno, Tonapah, Winnemucca, in NH: Concord, Exeter, Nashua, Portsmouth, in NJ: Caldwell, Dherry Hill, East Brunswick, Morristown, North Caldwell, in NM: Albuquerque, Carlsbad, Farmington, Gallup, Grants, Las Cruces, Santa Fe, Silver City, in NY: Albany, Buffalo, Ithaca, Jamestown, Lake Placid, Liverpool, Loudonville, New York City, Pittsford, Plainview, Queens, Rochester, Scarsdale, Syracuse, Vestal, Williamsville, Yorktown, in NC: Asheville, Charlotte, Durham, Fayetteville, Goldsboro, Greensboro, Hickory, Kinston, Raleigh, Skyland, Wilmington, Winston-Salem, in ND: Bismarck, Fargo, Minot, in OH: Akron, Cincinnati, Cleveland, Columbus, Dayton, Dublin, Fairborn, Kirtland, Perrysburg, Reynoldsburg, Tallmadge, Toledo, Westlake, Winterville, In OK: Lawton, Muskogee, Norman, Oklahoma City, Stillwater, Tulsa, in OR: Beaverton, Bend, Brookings, Central Point, Coos Bay, Corvallis, Eugene, Grants Pass, Gresham, Hermiston, Hillsboro, Keizer, Klamath Falls, LaGrande, Lake Oswego, Lebanon, Minnville, Medford, Newport, Nyssa, Ontario, Oregon City, Portland, Prineville, Roseburg, Salem, Sandy, The Dallas, in PA: Altoona, Broomall, Clarks Summit, Erie, Kane, Philadelphia(Broomall), Pittsburgh, Reading, Scranton(Clarks Summit), State College(Altoona), York, in RI: Providence, Warwick, in SC: Charleston, Columbia, Florence, Greenville, North Augusts, in SD: Gettysburg, Rapid City, Rosebud, Sioux Falls, in TN: Chattanooga, Franklin, Kingsport, Knoxville, Madison, Memphis, Nashville, in TX: Abilene, Amarillo, Austin, Bay City, Beaumont, Bryan, Conroe, Corpus Christi, Dallas, Denton, Duncanville, El Paso, Ft. Worth, Friendswood, Harlingen, Houston, Hurst, Katy, Kileen, Kingwood, Longview, Lubbock, McAllen, Odessa, Orange, Pasadena, Plano, Port Arthur, Richland Hills, San Antonio, Sugarland, In UT: American Fork, Altamont, Beaver, Blanding, Bloomington, Bluffdale, Bountiful, Brigham City, Canyon Rim, Castle Dale, Cedar City, Delta, Duchesne, Escalante, Farmington, Ferron, Fillmore, Granger, Heber, Helper, Highland, Holladay, Hunter, Huntington, Hurricane, Hyrum, Kanab, Kaysville, Kearns, Laketown, Layton, Lehi,

Loa, Logan, Magna, Manti, Mapleton, Midway, Moab, Monticello, Moroni, Mt. Pleasant, Murray, Nephi, Ogden, Orem, Panguitch, Parowan, Pleasant Grove, Price, Provo, Richfield, Riverton, Roosevelt, Rose Park, Salt Lake City, Sandy, Santaquin, South Jordan, Springville, St. George, Syracuse, Tooele, Trementon, Tropic, Vernal, Wellington, Wendover, West Jordan, West Valley City, in <u>VA</u>: Annandale, Bassett, Charlottesville, Chesapeake, Dale City, Falls Church, Fredericksburg, Hamilton, Martinsville, McLean, Newport News, Norfolk, Oakton, Pembroke, Richmond, Roanoke, Salem, Virginia Beach, Waynesboro, Winchester, in <u>VT</u>: Berlin, Montpelier,

___In <u>WA</u>: Auburn, Bellevue, Bellingham, Bremerton, Centralia, Colville, Edmonds, Ellensburg, Elma, Ephrata, Everett, Federal Way, Ferndale, Lake Stevens, Longview, Lynnwood, Marysville, Moses Lake, Mt. Vernon, North Bend, Olympia, Othello, Port Angeles, Pullman, Puyallup, Quincy, Renton, Richland, Seattle, Silverdale, Spokane, Sumner, Tacoma, Vancouver, Walla Walla, Wenatchee, Yakima, in <u>WV</u>: Charleston, Fairmont, Huntington, in <u>WI</u>: Appleton, Eau Clair, Hales Corner, Madison, Milwaukee, Shawano, Wausau, in <u>WY</u>: Afton, Casper, Cheyenne, Cody, Gillette, Green River, Jackson Hole, Kemmerer, Laramie, Lovell, Lyman, Rawlins, Riverton, Rock Springs, Sheridan, Urie, Worland.

The FHL is constantly adding new branches so this list will probably be out-of-date by the time you read it. An SASE and a $2 fee to the FHL (address in first paragraph above) will bring you an up-to-date listing of FHC.

When you go to FHL or FHC, <u>first</u> ask for the IL International Genealogical Index and examine it for the name of your ancestor, then if you are at FHL, request the record. If you are at FHC, ask them to borrow the microfilm containing the record from FHL. The cost is only a few dollars, and when your microfilm arrives (usually 4 to 6 weeks), you will be notified so that you can return and examine it. <u>Second</u>, ask for the Surname Catalog. Examine it for the surname of your ancestor. If you think any of the references relate to your ancestral line, and if you are at FHL, request the record. If you are at FHC, ask them to borrow the record for you. <u>Third</u>, ask for the Listings of Indexes to the Family Group Records Collection which will be found in the Author/Title Section of the FHL Catalog. There are several listings, so be sure you see them all. Locate the microfilm number which applies to the index of the surname you are seeking. If you are at FHL, request the microfilm. If you are at FHC, ask them to borrow the microfilm for you. When it comes, examine the microfilm to see if any records of your surname are indicated. If so, obtain them and see if they are pertinent.

Fourth, ask for the Ancestral File and look up the name you are seeking. If it is there, you will be led to sources of information, either people who are working on the line, or records pertaining to the line. Be careful with the material in this file, because in some of the cases, there appears to be no documentation. Fifth, if you are seeking a person who died after 1937, request the Social Security Death Index and look her/him up in it. Sixth, ask for the IL Locality Catalog. Examine all listings under the main heading of ILLINOIS. Then examine all listings under the subheading of the county you are interested in. These county listings will follow the listings for the state of IL. Toward the end of the county listings, there are listed materials relating to cities and towns in the county. Be sure not to overlook them. If you are at FHL, you can request the materials which are of interest to you. If you are at FHC, you may have the librarian borrow them for you. A large number of the records referred to in Chapter 2 and those listed under the counties in Chapters 4 and 5 will be found in the IL locality catalog.

The FHL and each FHC also have a set of Combined Census Indexes. These indexes are overall collections of censuses and other records for various time periods. Set 1 covers all colonies and states 1607-1819, Set 2 covers all states 1820-9, Set 3 covers all states 1830-9, Set 4 covers all states 1840-9, Set 5 covers the southern states 1850-9, Set 6 covers the northern states 1850-9, Set 7 covers the midwestern and western states 1850-9, Set 7A covers all the states 1850-9, and further sets cover various groups of states 1860 and after. Additional details concerning the records in FHL and FHC along with instructions for finding and using them will be found in:

__J. Cerny and W. Elliott, THE LIBRARY, A GUIDE TO THE LDS FAMILY HISTORY LIBRARY, Ancestry Publishing, Salt Lake City, UT, 1988.
__J. C. Parker, GOING TO SALT LAKE CITY TO DO FAMILY HISTORY RESEARCH, Marietta Publishing Co., Turlock, CA, latest edition.

7. The National Archives (NA)

The National Archives and Records Service (NA), located at Pennsylvania Avenue and 8th Street, Washington, DC 20408, is the central national

repository for <u>federal</u> records, many being of importance to IL genealogical research. The NA does not concern itself with colonial records
(pre-1776), state, county, city, or town records. Among the most
important NA records which pertain to IL are the following:
___Census records: Federal census records for IL 1820-80, 1900-20, see
    Section 7, Chapter 2
___Non-population census schedules: farm, manufacture, and mortality
    records for IL, 1850-80, see Section 7, Chapter 2
___Military records: Service, bounty land, pension, claims records, and in-
    dexes for the Revolution, War of 1812, Mexican War, Civil War,
    Spanish-American War, see Sections 24-26, Chapter 2
___Land records: Land claims, warrant applications, land warrant
    redemptions, land sales, surveys, land grants for IL, 1804-, records are
    in ISA, NA, Bureau of Land Management in Springfield, VA,
    Chicago Branch of the NA, and the NA in Washington, DC, see
    Section 21, Chapter 2
___Naturalization records: For US District and Circuit Courts in IL,
    records are in the Chicago Branch of the NA, also a large
    naturalization index for northern IL, see Section 28, Chapter 2
___Court Records of Territories and of Federal District and Circuit
    Courts: For Northwest Territory(1787-1801), IN Territory (1804-
    1816), and IL Territory (1809-18) at NA, for IL (1819-1982) in the
    NAGL, see Section 11, Chapter 2
Details on all of these have been given in the pertinent sections of
Chapter 2. Further detail on them may be obtained in:
___NA Staff, GENEALOGICAL RESEARCH IN THE NATIONAL
    ARCHIVES, NA, Washington, DC, 1982.
___L. D. Szucs and S. H. Luebking, THE ARCHIVES, A GUIDE TO
    THE NATIONAL ARCHIVES FIELD BRANCHES, [REGIONAL
    CENTERS], Ancestry Publishing, Salt Lake City, UT, 1988.

The numerous records of the NA may be examined in Washington in
person or by a hired researcher. Microfilm copies of many of the major
records and/or their indexes may also be seen in National Archives
Regional Centers (NARC) which are located in or near Anchorage (654
West Third Avenue, Anchorage, AK 99501), Atlanta (1557 St. Joseph
Ave., East Point, GA 30344), Boston (380 Trapelo Rd., Waltham, MA
02154), Chicago (7358 S. Pulaski Rd., Chicago, IL 60629), Denver (Bldg.
48, Federal Center, Denver, CO 80225), Fort Worth (501 West Felix St.,
Ft. Worth, TX 76115), Kansas City (2312 E. Bannister Rd., Kansas City,
MO 64131), Los Angeles (24000 Avila Rd., Laguna Niguel, CA 92677),
New York (201 Varick St., New York, NY 10014), Philadelphia (9th and

Market Sts., Philadelphia, PA 19107), San Francisco (1000 Commodore Dr., San Bruno, CA 94066), and Seattle (6125 Sand Point Way, NE, Seattle, WA 98115).

Take special note of the National Archives-Great Lakes Region in Chicago, IL. It holds many IL census records, Revolutionary War service, pension, and bounty land records, records of US Courts of IL, naturalization records in US Circuit and District Courts, Internal Revenue tax records 1862-66, IL Union service records 1861-65, and the IL non-population census schedules.

Many of the NA records pertaining to IL, as was noted in detail in Chapters 2 and 3, are also available at ISHL, ISA, NL, NARC, NAGL, and the FHL (FHC), and some are available at LGL and RL. In addition, practically any local library in the US can borrow NA microfilms for you from AGLL (American Genealogical Lending Library, PO Box 329, Bountiful, UT 84011). Or you may borrow from them directly. Included are NA census records and military records (Revolutionary War, War of 1812, Mexican War, Civil War).

8. IL Regional Archives Depositories (IRAD)

The ISA administers seven regional depositories located on university campuses in IL. Local governments (county, city, town, village, township) are invited to deposit records in these depositories for safe-keeping and to make them accessible to researchers. The ISA publishes a guide to these collections which is updated often:
___R. E. Bailey, E. S. Evans, B. Heflin, and K. R. Moore, editors, A SUMMARY GUIDE TO LOCAL GOVERNMENTAL RECORDS IN THE IL REGIONAL ARCHIVES, ISA, Springfield, IL, latest edition.
The IL Regional Archives Depositories (IRAD) which are in the IL Regional Archives Depository System are as follows. Listed after each are the counties which may deposit records there.
___(1) IRAD-NIU, Swen Parson Hall, Northern IL University, DeKalb, IL 60115. Telephone 1-815-753-1779. Counties served: Boone, Bureau, Carroll, DeKalb, DuPage, Jo Daviess, Kane, Kendall, Lake, LaSalle, Lee, McHenry, Ogle, Stephenson, Whiteside, Will, Winnebago.
___(2) IRAD-WIU, University Library, Western IL University, Macomb, IL 61455. Telephone 1-309-298-2717. Counties served: Adams,

Brown, Calhoun, Fulton, Hancock, Henderson, Henry, Knox, Mc-Donough, Mercer, Peoria, Pike, Rock Island, Schuyler, Stark, Warren.
___(3) IRAD-ISU, Williams Hall, IL State University, Normal, IL 61761. Telephone 1-309-452-6027. Counties served: Champaign, DeWitt, Ford, Grundy, Iroquois, Kankakee, Livingston, Logan, Marshall, Mc-Lean, Piatt, Tazewell, Vermilion, Woodford.
___(4) IRAD-SSU, Brookens Library, Sangamon State University, Springfield, IL 62794. Telephone 1-217-786-6520. Counties served: Bond, Cass, Christian, Fayette, Greene, Jersey, Macon, Macoupin, Mason, Menard, Montgomery, Morgan, Sangamon, Scott.
___(5) IRAD-EIU, Booth Library, Eastern IL University, Charleston, IL 61920. Telephone 1-217-581-6093. Counties served: Clark, Clay, Coles, Crawford, Cumberland, Douglas, Edgar, Edwards, Effingham, Jasper, Lawrence, Moultrie, Richland, Shelby, Wabash, Wayne.
___(6) IRAD-SIU, Morris Library, Southern IL University, Carbondale, IL 62901. Telephone 1-618-453-3040. Counties served: Alexander, Clinton, Franklin, Gallatin, Hamilton, Hardin, Jackson, Jefferson, Johnson, Madison, Marion, Massac, Monroe, Perry, Pope, Pulaski, Randolph, St. Clair, Saline, Union, Washington, White, Williamson.
___(7) IRAD-UNI, University Library, Northeastern IL University, 5500 N. St. Louis Ave., Chicago, IL 60625-4699. Telephone 1-312-794-6279. County served: Cook.

Figure 28 displays the IRADs and the counties they serve in geographical form. In chapters 4 and 5, detailed listings of the records held by the IRADs will be given for each county.

9. Regional libraries (RL)

Regional libraries (RL) in IL are defined as those libraries which have sizable genealogical collections for the region, rather than just for the immediate locality. A number of these have been treated in the following series of articles:
___IL Libraries 68(4) (Apr 1986) 243-284, 70(9) (Sep 1988) 484-536, 74(5) (Nov 1992) 393-484.
Some of the more important regional libraries are:
___Belleville Public Library, 121 East Washington Street, Belleville, IL 62220, Phone 1-(618)-234-0441. Bibliography of Archives Collection and Supplement available from them.
___Centralia Public Library, 515 East Broadway, Centralia, IL 62801, Phone 1-(618)-532-5222.

160

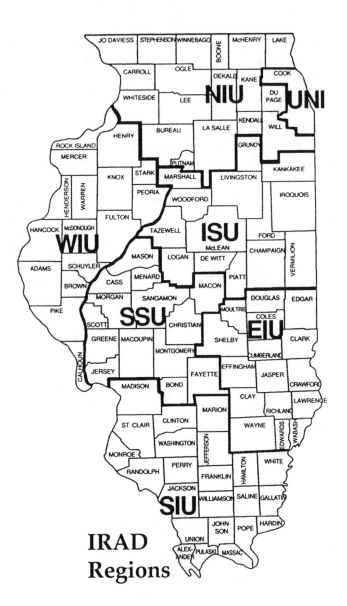

IRAD
Regions

Figure 28. IL Regional Archives Depositories. Map reproduced by permission of the Office of IL Secretary of State George H. Ryan.

___Danville Public Library, 307 N. Vermilion St., Danville, IL 61832, Phone 1-(217)-446-7420.

___Galesburg Public Library, 40 East Simmons Street, Galesburg, IL 61401, Phone 1-(309)-343-6118.

___Kankakee Public Library, 304 South Indiana Avenue, Kankakee, IL 60901, Phone 1-(815)-939-4564.

___Lincoln Library, 326 South 7th Street, Springfield, IL 62701, Phone 1-(217)-753-4910.

___Moline Public Library, 504 17th Street, Moline, IL 61625, Phone 1-(309)-762-6883.

___Peoria Public Library, 107 N.E. Monroe Street, Peoria, IL 61602, Phone 1-(309)-672-8858.

___Quincy Public Library, 526 Jersey Street, Quincy, IL 62301, Phone 1-(217)-222-0226.

___Rockford Public Library, 215 North Wyman Street, Rockford, IL 61101, Phone 1-(815)-965-6731.

___Shawnee Library System, Greenbriar Road, Carterville, IL 62918, Phone 1-(618)-985-3711. Bibliography of Genealogy Collection and Supplement available from them.

___South Suburban Genealogical and Historical Society Library, 320 East 161st Place, South Holland, IL 60473, Phone 1-(708)-333-9474.

___Starved Rock Library, 900 Hitt St., Ottawa, IL 61350, Phone 1-(815)-434-7537.

___University of IL Library, IL Historical Survey, 1408 West Gregory Drive, Urbana, IL 61801, Phone 1-(217)-333-1777. Guides to genealogical holdings and manuscripts available from them.

___Urbana Free Library, 201 South Race Street, Urbana, IL 61801, Phone 1-(217)-367-4025.

___Wheaton Public Library, 225 North Cross Street, Wheaton, IL 60187, Phone 1-(708)-668-1374.

___Winnetka Public Library, 768 Oak Street, Winnetka, IL 60093, Phone 1-(312)-446-7220.

When a visit is made to any of these libraries, your _first_ endeavor is to search the card and/or computer catalogs. You can remember what to look for with the acronymn SLANT. A detailed treatment of its use was given back in Section 1 of this chapter. This procedure should give you very good coverage of the library holdings which are indexed in the catalog. The _second_ endeavor at any of these libraries is to ask about any special indexes, catalogs, collections, finding aids, or materials which might be pertinent to your search. You should make it your aim particularly to inquire about Bible, cemetery, church, map, manuscript, military, mortuary, and newspaper materials. In some cases, microform (microfilm, microfiche, microcard) records are not included in the regular catalog but are separately indexed. It is important that you be alert to this possibility.

10. Local repositories

Local libraries, court houses, and other repositories (LL, CH, LR) are located in every county seat, and sometimes libraries and other repositories will be found in other towns in the county. The most significant libraries are listed under the counties in Chapters 4 and 5. At the libraries, it is important for you to inquire about other record repositories in the county: cemeteries, churches, mortuaries, newspaper offices, organization offices, schools, society offices. Please look back at the last third of Section 1 for information about Court Houses, and remember that they should be visited only after going to the library.

11. Large genealogical libraries (LGL)

Spread around the US there are a number of large genealogical libraries (LGL) which have at least some IL genealogical source materials. In general, those libraries nearest and/or west of IL are the ones that have the larger IL collections, but there are exceptions. Among the largest genealogical libraries, which you may check for IL holdings, are the following:

___In AL: Birmingham Public Library, Library at Samford University in Birmingham, AL Archives and History Department in Montgomery, in AZ: Southern AZ Genealogical Society in Tucson, in AR: AR Genealogical Society in Little Rock, AR History Commission in Little Rock, Little Rock Public Library, in CA: CA Genealogical Society in San Francisco, Los Angeles Public Library, San Diego Public Library, San Francisco Public Library, Sutro Library in San Francisco,

___In CO: Denver Public Library, in CT: CT State Library in Hartford, Godfrey Memorial Library in Middletown, in DC: Library of Congress, DAR Library, National Genealogical Society Library in Washington, in FL: FL State Library in Tallahassee, Miami-Dade Public Library, Orlando Public Library, Tampa Public Library, in GA: Atlanta Public Library, in ID: ID Genealogical Society, in IL: Newberry Library in Chicago, in IA: IA State Department of History and Archives in Des Moines, in KY: KY Historical Society in Frankfort, Filson Club in Louisville,

___In LA: LA State Library in Baton Rouge, in ME: ME State Library in Augusta, in MD: MD State Library in Annapolis, MD Historical Society in Baltimore, in MA: Boston Public Library, New England Historic Genealogical Society Library in Boston, in MI: Detroit Public Library, in MN: MN Public Library, in MS: MS Department of Archives and History in Jackson, L. W. Anderson Genealogical Library in Gulfport, in MO: Kansas City Public Library, Mid-Continent Public Library in Independence, St. Louis Public Library, In NE: NE State Historical Society in Lincoln, Omaha Public Library, in NV: Washoe County Library in Reno, in NY: NY Public Library, NY Genealogical and Biographical Society in NY City, in NC: NC State Library in Raleigh, in OH: OH Historical Society and State Library of OH both in Columbus, Western Reserve Historical Society in Cleveland, Public Library in Cincinnati, in OK: OK State Historical Society in Oklahoma City, in OR: Genealogical Forum of Portland, Portland Library Association, in PA: Historical Society of PA in Philadelphia, PA State Library in Harrisburg,

___In SC: The South Caroliniana Library in Columbia, in SD: State Historical Society in Pierre, in TN: TN State Library and Archives in Nashville, in TX: Dallas Public Library, Fort Worth Public Library, TX State Library in Austin, Houston Public Library, Clayton Library in Houston, in UT: Brigham Young University Library in Provo, in VA: VA Historical Society Library and VA State Library in Richmond, in WA: Seattle Public Library, in WV: WV Department of Archives and History in Charleston, in WI: Milwaukee Public Library, State Historical Society in Madison.

When you visit a LGL, the general procedure described earlier in this chapter should be followed: First, search the card catalog. Look under the headings summarized by SLANT: subject, location, author, name, title. Then, second, inquire about special indexes, catalogs, collections, materials, and microforms.

The above list of LGL is not inclusive. There may be other medium-sized and large libraries near you. Just because they do not appear in the above list, do not fail to check out their IL genealogical holdings.

List of Abbreviations

CCB	=	Cook County Building, Chicago
CCH	=	Chicago City Hall
CH	=	Court House(s)
CHSL	=	Chicago Historical Society Library
CJCLDS	=	Church of Jesus Christ of Latter Day Saints
CPL	=	Chicago Public Library
D	=	Federal mortality censuses
DC	=	Daley Center, Chicago
E	=	Early inhabitant lists
F	=	Federal Farm and Ranch censuses
FHC	=	Family History Center(s), branches of FHL
FHL	=	Family History Library, Salt Lake City, UT
IL	=	Illinois
IRAD	=	IL Regional Archives Repository(ies)
IRAD-EIU	=	IRAD at Eastern IL University, Charleston
IRAD-ISU	=	IRAD at IL State University, Normal
IRAD-NIU	=	IRAD at Northern IL University, DeKalb
IRAD-SIU	=	IRAD at Southern IL University, Carbondale
IRAD-SSU	=	IRAD at Sangamon State University, Springfield
IRAD-UNI	=	IRAD at Northeastern IL University, Chicago
IRAD-WIU	=	IRAD at Western IL University, Macomb
ISA	=	IL State Archives, Springfield
ISGS	=	IL State Genealogical Society, Springfield
ISGSQ	=	IL State Genealogical Society Quarterly
ISHL	=	IL State Historical Library, Springfield
ISHS	=	IL State Historical Society, Springfield
ISL	=	IL State Library, Springfield
LL	=	Local Library(ies)
LR	=	Local Repositories
M	=	Federal Manufactures censuses
NA	=	National Archives, Washington, DC
NAGL	=	National Archives - Great Lakes Region, Chicago
NARC	=	National Archives Regional Centers
NL	=	Newberry Library, Chicago
P	=	1840 Revolutionary War pension census
R	=	Regular federal censuses
RL	=	Regional Library(ies)
S	=	IL State censuses
T	=	IN and IL Territorial censuses

Chapter 4

RESEARCH PROCEDURE, COOK COUNTY, AND CHICAGO

1. Introduction

Now you should have a good idea of IL history, its genealogical records, and the locations and availabilities of these records. The emphasis in the first three chapters was on records at levels higher than the county. Detailed information on national, state-wide, and regional records was given, but county records were normally treated only in general. We now will turn our focus upon the county records, treating them in detail. We will also emphasize non-governmental records available at the county level (such as Bible, biography, cemetery, directories, DAR, ethnic, genealogies, histories, manuscripts, maps, mortuary, newspaper, and periodicals). The reason for all this attention to county records is that these records are more likely to contain more information on your ancestors than any other type. Such records were generally recorded by people who knew your forebears, and they often relate to the personal details of her/his life. Further, there are likely to be more original records in the counties, especially those kept by local governmental agencies and churches.

In the state of IL, most of the original governmental records of the counties and cities remain within the counties and in the appropriate IRAD. Some of these original county/city governmental records and some non-governmental records have been microfilmed by the FHL, and the microfilms are available at FHL, and by interlibrary loan through the many FHC branches throughout the US. Microfilms of some of these original records are also available at the ISA (for about 40 counties). Some of the original county/city governmental records and numerous non-governmental records have been published either in printed volumes or as typescripts. Most of these publications are available at ISHL, and NL. Some are available at ISA, LGL, RL, and LL.

The next two chapters, Chapters 4 and 5, will deal with county and city records in detail. We will first discuss procedures for finding the county in which your IL progenitor(s) lived. This is important because knowing that your ancestors were simply from IL is not enough to permit genealogical research. You need to know the county or city since many genealogically-applicable records were kept on a local basis, and since you will often find more than one person in IL bearing the name of your ancestor. In such a case, the county/city location will often let you tell them apart. After discussing ways to find the county, we will <u>second</u> suggest approaches for doing IL genealogy, recommending the order in which the various repositories should be used. Then, <u>thirdly</u>, we will treat in detail the county and city records of Cook County and Chicago (in Chapter 4). Cook County has a population larger than many states of the US. This warrants some detail on this notable section of IL.

In Chapter 5, space will be devoted to the county reords of the other 101 counties of IL. Particular attention will be paid to the microfilmed and published records which are available outside of the county. You must not forget, however, that many of the important original records are in the county and IRAD, and that it is utterly necessary to base your genealogy on such records. Non-original records have too great a possibility of being incomplete and/or in error.

2. Finding the county

As you will recall from Chapter 1, official IL record keeping began with the early French settlements. A few records were then kept by the British, and a few when IL came to be included in IL County, VA. Counties were established in the Northwest Territory beginning in 1788, and they kept records from the start. In 1800 the IN Territory split from the Northwest Territory, and its counties also kept records from the start. Then, in 1809, the IL Territory was split from the IN Territory, and county record keeping continued. As the population increased, more counties were established, and more and more of the keeping of records was shifted to them. It is, therefore, of considerable importance for you to know your IL predecessor's county in order to direct yourself efficiently to many of the pertinent records. It is also important because the local county officials probably knew your ancestor personally, and further, kept more detailed records on him, his family, his property, and his activities than did the territory or state. If you happen to know your ancestor's county, you may skip the remainder of this section. If not, your first priority must be a successful search for the county. The most efficient method for discovering the county depends on the time period during which your forebear lived in IL. We will discuss county-finding techniques for three periods of time in IL history: (a) 1673-1820, (b) 1820-1916, and (c) 1916-present.

If your forebear's time period was <u>1673-1820</u>, you should look in the following major sources for your progenitor's name. Items more generally available (indexes in FHC, published and microfilm indexes in LGL) will be listed before those available chiefly in IL repositories (ISHL-ISA, NL) or available by ordering from FHL through FHC.

___(1a) INTERNATIONAL GENEALOGICAL INDEX (IGI), IL SECTION; FAMILY SEARCH; ANCESTRAL FILE; FAMILY GROUP RECORDS COLLECTION; all available at FHL and at FHC.

___(2a) F. Rider, AMERICAN GENEALOGICAL[-BIOGRAPHICAL] INDEX, Godfrey Memorial Library, Middletown, CT, 1942-, 2 series, 1st with 48 volumes, 2nd containing over 200 volumes.

___(3a) M. Kaminkow, GENEALOGIES IN THE LIBRARY OF CONGRESS, Magna Carta, Baltimore, MD, 1972-7, 3 volumes, plus SUPPLEMENTS; also A COMPLEMENT TO GENEALOGIES IN THE LIBRARY OF CONGRESS [GENEALOGIES IN OTHER LIBRARIES], Magna Carta, Baltimore, MD, 1981.

___(4a) The IL federal land grant index for IL: PUBLIC DOMAIN LAND SALES RECORD LISTING. See Section 21, Chapter 2, for full references.

___(5a) IL colonial, pioneer, and territorial lists by Belting, Alvord, Franklin, Carter, the Hammes Collection in the ISA, and the Name Index to Early IL Records in the ISA. See Sections 7, 17, and 33, Chapter 2, for full references.

___(6a) Early marriage indexes on computer disks, and in the Pre-1900 Marriage Index at the ISA and FHL. See Section 23, Chapter 2, or full references.

___(7a) Revolutionary War and War of 1812 veterans' records by Cliff, Meyer, Devanny, Walker, Chatten, Hammes, and Volkel, and the IL Roll of Honor. See Sections 24-25, Chapter 2, for full references.

___(8a) Biographical references such as The Genealogical Index of the Newberry Library, and the biography indexes in the ISA and NL. See section 4, Chapter 2 for details.

___(9a) Compiled county history indexes in the ISA and ISHL, and the card and computer catalogs in the same repositories. See Sections 10 and 18, Chapter 2.

___(10a) Applications for IL Prairie Pioneer Certificates, and the resulting publications. See Section 18, Chapter 2.

If these indexes fail to locate your predecessor's county, two further steps should be taken: (a) explore other indexes in ISHL-ISA-NL [see pertinent sections of Chapter 2], and (b) if your ancestor was early, since there were only a few counties constituted before 1820 and the population was not large, a search of major indexes of these counties is not a forbidding route to take.

For the time period <u>1820-1916</u>, the census record indexes should constitute your first search, then other materials can be invoked, if needed. These follow:

___(1b) CENSUS INDEXES, 1820-1910, as detailed in Section 7, Chapter 2.

___(2b) ITEMS 1a, 2a, 3a, 4a, 6a, 8a, and 9a from the list above.

___(3b) The Name Index to Early IL Records in the ISA. See Section 7, Chapter 2.

___(4b) The Index to the Compiled Service Records of IL Union Soldiers in the Civil War. See Section 26, Chapter 2.

For the time period from <u>1916-</u> forward, family members usually know the county. However, if they do not, the state-wide birth and death records provide the best source. Should you not find your ancestor in them, then some of the other sources listed below can be employed.

___(1c) INDEXES TO BIRTH RECORDS (1916-) AND DEATH RECORDS (1916-). See Sections 5 and 13, Chapter 2.

___(2c) CENSUS INDEX, 1920, as detailed in Section 7, Chapter 2.

___(3c) ITEMS 1a, 3a, 8a, and 9a from the list above.

___(4c) Social Security Administration, SOCIAL SECURITY DEATH INDEX, 1937-88, on four computer compact discs, at FHL and FHC.

The work of locating your IL ancestor can generally be done from where you live or nearby. This is because the key items are either indexes or indexed records which means that they can be scanned rapidly. Also, many are in published form (books or microfilms), which indicates that they are in numerous LGL outside of IL, as well as being available through FHC. Therefore, you should not have to travel too far to find many of the indexes you need. Some of the important indexes in IL repositories can be searched for you upon written request (enclose SASE). Or, if you prefer, all the above resources can be examined for you by a hired researcher in Springfield and Chicago. This ought not to cost too much because the searches can all be made in very short time, and your hired researcher can stop when the county has been identified.

3. Research approaches Having identified the county of your forebear's residence, you are in position to ferret out the details. This means that you need to identify what non-governmental, federal, state, and county records are available, then to locate them, and finally to examine them in detail. The most useful non-governmental records have been discussed in Chapter 2 (atlas, Bible, biography, cemetery, church, city directory, county/city history, court, DAR, ethnic, gazetteer, genealogical compilation, genealogical index, genealogical periodical, land, manuscript, map, mortuary, newspaper, regional publication). The federal governmental records which are most important for consideration have also been treated in Chapter 2 (census, court, military, naturalization). State governmental records which are of the greatest utility for genealogical research are examined in Chapter 2 (birth, court, death, divorce, land, marriage, military, tax). And the types of records which were generated by IL's counties are listed in Chapter 3 (Section 1), and they were discussed in general in Chapter 2. To remind you of the various types of county governmental records, the list from Chapter 3 is repeated here:

___County Board (sometimes called Commissioners or Supervisors): county government, tax regulations, roads, appropriations, pensions, relief

___County Clerk (other titles sometimes): records on tax, valuations, collections, vital statistics (births, marriages, deaths), licenses, elections, bonds of officers, militia, estrays, brands and marks, indentures, maps, plats

___Recorder: deeds, mortgages, soldiers, veterans burials, name changes, land patents, leases, bonds of officers, corporations, plats, maps, surveys

___County Court (and predecessors): civil, criminal, naturalizations, adoptions, insanity, sometimes probate

___Probate Court: probates, wills, estates, guardians

___Circuit Court: civil, criminal, chancery, naturalization, appeals

___Coroner: inquests

___Sheriff: arrests, jail records, warrants, executions (doing tasks assigned by the court), property sales, tax collection

___Surveyor: surveys, maps, plats

___Treasurer: finances, receipts, disbursements

___State's attorney: indictments, grand juries, imprisonments

___County home: inmates, admissions, dismissals, finances

___Superintendant of schools: finances, teachers, pupils

County and city governmental record originals are found in the counties, usually at the CH or in a special repository, and in the appropriate IRAD. Many microfilm copies of county and city governmental records are located at FHL (available through FHC), and at ISA. Most published (printed and typescript) county and city governmental records are at ISHS, NL, and FHL(FHC). Some will be found at LGL, RL, and LL. Both the major microfilmed records and the major types of published records (both governmental and non-governmental) for the 102 IL counties will be listed in detail in later sections of this and the next chapter. These listings have been obtained from the catalogs at FHL, ISA, ISHS, NL, and the ILLINET program on internet.

The general approach for doing an utterly thorough job of researching an IL ancestor is to follow this pattern:

___1st, check all family sources (oral, records, mementos, Bible), making a continuing effort to contact more and more of the many descendants of the ancestor

___2nd, locate your forebear's county (Section 2, this Chapter)

___3rd, use the nearest LGL (catalogs, indexes, publications, microfilms)

___4th, use the nearest FHC or the FHL (IGI, Ancestral File, Family Group Records Archives, FHL Catalog surname and locality indexes, integrated census indexes, social security index), if at FHC, order the pertinent microfilms

___5th, borrow any major federal records you have not seen from AGLL (census, military)

___6th, either go to Springfield, IL (ISL-IHS-ISA), or hire a researcher in Springfield to look at microfilms and publications you have not seen. Also visit or hire a researcher in Chicago, if called for.

___7th, either visit the county, or hire a researcher in the county to look in the LL (catalogs, indexes, manuscripts, local records), and to visit offices of cemeteries, churches, mortuaries, newspapers, and organizations to obtain records you have not seen

___8th, then you or your researcher should go to the CH, offices of the county and city record keepers, and county and city record repositories, and IRAD to examine records you have not seen, and to examine the originals of records you have seen in secondary form.

___9th, use the NARB and NA (for further federal census, court, military, and naturalization materials)

___10th, address inquiries to pertinent Church Archives, if church records have still not been found

The precise way in which you use this scheme will be determined chiefly by how far you are from Salt Lake City, UT (FHL) and Springfield, IL (ISHL-ISA), and the relevant IL county. The major idea that you need to recognize is that eventually you will have to go to IL, or you will need to hire a researcher there, perhaps two, one for Springfield, and one for the county.

In using the above steps to set forth your own research plan, you ought to think about three items. The first is expense. You need to balance the cost of a hired researcher over against the cost of personal visits (to Springfield and to the county): travel, meals, lodging. You need also to compare the costs of borrowing microfilms from your nearest FHC (a few dollars per roll) to a trip to Salt Lake City, where the films can be read off-the-shelf at no charge. Of course, your desire to visit your ancestor's area, and your desire to look at the records yourself may be an important consideration.

The second item is a reminder about interlibrary loans. With the exception of the microfilms of FHL (available through FHC) and those of AGLL (available personally or through your local library), very few libraries and practically no archives will lend out genealogical materials. The third item is also a reminder. Correspondence with librarians, governmental officials, and archivists is ordinarily of very limited use. The reason is that these helpful and hard-working federal, state, local, and private employees do not have time to do any detailed work for you because of the demanding duties of their offices. In some cases, these people will have time to look up one specific item for you (a land grant, a catalog entry, a deed record, a will, a military record) if an overall index is available. Please do not ask them for detailed data, and please do not write them a long letter. If you do write, enclose a long SASE, a check for $5 with the payee line left blank, and a brief request (no more than one-third page) for one specific item in an index or catalog. Ask them to use the check if there is a charge for their services or for copying, and if they do not have time to look themselves, that they hand the check and your letter to a researcher who can do the work.

4. Cook County information

In the following sections of this chapter, you will find some detailed information about Cook County and about Chicago, the very large city which occupies most of the county. These sections will deal with Cook County and Chicago history, Cook County and Chicago record repositories, and Record Notes on Cook County and Chicago. Then, in Chapter 5, listings of many of the major records of the other IL counties will be presented. Cook County and Chicago are being given special treatment because the population of the metropolitan area (over 8.5 million) exceeds that of many US states, and represents more than half of the people who live in IL (11.8 million). The development of Chicago involved very large numbers of individuals and thus had a powerful influence upon the history of the state.

No one, absolutely no one, should attempt research in the Chicago/Cook County area without consulting a very valuable guidebook. This volume goes into far more detail than can be included in the following treatment:

___L. D. Szucs, CHICAGO AND COOK COUNTY: A GUIDE TO RESEARCH, Ancestry, Salt Lake City, UT, 1996.

5. Cook County and Chicago History

Just north of the southwest corner of Lake MI a small river enters the lake. Not too far up the river, there is a short portage which takes you to the Des Plaines River, which flows into the IL River, which flows into the MS River, which flows south to the Gulf of Mexico. This portage thus acts as a water gateway to the vast areas to the west and the south. Its importance was recognized by the Indians who used it long before any Europeans came into the area. The portage and the river were known as Chicagou, which means strong or powerful in the Algonquin language. Many trails led to this spot, and numerous wars were fought over it. A French explorer-fur-trader, who reached Lake MI in 1634, reported a river which left the lake and connected with a distant southern sea. Some French fur traders probably used the portage earlier, but its first definitive description came from the explorations of Joliet and Marquette who camped at the mouth of the river in 1673. Joliet's report recommended that a canal be dug across the portage. French fur traders and missionaries increasingly used the portage. In 1681 LaSalle used the portage when he made his trip to the mouth of the MS River, claiming all connecting territory for France. A mission to convert Indians, the Mission of the Guardian Angel, was built at Chicago in 1696, and it ministered to two nearby Miami villages. A conflict between the French government and the Jesuits who were running the mission resulted in its closure in 1700.

During the next eight decades, the Chicago area was a no-man's land between warring Indian tribes, with the Potawatomis laying claim to northern IL after the French had been defeated by the British in the French and Indian War. Right after the American Revolution, in 1784, an Afro-Frenchman, DuSable, built a trading post near the mouth of the Chicago River. This established the first permanent settlement. The Indian defeat by Wayne at the Battle of Fallen Timbers in 1795 led to the cession to the US of a plot of land six miles square at Chicago. In 1804, the US built Fort Dearborn on the land, and a small community began to gather around the fort, and trading with the Indians increased. The British in Canada began inciting the Indians, and in 1810 the Potwatamies initiated hostile actions toward IL settlers. Fort Dearborn was ordered evacuated in 1812, and as the soldiers and their families left, they were massacred and the fort was burned by the Indians.

Fort Dearborn was rebuilt in 1816 after the War of 1812, and settlers who had left returned. IL was admitted to the Union in 1819, with the provision that its northern boundary be moved to include Chicago so as to give IL a port on Lake MI. Not many people came to settle the site, however. The state of IL in 1829 obtained a land grant from the US government along a strip ten miles wide from Lake MI through the portage to the Des Plaines River. Alternate sections along the strip were to be sold to finance a canal along the route. Two towns were plotted at the two ends of the strip, LaSalle and Chicago, and land sales were started. The Chicago survey was completed in 1830 and it was legally constituted as a settlement, with a population of about 50. The next year, the place was designated as the county seat of the newly-created Cook County. In 1832, the Black Hawk War erupted, and Fort Dearborn became the refuge for frightened frontier people. When the IL militia subsequently drove the Black Hawks out, settlement began to increase in Chicago. This was accelerated by the building of a harbor in 1833, the same year in which the Potawatamie agreed to leave IL, and in which Chicago was incorporated as a village. There were now about 350 residents, and the first newspaper was started.

With the removal of the Indian threat, the population of Chicago tripled by 1835. Stage lines began to serve the village, a bank was organized, a land office was opened, pigs and cattle and grain were brought in from the west, slaughterhouses and mills were operating, and shipments to the east were rising. The land craze which resulted was evidenced by the sale of over $2.5 million in canal lots, as construction on the canal was about to begin. Catholic, Baptist, Presbyterian, Methodist, and Episcopal churches had been established, and others would follow shortly. Calls were sent out for canal laborers, and immigrants began to arrive: 900 Irish, plus 800 Germans, Swedes, and Norwegians. The village was incorporated as a city in 1837, the population being about 4100. By 1843, the population had grown to about 7600, trade and food processing were growing rapidly, about 700 ships cleared the port, but the city was a mess. Its streets were mudholes (no paving) and pigstys (garbage), sanitation (water, sewers) was nil, saloons and brothels and gambling houses abounded, many of the houses were little more than flimsy wooden shacks, and crime was high. The city had a sizable preponderance of men, and the newspapers promised a good marriage to any young woman who would move to Chicago.

The year 1848 was an exceptionally important one because, in that year, the IL and MI canal was completed and the first railroad, the Chicago and Galena Union Railroad was finished. The population in 1850 was about 30,000. By 1853, there were about 60,000 people in Chicago, and more rail lines had reached the city, there being ten extending in all directions by 1856. Almost 100 trains a day entered or left the city. The transportation facilities provided links with the fertile prairies and with the eastern markets. So Chicago became a major center for processing and shipping food, especially grain and meat, for producing and selling lumber, for marketing consumer goods from the east, and for manufacturing agricultural machinery. In that one year, over 100,000 immigrants passed through Chicago on their way west. Crime had become so rampant by 1857 that the police conducted raids, made numerous arrests, and destroyed many gambling dens, houses of prostitution, saloons, and fencing operations. However, the reforms were short-lived, and soon preachers were decrying the complicity between the authorities and vice and crime by which the city was cursed and degraded.

As of 1860, Chicago had changed from a farmers' retail market to a regional wholesale and manufacturing center. Its population had risen to over 109,000, it had 15 railroads, 36 wholesale houses, and about 500 factories. All of this was expanded during the Civil War (1861-65) with Chicago serving as a major supplier for the military. The city sent 15,000 men into the Union forces, including large numbers of Irish, Germans, and Swedes. By 1870, Chicago had about 299,000 inhabitants, and 79 blocks of stores and wholesale houses in the center. North, there were farm machinery factories, and beyond them the houses of the wealthy. West, there were breweries, distilleries, tanneries, flour mills, iron works, and founderies. South, there were 500 acres of lumber processing mills and lumber yards, and beyond them, factories, about 14 miles of docks, stockyards, and meat-packing plants. To the east of these were railroad yards, carshops, boiler factories, and iron plants. One consequence of this rapid expansion was a shabby, congested city. Most people lived in small wood-framed houses, wood shacks, or wooden tenements (with no water or sewage facilities) located near the plants where they worked. In the southwest was an Irish community, in the north Swedish, and in the northwest German. The population of the city was about 155,000 native American and 144,000 foreign born, 295,000 white and 4000 Afro. Of the foreign-born, about 53,000 were German, 40,000 Irish, 10,000 English, 10,000 Canadian, 6000 Norwegian, 6000 Swedish, 4000 Scottish, 2000 French, 1000 Danish, 1000 Swiss, 1000 Welsh, and the rest from other nations.

The fires which Chicago experienced in 1839, 1849, and 1857 pale into insignificance compared with the one that broke out in the fall of 1871. A raging wind-fanned fire roared through the wooden structures of the city, then spread to buildings of stone and brick, almost completely destroying everything in a band about 1.0 miles wide and 3.5 miles long along the lakeshore in the center of the city. Almost 300 people were killed, about 100,000 were left homeless, and over 18,000 homes, stores, hotels, churches, factories, and governmental buildings were destroyed. Practically all county and city records burned up in this 27-hour conflagration, which was finally stopped by rain. Almost immediately, a system of relief was organized, and assistance (4 million dollars, food, clothing, supplies) was received from all over the world. The rebuilding of the city was almost a miracle in its rapidity, and excellent planning and hard work brought about a new Chicago of brick, stone, and pavement. Within four years, very little evidence of the calamity could be found. And the growth in population, commerce, and industry continued.

The rapid growth of the manufacturing enterprises in Chicago generated some difficulties between management and the laboring people. The city experienced a series of strikes, some of them emanating in riots and other forms of violence. The 1880 population was about 503,000, that for 1890 was about 1,100,000, and in 1900 it reached about 1,700,000. In 1893, Chicago celebrated the 400th anniversay of North America by staging a gigantic fair, the Columbian Exposition. In World War I, Chicago once again made a tremendous contribution of men and supplies, their iron and steel industry being expanded greatly. Manufacturing brought many Afro-Americans into the city, and there were some racial tensions which led to rioting in 1919. The 1920s in Chicago brought continuing prosperity, the era of prohibition, and the gangland crime syndicate with its blackmail and murders. In the midst of the Depression which began in 1929, Chicago celebrated its 100th anniversary with the 1933 World's Fair, which attracted over 100 million visitors. In World War II, true to its history, Chicago was a major center for the production of war goods. Since then, the city has had a civic building boom, a series of successful slum clearance projects, and a considerable amount of flight to the suburbs. It is today one of the main tourist attractions of the midwestern US, with its planetarium, museums, parks, sports, shopping, theaters, music, and libraries.

6. Cook County and Chicago Record Repositories

The major repositories in Chicago and Cook County for genealogical research will be treated in this section. These repositories include (a) the Cook County Bureau of Vital Statistics, (b) the Circuit Court of Cook County Archive s, (c) the Cook County Recorder and Treasurer, (d) the Chicago Historical Society Library, CHS, (e) the Chicago Public Library, CPL, (f) the Family History Centers in the area, FHC, (g) the IL Regional Archives serving Cook County, IRAD-UNI, (h) the National Archives Great Lakes Branch, NAGL, and (i) the Newberry Library, NL.

Cook County Bureau of Vital Statistics

The Cook County Bureau of Vital Statistics is located at 118 North Clark Street, Chicago, IL 60602. Its telephone number is 1-(312)-443-7790. It is open 8:30am-5:00pm Monday-Friday. The Bureau houses vital records (birth, marriage, death) along with indexes for them. The Bureau can issue copies of marriage records, birth records 75 years old or older, and death records 20 years old or older. You cannot search the indexes yourself, but the Bureau for a fee will make a three-year search of an index and, if a record is found, a copy of it. The records date from 1871, but it is well to remember that the earlier records tend to be more incomplete that the later ones.

Circuit Court of Cook County Archives

The Circuit Court of Cook County maintains an Archives for the preservation of non-current records of the Court. The Archives Department is located in Room 1113, Richard J. Daley Center, Chicago, IL 60602. The hours are 8:30am-4:30pm, Monday-Friday and the telephone number is 1-(312)-629-6601 or 6628. Many of the holdings date from 1871. The major records that are held are listed below. These have been obtained from the Archives leaflet and a conference with the archivists.

___Naturalization Records, 1871-1929, from the Superior, Circuit, County, and Criminal Courts, indexed in the NA Soundex Microfilm Naturalization Index, 1840-1950.

___Probate Cases, 1871-1967, from the County and Probate Courts, indexes include Deceased Indexes (1871-1967), Minors Indexes (1871-1976), Incompetents Indexes (1911-76), Wills Indexes (1850-1993), Docket Books (1871-1993). Case files, wills, and most docket books stored off-site, must be requested.

___Law and Chancery Cases, 1871-1964, from Circuit and Superior Courts, indexed in Plaintiff and Defendant Indexes (1871-1964), Docket Books and Clerk's Record Books (1871-present). Docket Books and Clerk's Record Books stored off-site, must be requested. Contain divorce, law, and chancery cases.

___Divorce Cases, 1871-1979, from Circuit and Superior Courts, indexed in Plaintiff and Defendent Indexes (1871-1964), Divorce Division Index (1964-1979), Docket Books and Clerk's Record Books (1871-present). Docket Books and Clerk's Record Books stored off-site, must be requested.

___Criminal Felony Cases, 1871-1900, 1927-1982, indexed in Criminal Indictment Indexes (1871-1983), Docket Books and Clerk's Record Books (1871-present). Docket Books and Clerk's Record Books stored off-site, must be requested.

___County Court Cases, 1871-1982, indexed in County Court Case File Indexes (1871-present), Docket Books and Clerk's Record Books. County Court Case File Indexes in Room 1201. Docket Books and Clerk's Record Books stored off-site, must be requested.

Adoption Case Records, Mental Health Case Records, and Juvenile Case Records are also held in the Archives, but they are closed without special permission from the Court.

Cook County Recorder and Treasurer

Land records in Cook County are held in the office of the Recorder of Deeds, Cook County Building, Room 120, 118 North Clark Street, Chicago, IL 60602. The telephone number is 1-(312)-443-5060, and the hours are 9:00am-5:00pm, Monday-Friday. Deeds and other land instruments are filed in the Recorder's Office under the piece of property. In other words, land transactions are indexed according to the legal description of the land. Your first job, then, is to obtain a legal description of the property. This may be obtained in Room 112 which is the County Treasurer's Office. The description is then taken to the Tract Department in the basement of Room 120, where you will be sent to a certain ledger. In the ledger, you will see the transactions pertaining to the piece of property. Each transaction will show the grantor and the grantee. When you see the transaction that you want, copy the document number. Take the document number to the Microfiche Area (also in the basement), where you will be led to a paging book which will give you a reference to the microfilm you need. Obtain the microfilm from the attendant, find the document on it, then order the document. See Szucs for considerable more detail on this somewhat-complicated process.

Chicago Historical Society Library

The Chicago Historical Society, CHS, is located at Clark Street and North Avenue, Chicago, IL 60614. The telephone number is 1-(312)-642-4600, and the hours are 9:30am-4:30pm, Tuesday-Saturday. The Library holds a number of useful items for genealogical research, especially in its collections of Chicago books, histories, biographies, directories, newspapers, periodicals, maps, atlases, and manuscripts. When you enter, check your hat, coat, briefcase, large purse, parcels at the check stand on the first floor, then obtain an admission card to the research collections. Take the elevator to the third floor, enter the Library Reading Room, then fill out a Library Research Application. The major finding aids in this room are:

___Main Library Card Catalog, search by name, location, subject, author, title. When the card reads Reference, the item is on the shelves in the Reading Room. All other items must be requested.

___Periodicals Card Index, search by name of periodical.

___Winslow Chicago Chronology Index, search by event, card will give the date.

___Loose-leaf Finding Aid Notebook, a copy on each table. Contents include lists of: Chicago Fire Insurance Atlases, Chicago Newspapers on Microfilm, Newspapers by Date, Clipping File Subject Headings (Afro-Americans, Asssociations, Biography, Collective Biography, Cemeteries, Communities, Churches, Foreign Population)

___Card Catalog of Ship Disasters, search by name of ship.

___IL Newspaper Project List, ask for list at the desk.

___Map Notebook, search by date and type, ask for notebook at desk.

In the adjacent Manuscript Room, you will find this:

___Manuscript Card Catalog, search by name, location, subject, author, title. Manuscript Collections acquired after 1980 are not in this catalog. Ask an archivist to search the computer catalog for these.

Chicago Public Library

The Chicago Public Library, CPL, is located at 400 South State Street, Chicago, IL 60605. Its hours are 9:00am-7:00pm Monday, 11:00am-7:00pm Tuesday,

9:00am-5:00pm Wednesday, 11:00am-7:00pm Thursday, 9:00am-5:00pm Friday-Saturday, and 1:00pm-5:00pm Sunday. There are four areas in the CPL that are of special interest to genealogists:
___General Information Services Division, 3rd Floor, telephone 1-(312)-747-4300.
___Government Publications Department and the Municipal Reference Center, 5th Floor South, telephone number for government publications 1-(312)-747-4500, telephone number for municipal references 1-(312)-747-4526.
___Social Sciences Division, 5th Floor North and Sixth Floor, telephone number 1-(312)-747-4600.
___Special Collections and Preservation Division, 9th Floor, telephone number 1-(312)-747-4876. Reading Room hours: 12:00n-6:00pm Monday-Tuesday, 12:00n-4:00pm Wednesday, 12:00n-6:00pm Thursday, 12:00n-4:00pm Friday-Saturday, and 1:00pm-5:00pm Sunday.
The CPL issues a special leaflet on each of this areas. It is advisable to make good use of them when you visit.

In all of the above sections of the Library, you will find the major computer-based finding aid:
___CARL, the CPL Computer Catalog, search by Word, Name, Location, Subject, Author, Title.
In the General Information Services Division (3rd Floor), you will find CARL, the Circulation Department (for book check-out and return), and the Newspapers and Periodicals Center. This center manages a sizeable collection of old Chicago newspapers, journals, and periodicals. Finding aids for locating newspapers and periodicals are as follows:
___Newspaper Holdings List, available at the desk.
___Serials Holdings List, available at the desk.

On the 5th Floor South, there are located the Government Publications Department and the Municipal Reference Collection along with CARL. The Government Publications Department is a depository for Federal, IL State, and Chicago City publications. This means that they have all publications issued by these governments. Federal publications include military and civilian employee registers, gazetteers, maps, and the CIS US Serial Set Index (including petitions to the Federal government for assistance). CARL does not include Federal publications, so you must use several other indexes that the Department provides. The IL State publications consist of items dating back into the early 1800s. These include the ISA Marriage Record Index. They can be identified in CARL and in a card catalog located in the Department. Notable among the holdings are IL statutes, administrative codes, and registers, and US topographic maps of IL. The Municipal Reference Collection consists of such items as Chicago ordinances, government, budgets, maps, the Board of Education Reports (those for 1867-95 include high school graduates), and the Journal of the City Council(1861-).

The Social Sciences Division occupies the 5th Floor North and all of the 6th Floor. Stations with CARL are also located in this division. There are several collections of value to family searchers in this division: Biography, Genealogy, History, Maps, and Periodicals. Included are Chicago City directories (1839-), Chicago telephone directories (1878-), US censuses, census indexes, IL county histories, passenger and immigration lists and indexes, and genealogical reference works,

The Special Collections Department (on the 9th Floor) has many specialized items dealing with Chicago history. Notable among these are the Neighborhood History Research Collection and the Civil War Research Collection. The Neighborhood History Research Collection is made up of about 120 linear feet of manuscript, printed, and photgraphic materials collected by neighborhood historical societies in the 1930s and 1940s. The collections, which come from Southside and Westside communities, almost all have good biographical information. Guides to the collections are available in the Reading Room of the Department. There is a similar Northside Collection at the Sulzer Regional Library, 4455 North Lincoln Avenue, Chicago, IL 60625 [telephone 1-(312)-728-8652]. The Civil War Research Collection consists of official records of the Union and Confederate armies and navies, service records of IL Union soldiers, and IL regimental histories.

| Family History Centers |

Read the material in Section 5 of the previous chapter. This will describe for you the genealogical materials, catalogs, and indexes available through FHCs, namely, the extensive collection at the FHL in Salt Lake City. FHCs in the Chicago area include:

___Chicago Heights FHC, 402 Longwood Drive.
___Napierville FHC, 25 West 341 Ridgeland Road.
___Orland Park FHC, 13150 South 88th Avenue.
___Schaumburg FHC, 1320 West Schaumburg Road.
___Wilmette FHC, 2801 Lake Avenue.

The NL also has the numerous indexes and catalogs of the FHL.

Among the records for Cook County/Chicago which are available on microfilm from FHL through its FHCs are:

___Cook County genealogical records, bible records, and family lineages.
___Eight biographical compendia.
___Cemetery directories and some cemetery records.
___Cook County state and federal censuses.
___Records of a few churches.
___Cook County Circuit Court, Burned Record Series, 1871-1932.
___Six Cook County genealogy collections.
___Three Cook County genealogical periodicals.
___Cook County Court, Grants of Guardianship, 1877-1923.
___Cook County Probate Court, Documentary Record of Guardians, 1877-1923.
___Seven Cook County histories.
___Cook County military veteran burials.
___Cook County Civil War military census, 1861-62.
___Cook County pensioners, 1883.
___Cook County Circuit Court, Naturalization Records, 1871-1929.
___Cook County Superior Court, Naturalization Records, 1906-29.
___Cook County Court, Probate Records, 1871-1931.
___Cook County Court, Record of Wills, 1877-1928.
___Cook County Clerk, Birth Records, 1871-1922.
___Cook County Clerk, Death Certificates and Records, 1871-1922.
___Cook County Clerk, Marriage Licenses, 1871-1920.
___Cook County Coroner, Death Records, 1879-1904.
___About 20 Chicago biographical compendia.
___Some Chicago cemetery records.
___Numerous Chicago church records.
___Chicago city directories, 1839-1928/9.
___Some Chicago funeral home records.
___Chicago Genealogical Society's ancestor file, compiled 1974-84.
___Five Chicago genealogical periodical entries.
___Over 30 Chicago histories.
___Chicago deed records, 1872-85.
___IL State Canal land sales records, 1830-84.
___Maps of Chicago, 1852, 1872, 1876.
___Confederate prisoner deaths at Camp Douglas, 1862-65.
___Over twenty works on minorities in Chicago.
___Some collected Chicago obituaries.
___Chicago City Council proceedings, 1833-71.

___Chicago birth certificates and registers, 1871-1922.
___Chicago death certificates and records, 1871-1945.
___Vital records from Chicago newspapers, 1833-48.
___Deaths and marriages taken from selected Chicago newspapers, 1833-89.
___Chicago voters, 1888-90, 1892.

Illinois Regional Archives: IRAD-UNI

The IRAD unit which serves Chicago and Cook County is located at the Ronald Williams Library, Northeastern IL University, 5500 North St. Louis, Chicago, IL 60625. The IRAD-UNI is open 9:00am-4:00pm Monday-Friday, but hours can be decreased when the University is not in session, so be sure to call them at 1-(312)-794-6279. The major genealogically-related records which IRAD-UNI holds for Cook County are as follows:

___Probate Records (administrator, guardian, probate, will) 1877-1922, no indexes
___Chicago Atlases 1872-1950
___Chicago City Council Records 1833-1971
___Chicago Voter Register Index 1888-92
___Chicago Burned Record Files 1872-1904, indexed
___Naturalization Records 1871-1929, some indexed
___Chicago Marriage Record Index 1830-1900
___Chicago Street History and Name Changes, 8 binders
___Lakeview City Records 1857-94
___Lake Town Records 1853-89
___Village Records for Beverly, Clearing, Edison Park, Fernwood, Hyde Park, Jefferson, Morgan Park, Mount Greenwood, Norwood Park, Rogers Park, Washington Heights, West Ridge, and West Roseland

A more up-to-date listing of the holdings at IRAD-UNI can be obtained by writing IRAD, IL State Archives, Springfield, IL 62756.

National Archives - Great Lakes Region

The National Archives has a regional branch in the Chicago Area. It is known as the National Archives-Great Lakes Region. The facility is located at 7358 South Pulaski Road, Chicago, IL 60629, and the telephone number is 1-312-581-7816. Its open times are 8:00am-4:15pm, Monday, Wednesday, Thursday, and Friday, and 8:00am-8:30pm on Tuesday. Do not fail to call before you go because the times may change. Details on the holdings of this repository are provided in:

    ___L. D. Szucs and S. H. Luebking, THE ARCHIVES; A GUIDE TO THE NATIONAL ARCHIVES FIELD BRANCHES, Ancestry, Salt Lake City, UT, 1988.

Among their records which pertain to IL are the following:

    ___Federal Census Records for IL, 1820-80, 1900-20

    ___Non-population Census Records for IL, 1850-80

    ___Federal Mortality Schedules for IL, 1850-80

    ___Northern District Naturalization Record Index, 1840-1950, an index of naturalizations in federal, state, and county courts, includes those for Cook County for 1871-1950

    ___Cook County Naturalization Petitions, 1871-1906

    ___Licensing and Enrollment Records of Commercial Maritime Vessels, for IL 1856-1952

    ___Purchases of Federal Land in IL, 1814-85

    ___Internal Revenue Tax Assessments for IL, 1862-73, 1905-1919

    ___Selective Service Records for IL, 1917-19, 1942-47

    ___US District and Circuit Court Records for IL, 1819-1982

    ___War of 1812 Service Record Index, Bounty Land Records, and Bounty Land Record Indexes

    ___Mexican War Service Record Index

    ___Civil War Service Record Index for IL

    ___Spanish-American War Service Record Index

    ___Selective Service Registration Records for IL

    ___Index to IL Public Domain Land Sales

Newberry Library

A detailed discussion of the Newberry Library and its holdings was presented in Section 4 of the previous chapter. Please review that material. Take special note that the Newberry Library's collection is especially rich in the following sorts of publications for Chicago and Cook County: atlases, biographies, business records, cemetery records, census records, church records, directories, ethnic sources, gazetteers, maps, military records, newspapers, organization records, and society records.

---

7. Supplementary Notes on Records of Cook County and Chicago

Chapter 2 presented many categories of records available for research in IL. These categories are repeated below along with special notes which apply to Cook County and Chicago.

| Bible Records | See Section 3, Chapter 2. Bible records for Cook County/Chicago will be found in the DAR books and in the card and computer catalogs of ISHL, FHL(FHC), NL, RL, and the LL in the Chicago |

area.

| Biographies | See Section 4, Chapter 2, and Szucs. Biographical references and information for Cook County/Chicago can be located in the regular and special biography catalogs and indexes in ISA, ISHS, CHS, CPL, and |

NL, the Illinet Computer Catalog (on the World Wide Web), the Biography and Genealogy Master Index, the Genealogical Index of the Newberry Library, and the Neighborhood Collections at CPL and the Sulzer Regional Library (CPL Subsection, Section 6, Chapter 4). Among the more useful general volumes to which the indexes refer are:

__BIOGRAPHICAL SKETCHES OF THE LEADING MEN OF CHICAGO, 1868.

__BIOGRAPHICAL SKETCHES OF SOME OF THE EARLY SETTLERS OF THE CITY OF CHICAGO, Fergus Printing Co., Chicago, IL, 1876.

__D. W. Wood, CHICAGO AND ITS DISTINGUISHED CITIZENS, George and Co., Chicago, IL, 1881.

__J. J. Flinn, HANDBOOK OF CHICAGO BIOGRAPHY, Chicago, IL, 1893.

__PORTRAIT AND BIOGRAPHICAL RECORD OF COOK COUNTY, IL, Lake City Publ. Co., Chicago, IL, 1894.

__ALBUM OF GENEALOGY AND BIOGRAPHY, COOK COUNTY, IL, LaSalle Book Co., Chicago, IL, 1895-9.

__J. Moses, HISTORY OF CHICAGO, Munsell, Chicago, IL, 1895.

__BIOGRAPHICAL DICTIONARY AND PORTRAIT GALLERY OF REPRESENTATIVE MEN OF CHICAGO, American Biographical Publ. Co., Chicago, IL, 1895.

__J. B. Bradwell, PIONEERS OF CHICAGO, Chicago Legal News Co., Chicago, IL, 1896.

__A HISTORY OF THE CITY OF CHICAGO, Interocean, Chicago, IL, 1900.

__NOTABLE MEN OF CHICAGO AND THEIR CITY, Chicago, IL, 1910.

___WHO'S WHO IN CHICAGO, Marquis, Chicago, IL, volumes since 1905-forward.

___N. Bateman, HISTORICAL ENCYCLOPEDIA OF IL, COOK COUNTY EDITION, Munsell, Chicago, IL, 1905.

___A. N. Waterman, HISTORICAL REVIEW OF CHICAGO AND COOK COUNTY AND SELECTED BIOGRAPHY, Lewis Publ. Co., Chicago, IL, 1908, 3 volumes.

___NOTABLE MEN OF CHICAGO AND THEIR CITY, Chicago Daily Journal, Chicago, IL, 1910.

___J. W. Leonard, THE BOOK OF CHICAGOANS, Marquis, Chicago, IL, 1911.

___J. S. Currey, CHICAGO, ITS HISTORY AND ITS BUILDERS, Clarke Publ. Co., Chicago, IL, 1912.

___C. J. Herringshaw, CITY BLUE BOOK OF BIOGRAPHY, Herringshaw, Chicago, IL, 1914-17.

___E. Poole, GIANTS GONE: MEN WHO MADE CHICAGO, McGraw-Hill, New York, NY, 1943.

In addition to the above general biographical compendia the finding aids will lead you to a number of biographical collections dealing with special organizational or occupational groups. Among the most useful of these are:

___(Irish) C. Ffrench, BIOGRAPHICAL HISTORY OF THE AMERICAN IRISH IN CHICAGO, American Biographical Publ. Co., Chicago, IL, 1897.

___(German) CHICAGO UND SEIN DEUTSCHTHUM, German-American Biographical Publ. Co., Cleveland, OH, 1901.

___(German) E. Dietzsch, DEUTSCHE MÄNNER, Stern and Co., Chicago, IL, 1885.

___(Czech/Slovak) CZECH AND SLOVAK LEADERS IN METRO-POLITAN CHICAGO, Slavonic Club, Chicago, IL, 1934.

___(Polish) TO NEW YORK, CHICAGO, AND SAN FRANCISCO, Interpress, Warsaw, Poland, 1986.

___(Polish) T. L. Hollowak, POLISH DIRECTORY FOR THE CITY OF CHICAGO, 1903, Polish Genealogical Society, Chicago, IL, 1981.

___(Jewish) H. L. Meites, HISTORY OF THE JEWS OF CHICAGO, Chicago Jewish Historical Society, Chicago, IL, 1924.

___(Jewish) THE CHICAGO JEWISH CCOMMUNITY BLUE BOOK, Sentinel Publ. Co., Chicago, IL, 1918.

___(Liquor tradesmen) HISTORY OF CHICAGO AND SOUVENIR OF THE LIQUOR INTEREST, Belgravia Publ. Co., Chicago, IL, 1891.

___(Police) J. J. Flinn, HISTORY OF THE CHICAGO POLICE, Police
Book Fund, Chicago, IL, 1887.

___(Lawyers) BENCH AND BAR OF CHICAGO, American Biograph-
ical Publ. Co., Chicago, IL, 1883.

___(Lawyers) GUNTHORP'S LEGAL DIRECTORY OF CHICAGO,
Leonard and Gunthorp, Chicago, IL, 1900.

___(Lawyers) F. B. Wilkie, SKETCHES AND NOTICES OF THE
CHICAGO BAR, Western News Co., Chicago, IL, 1871.

___(Musicians/Artists) F. C. Bennett, HISTORY OF MUSIC AND ART
IN IL, Historical Publ. Co., Philadelphia, PA, 1904.

___(Railroaders) CHICAGO, ROCK ISLAND, AND PACIFIC RAIL-
WAY SYSTEM AND REPRESENTATIVE EMPLOYEES,
Biographical Publishing Co., Chicago, IL, 1900.

___(World War I Military) FIGHTING MEN OF IL, Publishers
Subscription Co., Chicago, IL, 1918.

___(Druggists) ANNIVERSARY VOLUME, Chicago Veteran Druggest
Assn., Chicago, IL, 1904.

___(Republicans) R. P. O'Grady, CHICAGO AND COOK COUNTY
OFFICIAL REPUBLICAN DIRECTORY, The Author, Chicago, IL,
1900.

___(Stockbrokers) THE CHICAGO STOCK EXCHANGE, Excelsior
Print Co., Chicago, IL, 1894.

___(Personnel in construction, manufacturing, banking, commerce, and
railroading) INDUSTRIAL CHICAGO, Goodspeed Publishing Co.,
Chicago, IL, 1891.

| Birth Records |

See Section 5, Chapter 2, the Subsection on the
Cook County Bureau of Vital Statistics in Section 6,
Chapter 4, and Szucs. Chicago/Cook County birth
records are held at the Cook County Bureau of Vital
Statistics. They date from 1871, but the earlier ones are not as complete
as the later. Some of the records are available from FHL(FHC).

| Cemetery Records |

See Section 6, Chapter 2, and Szucs. There are
now over 200 cemeteries in Cook County. A
good listing is provided by Szucs. In the early
years, there were several cemeteries in the
central city, but these graves were moved to suburban cemeteries, chief
among which were Calvary, Graceland, Hebrew Benevolent, Oak Woods,
Rose Hill, and Wunders. A report by Danemark discusses the early
cemeteries:

___ B. Danemark, EARLY CHICAGO CEMETERIES, CHS, Chicago, IL, 1971.

A number of cemeteries in Cook County have been read, and the results published. Examine the indexes at ISA, ISHL, NL, and CHS, as well as the DAR books for references to these. Death records often mention the cemetery of burial, especially obituaries and death certificates.

Census Records

See Section 7, Chapter 2, and Szucs. Census records are available for Chicago/Cook County for 1820-1920 (except 1890), the Cook County area being in Clark County in 1820. They have all been indexed. The records and/or the indexes are available at CPL, CHS, NAGL, NL, ISA, ISHL, AGLL, and FHL(FHC). The 1850/60/80 mortality schedules are available for Chicago/Cook County, but the ones for 1870 are missing. Those for 1850/60 have been indexed by Volkel. The unindexed 1850/60/70/80 farm and manufactures censuses are available at ISA, and some of them at the NL. A number of the IL state censuses have been indexed in the card catalogs at ISA. The 1857 and 1871 Chicago city directories act as pseudo-censuses in that they provide additional information, including some birthplaces, sometimes the years of residency in Chicago, and numbers of persons in the household.

Church Records

See Section 8, Chapter 2, and Szucs.. The WPA Historical Records Survey GUIDE TO CHURCH VITAL STATISTICS RECORDS is an exceptionally valuable aid for locating your ancestor's possible church in Chicago/Cook County. The GUIDE also describes what records are available for each church. The records of many Catholic parishes in Chicago/Cook County have been microfilmed, and they are available at NL or the FHL(FHC). The major denominations in Chicago in the early 1900s were Catholic, Lutheran, Methodist, Jewish, Presbyterian, and Baptist, with the Catholics far outnumbering all the others combined. Some good lists of churches of several of these denominations will be found in the book by Szucs. The many Chicago city directories also name contemporary churches. Records for Chicago churches may be sought in the churches themselves, ISA, ISHL, NL, and CHS.

City Directories

See Section 9, Chapter 2, and Szucs. The first Chicago city directory appeared in 1839, and since then fairly regularly up until 1917, and after that in 1923 and 1928/9. In some of the years no directory was published, and in other years, more than one was published. Those of 1859 and 1871 are especially useful since they include data other than name of head of household, occupation, and home and/or business address. The issue of 1859 includes birthplace and years residing in Chicago, and the issue of 1871 includes the number of males and the number of females in the household, and the householder's years of residency in Chicago. City directories are available at CHS, CPL, and NL. Those up to 1861 have also been put on microfiche and those after that on microfilm.

In addition to city directories, there have also been directories of special groups in Chicago or Cook County. These may be found in NL and CHS: telephone directories, community directories, business directories, and directories of physicians, attorneys, politicians, postmasters, fraternity men, press club members, city officials, school officials and teachers, fashionable ladies, importers and wholesalers, manufacturers, real-estate dealers, merchants, black business and professional men and women, and socially-inclined women. Lists of some of these are presented in the book by Szucs.

City and County Histories

See Section 10, Chapter 2. City and county histories for Chicago and Cook County will be found in ISHS, NL, CHS, CPL, and FHL(FHC). The best multi-volumed histories are:

___A. T. Andreas, HISTORY OF CHICAGO FROM THE EARLIEST PERIOD TO THE PRESENT TIME, Andreas, Chicago, IL, 1884-86, 3 volumes.

___B. L. Pierce, A HISTORY OF CHICAGO, Knopf, New York, NY, 1937-57, 3 volumes. Chicago up through 1893.

Of lesser import, but still useful are:

___J. Kirkland, THE STORY OF CHICAGO, Dibble Publ. Co., Chicago, IL, 1892-94, 2 volumes.

___J. Moses and J. Kirkland, HISTORY OF CHICAGO, IL, Munsell, Chicago, IL, 1895, 2 volumes.

Among the best one-volumed treatments are:

___L. Lewis and H. J. Smith, CHICAGO: THE HISTORY OF ITS REPUTATION, Harcourt, Brace, and Co., Chicago, IL, 1929.

___E. Dedmon, FABULOUS CHICAGO, Atheneum, Chicago, IL, 1981.

Important works on the frontier and pioneer period in Chcago and its region are:

___M. M. Quaife, CHICAGO AND THE OLD NORTWEST, 1673-1835, Univ of Chicago Press, Chicago, IL, 1913.

___A. H. Meyer, CIRCULATION AND SETTLEMENT PATTERNS OF THE CALUMET REGION OF NORTHWEST IN AND NORTHEAST IL, in Annals of the Association of American Geographers, 44(Sep. 1954), 46(Sep. 1956).

Bibliographies of historical works on Chicago/Cook County, which may be consulted for detailed studies on various topics are:

___F. Jewell, ANNOTATED BIBLIOGRAPHY OF CHICAGO HISTORY, CHS, Chicago, IL, 1979.

___P. R. Duis, CHICAGO, in J. Hoffmann, A GUIDE TO THE HISTORY OF IL, Greenwood Press, Westport, CT, 1991, pages 119-139.

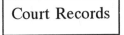

| Court Records |

Refer to Section 11, Chapter 2, the Sub-sections on the Circuit Court of Cook County Archives and the Family History Centers in Section 6 of this Chapter, and Szucs. There you will find described the most accessible of the Chicago/Cook County court records.

| DAR Records |

Please review Section 12, Chapter 2. Several of the DAR volumes apply to Chicago/Cook County. Do not fail to consult them. They are available at the DAR Library in Washington, ISHL, and NL.

| Death Records |

See Section 13, Chapter 2, the Subsection on the Cook County Bureau of Vital Statistics in Section 6, Chapter 4, and Szucs. Chicago/Cook County death records are held at the Cook County Bureau of Vital Statistics. They date from 1871, but the earlier ones are not as complete as the later. Some of the records are available from FHL(FHC).

| Divorce Records |

Consult Section 14, Chapter 2, and the Subsection on the Circuit Court of Cook County Archives in Section 6, Chapter 4. Chicago/Cook County divorce records are accessed through the Divorce Case indexes available in the Circuit Court of Cook County Archives.

| Emigration and Immigration Records |

Reread Section 15, Chapter 2.

Ethnic Records	Check Section 16, Chapter 2. People from other countries have come to Chicago in large numbers and have had a profound influence upon its history.

The following book presents a good review of the most important groups:

___L. D. Scuzs, CHICAGO AND COOK COUNTY: A GUIDE TO RESEARCH, Ancestry, Salt Lake City, UT, 1996, pages 240-280.

Further important readings include:

___P. d'A. Jones and M. G. Holli, ETHNIC CHICAGO, Eerdman's Publ. Co., Grand Rapids, MI, 1981. Contains chapters on Germans, Irish, Italians, Japanese, Jews, Ukrainians.

___C. Pence, ETHNIC RESOURCES IN THE ISHL, IL Libraries 74(Nov 1992), No. 5. Also all other articles in this issue.

___Chicago Department of Development and Planning, HISTORIC CITY, THE SETTLEMENT OF CHICAGO, The Department, Chicago, Il, 1976.

Important contacts and references for assistance in searching specific groups include the following. References have been obtained from Illinet, the catalogs of NL, CPL, CHS, the Chicago telephone directory, and the books by Bentley and Szucs.

___(Afro-American) The Afro-American Genealogical and Historical Society of Chicago, PO Box 377651, Chicago, IL 60637. Also see articles in IL Libraries 74(Nov 1992), No. 5.

___(Czech/Slovak) Czechoslovak Society of America, 122 West 22nd St., Oak Brook, IL 60521. Also see articles in IL Libraries 74(Nov 1992), No. 5.

___(Dutch) See article in IL Libraries 74(Nov 1992), No. 5.

___(German) See R. L. Otto, GERMAN RESEARCH, in L. D. Scuzs, CHICAGO AND COOK COUNTY: A GUIDE TO RESEARCH, Ancestry, Salt Lake City, UT, 1996, pages 254-264. Also see articles in IL Libraries 74(Nov 1992), No. 5.

___(Irish) Irish-American Heritage Center, 4626 North Knox Avenue, Chicago, IL 60630. See K. J. Betit and T. M. Cook, THE IRISH IN CHICAGO, in The Irish at Home and Abroad, 2(1994/5), No. 2, Salt Lake City, UT, 1994, pages 46-53. Also see articles in IL Libraries 74(Nov 1992), No. 5.

___(Italian) Italian-American Heritage Center, 263 North York Road, Chicago, IL 60126.

___(Jewish) The Jewish Genealogical Society of IL, PO Box 515, Northbrook, IL 60065. Chicago Jewish Historical Society, 618 South Michigan Avenue, Chicago, IL 60605.

___(Lithuanian) Balzekas Museum of Lithuanian Culture, 6500 South Pulaski Road, Chicago, IL 60629. See also the article in IL Libraries 74(Nov 1992), No. 5.

___(Polish) Polish Museum of America, 984 North Milwaukee Avenue, Chicago, IL 60622. Polish Genealogical Society of America, same address. See also the article in IL Libraries 74(Nov 1992), No. 5.

___(Swedish) Swedish-American Historical Society, 5125 Spaulding Avenue, Chicago, IL 60625. Swedish-American Archives of Greater Chicago, North Park College, Foster and Kedzie Avenues, Chicago, IL 60625. Also see articles in IL Libraries 74(Nov 1992), No. 5.

___(Ukrainian) Ukrainian National Museum, 2453 West Chicago Avenue, Chicago, IL 60622.

Finally, do not overlook the Neighborhood Collections at CPL and the Sulzer Regional Library (CPL Subsection, Section 6, Chapter 4).

Gazetteers, Atlases, and Maps

Consult Section 17, Chapter 2, and the Chicago Gazetteer chapter in Szucs. The best sources of atlases, gazetteers, and/or maps for Chicago/Cook County are the CHS (best collection), CPL, IRAD-UNI (atlases), NL, and the Cook County Clerk's Maps and Tax Redemption Department. One of the main problems that Chicago researchers often face is that the street numbering was changed in 1909. Both the CHS and the CPL have guides which relate the old and the new numbers, and there are guides in CPL which assist with street name changes.

Genealogical Indexes and Compilations

Please look at Section 18, Chapter 2 again. There are some special indexes and compiled records which apply to Chicago/Cook County. Some of the better ones which have not been previously noted are:

___S. Fink, CHICAGO MARRIAGE AND DEATH INDEX, typescrript by the compiler and in his custody. Records compiled from Chicago newspapers: marriages (1833-71), deaths (1856-89). Available on microfilm from FHL(FHC) and at NL.

___Chicago Genealogical Society, VITAL RECORDS FROM CHICAGO NEWSPAPERS, 1833-48, The Society, Chicago, IL, 19xx-, 7 volumes to date.

___Chicago Genealogical Society, CHICAGO ANCESTOR FILE, 1974-84, The Society, Chicago, IL, 1985. With supplements published in the Society's journal The Chicago Genealogist. More than 10,000 Chicago ancestors submitted by their descendants.

Genealogical Periodicals

Check out Section 19, Chapter 2. Among the better of the genealogical periodicals published in Chicago/Cook County are those listed below. These references have been obtained from the FHL catalog, the NL catalog, the Genealogical Helper, and the book by Bentley:

___BULLETIN OF THE POLISH GENEALOGICAL SOCIETY OF AMERICA, quarterly, The Society, Chicago, IL.

___CHICAGO GENEALOGIST, quarterly, Chicago Genealogical Society, Chicago, IL. Also a NEWSLETTER.

___SEARCH, quarterly, Jewish Genealogical Society of IL, Northbrook, IL.

___NEWSLETTER OF THE NORTH SUBURBAN GENEALOGICAL SOCIETY, The Society, Winnetka, IL.

___NEWS FROM THE NORTHWEST, newsletter of the Northwest Suburban Council of Genealogists, Mt. Prospect, IL.

___NEWSLETTER OF THE POLISH GENEALOGICAL SOCIETY OF AMERICA, The Society, Chicago, IL.

___WHERE THE TRAILS CROSS, quarterly, South Suburban Genealogical Society, South Holland, IL. Also a NEWSLETTER.

___RELATIVELY SPEAKING, newsletter of the Tinley Moraine Genealogical Society, Tinley Park, IL.

In addition to the voluminous records of Chicago found in the above periodicals, especially the CHICAGO GENEALOGIST, the IL State Genealogical Society Quarterly has a number of references that could be of assistance [listed as Volume:Page or Volume(Issue):Page] --
1(4):43, 2:70, 2:129, 5:217, 5:221, 9:26, 9:27, 9:77, 10:147, 10:154, 11:72, 11:95, 12:91, 13:27, 13:101, 13:142, 14:187, 14:190, 14:192, 15:20, 15:50, 15:255, 15:275, 16:42, 16:170, 17:8, 17:195, 18:26, 18:86, 18:96, 19:167, 20:88, 21:80, 21:221, 23:47, 23:96, 23:47, 23:96, 23:194, 24:27, 24:32, 24:66, 24:132, 24:235, 24:210, 25:15, 25:18, 25:33, 25:67, 25:71, 25:96, 25:136.

Genealogical and Historical Societies

See Section 20, Chapter 2. The following genealogical societies are ones which are active in Chicago/Cook County. The listings have been gleaned from the FHL catalog, the NL catalog, the Genealogical Helper, and the book by Bentley:

___Afro-American Genealogical and Historical Society of Chicago, PO Box 377651, Chicago, IL 60637.

___Chicago Genealogical Society, PO Box 1160, Chicago, IL 60690.

___Des Plaines Genealogical Questors, 789 Pearson St., Des Plaines, IL 60016.

___Dunton Genealogical Society, Arlington Heights Memorial Library, 500 North Dunton Avenue, Arlington Heights, IL 60004.

___Green Hills Genealogical Society, Green Hills Library, 8611 West 103rd Street, Palos Hills, IL 60465.

___Jewish Genealogical Society of IL, PO Box 515, Northbrook, IL 60065.

___Lithuanian-American Genealogical Society, Balzekas Museum of Lithuanian Culture, 6500 South Pulaski Road, Chicago, IL 60629.

___North Suburban Genealogical Society, Winnetka Public Library, 768 Oak Street, Winnetka, IL 60093.

___Northwest Suburban Council of Genealogists, PO Box AC, Mt. Prospect, IL 60056.

___Polish Genealogical Society of America, Polish Museum of America, 984 North Milwaukee Avenue, Chicago, IL 60622.

___Poplar Creek Genealogical Society, 200 Kosan Circle, Streamwood, IL 60103.

___Schaumburg Genealogical Society, Schaumburg Public Library, 32 West Library Lane, Schaumburg, IL 60194.

___South Suburban Genealogical Society, PO Box 96, South Holland, IL 60473.

___Tinley Moraine Genealogical Society, PO Box 521, Tinley Park, IL 60477.

___Western Springs Genealogical Society, Western Springs Historical Society, Grand Avenue School, 4211 Grand Avenue, Western Springs, IL 60558.

There are numerous historical societies in Chicago/Cook County. Some of these have been mentioned in the Sub-section on ethnic groups. Others are listed in the Directory of the American Association for State and Local History, the book by the Association of IL Museums and Historical Societies, and the book by Bentley, all of which have been referenced in Section 20, Chapter 2.

| Land Records | See Section 21, Chapter 2, and the excellent discussion of the saving of the abstract companies' records during the fire in 1871 from Chamberlin as quoted by Szucs. The original land grants for the Chicago |

area may be accessed through the IL Public Domain Land Sales Record Listing (alphabetically arranged). However, the land transfer records (deeds, mortgages) were lost in the 1871 fire. After the fire, owners could submit evidence of ownership and receive a court order which could be recorded. These documents are in the Burned Record Series, which are available at IRAD-UNI, the Circuit Court of Cook County Archives, and the FHL(FHC). There is another source of land transfer records for Cook County in the period before the fire. Many of the records of three abstract companies (commercial firms which keep records of land titles and their transfers) were saved from the fire. These records are now owned by the:

___Chicago Title Insurance Company, 171 North Clark, Chicago, IL 60602.

The company will track land transfers, grantors, and grantees by searches which they offer for sale. The obtaining of land records for the period after the fire has been discussed in the Subsection entitled Cook County Recorder and Treasurer in Section 6 of this chapter.

| Manuscripts | See Section 22, Chapter 2. The major manuscript repositories in the Chicago/Cook County area are the CHS, University of IL at Chicago, University of Chi- |

cago, NL, CPL, and several other universities, colleges, theological seminaries, and ethnic libraries. Excellent articles on the holdings of these repositories by Pugh, Bamberger, Meyer, Haskell, and Leonard will be found in:

___J. Hoffmann, A GUIDE TO THE HISTORY OF IL, Greenwood Press, Westport, CT, 1991, pages 205-306.

| Marriage Records | Consult Section 23, Chapter 2, the Subsection on the Cook County Bureau of Vital Statistics in Section 6, Chapter 4, and Szucs. |

Chicago/Cook County birth records are held at the Cook County Bureau of Vital Statistics. They date from 1871, but the earlier ones are not as complete as the later. Some of the records are available from FHL(FHC). Do not forget the newspaper abstracts by Fink.

| Military Records | Please review Sections 24, 25, and 26 in Chapter 2. There is a special Cook County index to the Honor Roll of Veterans Buried in IL: |

___INDEX TO THE ROLL OF HONOR, COOK COUNTY, IL, Markham Publications, Salt Lake City, UT, 1988.

Of value for the Civil War are:

___L. D. Szucs, K. Bobko, J. Stoddard, and S. Murdoch, LIST OF PENSIONERS--CHICAGO AND COOK COUNTY, IL--JANUARY 1, 1883, Chicago Genealogical Society, Chicago, IL, 1985.

___K. Vandenberg, RESEARCH SERIES, VOLUME 2: ABLE-BODIED MEN, MILITARY CENSUS, 1861-62, South Suburban Genealogical and Historical Society, South Holland, IL, 1991. Enrollees in some townships of Cook County.

| Mortuary Records |

There are many mortuaries in Chicago/Cook County. A survey of almost 400 of them and their records has been made:

___K. Vanderburg, SURVEY OF FUNERAL HOMES IN COOK COUNTY, South Suburban Genealogical and Historical Society, South Holland, IL.

Some microfilmed records and some original records of mortuaries are available at CHS, ISA, FHL(FHC), and the South Suburban Genealogical and Historical Society. However, most must be sought at the individual mortuaries.

| Naturalization Records |

Consult Section 28 of Chapter 2. Naturalization records for Chicago/Cook County will be found in IRAD-UNI, NAGL, FHL(FHC), and the Circuit Court of Cook County Archives. Remember that those before 1871 were destroyed and that the NAGL has an index to naturalizations filed with local, state, and federal courts in Chicago/Cook County, as well as some surrounding areas.

___Soundex Index to Naturalizaton Petitions in the Northern District of IL and Immigration and Naturalization Service District Number 9, 1840-1950, an index of naturalizations in federal, state, and county courts, includes those for Cook County for 1871-1950, RG85, NAGL, Chicago, IL.

They also hold copies of Cook County naturalization petitions for 1871-1906.

| Newspapers |

See Section 29, Chapter 2. Collections of Chicago/Cook County newspapers will be found in CHS, CPL, NL, and the ISHL. For listings of many of these consult the book by Szucs.

| Tax and Voter Lists |

The older records of the Cook County tax assessor are in a remote warehouse, making them essentially unavailable at the time of this writing. Internal Revenue tax assessment lists for 1862-66 can be used at NAGL. A voter list for Cook County in 1826 was published in the Chicago Genealogist, December 1969 issue. And voters in the first city election in Chicago have been published in the Chicago Genealogical Society's book entitled GENEALOGICAL SOURCES IN CHICAGO, IL, 1835-1900, which was issued in 1982. Voter lists for 1888/90/92 are located at IRAD-UNI.

| Will and Probate Records |

Read Section 34, Chapter 2. The older will and probate records for Chicago/Cook County are in the Circuit Court of Cook County Archives. Please review the section on the Archives which appeared earlier in this chapter. Many of these records are on microfilm at FHL(FHC). IRAD-UNI holds some original records and many microfilmed ones. In addition, there are some useful publications:

___J. Barekman, INDEX TO COOK COUNTY WILLS, 1850-1915, in Chicago Genealogist, Fall 1972, and issues which followed. Notice that this is an index only. Records corresponding to the pre-1871 entries have not been found.

___D. McClure and L. D. Szucs, PROBATE COURT RECORDS, COOK COUNTY, IL, DOCKET BOOK A, 1871-72, Authors, St. Petersburg, FL, 1994.

___D. McClure, PROBATE COURT RECORDS, COOK COUNTY, IL, Chicago Genealogical Society, Chicago, IL, 1992.

Some guardian records are at IRAD-UNI and FHL(FHC) has some on microfilm.

| WPA Records |

The Works Progress Administration and Historical Records Survey included a number of pertinent items in their work in Chicago and Cook County. These include:

___Guide to Church Vital Statistics Records, published 1941.

___Inventory of Cook County Archives, 1936-42, manuscripts in ISA, Record Group 954.7.

___Inventories of Municipal Archives in Cook County, 1936-41, including Chicago, Bellwood, Berwyn, Blue Island, Brookfield, Cicero, Crestwood, Des Plaines, Dixmoor, Evanston, Forest Park, Franklin Park, La Grange, Lyons Township, Maywood, Melrose Park, Oak

Park, Park Ridge, River Forest, Riverside, Summit, Tinley Park, Westchester, and Westmont, manuscripts in ISA, Record Group 954.11.

___Chicago and Cook County Deaths, 1871-1933, alphabetically arranged, on microfilm at FHL(FHC), not complete.

8. Pre-Fire (Pre-1871) Records

As you have undoubtedly realized by now, Chicago/Cook County research for the years before 1871 is usually difficult because of the massive destruction of records in the great fire. Below is presented a summary of the records which are available for this pre-1871 period. They are arranged according to the categories used in the previous section. See the previous section for details, since this summary is only a check list to keep you from overlooking possible sources.

___Bible: some available.

___Biography: one book available for 1868, later ones useful because they refer to events of previous years.

___Birth: not available.

___Cemetery: many available, very useful.

___Censuses: federal 1820-70, mortality 1850/60, farm and manufactures 1850/60/70, state 1840/55/65.

___Church: many available, very useful.

___City Directories: available for 1839-71, very valuable, especially those of 1859 and 1871, since they contain added data. There are also fraternal and occupational directories and records which may give pre-1871 information.

___City Histories: nothing very useful written before 1871, but later volumes sometimes refer to persons as of earlier dates.

___Court: most local records destroyed, but the Burned Record Series refers to earlier dates. Also see the Federal District and Circuit Court records 1819-. Chicago City Council Proceedings available 1833-71, but not always helpful. Later court records sometimes refer to pre-1871 events.

___DAR: some typescripts available.

___Death: not available. Post-1871 death certificates may refer to pre-1871 births and marriages.

___Divorce: not available.

___Emigration, immigration: city directories of 1859 and 1871 carry possible clues to immigration dates.

___Ethnic: see the Neighborhood Collections at CPL and the Sulzer Regional Library.

___Gazetteers, atlases, maps: Some available.

___Genealogical compilations and indexes: see Chicago Genealogical Society's Ancestral File, vital records abstracted from Chicago newspapers, and DAR volumes.

___Land: check land records held by the Chicago Title Company, IL Public Domain Land Sales records, the Chicago Burned Record Series, and IL State Canal land sales.

___Manuscript: many available, some of them helpful.

___Marriage: not available.

___Military: see Civil War military census 1861-62, Civil War Roll of Honor, federal records for War of 1812, Mexican War, and Civil War.

___Mortuary: some available.

___Naturalization: not available, except some may be in Homestead records filed in other places at later dates.

___Newspaper: vital records collected from Chicago newspapers, 1833-89. Also many pre-1871 newspapers survived.

___Tax: internal revenue assessments, 1862-73.

___Will and probate: not available. Post-1871 wills and administrations may give clues to pre-1871 events.

Chapter 5

OTHER IL COUNTY LISTINGS

| **1. Introduction** | In this chapter, listings of many of the major records of the other IL counties will be presented. The records are mostly county based, many of them being governmental records, and many being non-governmental or private records. |

In addition, libraries and genealogical societies in the counties will be shown because they are often valuable sources of ancestral information.

Please take a look at the next section (Section 2) which will serve as an example of the format of the county listings. This section deals with Adams County. First, the name of the county is given, then the dates on which the county was formed and organized (if they differ), along with the parent county or counties. This is followed by the name of the county seat and the zip code of the CH. After this, you will find notes regarding losses of county records, if such has occurred.

Then you will find a listing of CENSUS records which are available for the county. T stands for territorial, R for regular federal, S for state, P for 1840 federal pensioners, F for federal farm and ranch, M for federal manufactures and industrial, D (death) for federal mortality. Next will be found the records which are available at the FHL, and therefore are obtainable through FHCs. Following this, there are the records which are available at the appropriate IRAD-XXX. The XXX stands for the appropriate IRAD. Then, there is a list of articles in ISGSQ which pertain to the county. These are listed as Volume:Page, for example, 21:56 means volume 21, page 56. For Volume 1 only, the listings will appear as follows- 1(4):77. This means volume 1, issue 4, page 77. The ILLINET PUBLISHED RECORDS section then lists the major genealogical publications that are available for the county. These publications have been taken from the World Wide Web ILLINET Catalog (htttp//:www.library.sos.state.il,us/), a catalog which combines the holdings of over 800 IL libraries.

Next, there appears a summary of an INVENTORY of county records as they were shortly after the turn of the century (according to Pease). This list is meant to give you an idea of the records that should be sought in the CH. It is not intended to be complete, but to show you what was available during the 19th century, which is the time when most people are seeking their ancestors. Some of the records may have since been transferred or even lost, and other types have since been added. Finally, there is a LIBRARY section, a GENEALOGICAL SOCIETY section, and a GENEALOGICAL PUBLICATION section in which pertinent information for the county is given. Please be aware that addresses can change.

Now, a few remarks about the listings of county records need to be made. The listings are not complete, but are meant to give you a good general idea of the materials which are available. The emphasis in the listings has been in the pre-1900 period, since this is the time domain of major concern to most researchers. Further, when a set of inclusive dates is given, such as (1817-1903), it does not necessarily mean that every year is included; there may be a few gaps. Another important item to take careful notice of is that the dates in the county listings show when separate record books or files were set up for various types of records. The date does not necessarily mean that there were no records of that sort before the date. For example, in Adams County deed records begin in 1825, but separate mortgage records do not begin until 1885. This does not mean that there were no mortgage records before 1885. Such records were probably filed with the deed records prior to that.

Do not forget that the listings of records under the names of the counties in this chapter represent only a fraction of what is available in the counties. A visit to the IL county (or a hired searcher) and a search of its records is an absolute must if you want to do a thorough investigation. Even though the microfilmed and published records are often those of greatest genealogical utility, the records which have not been put into microfilm or published form are very valuable, particularly the court records, and among them, especially the probate and case packets or files. These records are usually only in the county. And, equally important, the CH is often the only place where many of the original records can be viewed, an activity that is necessary for complete documentation.

---

2. Adams County

Adams County, formed 1825 from Pike County, County Seat Quincy (521 Vermont, 62306).

CENSUSES: 1830R, 1840RSP, 1850-RFMD, 1855S, 1860RFMD, 1865S, 1870RFM, 1880RFMD, 1900R, 1910R, 1920R.

FHL(FHC) RECORDS: atlas (1872, 1901), Baptist (1843-1970), biography (1869/79/92, 1905/19), birth (1864-1915), CJCLDS (1840-51), cemetery, chancery court (1825-1935), Christian Church (1835-1974), circuit court (1826-1964), commissioner's court (1825-49), Congregational (1830-1960), coroner (1825-1928), death (1877-1990), deed (1825-86), divorce (1825-1935), early record index, Episcopal (1871-1974), Evangelical Lutheran (1856-1965), guardian (1827-1937), history (1869/79/82, 1905/19/75), inventory (1939), land (1823-72), Lutheran (1851-1962), marriage (1825-1926), Methodist (1827-1958), military (1861-62), mortgage (1885-1911), naturalization (1826-1943), newspaper abstract (1835-50), obituary (1875-1953), original land entry (1817-60), poor (1827-1964), Presbyterian (1845-1909), probate (1827-1964), survey (1834-73), tax (1841-44, 1850), United Church of Christ (1858-1970), will (1836-1943), WPA.

IRAD-WIU RECORDS: circuit court (1826-1974), court (1830-1919), deed (1825-1948), estray (1875-88), poor (1873-1947), probate (1826-1969), will (1837-1964).

ILLINET PUBLISHED RECORDS: atlas (1872, 1901/10/13), biography (1879/92, 1905/19), cemetery, coroner, (1837-1906), directory (1886), early records index (to 1850), genealogical periodical, history (1879, 1905/19/48/55/74), inventory, lawyers and judges, map (1889), marriage (1825-99), medical society (1850-1945), surname index, tax (1841), veteran's burial, WPA.

ISGSQ ARTICLES: 2:205, 6:99, 9:99, 12:137, 15:99, 17:41, 17:47, 17:82, 17:101, 17:141, 22:165, 24:46, 24:146.

COUNTY INVENTORY: birth (1877-), board of supervisors (1849-), cemetery deed (1861-), circuit court (1825-), county court (1872-), county commissioners (1825-38), death (1877-), deed (1818-), guardian (1827-), insanity (1883-), marks and brands (1825-95), marriage (1825-), militia (1861-62), mortgage (1836-), naturalization (1840-1906), original land entry (1815-60), physicians (1877-), powers of attorney (1855-), probate (1825-), road (1826-71), tax (1822-), will (1826-).

LIBRARY: Quincy Public Library, 526 Jersey St., Quincy, IL 62301.

GENEALOGICAL SOCIETY: Great River Genealogical Society, Quincy Public Library, 526 Jersey St., Quincy, IL 62301.

GENEALOGICAL PUBLICATION: Above society publishes The Yellow Jacket.

3. Alexander County

Alexander County, formed 1819 from Union County, County Seat Cairo (2000 Washington Ave., 62914).

CENSUSES: 1820RS, 1830R, 1840RP, 1850RFMD, 1855S, 1860RFMD, 1865S, 1870RFM, 1880RFMD, 1900R, 1910R, 1920R.

FHL(FHC) RECORDS: biography (1883) birth (1878-1915), Catholic (1840-74), cemetery, circuit court (1842-73), city directory (1864-), Civil War soldiers, commissioners (1819-1929), death (1879-1917), deed (1818-1917), genealogical compilations, history (1883, 1910), marriage (1819-1918), Methodist (1863-1910), naturalization (1857-1941), obituary (1879-88), original land entry (1816-57), probate (1819-1902), Revolutionary soldiers.

IRAD-SIU RECORDS: birth (1878-1917), circuit court (1842-73), court (1873-1930), death (1878-1915), deed (1818-1944), plat (1853-1939), marriage (1819-1944), naturalization (1857-1941), original land entry (1816-57), probate (1819-1944), tax (1867-73).

ILLINET PUBLISHED RECORDS: biography (1883), cemetery, genealogical compilations, history (1883, 1973/85/89/90), marriage (to 1871), plat (1900).

ISGSQ ARTICLES: 24:131.

COUNTY INVENTORY: birth (1878-), Cairo assessments (1882-), Cairo court of common pleas (1859-69), Cairo deed (1856-65), Cairo entry book (1856-65), circuit court (1821-), coroner (1843-), county court (1872-), county commissioners (1819-), death (1878-), deed (1819-), entry (1860-), estray (1863-83), guardian (1842-), insanity (1893-), marks and brands (1858-96), marriage (1819-), militia (1861-62), mortgage (1819-), naturalization (1865-), polls (1868-), physicians (1877-), plat (1856-), probate (1819-), road (1848-75), tax (1837, 1851-), will (1819-).

LIBRARY: Cairo Public Library, 1609 Washington Ave., Cairo, IL 62914.

GENEALOGICAL SOCIETY: Genealogical Society of Southern IL, John A. Logan College, Route 2, Box 145, Carterville, IL 62918.

GENEALOGICAL PUBLICATION: Above society publishes Saga of Southern IL. Also Newsletter.

---

4. Bond County — Bond County, formed 1817 from Madison County, County Seat Greenville (PO Box 407, 62246).

CENSUSES: 1818T, 1820RS, 1830R, 1840-RSP, 1850RFMD, 1855S, 1860RFMD, 1865S, 1870RFM, 1880RFMD, 1900R, 1910R, 1920R.

FHL(FHC) RECORDS: biography (1882/93, 1915), birth (1877-1915), cemetery, death (1878-1915), deed (1817-1921), genealogical compilations, history (1882, 1915/79/93), marriage (1817-1927), Methodist (1820-1987), naturalization (1858-1906), newspaper abstract, probate (1817-1965), tax (1853-1966), will (1854-1922).

IRAD-SIU RECORDS: marriage (1817-1916), poor (1890-91), probate (1837-55).

ILLINET PUBLISHED RECORDS: ancestor charts, atlas (1875, 1900), biography (1882/92, 1915/28/79/93), cemetery, early marriage, gazetteer, genealogical periodical, history (1882, 1915/28/65/79/93), marriage (1817-90), plat (1900).

ISGSQ ARTICLES: 1(4):18, 2:86, 3:157, 6:61, 6:127, 6:129, 6:157, 6:163, 6:187, 6:203, 7:64, 7:129, 8:36, 8:62, 8:67, 10:217, 11:112, 13:217, 22:28, 22:77, 24:2.

COUNTY INVENTORY: apprentice (1836-65), birth (1877-), circuit court (1818-), coroner (1876-1905), county court (1857-), county commissioners (1817-89), county supervisers (1889-), death (1877-), deed (1817-), entry (1815-75), insanity (1879-), jury (1872-), marriage (1817-), mortgage (1856-), naturalization (1866-1906), polls (1823-88), physicians (1877-), plat (1855-1907), probate (1817-), road (1839-), survey (1855-1907), tax (1853-), will (1817-).

LIBRARY: Greenville Public Library, 414 West Main St., Greenville, IL 62246.

GENEALOGICAL SOCIETY: Bond County Genealogical Society, PO Box 172, Greenville, IL 62246.

GENEALOGICAL PUBLICATION: Above society publishes BCGS News.

5. Boone County

Boone County, formed 1837 from Winnebago County, County Seat Belvidere (521 North Main St., 61008).

CENSUSES: 1840RP, 1850RFMD, 1855S, 1860RFMD, 1865S, 1870RFM, 1880RFMD, 1900R, 1910R, 1920R.

FHL(FHC) RECORDS: atlas (1871/86/92, 1905), biography (1877/92, 1909/90), birth (1877-1916), cemetery, city directory (1896-7), Civil War (1861-65), death (1877-1909), early settler, genealogical compilations, guardian (1839-1962), history (1877, 1909), marriage (1838-1923), military land (1839-53), naturalization (1866-1943), newspaper abstract, poor (1837-1947), probate (1839-1962).

IRAD-NIU RECORDS: original land entry (1838-1966).

ILLINET PUBLISHED RECORDS: atlas (1871/86/92, 1900/05), biography (1877/92, 1909), birth (1877-1948), cemetery, death (1877-1955), directory (1885), genealogical compilations, history (1877, 1909/76

/85), marriage (1838-1909), obituary (1851-99), pioneers (before 1841), probate (1839-1962).

ISGSQ ARTICLES: 6:162, 10:31, 16:136, 21:72, 22:76, 22:96, 22:167, 25:96.

COUNTY INVENTORY: birth (1877-), circuit court (1838-), county court (1854-), county commissioners (1836-49), county supervisors (1849-), death (1877-), deed (1838-), entry (1838-), insanity (1885-), marriage (1838-), militia (1861-62), mortgage (1838-), naturalization (1850-1906), physicians (1877-), probate (1837-), survey (1858-), tax (1850-), will (1837-).

LIBRARY: Ida Public Library, 320 North State St., Belvidere, IL 61008.

GENEALOGICAL SOCIETY: Winnebago-Boone Counties, Genealogical Society, PO Box 10166, Rockford, IL 61131.

GENEALOGICAL PUBLICATION: Above society publishes Twigs and Branches, also a Newsletter.

6. Brown County

Brown County, formed 1839 from Schuyler County, County Seat Mt. Sterling (62353).

CENSUSES: 1840RSP, 1850RFMD, 1855S, 1860RFMD, 1865S, 1870RFM, 1880RFMD, 1900R, 1910R, 1920R.

FHL(FHC) RECORDS: atlas (1903), biography (1892), cemetery, chancery court (1853-1924), genealogical compilations, guardian (1858-1939), history (1972), inventory, marriage (1839-61), naturalization (1857-1948), poor (1881-1963), probate (1839-1964), tax (1817-53), will (1869-1963), WPA.

IRAD-WIU RECORDS: marriage (1839-50), poor (1882-1963), probate (1850-67).

ILLINET PUBLISHED RECORDS: atlas (1903).biography (1882/92, 1972/95), cemetery (1825-1972), genealogical compilations, history (1882, 1955/72), inventory, marriage (1839-61), WPA.

ISGSQ ARTICLES: 2:9, 24:46, 22:76, 22:167.

COUNTY INVENTORY: birth (1878-), circuit court (1837-), county court (1850-62, 1872-), county commissioners (1839-83), county supervisors (1880-), death (1878-), deed (1839-), estray (1839-90), entry (1839-), guardian (1858), insanity (1874-), marriage (1839-), naturalization (1857-90), physicians (1877-), probate (1839-), survey (1837-), tax (1847, 1853-), will (1849-).

LIBRARY: Mt. Sterling Public Library, 143 West Main St., Mt. Sterling, IL 62353.

GENEALOGICAL SOCIETY: Versailles Area Genealogical and Historical Society, PO Box 92, Versailles, IL 6237; Schuyler-Brown Genealogical Society, 200 South Congress, Rushville, IL 62681.

7. Bureau County

Bureau County, formed 1837 from Putnam County, County Seat Princeton (PO Box 366, 61356).

CENSUSES: 1840RP, 1850RFMD, 1855S, 1860RFMD, 1865S, 1870RFM, 1880RFMD, 1900R, 1910R, 1920R.

FHL(FHC) RECORDS: atlas (1876), biography (1877/85/96, 1906), birth (1864-1915), cemetery, Civil War (1861-65), county directory (1858), DAR, genealogical compilations, history (1860/72/77/85, 1906), naturalization (1837-1908), newspaper abstract (1858-77), tax (1877).

IRAD-NIU RECORDS: Civil War (1861-65), naturalization (1837-1923).

ILLINET PUBLISHED RECORDS: atlas (1875, 1905/16), biography (1867/85/96, 1906), cemetery, county directory (1858-9, 1916), DAR, death (1858-77), early marriage, Evangelical Lutheran (1849-1979), history (1857/60/67/72/85, 1906/07/28/54/78). map (1867/75), marriage (1858-77), plat (1900/16), tax (1877), voter (1877).

ISGSQ ARTICLES: 6:13, 10:196, 13:99, 13:203.

COUNTY INVENTORY: birth (1878-), cemetery, circuit court (1837-), Civil War bounty (1864-66), Civil War soldier (1861-65), coroner (1840-), county court (1872-), county commissioners (1837-50), county supervisor (1850-), death (1878-), deed (1837-), estray (1837-), guardian (1858-), insanity (1873-), jury (1872-), marks and brands (1837-1903), marriage (1837-), mortgage (1837-), naturalization (1848-1906), original land entry (1837-), physicians (1877-), plat (1864-), poll (1848-72), probate (1837-), road (1837-52), survey (1839-1908), tax (1838-39, 1844-), will (1837-).

LIBRARY: Matson Public Library, 15 Park Avenue West, Princeton, IL 61356.

GENEALOGICAL SOCIETY: Bureau County Genealogical Society, PO Box 402, Princeton, IL 61356.

GENEALOGICAL PUBLICATION: Above society publishes Bureau County Genealogical Society Newsletter.

8. Calhoun County

Calhoun County, formed 1825 from Pike County, County Seat Hardin (PO Box 187, 62047).

CENSUSES: 1830R, 1840RSP, 1850RFMD, 1855S, 1860RFMD, 1865S, 1870RFM, 1880RFMD, 1900R, 1910R, 1920R.

FHL(FHC) RECORDS: biography (1891), birth (1878-1904), cemetery, circuit court (1825-50), Civil War (1861-65), coroner (1893-1915), death (1878-1903), deed (1825-1926), earmarks (1825-86), estray (1827-94), Evangelical Lutheran (1861-76), genealogical compilations, history (1934), marriage (1825-1982), naturalization (1849-1926), original land entry (1825-50), probate (1829-1916), survey (1847-50), tax (1846), will (1829-1916).

IRAD-WIU RECORDS: circuit court (1825-50), coroner (1893-1915), estray (1827-94), naturalization (1849-1926), original land entry (1825-50), probate (1834-43), survey (1847-52), tax (1846).

ILLINET PUBLISHED RECORDS: atlas (1900), biography (1891, 1967), cemetery, Civil War (1862-65), history (1930/33/39/67/75/81), newspaper, obituary (1875-99), undertaker (1878-1988).

ISGSQ ARTICLES: 22:168, 24:33.

COUNTY INVENTORY: birth (1877-), circuit court (1825-), county court (1872-), county commissioners (1825-), death (1878-), deed (1825-), earmarks (1825-86), estray (1827-94), guardian (1877-), inquest (1876-1910), insanity (1877-), juror (1895-), marriage (1825-), mortgage (1866-), naturalization (1866-1906), physicians (1877-), plat (1877-), probate (1848-), tax (1846, 1851-), will (1870-).

LIBRARY: South County Public Library District, PO Box 93, Brussels, IL 62013.

GENEALOGICAL SOCIETY: Calhoun/Pike Genealogical Society, PO Box 104, Pleasant Hill, IL 62366.

9. Carroll County

Carroll County, formed 1839 from Jo Daviess County, County Seat Mt. Carroll (PO Box 152, 61053).

CENSUSES: 1840RP, 1850RFMD, 1855S, 1860RFMD, 1865S, 1870RFM, 1880RFMD, 1900R, 1910R, 1920R.

FHL(FHC) RECORDS: biography (1878/89, 1913), cemetery, history (1878, 1930), inventory (1937), newspaper abstracts (1890-1907), Presbyterian (1854-58), WPA.

IRAD-NIU RECORDS: birth (1872-1942), coroner (1872-1906), court (1847-61), death (1877-1963), deed (1839-1968), estray (1865-1911), marriage (1839-1964), military (1861-66), naturalization (1869-1906), probate (1839-1967), tax (1840-61), will (1865-1967).

ILLINET PUBLISHED RECORDS: atlas (1900/08), biography (1878/89, 1913/75), cemetery, history (1878, 1913/56/68), inventory, map (1869), newspaper, plat (1893), WPA.

ISGSQ ARTICLES: 2:139, 3:5, 9:33, 12:225, 21:136, 22:168.

COUNTY INVENTORY: birth (1877-), board of supervisors (1849-), circuit court (1840-), coroner (1885-1905), county court (1872-), county commissioners (1839-48), death (1877-), deed (1837-), estray (1862-), guardian (1860-), insanity (1867-), jurors (1868-), marriage (1839-), militia (1861-62), mortgage (1854-), naturalization (1858-1906), original land entry (1840-), physicians (1877-), plat (1868-), probate (1839-), survey (1842-), tax (1849-), will (1865-).

LIBRARY: Mt. Carroll Township Public Library, 208 North Main St., Mt. Carroll, IL 61053.

GENEALOGICAL SOCIETY: Carroll County Genealogical Society, Savanna Public Library, 326 Third St., Savanna, IL 61074.

GENEALOGICAL PUBLICATION: Above society publishes Carroll County Genealogical Society Newsletter.

10. Cass County

Cass County, formed 1837 from Morgan County, County Seat Virginia (62691).

CENSUSES: 1840RP, 1850RFMD, 1855S, 1860RFMD, 1865S, 1870RFM, 1880RFMD, 1900R, 1910R, 1920R.

FHL(FHC) RECORDS: atlas (1840/65/99), Baptist (1831-1916), biography (1892, 1907/15), birth (1860-1915), cemetery, death (1878-1915), deed (1837-1940), Evangelical Lutheran (1893-1963), genealogical compilations, history (1915), jail (1872-1955), land (1823-1907), marriage (1837-1915), military (1861-1912), naturalization (1837-1921), poor (1887-1945), tax (1850-51), veterans' burial.

IRAD-SSU RECORDS: naturalization (1837-1921), poor (1887-1945), tax (1842, 1850-51), voter (1894-1912).

ILLINET PUBLISHED RECORDS: atlas (1840/74/99, 1900), Baptist, biography (1892, 1907/15/67), cemetery, genealogical compilations, history (1882, 1907/15/25/55/68), inventory, map (1856), marriage (1827-79), Presbyterian, tax (1836), WPA.

ISGSQ ARTICLES: 3:6, 4:94, 8:125, 8:220, 9:88, 19:215, 22:169.

COUNTY INVENTORY: birth (1871, 1878-), circuit court (1837-), county court (1872-), county commissioners and supervisors (1837-), death (1871, 1878-), deed (1837-), estray (1869-1905), guardian (1844-49, 1867-), insanity (1877-), land entry (1861-), marriage (1837-), military discharge (1865-), mortgage (1837-), naturalization (1859-94), physicians (1878-), probate (1837-), survey (1884-), tax (1845-), will (1867-).

LIBRARY: Virginia Memorial Publlic Library, 100 North Main St., Virginia, IL 62691.

HISTORICAL SOCIETY: Cass County Historical Society, PO Box 11, Virginia, IL 62691. Has a genealogy group.

HISTORICAL PUBLICATION: Above society publishes Cass County Historian, also Newsletter.

11. Champaign County

Champaign County, formed 1833 from Vermilion County, County Seat Urbana (204 East Elm St., 61801).

CENSUSES: 1840RSP, 1850RFMD, 1855S, 1860RFMD, 1865S, 1870RFM, 1880RFMD, 1900R, 1910R, 1920R.

FHL(FHC) RECORDS: atlas (1893), Baptist (1872-1945), Bible, biography (1886/87, 1900/05), birth (1878-1901), cemetery, county directory (1870-1), court (1833-72), death (1878-1915), deed (1833-1912), early settler, Evangelical Lutheran (1865-1943), genealogical compilations, history (1886, 1905/84/86), inventory (1938), landowner (1893), Lutheran (1882-1982), marriage (1833-1932), Methodist (1836-1970), military (1861-65), mortgage (1887-1902), naturalization (1858-1906), newspapers, newspaper abstracts, Presbyterian (1850-1943), probate (1833-1921), Quaker (1799-1909), United Church of Christ (1853-1978), will, WPA.

IRAD-ISU RECORDS: Civil War burial, death (1878-1949), deed (1833-1912), marriage (1833-1973), naturalization (1858-1906), probate (1833-1976), will (1864-1953).

ILLINET PUBLISHED RECORDS: atlas (1893, 1900/13), Baptist (1839-1989), Bible, biography (1878/86/87, 1900/05/18/83/95), cemetery, Christian Church (1878), Civil War, Congregational (1868-1938), county commissioners (1833-67), county supervisors (1868-1942), directory (1871, 1900), early settler (1815-60), Evangelical (1865-1943), Evangelical Lutheran (1874-1928), genealogical compilations, history (1871/76/78/86, 1905/18/60/63/84), internal revenue assessment (1862-66), inventory, landowner (1893), marriage, Mennonite (1889-1989), Methodist, microfilm birth (1878-1900), microfilm death (1878-1949), microfilm deed (1833-1927), microfilm marriage (1833-1932), microfilm probate (1833-1977), microfilm will (1851-1921), mortuary (1887-1902), newspapers, obituary, pioneer, plat (1893), Unitarian-Universalist (1859-1959), United Brethren, WPA.

ISGSQ ARTICLES: 1(4):4, 3:149, 6:148, 8:189, 9:69, 10:201, 11:41, 11:73, 18:220, 18:221, 19:16, 19:85, 19:29, 23:33, 23:99, 23:140, 25:33.

COUNTY INVENTORY: birth (1878-), board of supervisors (1860-), circuit court (1833-), Civil War bounty, county court (1872-), county commissioners (1833-60), death (1878-), deed (1833-), estray (1833-), guardian (1834-), indenture (1840-84), insanity (1864-), jury (1872-), marriage (1833-), military discharge (1861-65), militia (1861-62), mortgage (1836-), naturalization (1859-1906), original land entry (1833-), plat (1872-), probate (1833-), tax (1860-), will (1832-).

LIBRARY: Urbana Free Library, 201 South Race St., Urbana, IL 61801; University of IL Library, 1408 West Gregory Drive, Urbana, IL 61801.

GENEALOGICAL SOCIETY: Champaign County Genealogical Society, 201 South Race St., Urbana, IL 61801.

GENEALOGICAL PUBLICATION: Above society publishes Champaign County Genealogical Society Quarterly, also Newsletter.

12. Christian County

Christian County, formed 1839 from Sangamon and Montgomery Counties, created as Dane County but name was changed in 1840, County Seat Taylorville (PO Box 190, 62568).

CENSUSES: 1840RP, 1850RFMD, 1855S, 1860RFMD, 1865S, 1870RFM, 1880RFMD, 1900R, 1910R, 1920R.

FHL(FHC) RECORDS: biography (1880/93, 1904/18), birth (1877-1916), cemetery, DAR, death (1878-1917), deed (1839-1914), history (1880, 1904/18), land patent (1828-47), marriage (1839-1924), Methodist (1833-1954), military (1861-65), naturalization (1839-1906), Presbyterian, probate (1839-1919), plat (1891), will (1849-1919).

IRAD-SSU RECORDS: coroner (1870-1934), deed (1839-1968), jail (1868-1979), survey (1853-1962).

ILLINET PUBLISHED RECORDS: atlas (1869/91, 1900/11), biography (1880/93, 1904/18/68), cemetery, history (1880/93, 1904/18/68), map (1872/91/93, 1902/11), marriage (1839-66).

ISGSQ ARTICLES: 3:80, 10:88, 10:126, 13:203, 13:204, 22:28, 22:77, 24:2.

COUNTY INVENTORY: birth (1878-), circuit court (1839-), coroner (1874-94), county court (1872-), county commissioners and supervisors (1839-), death (1878-), deed (1839-), estray (1839-66), guardian (1852-), insanity (1870-), marriage (1839-), mortgage (1865-), naturalization (1857-1906), original land entry (1836-50), physicians (1877-), probate (1839-), survey (1852-69), tax (1849-), will (1849-).

LIBRARY: Taylorville Public Library, 121 West Vine St., Taylorville, IL 62568.

GENEALOGICAL SOCIETY: Christian County Genealogical Society, PO Box 174, Taylorville, IL 62568.

GENEALOGICAL PUBLICATION: Above society publishes Christian County Genealogical Quarterly, also Newsletter.

13. Clark County

Clark County, formed 1819 from Crawford County, County Seat Marshall (62441). Court house fire in 1902, some records lost.

CENSUSES: 1820RS, 1830R, 1840RSP, 1850RFMD, 1855S, 1860RFMD, 1865S, 1870-RFM, 1880RFMD, 1900R, 1910R, 1920R.

FHL(FHC) RECORDS: Baptist (1832-1944), Bible, biography (1907), birth (1877-1913), cemetery, DAR, death (1877-1911), deed (1816-1933), genealogical compilations, history (1883, 1907/78/81), inventory (1938), land grant, marriage (1825-1926), probate (1840-1976), veterans' burial, will (1840-1976), WPA.

IRAD-EIU RECORDS: nothing before 1936.

ILLINET PUBLISHED RECORDS: atlas (1900), biography (1883, 1907/81), birth, cemetery, history (1883, 1907/67/78/80/81), inventory, land grant, marriage (1819-99), mortuary, newspaper abstract (1861-77, 1894-1908), obituary (pre-1968), plat (1892, 1900), probate, WPA.

ISGSQ ARTICLES: 25:5, 25:33.

COUNTY INVENTORY: birth (1865-67, 1878-), board of supervisors (1853-), circuit court (1824-), county court (1872-), county commissioners (1833-53), death (1865-67, 1877-), deed (1818-), ear marks (1819-61), estray (1857-91), guardian (1820-), insanity (1893-), jury (1872-), land entry (1853-), marriage (1819-), militia (1861-62), mortgage (1848-), physicians (1877-), plat (1886-), probate (1820-), survey (1830-55, 1893-), tax (1901-), will (1859-).

LIBRARY: Marshall Public Library, 612 Archer ave., Marshall, IL 62441.

GENEALOGICAL SOCIETY: Clark County Genealogical Society, 309 Maple St., Marshall, IL 62441.

GENEALOGICAL PUBLICATION: Above society publishes Clark County Genealogical Society Newsletter.

14. Clay County

Clay County, formed 1824 from Wayne, Lawrence, Crawford, and Fayette Counties, County Seat Louisville (PO Box 160, 62858).

CENSUSES: 1830R, 1840RSP, 1850RFMD, 1855S, 1860RFMD, 1865S, 1870RFM, 1880-RFMD, 1900R, 1910R, 1920R.

FHL(FHC) RECORDS: biography (1884, 1909), birth (1862-1918), cemetery, Christian Church (1893-1985), commissioner's court (1825-41), death (1877-1918), deed (1825-1911), history (1884, 1909), marriage (1858-1919), military (1861-1910), naturalization (1868-1927), newspaper abstract, obituary, probate (1837-1925).

IRAD-EIU RECORDS: birth (1877-1918), death (1877-1915), deed (1825-1911), marriage (1825-45, 1858-1919), naturalization (1868-1927), probate (1837-1925), will (1865-1025).

ILLINET PUBLISHED RECORDS: atlas (1881), biography (1884, 1909), birth, cemetery, Civil War, death, history (1884, 1969), marriage (1825-95), newspaper abstracts, plat (1900), residents (1884).

ISGSQ ARTICLES: 3:75, 3:81, 4:71, 6:33, 11:204, 14:68, 15:179, 16:162, 21:232, 23:3, 25:33.

COUNTY INVENTORY: birth (1878-), circuit court (1825-), county court (1872-), county commissioners and supervisors (1825-), death (1877-), deed (1825-), estray (1835-1900), guardian (1864-), insanity (1893-), jury (1873-1910), marks and brands (1848-67), marriage (1825-), naturalization (1867-1910), original land entry (1825-), physicians (1878-), plat (1873-), probate (1837-), soldiers' discharge (1865-98), tax (1854-), will (1867-).

LIBRARY: Flora-Carnegie Library, 129 East North Ave., Flora, IL 62839; Cumberland Trail Library System, 12th and McCawley, Flora, IL 62839.

GENEALOGICAL SOCIETY: Clay County Genealogical Society, PO Box 94, Louisville, IL 62858.

GENEALOGICAL PUBLICATION: Above society publishes Clay Roots.

15. Clinton County

Clinton County, formed 1824 from Washington, Bond, and Fayette Counties, County Seat Carlyle (62231).

CENSUSES: 1830R, 1840RSP, 1850-RFMD, 1855S, 1860RFMD, 1865S, 1870RFM, 1880RFMD, 1900R, 1910R, 1920R.

FHL(FHC) RECORDS: biography (1881/94), birth (1877-1915), cemetery, death (1877-1915), deed (1818-1915), German immigrant, history (1881), land entry (1818-1920), marriage (1825-1937), naturalization (1857-1904), newspaper abstract, probate (1825-99), United Church of Christ (1859-1981), will (1857-1928).

IRAD-SIU RECORDS: birth (1877-1915), death (1877-1915), deed (1818-1920), marriage (1825-1937), land entry (1816-90), naturalization (1857-96), probate (1825-1969).

ILLINET PUBLISHED RECORDS: atlas (1900/13), biography (1881/94), cemetery, death (1877-1903), Freemasons, history (1881, 1913), marriage (1825-73), Odd Fellows, plat (1892).

ISGSQ ARTICLES: 6:76, 6:183, 7:140, 9:207, 13:44, 22:28, 22:77, 23:168, 24:2.

COUNTY INVENTORY: birth (1877-), board of supervisors (1874-), circuit court (1825-), coroner (1870-1900), county court (1872-), county commissioners (1825-74), death (1877-), deed (1825-), entry (1818-), estray (1831-38, 1857-82), guardian (1857-), insanity (1894-), jury (1872-), marriage (1825-), mortgage (1858-), naturalization (1858-1906), original land entry (1815-65), physicians (1877-), plat (1874-), probate (1825-), soldiers' discharge (1866-80), survey (1829-36, 1872-), tax (1842, 1848-), will (1850-).

LIBRARY: Case-Halstead Public Library, 571 Franklin St., Carlyle, IL 62231.

HISTORICAL SOCIETY: Clinton County Historical Society, 1091 Franklin St., Carlyle, IL 62231.

HISTORICAL PUBLICATION: Above society publishes Clinton County Historical Society Quarterly and Clinton County Museum Newsletter.

16. Coles County

Coles County, formed 1830 from Clark and Edgar Counties, County Seat Charleston (PO Box 207, 61920).

CENSUSES: 1840RSP, 1850RFMD, 1855S, 1860RFMD, 1865S, 1870RFM, 1880RFMD, 1900R, 1910R, 1920R.

FHL(FHC) RECORDS: atlas (1913), Baptist (1844-1905), biography (1879/87, 1906), birth (1878-1915), cemetery, Church of Christ (1886-1920), deed (1830-1919), genealogical compilations, history (1879, 1906/76), marriage (1830-1929), naturalization (1872-1946), plat (1892), will (1844-1925).

IRAD-EIU RECORDS: naturalization (1872-1946), tax (1880-1967).

ILLINET PUBLISHED RECORDS: assessor (1866), atlas (1900/13), biography (1879/87, 1906/76), birth, cemetery, Church of Christ, city directory (1898), Civil War burial, DAR, death, early marriage, genealogical compilationss, history (1879, 1906/65/76), internal revenue assessments (1862-66), marriage (1830-1929), Masons, mortality schedules (1850/60), newspaper, obituary, pioneers, plat (1893), Swedenborgians (1881-91), will (1844-80).

ISGSQ ARTICLES: 7:90, 21:3.

COUNTY INVENTORY: birth (1877-), board of supervisors (1870-), circuit court (1831-), county court (1873-), county commissioners (1832-69), death (1878-), deed (1831-), entry (1877-), estray (1831-1907), guardian (1875-), insanity (1859-1913), jury (1875-79, 1887-93, 1900-), marks and brands (1831-89), marriage (1831-), mortgage (1851-), naturalization (1850-98), physicians (1877-), plat (1836-58), probate (1832-), soldiers' discharge (1865-89), survey (1835-38, 1852-54), tax (1839-94), will (1843-).

LIBRARY: IRAD-EIU; Charleston Public Library, 712 Sixth St., Charleston, IL 61920.

GENEALOGICAL SOCIETY: Coles County, IL, Genealogical Society, PO Box 592, Charleston, IL 61920.

GENEALOGICAL PUBLICATION: Above society publishes Among the Coles.

17. Crawford County

Crawford County, formed 1816 from Edwards County, County Seat Robinson (PO Box 602, 62454).

CENSUSES: 1818T, 1820RS, 1830R, 1840RSP, 1850RFMD, 1855S, 1860RFMD, 1865S, 1870RFM, 1880RFMD, 1900R, 1910R, 1920R.

FHL(FHC) RECORDS: biography (1909), birth (1878-1981), cemetery, Christian Church (1847-83), circuit court (1817-1958), death (1877-1981-90), deed (1816-1939), genealogical compilations, history (1883, 1909), marriage (1817-1911), newspaper abstract, probate (1845-1923), Quaker (1818-1968), will (1818-1923).

IRAD-EIU RECORDS: birth (1877-1957), circuit court (1817-1958), death (1877-1958), deed (1817-1958), marriage (1817-1934), plat (1882-1957), probate (1844-1958), survey (1850-1933), swamp (1852-67), tax (1817-55), will (1818-1956).

ILLINET PUBLISHED RECORDS: atlas (1900), biography (1883, 1909/80), cemetery, DAR, genealogical compilations, history (1883, 1909/61/80/85) marriage (1817-73), newspaper abstracts, soldiers, will (1818-50).

ISGSQ ARTICLES: 3:9, 4:92, 7:46.

COUNTY INVENTORY: birth (1878-), board of supervisors (1868-), circuit court (1817-), county court (1872-), county commissioners (1817-67), death (1878-), deed (1816-), guardian (1848-), insanity (1886-93), jury (1872-), marriage (1817-), mortgage (1852-), physicians (1877-), plat (1882-), probate (1821-), survey (1862-), tax (1827-29, 1844-), will (1815-).

LIBRARY: Robinson Public Library District, 606 North Jefferson St., Robinson, IL 62454.

GENEALOGICAL SOCIETY: Crawford County Genealogical Society, 803 North Madison, Robinson, IL 62454.

GENEALOGICAL PUBLICATION: Above society publishes The Crawford County Genealogical Society Newsletter.

18. Cumberland County

Cumberland County, formed 1843 from Coles County, County Seat Toledo (PO Box 146, 62468), most records lost in an 1885 fire.

CENSUSES: 1850RFMD, 1855S, 1860RFMD, 1865S, 1870RFM, 1880RFMD, 1900R, 1910R, 1920R.

FHL(FHC) RECORDS: cemetery, history (1884, 1968/93), inventory, marriage (1878-88), mortgage (1882-87), Presbyterian (1889-1906), WPA.

IRAD-EIU RECORDS: justice of the peace (1857-1955), survey (1880-81).

ILLINET PUBLISHED RECORDS: atlas (1900), biography (1884, 1992), birth, cemetery, Evangelical United Brethren, history (1884, 1968/76/92), inventory, marriage (1885-93), Methodist, mortuary (1882-1929), obituary, original land entry (before 1841), residents (1884), WPA.

ISGSQ ARTICLES: 2:6, 6:154, 9:153.

COUNTY INVENTORY: birth (1885-), board of supervisors (1885-), circuit court (1885-), county court (1885-), death (1885-), deed (1885-), entry (1885-), estray (1887-), guardian (1885-), insanity (1885-), marriage (1885-), mortgage (1885-), naturalization (1892-), physicians (1884-), probate (1885-), survey (1884-), tax (1886-), will (1885-).

LIBRARY: Sumpter Township Library, Courthuse Square, Toledo, IL 62468.

GENEALOGICAL SOCIETY: Genealogical Society of Cumberland and Coles Counties, 1816 Walnut, Mattoon, IL 61938; Cumberland County Historical and Genealogical Society of IL, PO Box 393, Greenup, IL 62428.

GENEALOGICAL PUBLICATION: Second society above publishes The Happy Hunter.

19. DeKalb County

DeKalb County, formed 1837 from Kane County, County Seat Sycamore (110 East Sycamore St., 60178).

CENSUSES: 1840RP, 1850RFMD, 1855S, 1860RFMD, 1865S, 1870RFM, 1880-RFMD, 1900R, 1910R, 1920R.

FHL(FHC) RECORDS: atlas (1871/92, 1905/29), biography (1876/85/98, 1907), birth (1837-1903), Catholic (1865-1900), cemetery,

Congregational (1853-1953), death (1878-1903), history (1868/76/85, 1907), marriage (1837-77), naturalization (1860-1908), newspaper abstract, Presbyterian, tax (1840).

IRAD-NIU RECORDS: circuit court (1858-88), deed (1838-1930), entry (1847-1950), jail (1869-1951), jury (1858-86), justice of peace ((1869-1950), mortgage (1847-1946), tax (1860-1957).

ILLINET PUBLISHED RECORDS: atlas (1871, 1905), biography (1876/85/98/99, 1900/07), birth (1837-1903), cemetery, death (1878-1903), directory (1854-5/76), history (1868/76/85/99, 1907/63/72/86/87), map (1860/68/69), marriage (1837-70), naturalization, plat (1892, 1905), settlers, Swedish Evangelical Lutheran.

ISGSQ ARTICLES: 6:162, 22:270, 24:201.

COUNTY INVENTORY: birth (1877-), board of supervisors (1849-), circuit court (1838-), county court (1863-), county commissioners (1837-49), death (1878-), deed (1838-), entry (1847-), estray (1848-95), guardian (1871-), insanity (1893-), jury (1866-), marriage (1837-), militia (1861-63), mortgage (1847-), naturalization (1853-1906), original land entry (1840-55), physicians (1877-), plat (1859-), probate (1839-), soldiers' discharge (1864-1910), tax (1851-), will (1862-).

LIBRARY: DeKalb Public Library, 309 Oak St., DeKalb, IL 60115.

GENEALOGICAL SOCIETY: DeKalb County Historical-Genealogical Society, PO Box 295, Sycamore, IL 60178.

GENEALOGICAL PUBLICATION: Above society publishes The Cornsilk of DeKalb County, IL.

20. DeWitt County

DeWitt County, formed 1839 from McLean and Macon Counties, County Seat Clinton (201 West Washington St., 61727).

CENSUSES: 1840RP, 1850RFMD, 1855S, 1860RFMD, 1865S, 1870RFM, 1880-RFMD, 1900R, 1910R, 1920R.

FHL(FHC) RECORDS: atlas (1875), biography (1882/91, 1901/10), birth (1871-1930), cemetery, Christian Church (1873-1961), death (1878-1979), deed (1868-1913), history (1910), inventory, land owner (1875/94), marriage (1839-1928), Methodist (1877-1926), naturalization (1863-98), Presbyterian (1837-1926), probate (1862-1923), Universalist (1895-1968), will (1850-98), WPA.

IRAD-ISU RECORDS: birth (1877-1959), death (1878-1959), deed (1839-75), marriage (1839-1955), survey (1846-67), tax (1845-51).

ILLINET PUBLISHED RECORDS: atlas (1875, 1915), biography (1882/91, 1901/10/85), cemetery, DAR, history (1882, 1910/55/85), internal revenue assessment (1862-66), inventory (1941), map, marriage, mortuary, probate (1839-1950), plat (1891/94), settlement pattern, WPA.

ISGSQ ARTICLES: 5:123, 10:100, 16:53, 21:214, 21:231.

COUNTY INVENTORY: birth (1878-), board of supervisors (1859-), circuit court (1839-), county court (1872-), county commissioners (1839-59), death (1878-), deed (1839-), entry (1839-), estray (1872-96), guardian (1866-), insanity (1886-), jury (1872-), marriage (1839-), militia (1861-62), mortgage (1854-), naturalization (1854-1906), original land entry (1829-43), physicians (1877-), plat (1871-), probate (1839-), tax (1839-), will (1850-).

LIBRARY: Vespasian Warner Public Library District, 120 West Johnson St., Clinton, IL 61727.

GENEALOGICAL SOCIETY: DeWitt County Genealogical Society, PO Box 632, Clinton, IL 61727.

GENEALOGICAL PUBLICATION: Above society publishes The DeWitt County Genealogical Quarterly. Also Newsletter.

21. Douglas County

Douglas County, formed 1859 from Coles County, County Seat Tuscola (401 South Center St., 61953).

CENSUSES: 1860RFMD, 1865S, 1870RFM, 1880RFMD, 1900R, 1910R, 1920R.

FHL(FHC) RECORDS: atlas (1875/93, 1914), Baptist (1870-1941), biography (1884, 1900/10), birth (1859-1918), cemetery, Christian Church (1863-1963), deed (1839-1910, divorce (1825-1935), Evangelical and Reformed (1858-1968), history (1876/84, 1900/10), inventory, Lutheran (1870-1972), marriage (1857-1911), Methodist (1872-1980), military discharge (1865-90, 1919-50), naturalization (1860-1906), newspaper abstract (1880-1980), plat (1893), Presbyterian (1861-1975), probate (1869-1927), United Church (1870-1980), will (1869-1927), WPA.

IRAD-EIU RECORDS: jail (1872-1970), military discharge (1865-94).

ILLINET PUBLISHED RECORDS: atlas (1875, 1900/14), biography (1884, 1900/10/83), cemetery, DAR, history (1876/84, 1910), inventory (1939), marriage (1859-79), Methodist (1877-1900), naturalization, obituary, plat (1893), probate (1859-1963), Zion Evangelical (1862-1984), WPA.

ISGSQ ARTICLES: 3:8, 11:17, 15:267.

COUNTY INVENTORY: birth (1878-), board of supervisors (1859-), circuit court (1859-), coroner (1870-73, 1907-08), county court (1872-), death (1877-), deed (1859-), entry (1874-1912), estray (1859-), guardian (1859-), insanity (1883-), jury (1872-), marriage (1859-), mortgage (1871-), naturalization (1860-1904), physicians (1877-), probate (1859-), soldiers' discharge (1865-94), survey (1865-70), tax (1859-), will (1865-).

LIBRARY: Tuscola Public Library, 112 East Sale St., Tuscola, IL 61953.

GENEALOGICAL SOCIETY: Douglas County Genealogical Society, PO Box 113, Tuscola, IL 61953.

GENEALOGICAL PUBLICATION: Above society publishes Douglas Trails and Traces.

22. DuPage County

DuPage County, formed 1839 from Cook County, County Seat Wheaton (421 North County Farm Rd., 60189).

CENSUSES: 1840RP, 1850RFMD, 1855S, 1860RFMD, 1865S, 1870RFM, 1880-RFMD, 1900R, 1910R, 1920R.

FHL(FHC) RECORDS: atlas (1874), biography (1882/94, 1989), cemetery, genealogical compilations, history (1857/74/77/82, 1913/89), land owner (1835-1904), Lutheran (1837-1988), marriage (1839-1906), Presbyterian.

IRAD-NIU RECORDS: none.

ILLINET PUBLISHED RECORDS: atlas (1874, 1904), Bible, biography (1874/82/94, 1913), birth, cemetery, DAR, death, directory (1915-6), genealogical compilations, guidebook, history (1857/74/77/82/89/-93, 1913/76/85), original land entry, land owner (1835-1904), map (1851/70), marriage (1839-1906), newspaper, pioneer map, probate (1839-1900), Zion Evangelical Lutheran (1837-1988).

ISGSQ ARTICLES: 10:203, 12:193, 14:94, 17:8, 19:203, 21:99, 25:96.

COUNTY INVENTORY: birth (1878-), board of supervisors (1850-), circuit court (1839-), county court (1872-), county commissioners (1839-49), death (1878-), deed (1839-), entry (1839-), guardian (1859-), insanity (1871-), marriage (1839-), mortgage (1848-), naturalization (1861-1906), original land entry (1835-58), physicians (1877-), plat (1848-), probate (1839-), tax (1847-), will (1868-).

LIBRARY: Wheaton Public Library, 225 North Cross St., Wheaton, IL 60187.

GENEALOGICAL SOCIETY: DuPage County Genealogical Society, PO Box 133, Lombard, IL 60148; Fox Valley Genealogical Society, 705 North Brainard St., Naperville, IL 60563.

GENEALOGICAL PUBLICATION: First society above publishes The Review of the DuPage County Genealogical Society. Second society above publishes Fox Tales.

23. Edgar County

Edgar County, formed 1823 from Clark County, County Seat Paris (61944).

CENSUSES: 1830R, 1840RSP, 1850-RFMD, 1855S, 1860RFMD, 1865S, 1870RFM, 1880RFMD, 1900R, 1910R, 1920R.

FHL(FHC) RECORDS: atlas (1870/94, 1910), birth (1877-1908), cemetery, Civil War (1861-65), death (1877-1925), deed (1824-1920), genealogical compilations, history (1879, 1976), marriage (1823-1904), mortgage (1892-1902), naturalization (1872-1908), plat (1894), Presbyterian (1824-1925), probate (1823-1963), Quaker (1895-1956), will (1823-1963).

IRAD-EIU RECORDS: deed (1823-1919), marriage (1855), tax (1823-38).

ILLINET PUBLISHED RECORDS: Afro-American, atlas (1900/10), Bible, biography (1879/89/92, 1905), board of supervisors (1857-59), cemetery, Civil War soldiers, county commissioner (1823-49), DAR, death (1877-1925), genealogical compilations, history (1879/92, 1905/50/63/76), internal revenue assessment (1862-66), map (1870), marriage (1823-69, 1874-77, 1892-1957), military discharge, mortuary, newspaper abstract, obituary, plat (1894, 1910), probate (1823-1963).

ISGSQ ARTICLES: 2:209, 15:265, 25:71, 25:95.

COUNTY INVENTORY: birth (1877-), board of supervisors (1857-), circuit court (1823-), county court (1872-), county commissioners (1823-57), death (1877-), deed (1823-), ear marks (1823-86), entry (1875-), guardian (1858-), insanity (1886-), jury (1872-), marriage (1823-), mortgage (1854-), naturalization (1859-1906), original land entry (1816-55), physicians (1879-), plat (1880-), probate (1823-), soldiers' discharge (1865-84), tax (1831, 1840-), will (1829-).

LIBRARY: Edgar County Genealogy Library, 408 North Main St., Paris, IL 61944.

GENEALOGICAL SOCIETY: Edgar County Genealogical Society, PO Box 304,, Paris, IL 61944.

GENEALOGICAL PUBLICATION: Above society publishes The Edgar County Genealogical Society Newsletter.

24. Edwards County

Edwards County, formed 1814 from Madison and Gallatin Counties, County Seat Albion (62806).

CENSUSES: 1820R, 1825S, 1830R, 1840RP, 1850RFMD, 1855S, 1860RFMD, 1865S, 1870RFM, 1880RFMD, 1900R, 1910R, 1920R.

FHL(FHC) RECORDS: alien (1817-22), biography (1883), cemetery, death (1877-1933), deed (1815-88), Episcopal (1841-1956), genealogical compilations, history (1883, 1950/64/80/93), land (1855-74), marriage (1815-1936), military discharge (1866-1963), naturalization (1819-1915), newspaper index (1869-1906), obituary, probate (1815-85), veterans' graves (1865-1961), voter (1816-91), will (1815-1922).

IRAD-EIU RECORDS: alien (1817-22), board of supervisors (1815-64), birth (1877-1933), death (1877-1933), deed (1815-1978), marriage (1815-1968), military discharge (1866-1967), naturalization (1819-1917), plat (1874), probate (1815-85), survey (1831-1925), will (1815-1916).

ILLINET PUBLISHED RECORDS: atlas (1907), Bible, biography (1883, 1907/80), cemetery, death (1877-1933, early settlers, history (1822/83, 1907/09/45/62/64/80), map (1817/66/90/91), marriage (1815-44), obituary, original land sales, plat (1900), school (1865, 1873-75, 1868-80, 1883/88).

ISGSQ ARTICLES: 25:150.

COUNTY INVENTORY: birth (1877-), census of county (1825/35/61/65), circuit court (1815-), coroner (1884-), county court (1872-), county commissioners (1815-32), death (1877-), deed (1815-), estray (1841-86), guardian (1845-49, 1873-), indenture (1831-74), insanity (1893-), jury (1832-), map (1831), marks and brands (1815-75), marriage (1815-), military bounty (1866-67), military discharge (1863-66), naturalization (1854-), original land entry (1815-55), physicians (1878-), probate (1817-), survey (1875-), tax (1815/19 /25, 1829-), will (1815-).

LIBRARY: Albion Public Library, 6 North Fourth St., Albion, IL 62806.

GENEALOGICAL SOCIETY: Edwards County Genealogical Society, 212 West Main St., Albion, IL 62806; Genealogical Society of Southern IL, John A. Logan College, Box 145, Route 2, Carterville, IL 62918.

GENEALOGICAL PUBLICATION: Second society above publishes Saga of Southern IL. Also Newsletter.

25. Effingham County

Effingham County, formed 1831 from Fayette and Crawford Counties, County Seat Effingham (101 North Fourth St., 62401).

CENSUSES: 1840RSP, 1850RFMD, 1855S, 1860RFMD, 1865S, 1870RFM, 1880RFMD, 1900R, 1910R, 1920R.

FHL(FHC) RECORDS: biography (1883/93, 1910/12), birth (1877-1916), cemetery, county directory (1895), death (1878-1915), deed (1833-1945), early settler, federal land grants (1836-99), genealogical compilations, history (1883, 1903/10/82), inventory, land (1829-95), Lutheran (1860-81), marriage (1833-1920), military (1831-32, 1846-48, 1861-66, 1898-99), naturalization (1859-92), newspaper abstract, probate (1836-1920), tax (1854-58, 1890), will (1836-1982), WPA.

IRAD-EIU RECORDS: birth (1877-1916), county court (1859-70), death (1878-1915), deed (1833-1936), estray (1839-51), marriage (1839-1920), mortgage (1854-1905), naturalization (1840-1905), physician (1877-1939), probate (1838-1964), tax (1829-1965), will (1838-1920).

ILLINET PUBLISHED RECORDS: atlas (1899, 1900), biography (1893, 1910/12/82/87), cemetery, DAR, directory (1895, 1900), genealogical compilations, history (1883, 1910/12/74/82/84), inventory (1940), marriage (1833-1910), mortuary (1900-22), original land sales (1830-1903), plat (1899), probate (1836-82), soldiers (1831-32, 1846-48, 1861-66, 1898-99), tax (1845-55, 1890), will (1836-82), WPA.

ISGSQ ARTICLES: 2:81.

COUNTY INVENTORY: birth (1878-), circuit court (1833-), coroner (1875-1907), county court (1872-), county commissioners and supervisors (1833-), death (1878-), deed (1833-), entry (1833-), estray (1862-91), guardian (1871-), insanity (1879-), jury (1852-1906), marks and brands (1840-68), marriage (1839-), militia (1861-62), naturalization (1860-1906), physicians (1877-), probate (1835-), survey (1859-85), tax (1854-), will (1839-).

LIBRARY: Helen Matthes Library, 100 Market St., Effingham, IL 62401.

GENEALOGICAL SOCIETY: Effingham County Genealogical Society, PO Box 1166, Effingham, Il 62401.

GENEALOGICAL PUBLICATION: Above society publishes Crossroad Trails. Also Newsletter.

26. Fayette County

Fayette County, formed 1821 from Bond, Wayne, Clark, Crawford, and Jefferson Counties, County Seat Vandalia (PO Box 401, 62471).

CENSUSES: 1830R, 1835S, 1840RP, 1850RFMD, 1855S, 1860RFMD, 1865S, 1870RFM, 1880RFMD, 1900R, 1910R, 1920R.

FHL(FHC) RECORDS: Baptist (1869-1911), biography (1878, 1904/10), birth (1893), cemetery, death (1893), deed (1825-86), guardian (1867-1934), history (1878, 1904/10), landowner (1847/91), marriage (1821-97), naturalization (1838-1906), Presbyterian (1857-84), probate (1821-84), will (1859-1922).

IRAD-SSU RECORDS: birth (1860-1925), circuit court (1821-61), death (1877-1925), deed (1821-1972), estray (1821-92), jury (1847-58), marks and brands (1827-91), marriage (1821-1964), probate (1858), tax (1816-1904).

ILLINET PUBLISHED RECORDS: biography (1878, 1910), cemetery, history (1878, 1910), inventory (1939), marriage (1821-97), plat (1891, 1900), tax (1847), WPA.

ISGSQ ARTICLES: 6:64, 10:100.

COUNTY INVENTORY: adoption (1882-), birth (1877-), board of supervisors (1859-), circuit court (1821-), county court (1872-), county commissioners (1839-49), county commissioners' court (1849-57), death (1877-), deed (1821-), guardian (1867-), insanity (1882-), indenture (1827-62), jury (1872-84), marriage (1821-), militia (1861-62), mortgage (1821-), naturalization (1866-1903), physicians (1877-), probate (1821-), road (1821-75), survey (1844-49, 1856-), tax (1830-35, 1853-), will (1861-).

LIBRARY: Evans Public Library, 215 South Fifth St., Vandalia, IL 62471.

GENEALOGICAL SOCIETY: Fayette County Genealogical and Historical Society, Evans Public Library, 215 South Fifth St., Vandalia, IL 62471.

GENEALOGICAL PUBLICATION: Above society publishes Fayette Facts.

27. Ford County

Ford County, formed 1859 from Vermilion County, County Seat Paxton (220 West State St., 60957).

CENSUSES: 1860RFMD, 1865S, 1870-RFM, 1880RFMD, 1900R, 1910R, 1920R.

FHL(FHC) RECORDS: atlas (1884, 1901), biography (1892, 1908), birth (1870-1909), cemetery, death (1878-1901), deed (1859-1904), genealogical compilations, guardian (1859-1953), history (1908), Lutheran, marriage (1859-1983), naturalization (1859-1906), Presbyterian (1867-1904), probate (1859-1929), will (1860-1942).

IRAD-ISU RECORDS: tax (1833-76).

ILLINET PUBLISHED RECORDS: atlas (1884, 1900/01), biography (1884/92, 1908), cemetery, history (1884/92, 1908/84), internal revenue assessment (1862-66), marriage (1959-1915).

ISGSQ ARTICLES: 2:76, 3:106, 5:177, 10:157, 11:17, 11:135, 13:202, 22:170.

COUNTY INVENTORY: birth (1878-), board of supervisors (1859-), circuit court (1859-), county court (1872-), county commissioners *1825-38), death (1878-), deed (1859-), entry (1859-), GAR, guardian (1859-), insanity (1883-), jury (1872-), marriage (1859-), mortgage (1859-), naturalization (1859-1906), physicians (1878-), plat (1859-), probate (1859-), survey (1875-), tax (1859-), will (1862-).

LIBRARY: Paxton Carnegie Library, 254 South Market St., 60957.

HISTORICAL SOCIETY: Ford County Historical Society, 243 West State St., Paxton, IL 60957.

GENEALOGICAL PUBLICATION: Above society publishes FCHS Newsletter.

28. Franklin County

Franklin County, formed 1818 from White, Johnson, and Gallatin Counties, County Seat Benton (62812). A fire in 1843 destroyed many records.

CENSUSES: 1818T, 1820RS, 1830R, 1840RSP, 1850RFMD, 1860RFMD, 1865S, 1870RFM, 1880RFMD, 1900R, 1910R, 1920R.

FHL(FHC) RECORDS: Baptist (1856-1914), biography (1887), birth (1861-1915), cemetery, death (1877-1915), deed (1819-1907), history (1887, 1920), inventory, marriage (1835-1916), Methodist (1854-1915), naturalization (1886-1909), original land entry (1814-20), probate (1848-1970), tax (1853), will (1835-1922), WPA.

IRAD-SIU RECORDS: birth (1861-1916), death (1877-1915), marriage (1835-1924), naturalization (1886-1912), probate (1837-1970), will (1835-1922).

ILLINET PUBLISHED RECORDS: biography (1877, 1920), birth, court, cemetery, divorce (1837-75), guardian (1846-49), history (1887, 1900/12/18/20/35/54/65), insanity (1869-79), inventory (1941), map (1875, 1900), marriage (1836-93), naturalization, obituary (1850-84), plat (1900), probate, tax (1853/65), WPA.

ISGSQ ARTICLES: 6:14, 6:177, 8:207, 10:29, 12:189.

COUNTY INVENTORY: birth (1877-), board of supervisors (1872-), circuit court (1837-), coroner (1879-), county court (1872-), county commissioners (1838-72), death (1877-), deed (1835-), estray (1857-1910), guardian (1849-93), indenture (1850-75), insanity (1879-), jury (1862-), marriage (1835-), militia (1861-62), mortgage (1862-), physicians (1877-), plat (1880-), probate (1837-), soldiers' discharge (1866-99), survey (1885-), tax (1851-), will (1860-).

LIBRARY: Benton Public Library, Benton, Benton IL 62812.

HISTORICAL SOCIETY: Franklin County Historical Society, 304 East Webster St., Benton, IL 62812.

GENEALOGICAL SOCIETY: Genealogical Society of Southern IL, John A. Logan College, Box 145, Route 2, Carterville, IL 62918.

GENEALOGICAL PUBLICATION: Above society publishes Saga of Southern IL. Also Newsletter.

29. Fulton County

Fulton County, formed 1823 from Pike County, County Seat Lewistown (100 North Main, 61542).

CENSUSES: 1825S, 1830R, 1835S, 1840RSP, 1850RFMD, 1855S, 1860RFMD, 1865S, 1870RFM, 1880RFMD, 1900R, 1910R, 1920R.

FHL(FHC) RECORDS: almshouse (1877-1908), atlas (1871/95), biography (1879/90, 1908/88), CJCLDS (1876-77), cemetery, chancery court (1824-1926), circuit court (1835-1926), county court (1859-1925), early settler, funeral (1832-1976), genealogical compilations, guardian (1824-1926), history (1879, 1908/69/73/88), marriage (1824-1911), military (1861-62), military discharge (1865-1914), mortgage (1851-81), mortuary (1885-1985), naturalization (1859-1954), newspaper abstract, obituary (1830-1982), Presbyterian (1866-1990), probate (1827-1931), town lots (1834-94), will (1821-1963).

IRAD-WIU RECORDS: almshouse (1877-1908), board of supervisors (1829-1948), circuit court (1835-1926), county court (1849-1917), deed (1817-60), estray (1843-70), insanity (1870-1934), militia (1861-62), military discharge (1862-65), naturalization (1835-1958), physician (1877-1921), poor (1887-1955), probate (1827-1963), tax (1839-1962), will (1828-1924).

ILLINET PUBLISHED RECORDS: atlas (1871/95, 1900), biography (1879/90, 1908/88), cemetery, gazetteer, history (1879/90, 1908/69/73/88), map (1851), marriage (1824-61), newspaper abstracts, obituary, plat (1895), will (1821-63).

ISGSQ ARTICLES: 1(4):4, 2:12, 2:153, 5:152, 6:102, 6:197, 13:60, 13:121, 14:76, 19:215, 22:75, 23:66, 24:132.

COUNTY INVENTORY: adoption (1895-), birth (1878-), board of supervisors (1849-), circuit court (1824-), county court (1872-), county commissioners (1823-49), death (1878-), deed (1821-), entry (1821-), estray (1849-70), guardian (1859-), insanity (1870-), marriage (1824-), militia (1861-63), naturalization (1859-1906), original land entry, physicians (1877-), probate (1827-), road (1841-91), soldiers' discharge (1863-65), survey (1874-), tax (1840-), will (1835-).

LIBRARY: Lewistown Carnegie Public Library District, 321 West Lincoln Ave., Lewistown, IL 61752.

GENEALOGICAL SOCIETY: Fulton County Historical and Genealogical Society, 45 North Park Drive, Canton, IL 61520.

GENEALOGICAL PUBLICATION: Above society publishes The Fulton County Historical and Genealogical Society Newsletter.

30. Gallatin County

Gallatin County, formed 1812 from Randolph County, County Seat Shawneetown (PO Box K, 62984).

CENSUSES: 1818T, 1820RS, 1830R, 1840RP, 1850RFMD, 1855S, 1860RFMD, 1865S, 1870RFM, 1880RFMD, 1900R, 1910R, 1920R.

FHL(FHC) RECORDS: biography (1887, 1988), black (1815-49), circuit court (1817-83), deed (1813-1917), early settler, genealogical compilations, history (1887, 1968), land entry (1814-76), marriage (1813-1926), Methodist (1867-1938), naturalization (1859-1953), probate (1815-87), will (1814-1931).

IRAD-SIU RECORDS: birth (1878-1972), board of supervisors (1813-1904), circuit court (1814-1920), death (1878-1916), deed (1813-1911), marriage (1813-1926), naturalization (1839-1906), probate (1813-1928), servitude (1815-39), will (1814-1931).

ILLINET PUBLISHED RECORDS: biography (1883/87, 1988), cemetery, court (1813-20), early settler, genealogical compilations, history (1883/87, 1968), land (1850-51), marriage (1813-70), newspaper abstract, plat (1900), probate, tax (1817-19).

ISGSQ ARTICLES: 4:172, 5:69, 5:203, 6:91, 6:99, 6:123, 8:1, 10:4, 10:14, 10:67, 10:127, 10:197, 10:200, 10:215, 11:187, 13:181, 14:1, 14:136, 15:31, 16:93, 24:132.

COUNTY INVENTORY: birth (1878-), board of supervisors (1891-), circuit court (1813-), coroner (1874-98), county court (1872-), county commissioners (1813-91), death (1878-), deed (1813-), estray (1837-67), free blacks (1839-56), guardian (1872-), indentured blacks (1814-37), jury (1872-), marriage (1830-), mortgage (1860-), naturalization (1859-93), original land entry (1814-56), probate (1830-), survey (1854-71), tax (1845, 1850-), will (1814-46).

LIBRARY: Shawneetown Public Library, East Lincoln Blvd., Shawneetown, IL 62984.

HISTORICAL SOCIETY: Gallatin Co Historical Society, PO Box 693, Shawneetown, IL 62984.

HISTORICAL AND GENEALOGICAL PUBLICATION: Above society publishes Gallatin County History and Families.

GENEALOGICAL SOCIETY: Genealogical Society of Southern IL, John A. Logan College, Box 145, Route 2, Carterville, IL 62918.

GENEALOGICAL PUBLICATION: Above society publishes Saga of Southern IL. Also Newsletter.

31. Greene County

Greene County, formed 1821 from Madison County, County Seat Carrollton (62016).

CENSUSES: 1830R, 1840RP, 1850-RFMD, 1855S, 1860RFMD, 1865S, 1870-RFM, 1880RFMD, 1900R, 1910R, 1920R.

FHL(FHC) RECORDS: biography (1879/65, 1968/89), birth (1877-1981), board of supervisors (1848-1973), cemetery, county officials (1821-37), death (1877-1981), deed (1821-1929), early settler, estray (1866-1915), genealogical compilations, history (1879/85, 1968), land grants, marriage (1821-1981), military (1861-1981), militia (1861-62), naturalization (1860-1906), poor (1836-1981), probate (1836-1981), will (1836-1981).

IRAD-SSU RECORDS: almshouse (1874-1928), board of supervisors (1821-1972), circuit court (1821-40), deed (1824-29), entry (1821-53), estray (1831-1904), jail (1886-1972), military discharge (1861-1981), militia (1861-62), poor (1824-26), tax (1836-1981).

ILLINET PUBLISHED RECORDS: atlas (1873), biography (1879/85, 1905), cemetery, early record compilation, early settler, history (1879/85, 1905/75/77), map (1861), marriage (1821-1901), plat (1893, 1900).

ISGSQ ARTICLES: 7:197, 9:93, 9:149, 12:87, 13:163, 13:164, 18:74, 22:28, 22:77, 24:2, 25:71

COUNTY INVENTORY: birth (1877-), board of supervisors (1888-), circuit court (1822-), coroner (1839-), county court (1872-), county commissioners (1821-88), death (1877-), deed (1822-), entry (1822-), guardian (1850-), insanity (1871-), jury (1872-), marriage (1821-), militia (1861-62), mortgage (1869-), naturalization (1860-1906), original land entry (1821-71), physicians (1877-), probate (1821-), soldiers' discharge (1865), survey (1893-), tax (1833/43/45, 1847-), will (1836-).

LIBRARY: Carrollton Public Library, 509 South Main St., Carrollton, IL 62016.

GENEALOGICAL SOCIETY: Greene County Historical and Genealogical Society, 221 North Fifth St., Carrollton, IL 62016.

32. Grundy County

Grundy County, formed 1841 from LaSalle County, County Seat Morris (111 East Washington St., 60450).

CENSUSES: 1840RP, 1850RFMD, 1855S, 1860RFMD, 1865S, 1870-RFM, 1880RFMD, 1900R, 1910R, 1920R.

FHL(FHC) RECORDS: atlas (1874, 1909), biography (1882, 1900/14), birth (1877-1905), death (1878-1904), deed (1832-1902), history (1882, 1914), Lutheran (1887-1961), marriage (1841-1923), mortgage (1853-1920).

IRAD-ISU RECORDS: circuit court (1846-1963).

ILLINET PUBLISHED RECORDS: atlas (1874/92, 1900/09), biography (1882, 1900/14), cemetery, history (1882, 1900/14/68), map (1863), plat (1892).

ISGSQ ARTICLES: 8:65, 8:130.

COUNTY INVENTORY: birth (1877-), board of supervisors (1850-), circuit court (1841-), coroner (1859-), county court (1855-), county commissioners (1841-49), death (1877-), deed (1841-), entry (1842-), estray (1854-95), guardian (1858-), insanity (1874-), jury (1856-), marriage (1841-), military bounty (1861-65), militia (1861-62), naturalization (1845-1906), original land entry (1835-55), physicians (1877-), plat (1844-), probate (1841-), survey (1885), tax (1842-), will (1854-).

LIBRARY: Morris Area Public Library, 604 Liberty St., Morris, IL 60450.

GENEALOGICAL SOCIETY: Will/Grundy Counties Genealogical Society, PO Box 24, Wilmington, IL 60481.

GENEALOGICAL PUBLICATION: Above society publishes Will/Grundy County Genealogical Societies Quarterly. Also Newsletter.

33. Hamilton County

Hamilton County, formed 1821 from White County, County Seat McLeansboro (62859).

CENSUSES: 1830R, 1835S, 1840RSP, 1850RFMD, 1855S, 1860RFMD, 1865S, 1870RFM, 1880RFMD, 1900R, 1910R, 1920R.

FHL(FHC) RECORDS: cemetery, circuit court (1821-39), history (1887), marriage (1821-70), military (1845-48, 1861-65), naturalization (1860-1900), newspaper abstract, original land grants (1814-54), probate (1823-1970), tax (1858), will (1823-1933).

IRAD-SIU RECORDS: none.

ILLINET PUBLISHED RECORDS: atlas (1900/05), Baptist, biography (1887), cemetery, Catholic (1893-1993), death, history (1887, 1971), map (1876), marriage (1821-), Methodist (1852-1967), obituary, probate, will (1821-1915).

ISGSQ ARTICLES: 3:191, 4:56, 4:173, 4:195, 6:91, 7:3, 8:138, 11:1, 11:81, 11:82, 11:175, 13:29, 13:135, 13:202, 14:1, 17:148.

COUNTY INVENTORY: birth (1878-), circuit court (1821-), county court (1872-), county commissioners and board of supervisors (1840-), death (1878-), deed (1818-), entry (1851-), guardian (1865-), indentures (1845-72), insanity (1872-), jury (1874-), marriage (1821-), military census (1861-62), mortgage (1856-), naturalization (1863-94), original land entry (1817-55), physicians (1877-), probate (1823-), road (1878-85), soldiers' discharge (1865-1900), state census (1835), survey (1860-), tax (1826-27, 1831/35/45, 1853-), will (1826-).

LIBRARY: McCoy Memorial Library, South Washington St., McLeansboro, IL 62859.

GENEALOGICAL SOCIETY: Genealogical Society of Southern IL, John A. Logan College, Box 145, Route 2, Carterville, IL 62918; Frankfort Area Genealogical Society, PO Box 427, West Frankfort, IL 62896.

GENEALOGICAL PUBLICATION: First society above publishes Saga of Southern IL. Also Newsletter. Second society above publishes Facts and Findings.

34. Hancock County

Hancock County, formed 1825 from Pike County, organized 1829, County Seat Carthage (PO Box 39, 62321).

CENSUSES: 1830R, 1840RP, 1850-RFMD, 1855S, 1860RFMD, 1865S, 1870-RFM, 1880RFMD, 1900R, 1910R, 1920R.

FHL(FHC) RECORDS: adoption (1883-1904), atlas (1874, 1904), biography (1880/94, 1907/89), birth (1844-1947), CJCLDS (1836-59), cemetery (1770-1980), Christian Church (1877-1955), circuit court (1829-1963), commissioners (1829-47), Civil War soldier, coroner (1893-1912), county court (1849-55), DAR, death (1877-1947), deed (1817-1917), directory (1886), Evangelical Lutheran (1857-1957), genealogical compilations (several), guardian (1833-1972), history (1880/94, 1974/79/85), land entry (1836-37), landowner (1817-56), marks and brands (1829-1973), marriage (1829-1922), Methodist (1854-1991), military discharge (1865-1965), mortgage (1840-1904), naturalization (1850-1930), Nauvoo records and histories, newspaper abstract (1835-50), obituary (1893-1977), pioneer, plat (1836-1938), Presbyterian (1855-76), probate (1831-1972), Revolutionary veteran burial, road (1874-93), survey (1836-84), tax (1817-72), United Church of Christ (1805-52), will (see probate).

IRAD-WIU RECORDS: adoption (1883-1904), birth (1844-1947), board of commissioners (1829-47), cemetery (1831-74), circuit court (1827-1964), coroner (1893-1913), county court (1846-1922), death (1877-1931), deed (1817-1934), guardian (1835-1954), marks and brands (1829-

1973), marriage (1829-1940), military discharge (1865-1965), mortgage (1882-1924), naturalization (1851-1930), original land entry (1817-38), plat (1834-1938), probate (1830-42), survey (1836-84), tax (1817-1963).

ILLINET PUBLISHED RECORDS: atlas (1874, 1900/04), Baptist (1835-1985), biography (1880/94, 1907/21/44), cemetery, Christian Church (1875-1975), directory (1886, 1903), genealogical compilations, history (1846/80, 1921/68), map (1853/59), marriage, Methodist (1866-1991), naturalization (1851-66), newspaper abstract, obituary, pioneers, plat (1891, 1900).

ISGSQ ARTICLES: 2:78, 6:32, 7:74, 8:137, 9:96, 9:128, 17:41, 17:101. 24:132, 25:32, 25:66.

COUNTY INVENTORY: adoption (1884-), birth (1878-), board of supervisors (1850-), circuit court (1829-), county court (1872-), county commissioners (1830-49), death (1878-), deed (1829-), estray (1858-1909), guardian (1830-), insanity (1870-), jury (1872-), land entry (1839-), marks and brands (1829-1907), marriage (1829-), military discharge (1865-), militia (1861-62), mortgage (1840-), naturalization (1851-1906), original land entry (1817-50), physicians (1877-), plat (1836-49), probate (1830-), road (1839-), survey (1838-), tax (1846-), will (1836-).

LIBRARY: Carthage Public Library District, 538 Wabash St., Carthage, IL 62321.

HISTORICAL SOCIETY: Hancock County Historical Society, PO Box 68, Carthage, IL 62321.

HISTORICAL PUBLICATION: Above society publishes Hancock County Historical Society Newsletter.

GENEALOGICAL SOCIETY: LaHarpe Historical and Genealogical Society, PO Box 289, LaHarpe, IL 61450.

GENEALOGICAL PUBLICATION: The above society publishes Historical Society Newsletter.

35. Hardin County

Hardin County, formed 1839 from Pike County, County Seat Elizabethtown (PO Box 187, 62931). Most records destroyed in an 1884 fire.

CENSUSES: 1840RSP, 1850RFMD, 1855S, 1860RFMD, 1865S, 1870RFM, 1880RFMD, 1900R, 1910R, 1920R.

FHL(FHC) RECORDS: biography (1893, 1987/92), birth (1884-1942), cemetery, death (1884-1946), deed (1880-1904), directory (1876), entry of land (1814-85), genealogical compilations, history (1939/87), marriage (1884-1969), newspaper abstract, obituary, probate (1884-1926), Revolutionary veterans, tax (1878/90).

IRAD-SIU RECORDS: probate (1884-1926).

ILLINET PUBLISHED RECORDS: biography (1893, 1987), cemetery, church deed (1848-92), death (1884-1919), history (1876, 1939/70/82/87), newspaper abstracts, obituary, plat (1900), tax (1878).

ISGSQ ARTICLES: 5:153, 12:228, 20:72, 24:134.

COUNTY INVENTORY: birth (1884-), circuit court (1880-), county court (1884-), county commissioners (1884-), death (1884-), deed (1877-), guardian (1884-), insanity (1884-), jury (1884-), land entry (1865-), marriage (1884-), mortgage (1882-), original land entry (1814-54), physicians (1884-), probate (1846-49, 1884-), survey (1867-), tax (1884-), will (1884-).

LIBRARY: Rosiclare Memorial Public Library, Main St., Rosiclare, IL 62982.

GENEALOGICAL SOCIETY: Hardin County Historical and Genealogical Society, PO Box 72, Elizabethtown, IL 62931; Genealogical Society of Southern IL, John A. Logan College, Box 145, Route 2, Carterville, IL 62918.

GENEALOGICAL PUBLICATION: Second society above publishes Saga of Southern IL. Also Newsletter.

36. Henderson County

Henderson County, formed 1841 from Warren County, County Seat Oquawka (61469).

CENSUSES: 1840RSP, 1850RFMD, 1855S, 1860RFMD, 1865S, 1870RFM, 1880RFMD, 1900R, 1910R, 1920R.

FHL(FHC) RECORDS: atlas (1900), biography (1882/94, 1911), birth (1877-1901), cemetery, circuit court (1859-1939), DAR, death (1878-1902), deed (1841-93), guardian (1859-1939), history (1882, 1911), marriage (1841-1901), naturalization (1856-1944), newspaper abstract, obituary, plat (1900), Presbyterian (1834-1989), probate (1841-1939).

IRAD-SIU RECORDS: school administration (1838-1901).

ILLINET PUBLISHED RECORDS: atlas (1875, 1900/14), biography (1882/94, 1911), cemetery, church history, county record compilation, DAR, history (1882, 1911), marriage (1841-1900), newspaper abstracts.

ISGSQ ARTICLES: 3:76, 7:137, 8:151, 9:83, 9:157, 9:158, 10:27, 10:136, 11:195, 12:37, 12:135, 13:194, 14:85, 14:189, 16:156, 25:32, 25:66.

COUNTY INVENTORY: birth (1877-), circuit court (1841-), county court (1872-), county commissioners (1841-), death (1878-), deed (1841-), dog license (1881-1908), guardian (1859-), insanity (1878-91, 1894-), jury (1853-1909), land entry (1841-), marriage (1841-), military discharge (1865-), militia (1861-), mortgage (1857-), naturalization (1852-1906), physicians (1877-), probate (1841-), survey (1876), tax (1841-), will (1841-).

LIBRARY: Henderson County District Library, East Main St., Biggsville, IL 61418.

HISTORICAL SOCIETY: Henderson County Historical Society, Rural Route 1, Box 130, Oquawka, IL 61469.

37. Henry County

Henry County, formed 1825 from Fulton County, but not organized until 1837, County Seat Cambridge (61238). See Fulton and Knox Counties for the period 1825-36.

CENSUSES: 1830R, 1840RP, 1850RFMD, 1860RFMD, 1865S, 1870RFM, 1880RFMD, 1900R, 1910R, 1920R.

FHL(FHC) RECORDS: atlas (1875), biography (1877/85, 1901/10), birth (1877-1901), board of supervisors (1857-97), court (1844-1923), death (1877-1916), deed (1818-1912), guardian (1856-1928), history (1877, 1810/68), marriage (1837-1923), military (1861-65), military discharge, naturalization (1856-1954), newspaper abstract, poor (1889-1902), Presbyterian (1871-1909), probate (1840-1930), United Evangelical (1840-1964), veterans' burial, will (1852-1924).

IRAD-WIU RECORDS: board of supervisors (1837-1935), Civil War bounty (1862-65), coroner (1870-1905), physician (1877-1908), tax (1850, 1876-1902).

ILLINET PUBLISHED RECORDS: atlas (1875/93, 1911), biography (1877/85, 1901/10), birth (1877-1916), cemetery, death (1877-1902), history (1877/85, 1910/41/68/70/72), map (1858/60), marriage (1821-53), naturalization, plat (1893).

ISGSQ ARTICLES: 4:159, 8:191, 14:75, 15:104, 18:17, 25:33.

COUNTY INVENTORY: birth (1878-), circuit court (1837-), coroner (1870-1910), county court (1872-), county commissioners and supervisors (1837-), death (1877-), deed (1837-), estray (1838-71), guardian (1857-), insanity (1854-), land entry (1837-), marriage (1837-), military (1861-65), militia (1861-63), mortgage (1837-), naturalization (1872-1906), original land entry, physicians (1877-), probate (1839-), survey (1864-), tax (1849-), will (1852-).

LIBRARY: Cambridge Public Library District, 212 West Center St., Cambridge, IL 61238.

GENEALOGICAL SOCIETY: Henry County Genealogical Society, PO Box 346, Kewanee, IL 661443.

GENEALOGICAL PUBLICATION: Above society publishes Henry County Genie. Also Newsletter.

38. Iroquois County

Iroquois County, formed 1833 from Vermilion County, not organized until 1834, County Seat Watseka (550 South Tenth St., 60970). Many records destroyed by fire in 1865.

CENSUSES: 1840RP, 1850RFMD, 1855S, 1860RFMD, 1865S, 1870-RFM, 1880RFMD, 1900R, 1910R, 1920R.

FHL(FHC) RECORDS: atlas (1884, 1904/21), biography (1893, 1907), birth (1878-1900), cemetery, death (1878-1901), deed (1835-89), French-Canadian families, genealogical compilations, history (1880, 1907/68/85), map (1860), military (1861-65), naturalization (1859-1906), original land purchase (1831-82), Presbyterian (1857-1900).

IRAD-ISU RECORDS: only a few later records.

ILLINET PUBLISHED RECORDS: atlas (1884, 1900/04), biography (1880/93, 1907), Catholic (1856-79), cemetery, French-Canadian families, history (1880, 1907/55/68/76/85/93), internal revenue assessment (1862-66), map (1860), marriage, newspaper abstract, tax (1890).

COUNTY INVENTORY: birth (1877-), board of supervisors (1867-), circuit court (1835-), county court (1872-), death (1877-), deed (1834-), guardian (1862-), insanity (1885-), land entry (1856-), marriage (1866-), military discharge (1867-1902), mortgage (1834-), naturalization (1859-1906), physicians (1877-), plat (1865-), probate (1863-), survey (1836-), tax (1866-), will (1866-).

LIBRARY: Watseka Public Library, 201 S. Fourth St., Watseka, IL 60970.

GENEALOGICAL SOCIETY: Iroquois County Genealogical Society, 103 West Cherry St., Watseka, IL 60970. Maintains a genealogical library at this address.

GENEALOGICAL PUBLICATION: The above society publishes The Iroquois Stalker. Also Newsletter.

39. Jackson County

Jackson County, formed 1816 from Randolph and Johnson Counties, County Seat Murphysboro (62966), many records lost in an 1843 fire.

CENSUSES: 1818T, 1820RS, 1830R, 1840RP, 1850RFMD, 1855S, 1860RFMD, 1865S, 1870RFM, 1880RFMD, 1900R, 1910R, 1920R.

FHL(FHC) RECORDS: African-Methodist (1868-1968), Baptist (1834-1911), biography (1878/94, 1977/83), birth (1852-1915), cemetery, Christian Church (1894-1970), circuit court (1844-55), city directory (1896, 1905), county commissioner court (1823-35), court (1843-55), death (1877-

1917), deed (1843-95), Evangelical Lutheran (1849-1973), genealogical compilations, guardian (1858-1902), history (1878/94, 1977/83), inventory (1939), jury (1823-41), marriage (1843-1915), military (1862-63), naturalization (1859-1906), obituary (1893-1922), physician (1877-94), plat (1907), Presbyterian (1853-1928), probate (1840-1922), will (1843-1922), WPA.

IRAD-SIU RECORDS: birth (1852-1943), board of supervisors (1823-1954), circuit court (1844-56), court (1843-55), death (1877-1916), deed (1838-1936), jail (1873-1937), marriage (1842-1915), naturalization (1857-1906), physician (1877-94), probate (1840-1964), tax (1858-1970), voter (1865-74), will (1842-1964), WPA.

ILLINET PUBLISHED RECORDS: atlas (1900/07), biography (1878/94, 1983), cemetery, county court (1823-41), DAR, genealogical compilations, historical map (1944), history (1878/82/94, 1928/35/45/82/83), inventory (1939), jury (1823-41), land, marriage (1843-75), military (1862-63), naturalization, will.

ISGSQ ARTICLES: 9:42, 13:201, 24:134, 25:71.

COUNTY INVENTORY: adoption (1871-), birth (1878-), board of supervisors (1872-), circuit court (1843-), coroner (1845-), county court (1872-), county commissioners (1823-49), county commissioners court (1849-72), death (1878-), deed (1853-), estray (1857-96), guardian (1859-), indentures (1843-1910), insanity (1874-), jury (1872-), land entry (1857-), marks and brands (1867-), marriage (1842-), militia (1861-62), mortgage (1861-), naturalization (1858-1906), original land entry (1815-72), physicians (1877-), plat (1888-), probate (1843-), survey (1885-), tax (1850-), will (1843-).

LIBRARY: Sallie Logan Public Library, 1808 Walnut St., Murphysboro, IL 62966; Carbondale Public Library, 405 West Main St., Carbondale, IL 62901; Morris Library, Southern IL University at Carbondale, Carbondale, IL 62901.

HISTORICAL SOCIETY: Jackson County Historical Society, 1401 Walnut St., Murphysboro, IL 62966.

HISTORICAL PUBLICATION: Above society publishes Jacksonian Ventilator.

GENEALOGICAL SOCIETY: Genealogical Society of Southern IL, John A. Logan College, Box 145, Route 2, Carterville, IL 62918.

GENEALOGICAL PUBLICATION: Above society publishes Saga of Southern IL. Also Newsletter.

40. Jasper County

Jasper County, formed 1831 from Clay and Crawford Counties, County Seat Newton (100 West Jourdan St., 62448).

CENSUSES: 1835S, 1840RSP, 1850RFMD, 1855S, 1860RFMD, 1865S, 1870RFM, 1880RFMD, 1900R, 1910R, 1920R.

FHL(FHC) RECORDS: biography (1884/93, 1988), birth (1877-1903), cemetery, death (1877-1908), deed (1837-1915), guardian (1888-1935), history (1884/93, 1988), marriage (1835-1900), military, naturalization (1869-1906), probate (1835-1972), will (1850-1937).

IRAD-EIU RECORDS: tax (1871-1918).

ILLINET PUBLISHED RECORDS: atlas (1900/02), biography (1884/93, 1988), cemetery, history (1884, 1938/76/88), map (1901), marriage, military discharge, obituary, residents (1884).

ISGSQ ARTICLES: 2:213, 13:85, 14:31, 14:86.

COUNTY INVENTORY: birth (1877-), board of supervisors (1860-), circuit court (1835-), county court (1872-), county commissioners (1835-60), death (1877-), deed (1836-), estray (1835-58), guardian (1861-), insanity (1878-), jury (1872-), land entry (1850-), marks and brands (1839-68), marriage (1835-), militia (1861-62), mortgage (1854-), naturalization (1868-1906), original land entry (1837-72), physicians (1878-), plat (1885-), probate (1835-), tax (1860-), will (1850-).

LIBRARY: Newton Public Library, 100 South Van Buren St., Newton, IL 62448.

GENEALOGICAL SOCIETY: Jasper County Historical and Genealogical Society, 100 South Van Buren St., Newton, IL 62448.

GENEALOGICAL PUBLICATION: Above society publishes Our Heritage.

41. Jefferson County

Jefferson County, formed 1819 from White and Edwards Counties, County Seat Mt. Vernon (62864).

CENSUSES: 1820RS, 1830R, 1840RP, 1850RFMD, 1860RFMD, 1865S, 1870-RFM, 1880RFMD, 1900R, 1910R, 1920R.

FHL(FHC) RECORDS: Baptist (1866-1950), biography (1883/94, 1978), birth (1867-1915), death (1877-1915), deed (1822-1904), history (1883/94, 1978/93), marriage (1819-1916), mortgage (1857-61, 1874-1905).

IRAD-SIU RECORDS: board of supervisors (1819-49), deed (1822-1927).

ILLINET PUBLISHED RECORDS: atlas (1900), Baptist (1842-81), biography (1883/94, 1909/78), cemetery, circuit court, early settler, genealogical compilations, geography, history (1883, 1909/46/62/78/90), map (1876, 1900), marriage (1819-74), obituary.

ISGSQ ARTICLES: 5:123, 6:13, 6:14, 6:138, 7:140, 9:19, 9:85, 13:157, 15:17, 25:3.

COUNTY INVENTORY: birth (1877-), board of supervisors (1871-), circuit court (1819-), coroner (1875-), county court (1872-), county commissioners (1819-71), death (1877-), deed (1824-), estray (1864-1909), guardian (1858-), indenture (1820-79), insanity (1895-), jury (1846-57, 1872-), land entry (1864-), marriage (1819-), mortgage (1822-), naturalization (1869-1905), physicians (1877-), plat (1880-1901), probate (1831-), survey (1837-67), tax (1830, 1863-65, 1874-91), will (1866-).

LIBRARY: C. E. Brehm Memorial Public Library District, 101 South Seventh St., Mt. Vernon, IL 62864.

GENEALOGICAL SOCIETY: Genealogical Society of Southern IL, John A. Logan College, Box 145, Route 2, Carterville, IL 62918.

GENEALOGICAL PUBLICATION: Above society publishes Saga of Southern IL. Also Newsletter.

42. Jersey County

Jersey County, formed 1839 from Greene County, County Seat Jerseyville (201 West Pearl St., 62052).

CENSUSES: 1840RP, 1850RFMD, 1855S, 1860RFMD, 1865S, 1870RFM, 1880RFMD, 1900R, 1910R, 1920R.

FHL(FHC) RECORDS: atlas (1872), biography (1885, 1919), birth (1845-66, 1878-1900), cemetery, death (1878-1983), deed (1822-1924), early records, history (1885, 1901/19/91), marriage (1839-1943), naturalization (1854-1905), original land sales (1821-57), probate (1839-1940), United Church of Christ (1890-1902).

IRAD-SSU RECORDS: birth (1868-1967), death (1878-1967), guardian (1879-1922), land entry (1821-75), marriage (1839-1967), plat (1856), probate (1839-1964), will (1839-1964).

ILLINET PUBLISHED RECORDS: atlas (1872), biography (1885, 1919/91), cemetery, early records, history (1876/85, 1919/75/76/91), land tract sales (1821-57), plat (1893).

ISGSQ ARTICLES: 4:247, 14:195, 21:12, 22:28, 22:77, 24:2.

COUNTY INVENTORY: birth (1877-), board of supervisors (1879-), circuit court (1839-), county court (1872-), county commissioners and court (1839-77), death (1878-), deed (1839-), guardian (1856-), insanity (1878-93), land entry (1822-), marriage (1839-), mortgage (1839-), naturalization (1854-1906), original land entry (1831-57), physicians (1877-), probate (1839-), road (1872-), survey (1838-50, 1885-), tax (1845, 1849-), will (1856-).

LIBRARY: Jerseyville Public Library, 105 North Liberty St., Jerseyville, IL 62052.

GENEALOGICAL SOCIETY: Jacksonville Area Genealogical and Historical Society, 203 South Fayette St., Jacksonville, IL 62651.

GENEALOGICAL PUBLICATION: Above society publishes Jacksonville, IL Genealogical Journal.

43. Jo Daviess County

Jo Daviess County, formed 1827 from Henry, Mercer, and Putnam Counties, County Seat Galena (330 North Bench St., 61036).

CENSUSES: 1830R, 1840RSP, 1850-RFMD, 1855S, 1860RFMD, 1865S, 1870RFM, 1880RFMD, 1900R, 1910R, 1920R.

FHL(FHC) RECORDS: atlas (1872/93, 1913), biography (1878/89), birth (1877-1986), Brethren, cemetery, city directory (1854-59), deed (1829-1902), Galena, genealogical compilations, history (1878), inventory (1938), Lutheran (1847-84), marriage (1830-1917), military (1861-65), naturalization (1856-1929), newspaper abstract, plat (1893), Presbyterian (1844-95), will (1829-1921), WPA.

IRAD-NIU RECORDS: birth (1877-1988), circuit court (1853-83), death (1877-1964), deed (1825-1902), Galena (1831-1977), marriage (1833-1988), naturalization (1840-1929), will (1829-1924).

ILLINET PUBLISHED RECORDS: atlas (1872/93, 1900/13), biography (1876/78/89, 1904/20), cemetery, directory (1868, 1917), early settler, history (1876/78, 1904), inventory (1938), marriage, newspaper abstract, newspaper index (1828-46), plat (1893), WPA.

ISGSQ ARTICLES: 7:142, 8:127, 11:98, 16:242.

COUNTY INVENTORY: birth (1878-), board of supervisors (1858-), circuit court (1828-), Civil War volunteer (1861-62), county court (1872-), county commissioners (1827-58), death (1878-), deed (1828-), estray (1849-1906), guardian (1872-), insanity (1886-), land entry (1836-), license (1850-1905), marks and brands (1831-1905), marriage (1828-), militia (1861-63), mine (1825-27, 1832-37, 1840/47), mortgage (1842-), naturalization (1856-1906), original land entry (1843-53), plat (1837-), probate (1828-), road (1828-83), tax (1839-), will (1831-).

LIBRARY: Galena Public Library, 601 South Bench St., Galena, IL 61036.

GENEALOGICAL SOCIETY: Check the Stephenson County Genealogical Society, PO Box 514, Freeport, IL 61032.

44. Johnson County

Johnson County, formed 1812 from Randolph County, County Seat Vienna (PO Box 96, 62995).

CENSUSES: 1818T, 1820RS, 1830R, 1840RSP, 1850RFMD, 1855S, 1860RFMD, 1865S, 1870RFM, 1880RFMD, 1900R, 1910R, 1920R.

FHL(FHC) RECORDS: Baptist (1860-1963), biography (1893, 1925/90), birth (1878-1925), cemetery, Church of Christ (1847-1943), circuit court (1814-17, 1829-36), commissioner's court and supervisors (1813-61), death (1878-1933), deed (1814-1928), genealogical compilations, history (1925/90/92), marriage (1835-1926), Methodist (1886-1921), obituary, Presbyterian (1842-1947), probate (1859-1948), Revolutionary veteran.

IRAD-SIU RECORDS: birth (1878-1974), cicuit court (1829-35), death (1878-1933), deed (1809-1907), marriage (1834-1926), probate (1822-1973), territorial court (1813-17), will (1870-1904), WPA.

ILLINET PUBLISHED RECORDS: biography (1893, 1925), cemetery, county commissioner (1813-17), DAR, genealogical compilations, history (1893, 1925/77/90), marriage (1834-77), Methodist (1845-1928), obituary, plat (1900).

ISGSQ ARTICLES: 19:193, 20:34, 20:91, 22:97, 24:2, 24:134.

COUNTY INVENTORY: birth (1878-), circuit court (1814-), county court (1872-), county commissioners (1813-17), county commissioners court (1851-72), court of common pleas (1813-19), death (1878-), deed (1815-), guardian (1870-), insanity (1888-), land entry (1867-), marriage (1835-), mortgage (1861-), naturalization (1870/89/96), original land entry (1818-96), physician (1878-), plat (1887-), probate (1820-), survey (1864-), tax (1853-), will (1870-).

LIBRARY: Vienna Public Library, PO Box 616, Vienna, IL 62995.

GENEALOGICAL SOCIETY: Genealogical Society of Southern IL, John A. Logan College, Box 145, Route 2, Carterville, IL 62918.

GENEALOGICAL PUBLICATION: Above society publishes Saga of Southern IL. Also Newsletter.

45. Kane County

Kane County, formed 1836 from LaSalle County, County Seat Geneva (719 South Batavia St., 60134), a few records lost in 1892 fire.

CENSUSES: 1840RP, 1850RFMD, 1855S, 1860RFMD, 1865S, 1870RFM, 1880RFMD, 1900R, 1910R, 1920R.

FHL(FHC) RECORDS: biography (1878/88/98, 1904/08/16), birth (1877-1916), Catholic, cemetery, Congregational (1841-1951), death (1877-1919), directory (1857, 1858-59), early families (1833-85), GAR, gazetteer (1867), genealogical compilations, guardian (1837-1922), history (1878/88, 1904/08), Lutheran (1882-1982), marriage (1836-1923), naturalization

(1846-1954), newspaper abstract, obituary, Presbyterian, probate (1837-1922), tax (1848), United Church of Christ.

IRAD-NIU RECORDS: circuit court (1836-70), county court (1881-84), insanity (1893-99), naturalization (1872-1906), probate (1861-1946), will (1866-1946).

ILLINET PUBLISHED RECORDS: atlas (1872/92, 1900/04), biography (1878/88/98, 1904/08/93), cemetery, DAR, directory (1859/87), early family (1833-85), gazetteer (1867), history (1878/88, 1904/08/36/41/-68), map (1851/60), marriage (1836-1906), naturalization (1857-1955), newspaper index (1884-99), Presbyterian (1841-1935), school (1857-88), tax (1848).

ISGSQ ARTICLES: 6:165, 6:212, 7:22, 9:150, 10:91, 11:15, 11:65, 11:200, 11:213, 12:139, 13:7, 14:71, 14:90, 15:50, 15:248, 16:53, 16:225, 22:68, 23:32, 25:96.

COUNTY INVENTORY: adoption (1898-), birth (1877-), board of supervisors (1850-), circuit court (1836-), county court (1872-), county commissioners (1836-50), death (1878-), deed (1837-), estray (1847-1902), guardian (1865-), insanity (1850-), jury (1853-), land entry (1837-), marriage (1836-), military bounty (1861-65), military discharge (1865-1904), militia (1861-62), mortgage (1837-), naturalization (1853-), original land entry (1839-55), physicians (1877-), plat (1837-), probate (1837-), road (1836-), tax (1844, some years 1860-80, 1881-), will (1857-).

LIBRARY: Geneva Public Library District, 127 James St., Geneva, IL 60134.

GENEALOGICAL SOCIETY: Kane County Genealogical Society, PO Box 504, Geneva, IL 60134.

GENEALOGICAL PUBLICATION: Above society publishes The Kane County Chronicles.

46. Kankakee County

Kankakee County, formed 1853 from Iroquois and Will Counties, County Seat Kankakee (450 East Court St., 60901).

CENSUSES: 1855S, 1860RFMD, 1865S, 1870RFM, 1880RFMD, 1900R, 1910R, 1920R.

FHL(FHC) RECORDS: atlas (1883, 1900), biography (1883/93, 1906), birth (1877-1918), Catholic, cemetery, city directory (1890), death (1877-1916), early settler, French-Canadian family, older genealogical periodical, history (1883, 1906/32/55/68), marriage (1853-1922), military veteran (1861-65), Presbyterian (1851-1906).

IRAD-ISU RECORDS: circuit court (1871), probate (1866-69), tax (1851-1920).

ILLINET PUBLISHED RECORDS: atlas (1870, 1900/03), biography 1906/68/73), Catholic, cemetery, Civil War veteran, French-Canadian family, history (1883, 1906/25/55/68/73), map (1860).

ISGSQ ARTICLES: 1(2):32, 5:250, 25:96.

COUNTY INVENTORY: birth (1878-), board of supervisors (1853-), circuit court (1853-), county court (1872-), death (1878-), deed (1853-), guardian (1859-), insanity (1861-92), land entry (1853-), marriage (1853-), mortgage (1853-), naturalization (1855-1906), physicians (1878-), probate (1853-), tax (1855-), will (1853-).

LIBRARY: Kankakee Public Library, 304 South Indiana Ave., Kankakee, IL 60901.

GENEALOGICAL SOCIETY: Kankakee Valley Genealogical Society, PO Box 442, Bourbonnais, IL60914.

GENEALOGICAL PUBLICATION: Above society publishes The-a-Kiki.

47. Kendall County

Kendall County, formed 1841 from LaSalle and Kane Counties, County Seat Yorkville (110 West Ridge St., 60560).

CENSUSES: 1850RFMD, 1855S, 1860RFMD, 1865S, 1870RFMD, 1880-RFMD, 1900R, 1910R, 1920R.

FHL(FHC) RECORDS: biography (1877/76/88, 1914), birth (1877-1918), cemetery, death (1877-1903), deed (1841-1926), draft registration (1914-18), history (1877, 1914) Lutheran (1883-1953), map (1859), marriage (1841-1915), military veteran, newspaper abstract, obituary, tax (1842).

IRAD-NIU RECORDS: none.

ILLINET PUBLISHED RECORDS: atlas (1870, 1900/03), biography (1876/77, 1901/14), cemetery, history (1876/77, 1914/27/75/76), map (1851/59/90, 1900), plat (1900), taxpayer (1876).

ISGSQ ARTICLES: 6:23, 14:8, 25:96.

COUNTY INVENTORY: birth (1877-), board of supervisors (1859-), circuit court (1841-), county court (1872-), county commissioners (1841-59), death (1877-), deed (1841-), guardian (1858-), insanity (1894-), land entry (1865-), marriage (1841-77, 1891,), mortgage (1856-), naturalization (1855-1906), physicians (1878-1905), plat (1863-), probate (1841-), tax (1845-), will (1849-).

LIBRARY: Yorkville Public Library, 902 Game Farm Road, Yorkville, IL 60560.

GENEALOGICAL SOCIETY: Kendall County Genealogical Society, PO Box 123, Yorkville, IL 60560.

GENEALOGICAL PUBLICATION: Above society publishes The Homestead. Also Newsletter.

---

48. Knox County

Knox County, formed 1825 from Fulton County, organized 1830, County Seat Galesburg (200 South Cherry St., 61401).

CENSUSES: 1830R, 1840RSP, 1850 RFMD, 1855S, 1860RFMD, 1865S, 1870RFMD, 1880RFMD, 1900R, 1910R, 1920R.

FHL(FHC) RECORDS: atlas (1870), biography (1878/86/99, 1912), birth (1877-1900), cemetery, DAR, death (1877-1990), deed (1818-86), directory (1888), gazetteer (1888, 1983), history (1878/86/99, 1912/21), inventory (1938), map (1861), marriage (1830-1922), military veteran (1914-18), naturalization (1856-1906), obituary (1853-1910), probate (1832-1900), Swedes, tax (1855/65/75/85/90), will (1830-1959), WPA.

IRAD-WIU RECORDS: board of supervisors (1871-1955), deed (1818-63), estray (1864-1944), Galesburg (1841-1984).

ILLINET PUBLISHED RECORDS: atlas (1891, 1900/03), biography (1878/86/99, 1912/20/21), board of supervisors, cemetery, Civil War veteran, DAR, death (1878-1910), deed, directory (1868), gazetteer, genealogical compilations, history (1878/86/99, 1905/12/21/55), inventory (1938), land grant, map (1861/70/95), marriage (1830-1910), naturalization (1856-61), newspaper abstract, obituary, plat (1900), probate (1832-1900), Swedes, tax (1855/65/75/85/90).

ISGSQ ARTICLES: 3:230, 4:82, 5:229, 6:102, 7:152, 11:116, 12:137, 14:26, 14:217, 15:29, 16:101, 19:228.

COUNTY INVENTORY: birth (1877-), board of supervisors (1850-), circuit court (1830-), county court (1872-), county commissioners (1830-49), death (1877-), deed (1818-), guardian (1858-), insanity (1871-), jury (1872-), marks and brands (1845-85), marriage (1830-), militia (1861-62), military discharge (1866-99), mortgage (1842-), naturalization (1856-1906), original land entry (1817-57), physicians (1877-), plat (1890), probate (1835-), road (1830-52), tax (1833-), will (1835-).

LIBRARY: Galesburg Public Library, 40 East Simmons St., Galesburg, IL 61401.

GENEALOGICAL SOCIETY: Knox County Genealogical Society, PO Box 13, Galesburg, IL 61402.

GENEALOGICAL PUBLICATION: Above society publishes Knox County Genealogical Society Quarterly.

49. Lake County

Lake County, formed 1839 from McHenry County, County Seat Waukegan (18 North County St., 60085).

CENSUSES: 1840RP, 1850RFMD, 1860-RFMD, 1865S, 1870RFMD, 1880RFMD, 1900R, 1910R, 1920R.

FHL(FHC) RECORDS: biography (1877/91, 1902), birth (1866-1905), Catholic (1847-1920), cemetery, early settler, first land purchaser, German Evangelical Lutheran (1846-78), history (1877/91, 1902), marriage (1839-1918), military census (1862), mortuary (1868-1937).

IRAD-NIU RECORDS: circuit court (1840-98), tax (1851-1900).

ILLINET PUBLISHED RECORDS: atlas (1885/96, 1900/07), biography (1877/91, 1902/39/67), cemetery, early settler, genealogical compilations, historical map, history (1852/77, 1923/39/67/68/81/89), map (1841/61/73), marriage (1839-59), military (1862), original land purchase.

ISGSQ ARTICLES: 17:195, 18:26, 18:145, 18:229, 25:37.

COUNTY INVENTORY: birth (1877-), board of supervisors (1850-), circuit court (1840-), county court (1853-), county commissioners (1839-50), death (1877-), deed (1839-), guardian (1858-), insanity (1876-), jury (1872-), land entry (1839-), marriage (1839-), militia (1861-62), mortgage (1845-), naturalization (1864-1906), physicians (1877-), plat (1868-), probate (1839-), survey (1840-), tax (1850-), will (1849-).

LIBRARY: Waukegan Public Library, 128 North County St., Waukegan, IL 60085.

GENEALOGICAL SOCIETY: Lake County Genealogical Society, Cook Memorial Library, 413 North Milwaukee Ave., Libertyville, IL 60048; Zion Genealogical Society, Zion-Benton Public Library, 2400 Gabriel Ave., Zion, IL 60099.

GENEALOGICAL PUBLICATION: The first society above publishes The Lake County Genealogical Society Quarterly. Also Newsletter. The second society above publishes The Illuminator.

50. LaSalle County

LaSalle County, formed 1831 from Putnam County, County Seat Ottawa (707 Etna Rd., 61350).

CENSUSES: 1840RSP, 1850RFMD, 1855S, 1860RFMD, 1865S, 1870RFMD, 1880RFMD, 1900R, 1910R, 1920R.

FHL(FHC) RECORDS: biography (1877/86, 1900/06/24), birth (1858-1940), cemetery, circuit court (1831-75), death (1877-1915), deed (1831-1943), directory (1883), early settler, guardian (1847-1945), history (1877/86, 1906/14/24), Lutheran (1847-1983), marriage (1831-1916), military roster, naturalization (1840-1906), newspaper abstract, obituary, Presbyterian (1835-1909), probate (1831-1923).

IRAD-NIU RECORDS: circuit court (1831-75), county court (1836-1963), naturalization (1840-1906), probate (1831-1900), survey (1842-70), will (1847-1900).

ILLINET PUBLISHED RECORDS: atlas (1876, 1900/06), biography (1877/86, 1900/06/24/67), Catholic, cemetery, city directory (1902), county record compilation, DAR, directory (1858/59), history (1877/86, 1906/24/67/68/81/87/88/91), map (1895), marriage (1831-51), pioneer, plat (1892, 1900), resident (1831-1931).

ISGSQ ARTICLES: 4:87, 5:162, 7:85, 7:192, 8:22, 8:220, 9:121, 9:206, 11:6, 12:89, 12:224, 13:216, 14:7, 15:102, 24:97.

COUNTY INVENTORY: birth (1877-), board of supervisors (1849-), circuit court (1831-), county court (1854-), county commissioners (1831-49), death (1877-), deed (1831-), estray (1863-), guardian (1837-), insane (1867-), jury (1888-), land entry (1831-), marriage (1831-), military discharge (1865-98), militia (1861-65), mortgage (1831-), naturalization (1840-1906), physicians (1877-), plat (1833-), probate (1831-), survey (1833-1906), tax (1841-), will (1847-).

LIBRARY: Reddick Library, 1010 Canal St., Ottawa, IL 61350.

GENEALOGICAL SOCIETY: LaSalle County Genealogical Guild, 115 Glover St., Ottawa, IL 61350.

GENEALOGICAL PUBLICATION: Above society publishes Pastfinder and Gene View.

51. Lawrence County

Lawrence County, formed 1821 from Crawford and Edwards Counties, County Seat Lawrenceville (62439).

CENSUSES: 1830R, 1840RSP, 1850-RFMD, 1855S, 1860RFMD, 1865S, 1870RFMD, 1880RFMD, 1900R, 1910R, 1920R.

FHL(FHC) RECORDS: atlas (1875), biography (1883, 1910/68/72), birth (1877-1923), Brethren (1865-1965), cemetery, death (1878-1925), deed (1821-1936), genealogical compilations, history (1883, 1910/68/71), marriage (1821-49, 1878-1937), Presbyterian (1854-99), probate (1859-1929), will (1821-1929).

IRAD-EIU RECORDS: birth (1889-1970), death (1878-1972), deed (1821-1960), marriage (1821-1970).

ILLINET PUBLISHED RECORDS: biography (1883, 1910), birth, cemetery, DAR, history (1883, 1910), marriage.

ISGSQ ARTICLES: 6:223, 15:93, 24:92.

COUNTY INVENTORY: birth (1877-), board of supervisors (1857-), circuit court (1821-), county court (1872-), county commissioners (1823-57), death (1877-), deed (1821-), estray (1876-), guardian (1858-), insanity (1893-), jury (1869-), land entry (1818-54, 1872-), marks and brands (1857-92), marriage (1821-), militia (1861-), mortgage (1848-), plat (1888-), probate (1819-), tax (1853-), will (1821-).

LIBRARY: Lawrence Township Public Library, 814 12th St., Lawrenceville, IL 62439.

GENEALOGICAL SOCIETY: Lawrence County Genealogical Society, Rural Route 1, Box 44, Bridgeport, IL 62417.

52. Lee County

Lee County, formed 1839 from Ogle County, County Seat Dixon (61021).

CENSUSES: 1840RP, 1850RFMD, 1855S, 1860RFMD, 1865S, 1870RFMD, 1880RFMD, 1900R, 1910R, 1920R.

FHL(FHC) RECORDS: biography (1881/92/93, 1904/14), cemetery, Congregational (1871-81), DAR, genealogical compilations, history (1881/92/93, 1904/14), marriage (1839-73), old settler.

IRAD-NIU RECORDS: circuit court (1840-1940), coroner (1840-1941).

ILLINET PUBLISHED RECORDS: atlas (1900/15), biography (1881/92/93, 1904/14), cemetery, county records, history (1881/92/93, 1904/14), petition (1853), pioneer.

ISGSQ ARTICLES: 2:215, 25:33.

COUNTY INVENTORY: adoption (1895-), birth (1878-), circuit court (1840-), county court (1872-), county commissioners and supervisors (1839-), death (1878-), deed (1838-), entry (1839-), estray (1861-98), guardian (1858-), insanity (1872-), jury (1872-), marriage (1839-), military (1861-65), mortgage (1840-), naturalization (1858-1906), physicians (1877-), plat (1874-), power of attorney (1841-), probate (1839-), survey (1873-), tax (1847-), will (1848-).

LIBRARY: Dixon Public Library, 221 South Hennepin Ave., Dixon IL 61021.

GENEALOGICAL SOCIETY: Lee County Genealogical Society, PO Box 63, Dixon, IL 61021.

53. Livingston County

Livingston County, formed 1837 from La-Salle and McLean Counties, County Seat Pontiac (112 West Madison St., 61764).

CENSUSES: 1840RSP, 1850RFMD, 1855S, 1860RFMD, 1865S, 1870RFMD,1880 RFMD, 1900R, 1910R, 1920R.

FHL(FHC) RECORDS: atlas (1911), biography (1888, 1900), birth (1878-1900), cemetery, death (1878-1900), deed (1836-1921), directory (1878), history (1878/88, 1900/91), marriage (1837-1923), military discharge (1865-1945), naturalization (1854-1906), probate (1837-1905).

IRAD-ISU RECORDS: board of supervisors (1856-1975), tax (1862-1970).

ILLINET PUBLISHED RECORDS: atlas (1900/11), biography (1878/88, 1900/09/91), cemetery, history (1878, 19/09/91), internal revenue assessment (1862), map (1902), original land grant, plat (1893).

ISGSQ ARTICLES: 2:214, 8:13, 8:209, 9:87, 10:224, 11:6, 19:1, 19:166.

COUNTY INVENTORY: adoption (1876-), birth (1877-), circuit court (1839-), coroner (1877-), county court (1855-), county commissioners and supervisors (1837-38), death (1878-), deed (1838-), estray (1849-), guardian (1858-), insanity (1874-), land entry (1837-), marks and brands (1837-74), marriage (1837-), military discharge (1865-99), militia (1861-63), mortgage (1859-), naturalization (1853-1905), physicians (1872-), plat, probate (1838-), road (before 1858), survey (1843-), tax (1849-), will (1867-).

LIBRARY: Pontiac Public Library, 401 North Main St., Pontiac, IL 61764.

GENEALOGICAL SOCIETY: Odell Trails Genealogical and Historical Society, PO Box 82, Odell, IL 60460.

---

54. Logan County

Logan County, formed 1839 from Sangamon County, County Seat Lincoln (62656). A fire in 1857 destroyed most records.

CENSUSES: 1840RP, 1850RFMD, 1855S, 1860RFMD, 1865S, 1870RFMD, 1880RFMD, 1900R, 1910R, 1920R.

FHL(FHC) RECORDS: atlas (1873), biography (1878/86, 1911/82), board of health (1895-1908), burial (1891-99), cemetery, DAR, (1856-1965), genealogical compilations, guardian (1872-1963), history (1878/86, 1911/53/82), inventory (1938), Methodist (1866-1920), mortuary (1861-1910), naturalization (1859-1906), newspaper abstract, old settler, Presbyterian (1857-1906), probate (1855-1949), will (1855-1930), WPA.

IRAD-ISU RECORDS: circuit court (1857-1944), insanity (1856-1963), Lincoln (1853-1954), will (1855-1964).

ILLINET PUBLISHED RECORDS: atlas (1873/93, 1900/10), biography (1878/86, 1901/11/82/88), cemetery, DAR, directory (1880/87), history (1878/80/86, 1901/11/53/55/73/76/82/88), internal revenue assessment (1862-66), inventory (1938), map (1837/64/93), Methodist (1866-1920), mortuary, plat (1893), probate.

ISGSQ ARTICLES: 2:80, 10:79, 13:203, 14:221, 19:129, 19:215, 20:10, 20:26, 20:79, 20:156, 22:164, 22:193, 22:228.

COUNTY INVENTORY : adoption (1857-), birth (1878-), board of supervisors (1867-), circuit court (1857-), county court (1872-), county commissioners (1857-67), death (1878-), deed (1845-50, 1853-), estray, guardian (1857-), insane (1856-), jury (1872-), land entry (1830-68, 1879-), marks and brands (1857-99), marriage (1857-), military bounty (1863-65), military discharge (1865-1908), militia (1861-62), mortgage (1854-), naturalization (1857-1906), physicians (1877-), plat (1870-), probate (1857-), survey (1880-81), tax (1857-), will (1855-).

LIBRARY: Lincoln Public Library, 725 Pekin St., Lincoln, IL 62656.

GENEALOGICAL SOCIETY: Logan County Genealogical Society, PO Box 283, Lincoln, IL 62656.

55. Macon County

Macon County, formed 1829 from Shelby County, County Seat Decatur (253 East Wood Street, 62523).

CENSUSES: 1830R, 1840RSP, 1850-RFMD, 1855S, 1860RFMD, 1865S, 1870RFMD, 1880RFMD, 1900R, 1910R, 1920R.

FHL(FHC) RECORDS: atlas (1903), Baptist (1894-1921), biography (1880/93, 1910/03/30), birth (1850-1922), cemetery, Church of God (1875-1901), Christian Church (1896-1922), circuit court (1831-48), Congregational (1872-1934), death (1877-1922), deed (1830-93), genealogical compilations, history (1876/80, 1903/10/30/68), Lutheran (1883-1931), marriage (1829-1930), Methodist (1836-1972), military (1861-63), military discharge (1864-65), mortuary (1887-1928), naturalization (1858-1906), obituary, original land entry (1830-74), poor, Presbyterian (1852-1971), probate (1830-1972), tax (1865-66), veterans' burial (1853-1955), will (1847-1916).

IRAD-SSU RECORDS: board of supervisors (1840-1964), circuit court (1830-72), estray (1849-62), naturalization (1858-1906), probate (1847-1962), tax (1848-91), will (1847-1916).

ILLINET PUBLISHED RECORDS: atlas (1874, 1900/03), Bible, biography (1876/80/93, 1903/10/30/67), birth (1850-1900), cemetery, circuit court (1831-38), circuit court criminal (1831-71), DAR, death (1877-1922), genealogical compilations, history (1876/80, 1903/10/29/30/67/68/70/76), internal revenue assessments (1862-66), map (1891, 1908), marriage (1829, 1880-), militia, poor farm, plat (1891, 1900), probate, tax (1865-66), veterans' burial.

ISGSQ ARTICLES: 2:77, 2:90, 2:220, 7:195, 9:20, 10:121, 11:167, 12:93, 12:145, 15:34, 16:159, 24:136, 25:10.

COUNTY INVENTORY: birth (1878-), board of supervisors (1875-), circuit court (1829-), county court (1872-), county commissioners (1829-74), death (1878-), deed (1831-), entry (1829-), estray (1862-1907), guardian (1870-), insanity (1873-), marriage (1829-), military discharge (1864-), naturalization (1860-1906), physicians (1877-), probate (1829-), survey (1836-), tax (1843, 1856-), will (1844-).

LIBRARY: Decatur Public Library, 247 East North St., Decatur, IL 62523.

GENEALOGICAL SOCIETY: Decatur Genealogical Society, PO Box 1548, Decatur, IL 62526.

GENEALOGICAL PUBLICATION: Above society publishes Central IL Genealogical Quarterly. Also Decatur Genealogical Society Newsletter.

56. Macoupin County

Macoupin County, formed 1829 from Madison and Greene Counties, County Seat Carlinville (62626).

CENSUSES: 1830R, 1840RP, 1850-RFMD, 1855S, 1860RFMD, 1865S, 1870RFMD, 1880RFMD, 1900R, 1910R, 1920R.

FHL(FHC) RECORDS: atlas (1893-94), Baptist, biography (1879/91), birth (1859-1903), cemetery, commissioner's court (1829-49), death (1877-1910), deed (1831-1918), Everly Chapel (1887-1928), history (1879/82, 1986/91), inventory (1939), Lutheran (1858-1978), marks and brands (1829-80), marriage (1829-1900), Methodist (1868-1945), military (1861-63), naturalization (1849-87), obituary (1856-61, 1897-1960), original land purchasers, old settlers, physicians (1877-1915), Presbyterian (1851-85), probate (1835-1939), WPA.

IRAD-WIU RECORDS: board of supervisors (1829-1969), coroner (1835-1928), estray (1862-1915), jail (1870-1956), land patent (1819-68), marks and brands (1829-80), marriage (1876-1905), militia (1861-63), naturalization (1849-87), physician (1877-1935), police magistrate (1870-1960), tax (1842-60).

ILLINET PUBLISHED RECORDS: atlas (1875/93, 1900), Baptist, biography (1879/91, 1904/11/67), birth, cemetery, coroner (1841-1928), death (1877-78), early settlers, genealogical compilations, history (1879/91, 1911/79), marriage (1829-51), Methodist (1868-1945), newspaper abstracts, obituary (1856-61, 1866-71, 1881-89), original land purchasers.

ISGSQ ARTICLES: 2:148, 6:150, 12:81, 12:83, 12:137, 13:37, 14:143, 14:144, 14:145, 14:146, 14:147, 14:232, 14:233, 14:234, 15:65, 15:92, 16:83, 16:84, 19:229, 25:25, 25:72, 25:93, 25:131.

COUNTY INVENTORY: birth (1878-), board of supervisors (1875-), circuit court (1829-), coroner (1835-), county court (1872-), county commissioners (1829-74), death (1878-), deed (1829-), estray (1862-1907), guardian (1852-), insanity (1873-), land patent (1819-68), marks and brands (1829-80), marriage (1829-), militia (1861-63), naturalization (1849-1906), physicians (1877-), probate (1829-), soldiers' discharge (1864-85), survey (1836-), tax (1842-43, 1853-).

LIBRARY: Carlinville Public Library, 112 East First St., Carlinville, IL 62626.

GENEALOGICAL SOCIETY: Macoupin County Genealogical Society, PO Box 95, Staunton, IL 62088.

GENEALOGICAL PUBLICATION: Above society publishes Macoupin County Searcher.

57. Madison County

Madison County, formed 1812 from St. Clair and Randolph Counties, County Seat Edwardsville (155 North Main St., 62025).

CENSUSES: 1818T, 1820RS, 1830R, 1840RSP, 1850RFMD, 1855S, 1860RFMD, 1865S, 1870RFMD, 1880RFMD, 1900R, 1910R, 1920R.

FHL(FHC) RECORDS: atlas (1892), Baptist (1817-1901), biography (1882/94, 1912), birth (1878-1916, some before 1878), Catholic (1857-1920), cemetery, court (1813-21), death (1878-1915), deed (1814-1910), early settler, gazetteer (1866), genealogical compilations, genealogical handbook, guardian (1819-1981), history (1866/82, 1912/78/80/83), indentures (1805-26), land (1818-30), Lutheran (1854-1938), marriage (1813-1908), military discharge (1865-1918), naturalization (1816-1929), newspaper abstract, obituary, plat (1818-1981), probate (1818-1981), Swiss (1831-1981), United Church of Christ (1837-1989), will (1818-1922), WPA.

IRAD-WIU RECORDS: board of supervisors (1813-21), poor farm (1880-1958), probate (1813-1970).

ILLINET PUBLISHED RECORDS: atlas (1873/92, 1900/06), biography (1866/73/82/94, 1912/39/62/83), birth (1850-79), cemetery, coroner (1870-88), death (1878-81), directory (1866, 1900), early court (1813-18), early marriage, gazetteer (1866), genealogical compilations, genealogical guide, history (1866/73/82, 1900/02/12/25/62/75/78/86), indenture (1805-26), landowner (1892), map (1861), marriage, naturalization (1816-1900), poor.

ISGSQ ARTICLES: 4:142, 4:206, 5:164, 6:32, 7:64, 7:91, 7:129, 7:221, 8:31, 8:67, 8:76, 8:93, 11:48, 11:84, 11:149, 12:137, 14:143, 15:105, 16:53, 18:77, 20:193, 21:67, 22:28, 22:77, 24:2, 24:138, 24:199, 24:222, 25:93, 25:160.

COUNTY INVENTORY: adoption (1870-), birth (1877-), black (1813-60), board of supervisors (1876-), circuit court (1813-), coroner (1837-95), county court (1872-), county commissioners and court (1822-76), death (1877-), deed (1811-), early court (1813-18), estray (1817-), guardian (1851-), indenture (1813-93), insanity (1866-), land entry (1814-), marriage (1813-), military bounty (1864-66), militia (1862), mortgage (1811-), municipal court (1837-46), naturalization (1840-1906), physicians (1878-), probate (1813-), survey (1835-1908), tax (1814/20/27, 1833-), will (1818-).

LIBRARY: Edwardsville Public Library, 112 South Kansas St., Edwardsville, IL 62025.

GENEALOGICAL SOCIETY: Madison County Genealogical Society, PO Box 631, Edwardsville, IL 62025.

GENEALOGICAL PUBLICATION: Above society publishes The Stalker. Also Madison County Genealogical Society Newsletter.

---

58. Marion County

Marion County, formed 1823 from Fayette and Jefferson Counties, County Seat Salem (62881).

CENSUSES: 1830R, 1840RP, 1850RFMD, 1855S, 1860RFMD, 1865S, 1870RFMD, 1880-RFMD, 1900R, 1910R, 1920R.

FHL(FHC) RECORDS: biography (1881/94, 1909), birth (1854-1916), cemetery, death (1877-1915), deed (1823-1942), entry (1832-1900), landowner (1892), marriage (1821-1934), naturalization (1862-1906), Presbyterian (1879-1900), probate (1823-1909), will (1857-1917).

IRAD-SIU RECORDS: board of supervisors (1843-49), coroner (1870-83), jury (1871-78), naturalization (1866-1906), probate (1823-1973), tax (1849-1951), will (1854-1917).

ILLINET PUBLISHED RECORDS: atlas (1892, 1900), biography (1881/94, 1909/61), cemetery, history (1881, 1909/61/73/94), landowners (1892), map (1915), obituary.

ISGSQ ARTICLES: 3:76, 8:148, 11:18, 13:33, 16:80, 19:96, 24:113.

COUNTY INVENTORY: birth (1878-), board of supervisors, circuit court (1823-), county commissioner (1823-73), county court (1872-), death (1878-), deed (1823-), estray (1838-75), guardian (1866-), insanity (1893-), land entry (1819-96), marriage (1823-), mortgage (1857-), naturalization

(1865-1906), physician (1877-1907), plat (1894-), probate (1828-), survey (1837-53, 1885-1900), tax (1845-), will (1857-).

LIBRARY: Bryan-Bennett Library, 217 West Main St., Salem, IL 62881.

GENEALOGICAL SOCIETY: Marion County Genealogical and Historical Society, PO Box 342, Salem, IL 62881.

GENEALOGICAL PUBLICATION: Above society publishes Footprints in Marion County.

---

59. Marshall County

Marshall County, formed 1839 from Putnam County, County Seat Lacon (122 North Prairie St., 61540).

CENSUSES: 1840RP, 1850RFMD, 1855S, 1860RFMD, 1865S, 1870RFMD, 1880RFMD, 1900R, 1910R, 1920R.

FHL(FHC) RECORDS: biography (1896), cemetery, history (1860/80), IOOF.

IRAD-ISU RECORDS: none.

ILLINET PUBLISHED RECORDS: atlas (1873/90, 1900/11), biography (1880/96/97, 1907), cemetery, genealogical compilations, history (1860/80/97, 1907/53/64/65/67/68/76/83).

ISGSQ ARTICLES: 9:218, 11:45, 11:46, 11:47, 13:208, 14:74, 15:25, 19:67, 21:139, 25:33.

COUNTY INVENTORY: birth (1877-), circuit court (1839-), county court (1872-), county commissioners and supervisors (1839-), death (1879-), deed (1838-), entry (1838-), estrays (1839-1908), guardian (1856-), insanity (1893-), jury (1872-1903), marks and brands (1839-1910), marriage (1839-), military discharge (1865), militia (1861-62), naturalization (1862-1906), physicians (1877-), plat (1871-1904), poll (1850-90), probate (1839-), survey (1850-60, 1879, 1885-96), tax (1851-), will (1841-).

LIBRARY: Lacon Public Library, 205 Sixth St., Lacon, IL 61540.

GENEALOGICAL SOCIETY: Henry Historical and Genealogical Society, 610 North St., Henry, IL 61537.

GENEALOGICAL PUBLICATION: Above society publishes Newsletter.

---

60. Mason County

Mason County, formed 1841 from Tazewell and Menard Counties, County Seat Havana (62644). Courthouse fire in 1882 destroyed some records.

CENSUSES: 1850RFMD, 1855S, 1860RFMD, 1865S, 1870RFMD, 1880RFMD, 1900R, 1910R, 1920R.

FHL(FHC) RECORDS: atlas (1874, 1903), Baptist (1842-1951), biography (1874/76/94, 1902), birth (1878-1905), Catholic (1874-1960), cemetery, Christian Church (1886-1942), death (1877-1903), deed (1841-1920), directory (1869), early settlers, Episcopal (1885-1951), genealogical compilations, genealogical guidebook, guardian (1866-1906), history (1874/76/79/94, 1902/68), Lutheran (1863-1993), marriage (1841-1946), Methodist (1856-1982), mortuary (1882-1938), naturalization (1859-1906), plat (1891, 1903), Presbyterian (1867-1949), probate (1841-1973).

IRAD-SSU RECORDS: board of supervisors (1841-1960), Havana (1853-1983), militia (1861-62), naturalization (1855-1906).

ILLINET PUBLISHED RECORDS: atlas (1874, 1900/03/11), biography (1876/79/94, 1902), birth (1877-1900), cemetery, death (1878-1901), directory (1900), genealogical compilations, German, history (1876/79, 1902/68), marriage (1841-99), mortuary (1882-1921), naturalization (1859-1931), pioneer (1902), plat (1891), probate (1841-1973), survey (1823-24).

ISGSQ ARTICLES: 15:27, 16:77, 24:138.

COUNTY INVENTORY: birth (1878-), board of supervisors and county commissioners (1841-), circuit court (1841-), county court (1872-), death (1877-), deed (1841-), ear marks (1841-97), entry (1859-), guardian (1863-), insanity (1860-), marriage (1841-), military discharge (1865-1902), militia (1861-63), mortgage (1856-), naturalization (1860-1905), physicians (1877-), probate (1841-), survey (1842-), will (1866-).

LIBRARY: Havana Public Library, 201 West Adams St., Havana, IL 62644.

GENEALOGICAL SOCIETY: Mason County Genealogical and Historical Society, PO Box 246, Havana, IL 62644.

61. Massac County

Massac County, formed 1843 from Pope and Johnson Counties, County Seat Metropolis (62960).

CENSUSES: 1850RFMD, 1855S, 1860-RFMD, 1865S, 1870RFMD, 1880RFMD, 1900R, 1910R, 1920R.

FHL(FHC) RECORDS: Baptist (1851-68), biography (1893, 1900/87), birth (1864-1941), cemetery, Church of Christ (1847-1943), circuit court (1843-49), death (1878-1971), deed (1843-96), Evangelical (1854-1927), Evangelical Lutheran (1865-1925), history (1900/55/87), IOOF, Lutheran (1860-89), marriage (1843-1923), Methodist (1839-84), naturalization

(1862-1904), newspaper abstract (1849-69), obituary (1866-76), probate (1846-94), tax (1853-54).

IRAD-SIU RECORDS: circuit court (1843-49), estray (1843-95), marks and brands (1860-1911), naturalization (1862-1904), physician (1877-1934), poor (1878-1942), probate (1846-1964), tax (1848-94).

ILLINET PUBLISHED RECORDS: atlas (1900), biography (1893, 1900/67/87), cemetery, coroner (1869-1914), death (1878-1902), history (1900/55/67/83/90), Lutheran (1854-1927), marriage (1843-77), Masonic (1857-1987), obituary,

ISGSQ ARTICLES: 2:211, 4:234, 5:153, 14:12, 14:25, 20:60.

COUNTY INVENTORY: birth (1877-), circuit court (1843-), county court (1872-), county commissioners (1843-), death (1877-), deed (1842-), entry (1860-), estray (1862-95), guardian (1872-), insanity (1893-), jail (1879-1910), jury (1860-), marks and brands (1860-), marriage (1843-), military discharge (1868-72), militia (1861-62), mortgage (1860-), naturalization (1862-1906), original land entry (1836-66), physicians (1877-), plat (1892), probate (1843-), survey (1886-1910), tax (1843-), will (1861-).

LIBRARY: Metropolis Public Library, 317 Metropolis St., Metropolis, IL 62960.

GENEALOGICAL SOCIETY: Massac County Genealogical Society, PO Box 1043, Metropolis, IL 62960.

62. McDonough County

McDonough County, formed 1826 from Schuyler County, organized in 1830, County Seat Macomb (61455).

CENSUSES: 1830R, 1840RP, 1850-RFMD, 1855S, 1860RFMD, 1865S, 1870RFMD, 1880RFMD, 1900R, 1910R, 1920R.

FHL(FHC) RECORDS: atlas (1871, 1913), Baptist (1833-1991), biography (1885/94, 1907/84), Catholic (1872-1943), cemetery, church record collection (1830-1991), coroner (1860-1923), deed (1831-1904), genealogical compilations, history (1878/85, 1907/68/84/92), marriage (1830-1900), Methodist (1841-1991), newspaper abstract (1880-1912), obituary (1830-1980), poor (1863-1914), Presbyterian (1852-1992), tax (1857-69), town lots (1832-1938), will (1834-57).

IRAD-WIU RECORDS: board of supervisors (1830-1969), coroner (1831-1969), entry (1831-1969), estray (1850-1905), jury (1891-1954), militia (1843-46), physician (1877-1945), poor (1863-1914), tax (1835-1939), town lot (1832-1939).

ILLINET PUBLISHED RECORDS: atlas (1871/93, 1900), Bible, biography (1878/85/94, 1907/92), cemetery, coroner (1860-1923), church record collection, directory (1898), genealogical compilations, history (1878/85, 1907/26/36/38/67/76/84/92), map (1861), marriage (1830-89), Methodist (1891-1991), newspaper (1892-1912), obituary, petition (1853), pioneers, plat (1893), Presbyterian (1839-1964), residents (1859), will (1834-57).

ISGSQ ARTICLES: 8:153, 8:155, 9:89, 10:93, 10:137, 11:18, 11:210, 13:195, 13:196, 15:19, 15:78, 15:262, 15:274, 16:34, 16:86, 16:169, 17:41, 17:101, 18:37, 19:230, 20:18, 20:26, 20:31, 20:33, 20:44, 22:88, 22:134.

COUNTY INVENTORY: birth (1878-), board of supervisors and county commissioners (1830-), circuit court (1830-), county court (1872-), death (1878-), deed (1830-), entry (1830-), estray (1857-68), guardian (1858-), insanity (1870-), marriage (1830-), militia (1861-62), mortgage (1836-), naturalization (1854-1906), physicians (1877-), plat (1883-), probate (1833-), survey (1883-), tax (1837-), will (1834-).

LIBRARY: WIU; Macomb City Public Library, 235 South Lafayette St., Macomb, IL 61455.

GENEALOGICAL SOCIETY: McDonough County Genealogical Society, PO Box 202, Macomb, IL 61455.

GENEALOGICAL PUBLICATION: Above society publishes McDonough County Genealogical Society News Quarterly.

63. McHenry County

McHenry County, formed 1836 from Cook County, organized 1837, County Seat Woodstock (2200 North Seminary Ave., 60098).

CENSUSES: 1840RP, 1850RFMD, 1855S, 1860RFMD, 1865S, 1870RFMD, 1880RFMD, 1900R, 1910R, 1920R.

FHL(FHC) RECORDS: atlas (1872, 1908), Bible, biography (1877/85, 1922/68), birth (1878-1902), Catholic (1852-1909), cemetery, deeds (1841-1901), death (1878-1909), directory (1877/92), early settlers, genealogical compilations, guardian (1840-1957), history (1885, 1922/68), map (1862), marriage (1837-1923), naturalization (1851-1955), obituary, probate (1840-1986), will (1898-1922).

IRAD-NIU RECORDS: deed (1841-1945).

ILLINET PUBLISHED RECORDS: atlas (1872/92), 1900/08), biography (1877/85, 1903/94), cemetery, genealogical compilations (1972-/76/94), history (1877/85, 1903/22/42/68/94), marriage, map (1862), naturalization (1851-1906), plat (1892), veterans' burial.

ISGSQ ARTICLES: 7:75, 10:31, 10:88, 14:69, 23:67.

COUNTY INVENTORY: birth (1877-), board of supervisors (1848-), circuit court (1838-), county court (1872-), county commissioners (1837-

48), death (1877-), deed (1837-), guardian (1873-), insanity (1875-), jury (1872-), land entry (1838-), marriage (1837-), mortgage (1848-), naturalization (1858-1906), physicians (1877-), probate (1840-), survey (1885-), tax (1850-), will (1866-).

LIBRARY: Woodstock Public Library, 414 West Judd St., Woodstock, IL 60098.

GENEALOGICAL SOCIETY: McHenry County Illinois Genealogical Society, 1011 Green St., Woodstock, IL 60050.

GENEALOGICAL PUBLICATION: Above society publishes McHenry County Illinois Connection.

---

64. McLean County

McLean County, formed 1830 from Tazewell County, County Seat Bloomington (104 West Front St., 61701). Fire in 1900 destroyed some records.

CENSUSES: 1840RP, 1850RFMD, 1855S, 1860RFMD, 1865S, 1870RFMD, 1880RFMD, 1900R, 1910R, 1920R.

FHL(FHC) RECORDS: atlas (1874, 1914), biography (1887/99, 1908), birth (1860-1902), Christian Church (1847-1908), DAR, death (1878-1900), genealogical compilations, German, history (1874/79, 1908/24/82), marriage (1831-1912), veterans' burial.

IRAD-ISU RECORDS: Bloomington (1871-1965), coroner (1884-1975), deed (1841-1945), probate (1834-1944).

ILLINET PUBLISHED RECORDS: atlas (1874, 1900/14), Bible, biography (1877/79/87/99, 1908/71/80), birth (1860-99), cemetery, gazetteer (1866), genealogical compilations, geography (1976), history (1874/79, 1908/24/30/69/72), internal revenue assessment (1862-66), map (1866/95), marriage (1831-92), naturalization (1853-1955), newspaper abstract, obituary (1848-70), plat (1895, 1900), veterans' burials.

ISGSQ ARTICLES: 2:8, 3:154, 4:93, 6:100, 7:125, 7:150, 11:42, 12:72, 14:71, 19:69, 19:143, 19:215, 22:173, 22:232, 22:233, 25:33.

COUNTY INVENTORY: birth (1878-), board of supervisors (1858-), circuit court (1831-), county court (1872-), county commissioners (1831-58), death (1878-), deed (1831-), guardian (1872-), insanity (1887-), jury, land entry (1846-), marriage (1831-), military (1861-64), military discharge (1863-1907), mortgage (1850-), naturalization (1853-1906), original entry (1821-68), physicians (1877-), plat (1867-), probate (1831-), survey (1840-69), will (1838-).

LIBRARY: ISU in Normal; Bloomington Public Library, 205 East Olive St., Bloomington, IL 61701; McLean County Historical Society

Library, 200 N. Main St., Bloomington, IL 61701; Normal Public Library, 206 W. College Avenue, Normal, IL 61761.

GENEALOGICAL SOCIETY: McLean County Genealogical Society, PO Box 488, Normal, IL 61761.

GENEALOGICAL PUBLICATION: Above society publishes Gleanings from the Heart of the Cornbelt. Also Newsletter.

65. Menard County

Menard County, formed 1839 from Sangamon County, County Seat Petersburg (62675).

CENSUSES: 1840RP, 1850RFMD, 1855S, 1860RFMD, 1865S, 1870RFMD, 1880RFMD, 1900R, 1910R, 1920R.

FHL(FHC) RECORDS: biography (1902/05), birth (1877-85), cemetery, chancery court (1839-1971), county court (1839-1963), death (1877-1900), deed (1838-1934), history (1905), land sales (1824-70), marriage (1839-1900), Masonic, naturalization (1859-1909), newspaper abstract (1861-68, 1878-79), poor (1879-1940), probate (1839-1963), Revolutionary veteran burial, voter (1839-45).

IRAD-SSU RECORDS: circuit court (1839-60), estray (1839-70), militia (1861-63), naturalization (1859-1944), poor (1879-1945), tax (1824-66), will (1849-84).

ILLINET PUBLISHED RECORDS: atlas (1874/99, 1900), biography (1879, 1902/05/88), birth (1877-85), cemetery, county court (1839-1971), death (1877-1900), early voters, genealogical compilations, history (1879, 1902/05/55), history of churches, inventory (1941), marriage (1839-75), Methodist, military registration (1861), obituary, original land sales (1824-70), Presbyterian (1867-), probate (1839-1963), Revolutionary veteran burial.

ISGSQ ARTICLES: 2:156, 16:37, 19:215.

COUNTY INVENTORY: birth (1878-), circuit court (1839-), county court (1872-), county commissioners (1839-), death (1878-), deed (1839-), estray (1839-68, 1876-92), guardian (1868-), insanity (1872-), land entry (1865-), marriage (1839-), mortgage (1858-), naturalization (1859-1906), physicians (1877-), probate (1839-), tax (1845-), will (1861-84).

LIBRARY: Petersburg Public Library, 220 S. Sixth St., Petersburg, IL 62675.

HISTORICAL SOCIETY: Menard County Historical Society, 125 S. Seventh St., Petersburg, IL 62675.

66. Mercer County

Mercer County, formed 1825 from Pike County, organized 1835, County Seat Aledo (604 NE Fifth Ave., 61231).

CENSUSES: 1830R, 1840RP, 1850-RFMD, 1855S, 1860RFMD, 1865S, 1870RFMD, 1880RFMD, 1900R, 1910R, 1920R.

FHL(FHC) RECORDS: biography (1882), cemetery, history (1882), poor (1859-1986), Presbyterian (1874-1959).

IRAD-WIU RECORDS: deed (1834-1901), land entry (1834-1954), poor (1859-1986).

ILLINET PUBLISHED RECORDS: atlas (1875, 1900), biography (1882, 1903/14/77/85), cemetery, DAR transcripts, genealogical compilations, history (1882, 1903/14/55/77/78/85), plat (1892, 1900).

ISGSQ ARTICLES: 2:85, 8:192, 13:209, 17:215, 25:33.

COUNTY INVENTORY: birth (1878-), board of supervisors and county commissioner (1835-), circuit court (1836-), county court (1872-), death (1878-), deed (1835-), estray (1836-1907), guardian (1853-), insanity (1874-), jury (1872-), land entry (1835-), marks and brands (1836-1908), marriage (1835-), military discharge (1865-1900), mortgage (1844-89), naturalization (1840-1907), physicians (1877-), plat (1869-), probate (1837-), survey (1885-), tax (1843-), will (1850-).

LIBRARY: Mercer Carnegie Library, 200 North College Ave., Aledo, IL 61231.

HISTORICAL SOCIETY: Mercer County Historical Society, 1406 SE Second Ave., Aledo, IL 61231.

67. Monroe County

Monroe County, formed 1816 from St. Clair and Randolph Counties, County Seat Waterloo (100 South Main St, 62298).

CENSUSES: 1818T, 1820RS, 1830R, 1840RSP, 1850RFMD, 1855S, 1860RFMD, 1865S, 1870RFMD, 1880RFMD, 1900R, 1910R, 1920R.

FHL(FHC) RECORDS: Baptist (1806-1959), biography (1883/94, 1955), birth (1868-1915), Cahokia (1722-1820), cemetery, court (1807-38), death (1878-1915), deed (1816-1900), Evangelical (1839-1948), history (1883, 1976/78/83), Lutheran (1841-1976), marriage (1816-1915), naturalization (1854-1906), Presbyterian (1875-1972), probate (1820-85), United Church of Christ (1846-1983).

IRAD-SIU RECORDS: county order (1870-1912), deed (1816-1963), naturalization (1854-1906), probate (1819-94).

ILLINET PUBLISHED RECORDS: atlas (1875, 1900/01), Bible, biography (1883/94), cemetery, DAR, history (1883/94), marriage (1816-77), plat (1900).

ISGSQ ARTICLES: 2:146, 3:136, 3:137, 4:92, 8:76, 9:124.

COUNTY INVENTORY: birth (1878-), circuit court (1817-), county commissioner (1816-), county court (1872-), death (1878-), deed (1816-), estray (1861-78), guardian (1858-), insanity (1878-), land entry (1814-57, 1882-), marriage (1816-), mortgage (1865-), militia (1861-62), naturalization (1860-1904), physician (1877-), plat (1867-), probate (1820-), survey (1866-), tax (1841-), will (1815-).

LIBRARY: Morrison-Talbott Library, 219 Park St., Waterloo, IL 62298.

GENEALOGICAL SOCIETY: Monroe County Genealogical Research Group, Box 256, Route 3, Waterloo, IL 62298.

68. Montgomery County

Montgomery County, formed 1821 from Bond and Madison Counties, County Seat Hillsboro (62049).

CENSUSES: 1830R, 1840RP, 1850RFMD, 1855S, 1860RFMD, 1865S, 1870RFM, 1880RFMD, 1900R, 1910R, 1920R.

FHL(FHC) RECORDS: atlas (1874, 1912), Baptist (1818-1950), biography (1882, 1918), cemetery, Christian Church (1863-1982), genealogical compilations, history (1882, 1918), Litchfield (1859-1924), Lutheran (1807-1947), marriage (1821-95), naturalization (1862-1910), newspaper abstract (1895-1980), Presbyterian (1819-1982), probate (1850-1914), will (1849-1929).

IRAD-SSU RECORDS: birth (1862-1957), circuit court (1821-1955), deed (1821-1958), land entry (1837-52), Litchfield (1859-1965), marks and brands (1821-46), marriage (1821-32), military discharge (1862-65), physician (1877-1929), plat (1823-1958), probate (1849-1958), survey (1836-39), tax (1821-72), will (11858-1958).

ILLINET PUBLISHED RECORDS: atlas (1874, 1900/12), biography (1878/82/92, 1904/18), cemetery, directory (1900), genealogical compilations, history (1882, 1904/18), inventory (1939), marriage (1817-74), naturalizaton (1862-1910), newspaper abstracts (1895-1980), obituary, petition (1838).

ISGSQ ARTICLES: 1(3):37, 1(4):18, 2:4, 3:129, 3:157, 4:239, 6:157, 6:160, 7:196, 8:36, 10:1, 10:8, 10:217, 13:143, 15:246, 19:217, 22:25, 22:28, 22:77, 23:171, 23:230, 24:2, 24:138, 24:198.

COUNTY INVENTORY: birth (1877-), circuit court (1821-), county court (1872-), county commissioners and supervisors (1821-), death

(1877-), deed (1821-), estray (1821-88), guardian (1850-), insanity (1886-), land entry (1837-), marriage (1821-), militia (1860-62), mortgage (1859-), naturalization (1862-1906), original land entry (1819-32), physicians (1877-), probate (1821-), survey (1885-), tax (1830-47, 1854-), will (1867-).

LIBRARY: Hillsboro Public Library, 214 School St., Hillsboro, IL 62049; Litchfield Carnegie Public Library, 400 North State St., Litchfield, IL 62056.

GENEALOGICAL SOCIETY: Montgomery County Genealogical Society, Litchfield Carnegie Public Library, 400 North State St., Litchfield, IL 62056.

GENEALOGICAL PUBLICATION: Above society publishes the Montgomery County Genealogical Society Quarterly. Also Newsletter.

69. Morgan County

Morgan County, formed 1823 from Sangamon and Greene Counties, County Seat Jacksonville (300 West State St, 62650).

CENSUSES: 1830RS, 1835S, 1840RP, 1850RFMD, 1855S, 1860RFMD, 1865S, 1870RFM, 1880RFMD, 1900R, 1910R, 1920R.

FHL(FHC) RECORDS: biography (1878/85/89, 1906/76), birth (1858-1979), cemetery, DAR, death (1858-1938), deed (1823-1907), directory (1860-61/66/68-69), Episcopal (1834-79), genealogical compilation, history (1878/85/89, 1906/39/68/73), inventory (1939), land (1827-61), Lutheran (1850-1980), marriage (1827-1939), military (1861-65), naturalization (1835-84), plat (1894), Presbyterian (1855-60, 1875-1900), probate (1824-1929), tax (1836, 1839-42), veterans' burial.

IRAD-SSU RECORDS: board of supervisors (1828-70), estray (1827-37), land entry (1823-40), probate (1837-52), tax (1836-61).

ILLINET PUBLISHED RECORDS: atlas (1872, 1900), biography (1878/85/89, 1906), cemetery, directory (1900), genealogical compilation, history (1873/78/85/89, 1906/25/42/68), immigration, inventory (1939), marriage (1827-69), naturalization, plat (1894), probate (1837-49), tax (1836/40), War of 1812 veterans' burials.

ISGSQ ARTICLES: 3:72, 6:101, 8:204, 9:30, 9:199, 12:137, 14:135, 15:19, 22:28, 22:77, 23:86, 24:2, 25:67, 25:136, 25:172.

COUNTY INVENTORY: birth (1878-), board of supervisors and county commissioners (1827-), circuit court (1828-), coroner (1869-99), county court (1872-), death (1878-), deed (1824-), estray (1833-37, 1843-95), guardian (1827-), insanity (1878-), jury (1872-84), land entry (1823-34, 1847-), marriage (1827-), military discharge (1863-99), mortgage (1830-), naturalization (1836-48, 1856-1908), original land entry (1823-27), physicians (1865-), poll (1829-1907), probate (1843-), survey (1879-), tax (1835-), will (1824-).

LIBRARY: Jacksonville Public Library, 201 West College St., Jacksonville, IL 62650.

GENEALOGICAL SOCIETY: Jacksonville Area Genealogical and Historical Society, 203 South Fayette St., Jacksonville, IL 62651; Morgan County Genealogical Society, 629 South Diamond St., Jacksonville, IL 62650; Meredosia Area Historical and Genealogical Society, PO Box 304, Meredosia, IL 62665.

GENEALOGICAL PUBLICATION: First society above publishes Jacksonville Illinois Genealogical Journal.

70. Moultrie County

Moultrie County, formed 1843 from Shelby and Macon Counties, County Seat Sullivan (61951).

CENSUSES: 1850RFMD, 1855S, 1860RFMD, 1865S, 1870RFM, 1880-RFMD, 1900R, 1910R, 1920R.

FHL(FHC) RECORDS: atlas (1913), biography (1881/91, 1990), birth (1877-1956), cemetery, Church of Christ (1872-1961), death (1877-1973), deed (1849-1935), history (1881, 1990), marriage (1843-1981), Methodist (1885-1965), military discharge (1862-98), obituary, will (1862-1964).

IRAD-EIU RECORDS: death (1877-1927).

ILLINET PUBLISHED RECORDS: atlas (1875/96, 1900), biography (1881/91, 1990), cemetery, Christian Church (1860-74, 1889-1902), Church of Christ (1881-1905), history (1881, 1990), internal revenue assessment (1862-66), inventory (1941), marriage (1843-82), mortuary (1890-1924), obituary (pre-1920).

ISGSQ ARTICLES: 2:212, 3:111, 13(1)iv, 24:139.

COUNTY INVENTORY: birth (1877-), board of supervisors (1867-), circuit court (1849-), coroner (1897-), county court (1872-), county commissioners (1843-73), death (1877-), deed (1848-), ear marks (1845-72), estray (1858-69, 1875-), guardian (1860-), indenture (1859-65), insanity (1872-), jury (1866-), marriage (1843-), military discharge (1865-1907), mortgage (1864-), naturalization (1862-1906), physicians (1877-), probate (1845-), survey (1870-), tax (1853-), will (1845-).

LIBRARY: Sullivan City Public Library, 2 West Water St., Sullivan, IL 61951; Moultrie County Historical and Genealogical Society Library, 117 East Harrison St., Sullivan, 61951.

GENEALOGICAL SOCIETY: Moultrie County Historical and Genealogical Society, 117 East Harrison St., Sullivan, IL 61951.

GENEALOGICAL PUBLICATION: Above society publishes Moultrie County Heritage. Also Newsletter.

71. Ogle County Ogle County, formed 1836 from Jo Daviess and LaSalle Counties, enlarged in 1839 with more land from Jo Daviess County, County Seat Oregon (Washington and South Fourth Sts., 61061).

CENSUSES: 1840RP, 1850RFMD, 1855S, 1860RFMD, 1865S, 1870RFM, 1880RFMD, 1900R, 1910R, 1920R.

FHL(FHC) RECORDS: biography (1878/86/99, 1909), cemetery, Civil War veterans, court (1837-42), DAR, death (1878-1953), deed (1837-1934), Evangelical and Reformed (1894-1903), genealogical compilation, guardian (1858-1932), history (1878/86, 1909), inventory (1940), marriage (1837-1930), mortuary (1890-1920), naturalization (1839-1929), obituary, probate (1838-1940), will (1845-1934).

IRAD-NIU RECORDS: board of supervisors (1837-1915), birth (1857-1955), circuit court (1837-1915), Civil War bounty (1862-69), county court (1869-97), death (1878-1965), deed (1837-1942), estray (1837-1918), guardian (1858-95), jail (1859-91), jury (1838-88), land entry (1837-1962), land patent (1833-55), militia (1861-62), naturalization (1839-1930), poor (1878-1933), probate (1838-1940), survey (1854-1915), will (1866-1934).

ILLINET PUBLISHED RECORDS: atlas (1872, 1900/12), biography (1878/86/99, 1909), cemetery, directory (1854-55), genealogical compilations, history (1859/78/86, 1900/09/67), inventory (1940), marriage (1837-1900), obituary (1896-1980), plat (1893), veteran (1886).

ISGSQ ARTICLES: 6:193, 15:276, 17:1, 17:2, 19:210, 24:140, 25:151.

COUNTY INVENTORY: birth (1878-), board of supervisors and county commissioners (1837-), circuit court (1837-), county court (1872-), death (1878-), deed (1837-), estray (1858-), guardian (1858-), insanity (1872-), land entry (1837-), marriage (1837-), militia (1861-62), mortgage (1841-), naturalization (1856-1906), physicians (1877-), plat (1850-), probate (1837-), tax (1847-), will (1838-).

LIBRARY: Oregon Public Library District, 300 Jefferson St., Oregon IL 61061.

GENEALOGICAL SOCIETY: Ogle County Genealogical Society, PO Box 251, Oregon, IL 61061.

72. Peoria County Peoria County, formed 1825 from Fulton County, County Seat Peoria (324 Main St., 61602).

CENSUSES: 1830R, 1840RP, 1850RFMD, 1855S, 1860RFMD, 1865S, 1870RFM, 1880RFMD, 1900R, 1910R, 1920R.

FHL(FHC) RECORDS: atlas (1873/90), biography (1880/90, 1902/12), cemetery, city directory (1844/50/56-1935), early settler, Episcopal, genealogical compilations, history (1850/70/80/82, 1902/74), inventory (1942), newspaper abstract, obituary, poor (1848-1936), probate (1825-87), tax (1825).

IRAD-WIU RECORDS: deed (1817-62), poor (1848-1936), probate (1825-87).

ILLINET PUBLISHED RECORDS: atlas (1873/96, 1900), biography (1880/90, 1901/12), cemetery, circuit court (1827-46), court (1825-32), death (1837-63), directory (1877, 1900), genealogical compilations, history (1844/80, 1901/12/68), inventory (1942), map (1861/90), potters' field burials (1899-1926), probate (1825-87).

ISGSQ ARTICLES: 3:1, 3:82, 3:92, 4:234, 5:165, 7:218, 9:218, 12:137, 14:75, 19:215, 23:7, 23:71, 25:33.

COUNTY INVENTORY: adoption (1891-), birth (1878-), board of supervisors (1850-), circuit court (1828-), commissioners court (1858-72), county court (1872-), county commissioners (1825-50), death (1878-), deed (1825-), estray (1872-), guardian (1825-), insanity (1882-), land entry (1825-), marriage (1825-), military discharge (1863-95), militia (1861), mortgage (1836-), naturalization (1855-1906), physicians (1878-), probate (1825-), road (1836-56), tax (1844-), will (1849-).

LIBRARY: Peoria Public Library, 107 NE Monroe St., Peoria, IL 61602.

GENEALOGICAL SOCIETY: Peoria Genealogical Society, PO Box 1489, Peoria, IL 61655.

GENEALOGICAL PUBLICATION: Above society publishes Prairie Roots. Also Newsletter.

73. Perry County

Perry County, formed 1827 from Randolph and Jackson Counties, County Seat Pinckneyville (612 Virginia Court, 62274).

CENSUSES: 1830R, 1840RP, 1850RFMD, 1855S, 1860RFMD, 1865S, 1870RFM, 1880-RFMD, 1900R, 1910R, 1920R.

FHL(FHC) RECORDS: Baptist (1857-1966), biography (1883/94, 1988), birth (1878-1916), Catholic (1892-1968), cemetery, county commissioners (1828-35), death (1878-1915), deed (1827-1950), guardian (1860-86), history (1883, 1988), insanity (1852-1924), marriage (1827-1916), naturalization (1856-1909), Presbyterian (1857-86), probate (1864-89), will (1860-1917).

IRAD-SIU RECORDS: board of supervisors (1835-1971), coroner (1870-92), indentures (1834-81), insanity (1854-1939), land patent (1814-1903), marks and brands (1859-94), naturalization (1845-1909), probate (1828-58), tax (1827-40, 1856-99).

ILLINET PUBLISHED RECORDS: atlas (1900/02), biography (1883/94), cemetery, genealogical compilations, history (1883/94, 1956/88), marriage (1827-50, 1868-96), Presbyterian (1834-63).

ISGSQ ARTICLES: 2:146, 9:43, 1:134, 21:71, 22:27, 24:140.

COUNTY INVENTORY: birth (1878-), board of supervisors and county commissioners (1828-), circuit court (1827-), commissioners court (1849-72), county court (1872-), death (1878-), deed (1829-), ear marks (1827-94), estray (1834-1908), guardian (1860-), insanity (1885-), land entry (1818-96), marriage (1827-), mortgage (1864-), naturalization (1860-1906), physicians (1877-), poll (1828-60), probate (1828-), survey (1885-), tax (1853-), will (1867-).

LIBRARY: Pinckneyville Public Library, 312 South Walnut St., Pinckneyville, IL 62274.

GENEALOGICAL SOCIETY: Genealogical Society of Southern IL, c/o John A. Logan College, Box 145, Route 2, Carterville, IL 62918.

GENEALOGICAL PUBLICATION: Above society publishes the Saga of Southern IL. Also Newsletter.

74. Piatt County

Piatt County, formed 1841 from DeWitt and Macon Counties, County Seat Monticello (101 West Washington St., 61856).

CENSUSES: 1850RFMD, 1855S, 1860-RFMD, 1865S, 1870RFM, 1880RFMD, 1900R, 1910R, 1920R.

FHL(FHC) RECORDS: atlas (1875/96, 1910), biography (1891, 1903), birth (1877-1931), cemetery, Civil War veterans, death (1877-1915), deed (1841-1954), genealogical compilations, history (1903/68/87/89), inventory (1940), jury (1874-1908), marriage (1841-1971), Methodist, military (1860-64), military discharge (1865-1920), naturalization (1858-1927), newspaper abstract, probate (1843-87), tax (1835-54), will (1850-1918).

IRAD-ISU RECORDS: birth (1877-1974), circuit court (1841-1911), county court (1872-92), death (1877-1974), deed (1841-1918), guardian (1859-1915), mortgage (1865-91), naturalization (1858-1906), probate (1843-1901), tax (1835-54), will (1850-1961).

ILLINET PUBLISHED RECORDS: atlas (1875, 1900/05/10), biography (1883/91, 1903/17), birth (1877-1916), cemetery, Civil War veterans, court, genealogical compilations, history (1883/91, 1903/17/-55/68), internal revenue assessments (1862-66), inventory (1940), marriage

(1841-1910), naturalization, newspaper abstracts, obituary, physician (1822-1950), poor (1871-72, 1884-1940).

ISGSQ ARTICLES: 2:216, 21:231.

COUNTY INVENTORY: birth (1877-), board of supervisors (1860-), circuit court (1841-), county court (1872-), county commissioners (1843-60), death (1877-), deed (1840-), estray (1850-99), guardian (1864-), insanity (1880-), jury (1872-), land entry (1836-56), marks and brands (1847-80), marriage (1841-), military (1860), military discharge (1865-1905), naturalization (1858-1906), physicians (1877-), probate (1841-), survey (1843-), tax (1850-), will (1850-).

LIBRARY: Allerton Public Library, 201 North State St., Monticello, IL 61856.

GENEALOGICAL SOCIETY: Piatt County Historical and Genealogical Society, PO Box 111, Monticello, IL 61856.

GENEALOGICAL PUBLICATION: Above society publishes Piatt County Historical and Genealogical Society Newsletter.

75. Pike County

Pike County, formed 1821 from Madison, Bond, and Clark Counties, County Seat Pittsfield (62363).

CENSUSES: 1830R, 1840RP, 1850RFMD, 1855S, 1860RFMD, 1865S, 1870RFM, 1880-RFMD, 1900R, 1910R, 1920R.

FHL(FHC) RECORDS: atlas (1872, 1912), biography (1880/91, 1906), birth (1877-1915), cemetery, DAR, death (1877-1915), deed (1818-1910), genealogical compilations, general store (1859-73), guardian (1872-1933), history (1880, 1906/39/71), inventory (1938), marriage (1827-1923), naturalization (1848-94), obituary, probate (1821-73), town lot (1835-1945), tract (1817-1940), will (1850-1950).

IRAD-WIU RECORDS: deed (1818-61).

ILLINET PUBLISHED RECORDS: atlas (1872, 1900/12), biography (1880/91, 1906/67), cemetery, genealogical compilations, history (1877/80, 1906/55/67), inventory (1939), map (1860), marriage (1827-53).

ISGSQ ARTICLES: 1(4):32, 2:224, 3:77, 5:89, 6:126, 7:155, 9:45, 9:136, 9:151, 11:34, 12:125, 13:20, 13:155, 22:15, 22:164, 24:141, 25:10.

COUNTY INVENTORY: birth (1877-), board of supervisors (1850-), circuit court (1821-), coroner (1833-), county court (1872-), county commissioners (1821-50), death (1877-), deed (1820-), estray (1866-1904), guardian (1853-), insanity (1868-), jury (1872-), land entry (1817-57), marriage (1827-), military discharge (1865-1902), mortgage (1820-), naturalization (1851-1906), physicians (1877-), probate (1821-), survey (1834-), tax (1836-), will (1855-).

LIBRARY: Pittsfield Public Library, 206 North Memorial St., Pittsfield, IL 62363.

GENEALOGICAL SOCIETY: Pike and Calhoun Counties Genealogical Society, 207 North Main St., Pleasant Hill, IL 62366.

GENEALOGICAL PUBLICATION: Above society publishes A Peek at Pike.

76. Pope County

Pope County, formed 1816 from Johnson and Gallatin Counties, County Seat Golconda (62938).

CENSUSES: 1818T, 1820RS, 1830R, 1840RP, 1850RFMD, 1855S, 1860RFMD, 1865S, 1870RFM, 1880RFMD, 1900R, 1910R, 1920R.

FHL(FHC) RECORDS: Baptist (1860-1972), biography (1893, 1989), birth (1862-1930), cemetery, circuit court (1818-62), Civil War soldiers, county court (1816-50), death (1877-1917), deed (1810-1910), genealogical compilations, history (1893, 1989), IOOF (1860-1945), landowner (1820), marriage (1813-1960), military (1861-62), military discharge (1862-65), naturalization (1864-98), obituary (1858-1934), Presbyterian (1819-1917), probate (1816-1950), Revolutionary War veterans, tax (1816-65), will (1861-1916).

IRAD-SIU RECORDS: circuit court (1818-59), military (1861-65), naturalization (1864-98), tax (1825-65), will (1861-1916).

ILLINET PUBLISHED RECORDS: atlas (1900), biography (1893, 1986/89), cemetery, county court (1816-31), deed (1811-50), genealogical compilations, historical map, history (1900, 1986.89), IOOF (1860-1945), marks and brands (1816-56), marriage (1813-1909), military pension, newspaper abstracts, obituary, probate (1816-35).

ISGSQ ARTICLES: 2:155, 5:153, 7:138, 9:68, 12:41, 13:67.

COUNTY INVENTORY: birth (1877-), circuit court (1818-), county court (1872-), county commissioners (1816-), death (1877-), deed (1816-), estray (1863-80), guardian (1872-), indenture (1831-), insanity (1889-93), land entry (1816-56, 1869-), marriage (1816-), militia (1862), military discharge (1835-51, 1865-), mortgage (1861-), naturalization (1888-96), physicians (1877-), probate (1816-), tax (1829, 1853, 1857-), will (1862-).

LIBRARY: Golconda Public Library, Main Street., Golconda, IL 62938.

GENEALOGICAL SOCIETY: Genealogical Society of Southern IL, c/o John A. Logan College, Box 145, Route 2, Carterville, IL 62918.

GENEALOGICAL PUBLICATION: Above society publishes The Saga of Southern IL. Also Newsletter.

77. Pulaski County

Pulaski County, formed 1843 from Johnson and Alexander Counties, County Seat Mound City 62963.

CENSUSES: 1850RFMD, 1855S, 1860-RFMD, 1865S, 1870RFM, 1880RFMD, 1900R, 1910R, 1920R.

FHL(FHC) RECORDS: biography (1883, 1987/92), birth (1882-1919), cemetery, Civil War veterans, death (1882-1919), deed (1843-91), history (1883, 1987/92), marriage (1857-1936), naturalization (1877-1900), probate (1862-1973), Revolutionary War veterans.

IRAD-SIU RECORDS: board of supervisors (1873-1945), birth (1882-1926), circuit court (1857-1945), coroner (1883), death (1882-1926), deed (1842-1945), marriage (1861-1947), naturalization (1872-1900), probate (1862-1944), survey (1851-1940).

ILLINET PUBLISHED RECORDS: biography (1883, 1987/92), cemetery, genealogical compilations, history (1883, 1944/87/92), plat book (1900).

ISGSQ ARTICLES: 10:221, 15:124, 23:227.

COUNTY INVENTORY: birth (1883-), circuit court (1844-), county court (1872-), county commissioners (1860-), death (1883-), deed (1843-), guardian (1870-), jury (1872-), land entry (1894-), marriage (1861-), mortgage (1867-), naturalization (1874-1906), probate (1860-), survey (1855-86), tax (1868-), will (1898-).

LIBRARY: Mound City Public Library, 307 Central St., Mound City, IL 62963; Mounds Public Library, 130 South Blanche Ave., Mounds, IL 62964.

GENEALOGICAL SOCIETY: Genealogical Society of Southern IL, c/o John A. Logan College, Box 145, Route 2, Carterville, IL 62918.

GENEALOGICAL PUBLICATION: Above society publishes The Saga of Southern IL. Also Newsletter.

78. Putnam County

Putnam County, formed 1825 from Fulton County, organized in 1831, County Seat Hennepin (61327).

CENSUSES: 1830R, 1840RP, 1850-RFMD, 1855S, 1860RFMD, 1865S, 1870RFM, 1880RFMD, 1900R, 1910R, 1920R.

FHL(FHC) RECORDS: biography (1896), cemetery, genealogical compilations, history (1880), Quaker (1841-1991).

IRAD-NIU RECORDS: none.

ILLINET PUBLISHED RECORDS: biography (1880/97, 1967), genealogical compilations, history (1860/77/80/97, 1907).

ISGSQ ARTICLES: 1(3):3, 1(4):7, 2:13, 2:93, 3:71, 5:105, 12:137, 22:204.

COUNTY INVENTORY: birth (1878-), circuit court (1831-), county court (1872-), county commissioners (1836-), death (1878-), deed (1831-), estray (1832-70), guardian (1834-), insanity (1870-), jury (1872-), land entry (1832-), marks and brands (1831-92), marriage (1831-), militia (1861-63), mortgage (1842-), naturalization (1836-1906), physicians (1877-), plat (1874-), probate (1831-), survey (1836-), tax (1831-), will (1888-).

LIBRARY: Putnam County Library, 200 East High St., Hennepin, IL 61327.

HISTORICAL SOCIETY: Putnam County Historical Society, Box 74, Route 26 and Power Road, Hennepin, IL 61327.

HISTORICAL PUBLICATION: Above society publishes Putnam Past Times.

79. Randolph County

Randolph County, formed 1795 from St. Clair County, County Seat Chester (Taylor Street, 62263).

CENSUSES: 1818T, 1820RS, 1825S, 1830R, 1840RSP, 1845S, 1850RFMD, 1855S, 1860RFMD, 1865S, 1870RFM, 1880RFMD, 1900R, 1910R, 1920R.

FHL(FHC) RECORDS: atlas (1859/75), biography (1859/83/94, 1974/92), birth (1870-1915), Cahokia (1790-97, 1807-12), Catholic (1695-1735, 1741-1834), cemetery, county commissioner (1802-07, 1824-36), court (1737-1885), death (1877-1917), deed (1768-1851), directory (1859, 1871-72), early settler (1820/25), Evangelical Lutheran (1849-1972), genealogical compilations, German Evangelical (1839-1947), guardian (1844-49, 1869-79), history (1859/83, 1992), Kaskaskia (1714-1816), land (1722-1934), Lutheran (1846-1958), marks and brands (1849-84), marriage (1800-1927), Methodist (1885-1909), military land, naturalization (1833-1906), negro (1809-63), newspaper abstract (1814-32), obituary, orphans court (1804-09), Presbyterian (1821-1971), probate (1809-86), tax (1841, 1845-46), will (1800-1916).

IRAD-SIU RECORDS: board of supervisors (1809-58), circuit court (1790-1878), court (1722-1814), deed (1768-1851), Kaskaskia (1708-1816), marriage (1809-70), tax (1873-1943).

ILLINET PUBLISHED RECORDS: atlas (1875, 1900), biography (1859/75/94, 1936), birth (1792-1879), cemetery, commissioners court (1802-07), court (1815-78), death (1890-1900), directory (1859), early residents (1820/25), Hammes Collection (1720-1827), historical atlas, historical map, history (1859/83, 1936/68/95), marriage (1720-1870), naturalization, newspaper abstracts, original patent (1814-74), orphans court (1804-09), pioneers, probate, tax (1890).

ISGSQ ARTICLES: 2:144, 2:168, 6:32, 11:131, 11:187, 2:206, 14:110, 14:129, 15:139, 16:224, 19:26, 24:141.

COUNTY INVENTORY: birth (1877-), circuit court and court of common pleas (1768-), county court (1872-), county court of quarter sessions and county commissioners court (1801-), death (1877-), deed (1723-), estray (1877-), guardian (1850-), insanity (1893-), jury (1872-), Kaskaskia manuscripts, land entry (1815-), marks and brands (1849-73), marriage (1809-), militia (1861-63), mortgage (1865-), naturalization (1866-1903), negro (1804-62), physicians (1877-), probate (1796-), survey (1829-77), tax (1826-), will (1826-).

LIBRARY: Chester Public Library, 733 State St., Chester, IL 62233.

GENEALOGICAL SOCIETY: Randolph County Genealogical Society, Suite 306, 600 State Street, Chester, IL 62233; Marissa Genealogical and Historical Society, PO Box 47, Marissa, IL 62257.

GENEALOGICAL PUBLICATION: First society above publishes The Trails. Second society publishes Branching Out From St. Clair County.

80. Richland County

Richland County, formed 1841 from Clay and Lawrence Counties, County Seat Olney (62450).

CENSUSES: 1850RFMD, 1855S, 1860RFMD, 1865S, 1870RFM, 1880-RFMD, 1900R, 1910R, 1920R.

FHL(FHC) RECORDS: biography (1884/93, 1909), cemetery, early landowners, guardian (1855-1938), history (1884/93, 1909), Lutheran (1869-1959), marriage (1841-1915), newspaper abstracts, probate (1841-1917), will (1855-1938).

IRAD-EIU RECORDS: deed (1829-1975).

ILLINET PUBLISHED RECORDS: atlas (1875, 1900/01), biography (1884/93, 1909), cemetery, commissioners court (1841-52), history (1884, 1966/76), newspaper abstracts, Lutheran (1869-1959), obituaries, original landowners, residents (1884).

ISGSQ ARTICLES: 2:3, 14:102.

COUNTY INVENTORY: birth (1878-), board of supervisors (1859-), circuit court (1842-), Civil War veterans, coroner (1870-), county court (1872-), county commissioners (1841-59), death (1878-), deed (1841-), estray (1865-1910), guardian (1867-), insanity (1886-1900), jury (1872-), land entry (1836-), marriage (1840-), mortgage (1855-), naturalization

(1851-1906), physicians (1877-1906), probate (1841-), survey (1846-52, 1885-), tax (1855-), will (1867-).

LIBRARY: Olney Public Library, 400 West Main St., Olney, IL 62450.

GENEALOGICAL SOCIETY: Richland County Genealogical and Historical Society, PO Box 202, Olney, IL 62450.

GENEALOGICAL PUBLICATION: Above society publishes Footprints Past and Present. Also Newsletter.

---

81. Rock Island County

Rock Island County, formed 1831 from Jo Daviess County, organized in 1833, County Seat Rock Island (1404 Third Avenue 61201).

CENSUSES: 1840RSP, 1850RFMD, 1855S, 1860RFMD, 1865S, 1870RFM, 1880RFMD, 1900R, 1910R, 1920R.

FHL(FHC) RECORDS: atlas (1905), biography (1877/85/97, 1914), birth (1875-1978), cemetery, circuit court (1842-90), city directory (1855-59), county directory (1886), death (1878-1921), deed (1835-1927), genealogical compilations, history (1877/85/97, 1914), inventory (1939), marriage (1834-1925), naturalization (1851-1962), newspaper abstract, pioneers, Presbyterian (1874-1935), probate (1834-1983), will (1837-1934).

IRAD-WIU RECORDS: board of supervisors (1833-1958), circuit court (1833-90), guardian (1859-1925), insanity (1842-1947), land entry (1837-41), naturalization (1848-1962), probate (1834-1983), will (1837-1922).

ILLINET PUBLISHED RECORDS: atlas (1894, 1900/05), biography (1877/85/97, 1914), church directory, DAR, directory (1886, 1900), early settlers, genealogical research guide, historical guide, history (1877/85/97, 1914), inventory (1939), marriage (1833-1900), newspaper abstracts, pioneers, probate, Swedish immigration.

ISGSQ ARTICLES: 2:217, 4:1, 6:142, 6:195, 6:220, 7:31, 7:150, 8:194, 9:161, 9:195, 11:209, 11:221, 13:91, 18:140, 18:145, 19:169, 20:230, 21:10, 21:214, 21:215, 24:24, 24:142, 25:33.

COUNTY INVENTORY: adoption (1877-), birth (1877-), circuit court (1834-), county court (1872-), county commissioners and supervisors (1833-), death (1878-), deed (1835-), estray (1832-95), guardian (1850-), insanity (1852-), jail (1884-93), jury (1866-97), land entry (1834-), marks and brands (1833-73), marriage (1833-), military (1861-65), mortgage (1858-), naturalization (1854-1899), physicians (1877-), plat (1862-), police court (1866-69), poor (1879-), probate (1835-), survey (1854-77, 1883-), tax (1843-), veterans' discharge (1865-), will (1837-).

LIBRARY: Rock Island Public Library, 4th Avenue and 19th St., Rock Island, IL 61201; Swenson Swedish Immigration Research Center, Augustana College, Box 175, Rock Island, IL 61201.

GENEALOGICAL SOCIETY: Black Hawk Genealogical Society, PO Box 3912, Rock Island, IL 61204.

GENEALOGICAL PUBLICATION: Above society publishes Black Hawk Genealogical Society Quarterly.

82. St. Clair County

St. Clair County, formed 1790 as a county in the Northwest Territory, County Seat Belleville (10 Public Square, 62220).

CENSUSES: 1818T, 1820RS, 1830R, 1840RP, 1850RFMD, 1855S, 1860RFMD, 1865S, 1870RFM, 1880RFMD, 1900R, 1910R, 1920R.

FHL(FHC) RECORDS: atlas (1874, 1901), Baptist (1806-1909), biography (1881/92, 1907/92), birth (1843-70), Cahokia (1722-1812), cemetery, circuit court (1790-1857), city directory (1860, 1887-88), Civil War relief (1862-64), county court (1796-1818), death (1843-70), deed (1825-86), emancipation (1812-13, 1822-43), Evangelical (1836-1920), guardian (1796-1818), history (1881/92, 1907/78/83), inventory (1939), land (1799-1813), Lutheran (1848-1970), map (1893), marks and brands (1796-97, 1807-31), marriage (1791-1869), naturalization (1816-1905), newspaper abstracts, obituary, poor (1854-1955), United Church of Christ (1819-1993), will (1772-1964).

IRAD-SIU RECORDS: adoption (1858-1947), birth (1874-1923), board of supervisors (1798-1962), circuit court (1790-1913), Civil War relief (1862-64), court (1862-1963), deed (1786-1927), insanity (1876-1963), jail (1887-1955), jury (1859-71), land entry (1848-80), marriage (1807-1976), mortgage (1840-49, 1865-83), naturalization (1835-1903), plat (1817-1907), poor (1854-1955), probate (1817-1964), slaves (1805-32, 1846-63), survey (1829-74), tax (1842-61), territorial court (1796-1818), will (1794-1970).

ILLINET PUBLISHED RECORDS: atlas (1874, 1900/01), Baptist (1809-1909), biography (1881/92, 1907/14), birth and death (1843-70), cemetery, census substitute for 1890, city directory (1888), DAR, early settlers, genealogical compilations, Hammes Collection (1720-1827), historical atlas, history (1874/76/81, 1907/91), inventory (1939), land (1720-1827), Lutheran (1848-1959), marks and brands (1796-97, 1807-31), marriage (1791-1869), naturalization (1816-1905), probate (1772-1964), slave (1720-1863), tavern license (1808), United Church of Christ (1874-1979).

ISGSQ ARTICLES: 3:213, 4:91, 5:81, 5:145, 6:89, 9:159, 10:28, 10:225, 11:18, 11:88, 11:93, 11:131, 11:187, 13:31, 13:42, 13:155, 15:33, 15:139.

COUNTY INVENTORY: adoption (1858-), birth (1877-), board of supervisors (1885-), circuit court (1790-), county commissioners court (1837-84), county court (1872-), coroner (1866-), court of quarter sessions (1799-1801, 1805-08), death (1877-), deed (1790-), early court (1796-1817), estray (1858-1905), guardian (1821-), indentures (1821-), insanity (1864-), jury (1878-), land (1814-53), land entry (1867-), marriage (1807-), military pension (1862-64), mortgage (1790-), naturalization (1836-1906), physicians (1878-), plat (1854-), probate (1796-), soldiers discharge (1864-1903), tax (1840-), will (1772-).

LIBRARY: Belleville Public Library, 121 East Washington St., Belleville, IL 62220.

GENEALOGICAL SOCIETY: St. Clair County Genealogical Society, PO Box 431, Belleville, IL 62222; Marissa Genealogical and Historical Society, PO Box 47, Marissa, IL 62257.

GENEALOGICAL PUBLICATION: First society above publishes St. Clair County Genealogical Society Quarterly. Also Newsletter. Second society publishes Branching Out From St. Clair County.

83. Saline County

Saline County, formed 1847 from Gallatin County, County Seat Harrisburg (62946).

CENSUSES: 1850RFMD, 1855S, 1860-RFMD, 1865S, 1870RFM, 1880RFMD, 1900R, 1910R, 1920R.

FHL(FHC) RECORDS: Baptist (1854-1931), biography (1887), birth (1866-1939), cemetery, circuit court (1848-58), city directory (1898), death (1877-1939), deed (1847-1913), history (1887, 1947), inventory (1941), marriage (1847-1958), Methodist (1891-1904), mortuary, newspaper abstracts, obituary (1898-1906), poor (1847-88), probate (1847-1922), will (1847-1911), WPA.

IRAD-SIU RECORDS: deed (1848-72), land entry (1814-61), will (1847-1922).

ILLINET PUBLISHED RECORDS: atlas (1908), biography (1887), birth (1869-1915), cemetery, city directory (1898), DAR compilations, death (1877-1912), genealogical compilations, history (1887, 1934/47), inventory (1941), map (1875), marriage (1847-98), obituary, plat (1900), poor (1847-88), probate, will (1847-88), WPA.

ISGSQ ARTICLES: 10:44, 21:151.

COUNTY INVENTORY: birth (1878-), board of supervisors (1896-), circuit court (1848-), county court (1872-), county commissioners (1848-95), death (1878-), deed (1847-), divorce (1897-), guardian (1877-), insanity (1886-), jury (1859-72), land entry (1869-), marriage (1847-), mortgage (1847-), physicians (1878-), probate (1848-), tax (1853-), will (1847-).

LIBRARY: Mitchell Carnegie Library, 101 East Church St., Harrisburg, IL 62946.

GENEALOGICAL SOCIETY: Saline County Genealogical Society, PO Box 4, Harrisburg, IL 62946.

GENEALOGICAL PUBLICATION: Above society publishes The Shawnee.

84. Sangamon County

Sangamon County, formed 1821 from Madison and Bond Counties, County Seat Springfield (800 East Monroe St., 62701).

CENSUSES: 1830R, 1840RP, 1850-RFMD, 1855S, 1860RFMD, 1865S, 1870-RFM, 1880RFMD, 1900R, 1910R, 1920R.

FHL(FHC) RECORDS: atlas (1874/94, 1914), Baptist (1894-1945), biography (1876/77/81/91, 1912), birth (1860-78), board of supervisors (1821-76), cemetery, Christian Church (1866-1954), city directory (1855-56/66/74-75/77-78/87/91-92), Confederate deaths (1862-65), Congregational (1867-1947), court (1853-57), death (1868-1908), deed (1822-1917), divorce (1825-1899), early settlers (1876), gazetteer (1866), genealogical compilations, guardian (1821-1982), history (1881, 1904/12), inventory (1939), Jewish, land sales, marriage (1821-89), Methodist (1820-1981), military (1862-63), naturalization (1862-64, 1874-1906), obituary (1861-96), poll (1821-30), poor (1875-97), Presbyterian (1832-1969), probate (1821-1922), tax (1832-38), will (1821-1982), WPA.

IRAD-SSU RECORDS: circuit court (1821-1940), county court (1870-1950), deed (1822-1910), insanity (1878-1910), jury (1849-61), marriage (1821-1955), naturalizaton (1858-1906), probate (1821-1959), Springfield death (1886-1918), Springfield jail (1894-1967), tax (1827-38), town lots (1833-67).

ILLINET PUBLISHED RECORDS: atlas (1874, 1900), biography (1876/81/91, 1904/12), birth (1860-78), cemetery, city directory (1855/66), county directory (1887/89), deed (1822-32), divorce (1825-99), early land sales, gazetteer (1866, 1982), guardian (1825-1901), history (1866/76/81, 1904/12/21/35/64/74/76/83), internal revenue assessments (1862-66), inventory (1939), map (1858/99, 1901), marriage (1821-70, 1879-89), Methodist (1836-1936), military (1862-63), naturalization (1862-64), newspaper abstracts, obituary (1861-96), plat (1894), poor (1875-88), Presbyterian, probate (1821-1907), Revolutionary veteran burials, tax (1835), voter (1831-34/36),

ISGSQ ARTICLES: 1(4):19, 2:18, 2:20, 2:210, 4:98, 4:237, 5:95, 7:27, 7:123, 7:179, 8:63, 9:92, 11:41, 12:137, 13:9, 13:89, 13:219, 14:74, 14:148, 15:19, 15:257, 19:39, 22:28, 22:77, 22:87, 23:161, 24:2, 24:92, 24:142, 25:71.

COUNTY INVENTORY: apprentice (1834-64), birth (1877-), board of supervisors (1887-), circuit court (1821-), coroner (1863-88), county court (1872-), county commissioners (1821-87), death (1877-), deed (1822-), estray (1827-), guardian (1821-), insanity (1851-), jury (1840-), land entry (1823-39, 1885-), marriage (1821-), militia (1861-) mortgage (1855-), naturalization (1840-1906), physicians (1877-), poll (1821-91), plat book (1894), probate (1821-), soldiers' discharge (1865-92), survey (1841-), tax (1829-), will (1850-).

LIBRARY: ISHL, Lincoln Library, Springfield Public Library, 326 South Seventh St., Springfield, IL 62701.

GENEALOGICAL SOCIETY: IL State Genealogical Society, PO Box 10195, Springfield, IL 62791; Sangamon County Genealogical Society, PO Box 1829, Springfield, IL 62705.

GENEALOGICAL PUBLICATION: The first society above publishes the IL State Genealogical Society Journal.

85. Schuyler County

Schuyler County, formed 1825 from Pike and Fulton Counties, County Seat Rushville (62681).

CENSUSES: 1830R, 1840RSP, 1850-RFMD, 1855S, 1860RFMD, 1865S, 1870RFM, 1880RFMD, 1900R, 1910R, 1920R.

FHL(FHC) RECORDS: atlas (1872), board of supervisors (1856-1942), biography (1892, 1908), birth (1877-1979), cemetery, circuit court (1821-1940), death (1877-1923), early settler, guardian (1869-1900), history (1908/83/85) insanity (1867-1921), jail (1872-94), land grant (1817-48), marks and brands (1825-84), marriage (1825-1943), Methodist (1854-98), militia (1861), naturalization (1828-93), newspaper abstract, poor (1855-1921), probate (1827-1926), tax (1838), will (1827-1926).

IRAD-WIU RECORDS: board of supervisors (1825-1972), estray (1845-60), jail (1872-86), jury (1872-94), marks and brands (1826-1974), militia (1861), naturalization (1828-80), physician (11877-1903), poor (1855-1921), tax (1833-60).

ILLINET PUBLISHED RECORDS: atlas (1872, 1900), biography (1882/92, 1908), cemetery, genealogical compilations, history (1876/82/92, 1908/83), insanity (1867-1921), naturalization, plat (1892), probate (1827-87).

ISGSQ ARTICLES: 1(3):14, 2:7, 13:105, 13:106, 13:201, 13:203, 23:23, 23:91.

COUNTY INVENTORY: birth (1878-), circuit court (1825-), county court (1872-), county commissioners and board of supervisors (1825-), death (1878-), deed (1826-), ear marks (1826-73), estray (1827-92), guardian (1857-), insanity (1871-), jury (1853-63, 1876-), land entry (1817-), marriage (1825-), militia (1861-62), naturalization (1839-1902), physicians (1878-), probate (1850-), survey (1870-76), soldiers' discharge (1865), tax (1835-), will (1827-).

LIBRARY: Rushville Public Library, 104 North Monroe St., Rushville, IL 62681.

GENEALOGICAL SOCIETY: Schuyler-Brown Genealogical Society, 200 South Congress St., Rushville, IL 62681.

GENEALOGICAL PUBLICATION: Above society publishes the Schuyler-Brown Genealogical Society Newsletter.

86. Scott County

Scott County, formed 1839 from Morgan County, County Seat Winchester (62694).

CENSUSES: 1840RP, 1850RFMD, 1855S, 1860RFMD, 1865S, 1870RFM, 1880RFMD, 1900R, 1910R, 1920R.

FHL(FHC) RECORDS: atlas (1873), biography (1889), birth (1840-66, 1880-1929), cemetery, death (1841-66, 1877-1903), deed (1839-1901), guardian (1839-1940), history (1889, 1973), inventory (1938), marriage (1839-1915), naturalization (1859-1906), original land sales (1823-80), Presbyterian (1891-1900), probate (1852-1924), soldiers' discharge (1865-1935), will (1835-1936), WPA.

IRAD-SSU RECORDS: board of supervisors (1839-1980), deed (1839-74), marriage (1867-1927), naturalization (1864-1903), tax (1843-1954).

ILLINET PUBLISHED RECORDS: atlas (1873, 1900/03), biography (1889), cemetery, history (1873/76/89, 1976), inventory (1938), marriage (1839-1915), tax (1836).

ISGSQ ARTICLES: 3:155, 22:77, 24:2, 24:102.

COUNTY INVENTORY: birth (1878-), circuit court (1839-), county court (1872-), county commissioners (1839-), death (1878-), deed (1839-), guardian (1839-66), insanity (1878-), land entry (1839-), marriage (1839-), mortgage (1839-), probate (1839-), soldiers discharge (1865-86), tax (1843-), will (1835-).

LIBRARY: Winchester Public Library, 215 North Main St., Winchester, IL 62694.

GENEALOGICAL SOCIETY: Jacksonville Area Genealogical Society, PO Box 21, Jacksonville, IL 62650.

GENEALOGICAL PUBLICATION: Above society publishes Jacksonville Illinois Genealogical Journal.

87. Shelby County

Shelby County, formed 1827 from Fayette County, County Seat Shelbyville (62565), fire in 1894.

CENSUSES: 1830R, 1840RP, 1850-RFMD, 1855S, 1860RFMD, 1865S, 1870RFM, 1880RFMD, 1900R, 1910R, 1920R.

FHL(FHC) RECORDS: atlas (1875/95, 1914), biography (1881/91, 1910/69/71/84/86), birth (1848-1915), cemetery, Christian Church (1867-1941), death (1877-1917), deed (1827-1926), genealogical compilations, guardian (1857-69), history (1881, 1910/73), inventory (1940), Lutheran (1870-1970), marriage (1827-78), Methodist (1829-1911), naturalization (1858-1906), plat (1875/95), probate (1828-1922), tax (1833-91), veterans burials, WPA.

IRAD-EIU RECORDS: birth (1848-1915), circuit court (1828-71), death (1878-1917), deed (1827-1926), marriage (1827-1922), mortgage (1857-91), naturalization (1858-1906), poor (1870-1942), probate (1839-1922), will (1870-1918).

ILLINET PUBLISHED RECORDS: atlas (1875/95, 1914), biography (1881/91, 1900/10/69), birth (1848-82), cemetery, genealogical compilations, history (1881, 1900/10), inventory (1940), marriage (1827-78), newspaper abstracts (1897-1930), obituary (1897-1930), poor, probate (1839-57), public land sales, veterans burials, tax (1854/57).

ISGSQ ARTICLES: 7:173, 10:217, 11:17, 13:61, 24:198, 25:93.

COUNTY INVENTORY: adoption (1886-), birth (1877-), board of supervisors and county commissioners (1833-), circuit court (1828-), county court (1872-), death (1877-), deed (1827-), guardian (1859-), insanity (1893-), land entry (1835-), marriage (1829-), mortgage (1857-), naturalization (1855-1906), physicians (1877-), probate (1839-), survey (1868-1909), tax (1853-59, 1867-), will (1867-).

LIBRARY: Shelbyville Free Public Library, 154 North Broadway St., Shelbyville, IL 62565.

GENEALOGICAL SOCIETY: Shelby County Historical and Genealogical Society, 151 South Washington St., Shelbyville, IL 62565.

GENEALOGICAL PUBLICATION: Above society publishes Shelby County Ancestors. Also Newsletter.

88. Stark County

Stark County, formed 1839 from Knox and Putnam Counties, County Seat Toulon (130 West Main St., 61483).

CENSUSES: 1840RSP, 1850RFMD, 1855S, 1860RFMD, 1865S, 1870RFM, 1880RFMD, 1900R, 1910R, 1920R.

FHL(FHC) RECORDS: atlas (1873), biography (1857/76/97), birth (1865-1901), cemetery, death (1877-1901), deed (1839-1984), genealogical compilations, guardian (1858-1912), history (1857/60/76), marriage (1839-1982), naturalization (1851-1906), obituary (1885-1900), poor (1868-1941), probate (1840-1911).

IRAD-WIU RECORDS: poor (1868-1941), tax (1849-1934).

ILLINET PUBLISHED RECORDS: atlas (1873, 1900/07), biography (1876/87/97), cemetery, historical geography, history (1860/76/87/97, 1905/55), map (1900), marriage (1839-66),

ISGSQ ARTICLES: 14:75, 20:90, 21:83, 21:138, 211:152, 23:218, 23:355, 24:26.

COUNTY INVENTORY: birth (1877-), board of supervisors and county commissioners (1839-), circuit court (1839-), county court (1872-), death (1878-), deed (1839-), estray (1839-66), guardian (1870-), insanity (1893-), land entry (1842-), marks and brands (1840-1901), marriage (1839-), mortgage (1839-), naturalization (1864-1903), physicians (1878-), probate (1840-), survey (1839-), tax (1841-), will (1883-).

LIBRARY: Toulon Public Library, 306 West Jefferson St., Toulon, IL 61483.

GENEALOGICAL SOCIETY: Stark County Genealogical Society, PO Box 83, Toulon, IL 61483.

89. Stephenson County

Stephenson County, formed 1837 from Winnebago and Jo Daviess Counties, County Seat Freeport (15 North Galena Avenue, 61032).

CENSUSES: 1840RP, 1850RFMD, 1855S, 1860RFMD, 1865S, 1870RFM, 1880RFMD, 1900R, 1910R, 1920R.

FHL(FHC) RECORDS: atlas (1871), biography (1880/88, 1900/83), Brethren, cemetery, history (1880/88, 1900/10/72/83), inventory (1938), newspaper abstracts, plat (1894), Presbyterian (1873-96), Reformed (1878-1916), Rockford city directory (1857-60, 1902-), WPA.

IRAD-NIU RECORDS: deed (1837-1962).

ILLINET PUBLISHED RECORDS: atlas (1871), biography (1880/88, 1900/10/83), Brethren, cemetery, genealogical compilations, history (1854/80/88, 1900/10/11/83), inventory (1938), map (1859, 1900), plat (1894, 1900).

ISGSQ ARTICLES: 2:151, 9:73.

COUNTY INVENTORY: birth (1878-), board of supervisors (1850-), circuit court (1839-), county court (1872-), county commissioners (1837-50), death (1878-), deed (1837-), estray (1839-1901), guardian (1858-), insanity (1893-), jury (1872-), land entry (1845-), marriage (1837-), militia (1861-63), mortgage (1846-), naturalization (1849-1906), physicians (1878-), plat (1869-), probate (1839-), soldiers discharge (1864-77), survey (1840-), tax (1839-), will (1849-).

LIBRARY: Freeport Public Library, 314 West Stephenson St., Freeport, IL 61032.

GENEALOGICAL SOCIETY: Stephenson County Genealogical Society, PO Box 514, Freeport. IL 61032.

GENEALOGICAL PUBLICATION: Above society publishes Stephenson County SWOGHEN.

90. Tazewell County

Tazewell County, formed 1827 from Peoria County, County Seat Pekin (Fourth and Court Sts., 61554).

CENSUSES: 1830R, 1840RSP, 1845S, 1850RFMD, 1855S, 1860RFMD, 1865S, 1870RFM, 1880RFMD, 1900R, 1910R, 1920R.

FHL(FHC) RECORDS: atlas (1864/86, 1910), board of supervisors (1874-1906), biography (1872/79/94), cemetery, coroner (1869-1964), death (1877-1916), deed (1827-1920), Evangelical United Brethren (1850-1950), genealogical compilations, guardian (1862-1926), history (1872/79/94, 1974), map (1864), marriage (1827-1916), naturalization (1839-1906), plat (1864), probate (1827-1923), soldiers discharge (1864-91), will (1830-1924).

IRAD-ISU RECORDS: board of supervisors (1827-1915), coroner (1869-1964), land entry (1829-71), military (1861-62), naturalization (1839-1906), will (1864-1949).

ILLINET PUBLISHED RECORDS: atlas (1873, 1900/10), biography (1879/94, 1905), cemetery, DAR, genealogical compilations, history 1879/94, 1905/16), internal revenue assessments (1862-66), land (1827-38), map (1864), marriage (1827-59), naturalization (1839-1909), obituary, plat (1891).

ISGSQ ARTICLES: 3:107, 4:73, 4:93, 5:123, 10:229, 11:32, 11:99, 12:72, 12:137, 13:104, 13:159, 14:19, 19:215, 21:144, 21:150, 22:86.

COUNTY INVENTORY: atlas (1903), birth (1877-), board of supervisors (1849-), circuit court (1827-), coroner (1892-), county court (1872-), county commissioners (1827-48), death (1877-), deed (1827-), ear marks (1827-1900), estray (1847-98), guardian (1827-), insanity (1870-), land entry (1829-), marriage (1827-), militia (1861-62, 1864), mortgage

(1835-), naturalization (1839-1906), physicians (1877-), plat (1834-), power of attorney (1847-), probate (1827-), soldiers discharge (1861-91), survey (1835-), tax (1844-), tract (1828-41), will (1830-).

LIBRARY: Pekin Public Library, 301 South Fourth St. Pekin, IL 61554.

GENEALOGICAL SOCIETY: Tazewell County Genealogical Society, PO Box 312, Pekin, IL 61555.

GENEALOGICAL PUBLICATION: Above society publishes Tazewell Genealogical Monthly.

91. Union County

Union County, formed 1818 from Johnson County, County Seat Jonesboro (PO Box H, 62952).

CENSUSES: 1818T, 1820RS, 1830R, 1840RSP, 1850RFMD, 1855S, 1860RFMD, 1865S, 1870RFM, 1880RFMD, 1900R, 1910R, 1920R.

FHL(FHC) RECORDS: atlas (1881), Baptist (1892-1914), biography (1871/83), birth (1851-1915), cemetery, circuit court (1818-48), death (1877-1915), deed (1818-90), genealogical compilations, guardian (1818-1918), history (1871/83, 1983), land entry (1816-1904), marriage (1818-1907), military (1862), naturalization (1860-1904), negro (1835-44), obituary, probate (1818-1965), Revolutionary veterans, soldiers discharge (1863-66).

IRAD-SIU RECORDS: birth (1862-1916), circuit court (1818-48), county court (1861-72), deed (1818-1968), land entry (1816-98), marriage (1818-1900), military (1862), naturalizaton (1860-1904), negro (1835-44), plat (1871-80), probate (1818-1965), tax (1839-70), soldiers discharge (1865), will (1856-91).

ILLINET PUBLISHED RECORDS: atlas (1881, 1900/08), biography (1883, 1983/87), birth, cemetery, court (1818-46), DAR, genealogical compilations, geography (1974), guardian (1818-1918), history (1883, 1941/54/ 83/87/95), marriage (1818-80), map, mortuary (1837-1941), obituary (1858-83).

ISGSQ ARTICLES: 2:218, 9:18, 14:200.

COUNTY INVENTORY: birth (1877-), circuit court (1818-), coroner (1874-95), county court (1872-), county commissioners (1818-), death (1877-), deed (1818-), estray (1831-84), guardian (1859-), insanity (1885-), jury (1872-), land entry (1817-95), marriage (1818-), mortgage (1860-), naturalization (1860-1903), negro (1835-44), physicians (1877-), plat (1839-), probate (1821-), soldiers discharge (1865-1909), survey (1885-), tax (1857-), will (1856-).

LIBRARY: Jonesboro Public Library, 62952.

GENEALOGICAL SOCIETY: Union County Genealogical and Historical Research Committee, 101 East Spring St., Anna, IL 62906.

92. Vermilion County

Vermilion County, formed 1826 from Clark and Edgar Counties, County Seat Danville (6 North Vermilion St., 61832).

CENSUSES: 1830R, 1840RSP, 1850-RFMD, 1855S, 1860RFMD, 1865S, 1870RFM, 1880RFMD, 1900R, 1910R, 1920R.

FHL(FHC) RECORDS: atlas (1875, 1907), Baptist (1829-1968), biography (1889, 1903/11/30), birth (1877-1919), cemetery, DAR, death (1877-1917), deed (1826-1928), early settler, Evangelical Lutheran (1896-1923), history (1879, 1903/11/30), inventory (1940), map (1850), marriage (1823-1900), Methodist (1861-1946), naturalization (1860-1903), Presbyterian (1823-1947), Quaker (1826-1970), veterans home (1866-1937), will (1826-1977), will (1826-1977), WPA.

IRAD-ISU RECORDS: marriage (1826-58).

ILLINET PUBLISHED RECORDS: atlas (1875/95, 1900/07/15), Baptist (1829-1968), biography (1879/89, 1903/11/30/69/75/83), cemetery, DAR, early settler, genealogical compilations, history (1879/89, 1903/11-/30/40/68/69/75/83), internal revenue assessment (1862-66), inventory (1940), map (1867), marriage (1826-62, 1883-87), Methodist (1823-1937), naturalization (1860-1906), newspaper abstracts (1858-1936), obituary, Pleasant Grove Church (1879-1968), soldiers discharge, tax, will, WPA.

ISGSQ ARTICLES: 2:70, 18:65, 18:193, 19:6, 19:215, 20:157, 20:212, 24:95, 25:33.

COUNTY INVENTORY: birth (1877-), circuit court (1826-), county court (1872-), county commissioners (1826-), death (1877-), deed (1827-), ear marks (1826-87), estray (1853-1911), guardian (1856-), insanity (1884-), jury (1861-), land entry (1838-), marriage (1826-), mortgage (1858-), naturalization (1838-1906), original land entry, physicians (1877-), plat (1871-1905), probate (1826-), soldiers discharge (1865-), tax (1829/33/34/35/37/39, 1851-), will (1827-).

LIBRARY: Danville Public Library, 307 North Vermilion St., Danville, IL 61832.

GENEALOGICAL SOCIETY: Illiana Genealogical and Historical Society, PO Box 207, Danville, IL 61834.

GENEALOGICAL PUBLICATION: Above society publishes Illiana Genealogist.

93. Wabash County

Wabash County, formed 1824 from Edwards County, County Seat Mount Carmel (Fourth and Market Sts., 62863). Fire in 1857 resulted in loss of most records.

CENSUSES: 1830R, 1840RP, 1850-RFMD, 1855S, 1860RFMD, 1865S, 1870RFM, 1880RFMD, 1900R, 1910R, 1920R.

FHL(FHC) RECORDS: biography (1883, 1993), cemetery, Christian Church (1819-60), deed (1865-1907), early settler, genealogical compilations, guardian (1883-1914), history (1883, 1993), newspaper abstract.

IRAD-EIU RECORDS: birth (1877-1984), death (1865-1907), marriage (1857-1928).

ILLINET PUBLISHED RECORDS: atlas (1900), biography (1883, 1911/93), cemetery, genealogical compilations, history (1883, 1911/77/93), map (1866).

ISGSQ ARTICLES: 2:82, 3:205, 13:134.

COUNTY INVENTORY: birth (1877-), circuit court (1857-), coroner (1883-), county court (1872-), county commissioners (1825-32, 1844-), death (1877-), deed (1856-), estray (1857-84), guardian (1868-), insanity (1875-), land entry (1860-), marriage (1857-), military bounty (1866-67), militia (1861-62), mortgage (1857-), naturalization (1860-97), original land entry (1814-55), physicians (1877-), plat (1837-), probate (1857-), sheriff (1866-), soldiers discharge (1866-83), tax (1857-), will (1857-).

LIBRARY: Mount Carmel Public Library, 727 Mulberry St., Mount Carmel, IL 62863.

94. Warren County

Warren County, formed 1825 from Pike, Schuyler, and Peoria Counties, not organized until 1830-31, County Seat Monmouth (61462).

CENSUSES: 1830R, 1840RP, 1850-RFMD, 1855S, 1860RFMD, 1865S, 1870RFM, 1880RFMD, 1900R, 1910R, 1920R.

FHL(FHC) RECORDS: atlas (1872/93), Baptist (1833-1983), biography (1877/86, 1903/27), birth (1877-1983), cemetery, Church of Christ (1831-58), Christian Church (1839-1986), commissioner's court (1830-37), DAR, death (1877-1901), deed (1830-1901), early settler, genealogical compilation, guardian (1831-1983), history (1877/86, 1903/27), insanity (1878-1929), jail (1869-1926), marriage (1831-1983), Methodist (1859-1967), militia (1861-62), mortgage (1855-82), mortuary (1884-1900), naturalization (1858-1943), obituary, poor (1860-1928),

Presbyterian (1831-1964), probate (1831-1983), tax (1855-56), United Brethren, will (1844-1940).

IRAD-WIU RECORDS: circuit court (1832-1950), county court (1859-1929), estray (1831-54), guardian (1859-1964), insanity (1878-1964), jail (1869-1940), jury (1872-1955), mortgage (1855-1964), police magistrate (1875-1922), probate (1849-1969), sheriff (1877-1922), tax (1839-1950).

ILLINET PUBLISHED RECORDS: atlas (1872, 1900/12), biography (1877/86, 1903), birth (1876-1915), bounty land, cemetery, Christian Church, court, DAR, death (1876-1915), early settler, genealogical compilations, plat (1893), history (1877/86, 1903), map, marriage (1829-1915), mortuary, naturalization (1859-1929), obituary, poor (1860-1978), will (1831-1940),

ISGSQ ARTICLES: 3:108, 7:152, 8:195, 10:219, 10:225, 12:137, 13:156, 15:13, 15:236, 15:252, 15:277, 18:129.

COUNTY INVENTORY: birth (1877-), board of supervisors (1864-), circuit court (1831-), county court (1849-), county commissioners (1830-64), death (1877-), deed (1830-), estray (1831-78), guardian (1859-), insanity (1873-), jury (1872-), land entry (1830-), marks and brands (1830-1902), marriage (1831-), military bounty (1861-67), militia (1861-62), mortgage (1844-), naturalization (1860-1906), physicians (1877-), power of attorney (1850-), probate (1830-), tax (1835, 1838-), tract (1830-), will (1849-).

LIBRARY: Warren County Library, 60 West Side Square, Monmouth, IL 61462.

GENEALOGICAL SOCIETY: Warren County Genealogical Society, PO Box 761, Monmouth, IL 61462.

GENEALOGICAL PUBLICATION: Above society publishes Prairie Pioneers. Also Newsletter.

95. Washington County

Washington County, formed 1818 from St. Clair County, County Seat Nashville (St. Louis St., 62263).

CENSUSES: 1818T, 1820RS, 1830R, 1840RP, 1850RFMD, 1855S, 1860RFMD, 1865S, 1870RFM, 1880RFMD, 1900R, 1910R, 1920R.

FHL(FHC) RECORDS: biography (1879/94), cemetery, early settler, genealogical compilations, history (1879/94), United Church of Christ (1842-1992).

IRAD-SIU RECORDS: city council (1869-1965).

ILLINET PUBLISHED RECORDS: atlas (1900/06), biography (1879/94, 1980), DAR, history (1879/94, 1968/80), land entry.

ISGSQ ARTICLES: 2:185, 8:1147, 9:143, 11:29, 11:30, 15:17.

COUNTY INVENTORY: birth (1877-), board of supervisors (1883-), circuit court (1818-), coroner (1877-1905), county court (1872-), county commissioners (1818-83), death (1877-), deed (1817-), estray (1874-1905), guardian (1856-), insanity (1879-), jury (1872-), land entry (1815-66, 1870-), marks and brands (1818-78), marriage (1832-), militia (1861-62), mortgage (1871-), naturalization (1865-1906), plat (1879-), probate (1818-), survey (1834-), tax (1853-), will (1867-).

LIBRARY: Nashville Public Library, 203 South Kaskasia St., Nashville, IL 62263.

GENEALOGICAL SOCIETY: Washington County Genealogical Society, Route 1, Nashville, IL 62263.

96. Wayne County

Wayne County, formed 1819 from Edwards County, County Seat Fairfield (PO Box 187, 62837). Fire in 1886 destroyed many records.

CENSUSES: 1820RS, 1830R, 1840RP, 1850RFMD, 1855S, 1860RFMD, 1865S, 1870RFM, 1880RFMD, 1900R, 1910R, 1920R.

FHL(FHC) RECORDS: Baptist (1853-1958), biography (1884), birth (1886-1903), cemetery, death (1886-1916), history (1884), marriage (1855-1916), newspaper abstract (1852-79), Presbyterian (1821-57), will (1861-1950).

IRAD-EIU RECORDS: coroner (1888-1960), Fairfield city (1867-1984), physician (1887-1936).

ILLINET PUBLISHED RECORDS: atlas (1881, 1900/10), Bible, biography (1884, 1903), birth (1886-1903), cemetery, DAR, death (1880-1916), history (1884, 1903), marriage (1880-85, 1896-1906), naturalization, newspaper abstracts (1876-79), obituary (1880-90), plat (1900/10), Presbyterian (1821-57), will (1861-1950).

ISGSQ ARTICLES: 2:143, 3:79, 8:211, 13:205, 19:218, 22:143, 23:225.

COUNTY INVENTORY: birth (1886-), board of supervisors (1886-), circuit court (1819-), county court (1886-), death (1886-), deed (1886-), guardian (1887-), insanity (1893-), land entry (1886-), marriage (1886-), mortgage (1886-), naturalization (1867-1903), physicians (1878-), plat (1886-), probate (1886-), tax (1886-), will (1886-).

LIBRARY: Fairfield Public Library, 300 SE Second St., Fairfield, IL 62837.

97. White County

White County, formed 1815/16 from Gallatin County, County Seat Carmi (PO Box 339, 62821).

CENSUSES: 1818T, 1820RS, 1830R, 1840RSP, 1850RFMD, 1855S, 1860RFMD, 1865S, 1870RFM, 1880RFMD, 1900R, 1910R, 1920R.

FHL(FHC) RECORDS: Antioch Church (1867-1916), Baptist (1820-1954), biography (1883), birth (1877-1916), cemetery, circuit court (1816-34, 1848-55), court (1818-88), DAR, death (1878-1915), deed (1816-86), genealogical compilations, German Evangelical (1856-1919), history (1883), Hopewell Church (1819-68), land grants (1814-54), marriage (1816-1930),Methodist(1881-1944),naturalization(1842-98),Presbyterian (1868-96), probate (1816-1969), will (1816-1916).

IRAD-SIU RECORDS: deed (1814-1970), naturalization (1860-98), will (1816-1914).

ILLINET PUBLISHED RECORDS: Antioch Church (1867-1916), atlas (1900/01), biography (1883), cemetery, court (1860-88), history (1883), land grants (1814-54), map (1871), marriage (1816-1915), probate (1818-76), will (1816-1916).

ISGSQ ARTICLES: 22:144, 23:24.

COUNTY INVENTORY: birth (1878-), board of supervisors (1872-), circuit court (1817-), county court (1872-), county commissioners (1816-72), death (1878-), deed (1816-), guardian (1873-), insanity (1881-), jury (1872-), land entry (1816-60), marriage (1816-), mortgage (1857-), naturalization (1860-98), negro (1816-59), physicians (1878-), probate (1816-), survey (1885-), tax (1837-), will (1816-).

LIBRARY: Carmi Public Library, 201 North Church St., Carmi, IL 62821.

HISTORICAL SOCIETY: White County Historical Society, PO Box 121, Carmi, IL 62821.

GENEALOGICAL SOCIETY: Genealogical Society of Southern IL, c/o John A. Logan College, Box 145, Route 2, Carterville, IL 62918.

GENEALOGICAL PUBLICATION: Above society publishes The Saga of Southern IL. Also Newsletter.

98. Whiteside County

Whiteside County, formed 1836 from Jo Daviess and Ogle Counties, not organized until 1839/40, County Seat Morrison (200 East Knox St., 61270).

CENSUSES: 1840RSP, 1850RFMD, 1855S, 1860RFMD, 1865S, 1870RFM, 1880RFMD, 1900R, 1910R, 1920R.

FHL(FHC) RECORDS: biography (1877/83, 1900/08), birth (1877-81), cemetery, chancery court (1855-86), coroner (1871-1908), DAR, genealogical compilations, history (1877/83, 1900/08), land patent (1839-55), marriage (1856-8126), military (1861-65), military bounty (1865), militia (1861-62), newspaper abstract (1882-1909), obituary (1856-1909), poor (1871-1905), probate (1839-1943), tax (1848-79, 1890).

IRAD-NIU RECORDS: coroner (1892-1908), jail (1872-86), land patent (1832-70), militia (1861-66), military bounty (1865-66), tax (1848-1966), will (1842-1922).

ILLINET PUBLISHED RECORDS: atlas (1872, 1900/12), biography (1877/85, 1900), birth (1856-81), cemetery, DAR, history (1877/85, 1900/68), map (1896, 1909), marriage (1856-82), naturalization, obituary (1856-82), plat (1896, 1909), tax (1890).

ISGSQ ARTICLES: 7:31, 7:164, 10:154, 11:33, 13:145, 21:35, 23:152, 25:96.

COUNTY INVENTORY: birth (1877-), circuit court (1841-), county court (1872-), county commissioners and supervisors (1839-), death (1877-), deed (1839-), guardian (1852-), insanity (1878-), land entry (1857-), land patent (1839-78), marriage (1839-), military (1861-65), naturalization (1844-1906), plat (1854-), probate (1842-), survey (1885-), tax (1849-), will (1846-).

LIBRARY: Odell Public Library, 202 East Lincoln Way, Morrison, IL 61270; Sterling Public Library, 102 West Fourth St., Sterling, IL 61081.

GENEALOGICAL SOCIETY: Whiteside County Genealogists, PO Box 145, Sterling, IL 61081.

99. Will County

Will County, formed 1836 from Cook and Iroquois Counties, County Seat Joliet (302 North Chicago St., 60431).

CENSUSES: 1840RP, 1850RFMD, 1855S, 1860RFMD, 1865S, 1870RFM, 1880RFMD, 1900R, 1910R, 1920R.

FHL(FHC) RECORDS: 1901), Baptist, biography (1878/84/90, 1900/07), Catholic (1838-51, 1893-1925), cemetery, directory (1859-60, 1872-), history (1878/84/90, 1900/07/28/73), Lutheran (1836-1906), map (1870), military.

IRAD-NIU RECORDS: circuit court (1836-1938), marriage (1836-1901), probate (1837-1901), will (1837-1905).

ILLINET PUBLISHED RECORDS: atlas (1873, 1909), biography (1878/84/90, 1900/07/28/69), cemetery, Civil War roster, directory (1859-60, 1872-), early settlers, gazetteer (1939), history (1878/84/90, 1900/07/28

/55/57/69/93), landowners (1842), map (1862/98, 1900), pioneers, plat (1893).

ISGSQ ARTICLES: 4:94, 6:23, 10:199, 13:35, 13:127, 15:85, 18:163, 22:129, 25:71, 25:96.

COUNTY INVENTORY: adoption (1893-), birth (1877-), board of supervisors (1850-), circuit court (1836-), coroner (1836-), county court (1872-), county commissioners (1836-50), death (1877-), deed (1836-), estray (1836-82), guardian (1849-), insanity (1872-), jury (1888-), land entry (1835-70), marriage (1836-), militia (1861-62), mortgage (1836-), naturalization (1854-1906), physicians (1877-), plat (1836-), poll (1836-93), probate (1836-), survey (1835-39, 1848-55), tax (1836-), war bounty (1867-), will (1837-).

LIBRARY: Joliet Public Library, 150 North Ottawa St., Joliet, IL 60431.

GENEALOGICAL SOCIETY: Fox Valley Genealogical Society, PO Box 5435, Naperville, IL 60467; Northern Will County Genealogical Society, 603 Derbyshire Lane, Bollingsbrook, IL 60439; South Suburban Genealogical and Historical Society, PO Box 96, South Holland, IL 60473; Will/Grundy Counties Genealogical Society, PO Box 24, Wilmington, IL 60481.

GENEALOGICAL PUBLICATION: Fox Valley Society publishes Fox Tales; South Suburban Society publishes Where the Trails Cross, and also Newsletter; Will/Grundy Counties Society publishes Will/Grundy Genealogical Society Quarterly, and also Newsletter.

100. Williamson County

Williamson County, formed 1839 from Franklin County, County Seat Marion (200 Jefferson St., 62959).

CENSUSES: 1840RP, 1850RFMD, 1855S, 1860RFMD, 1865S, 1870RFM, 1880RFMD, 1900R, 1910R, 1920R.

FHL(FHC) RECORDS: Baptist (1849-78), biography (1876/87), birth (1877-1966), cemetery, Christian Church (1892-97), city history (1972), death (1877-1915), deed (1823-1928), early settler, gazetteer (1939), genealogical compilations, guardian (1860-91), history (1876/87, 1905/39), marriage (1839-1916), naturalization (1865-1903), newspaper abstracts, original land entry (1814-60), probate (1850-1971), Shake Rag Church (1880-90), veterans' burials, will (1853-1919).

IRAD-SIU RECORDS: county court (1874-97), naturalization (1864-1906), tax (1883-99), will (1853-1919).

ILLINET PUBLISHED RECORDS: atlas (1900/05/08), Baptist (1800-1964), biography (1876/87, 1905), cemetery, early settler, gazetteer

(1939), genealogical compilations, history (1876/87, 1905/39/89), immigration, map (1839/75), marriage (1839-65), newspaper abstracts, pensioners, tax (1868).

ISGSQ ARTICLES: 4:94, 4:235, 8:130, 18:32.

COUNTY INVENTORY: birth (1877-), board of supervisors (1908-), circuit court (1840-), coroner (1881-1905), county court (1872-), county commissioners (1839-1908), death (1877-), deed (1839-), estray (1867-1905), guardian (1860-), insanity (1880-), jury (1872-), land entry (1869-74), marriage (1839-), militia (1861-), mortgage (1860-), naturalization (1880-96), physician (1877-), plat (1891-), probate (1840-), survey (1862-), tax (1857-), tract (1817-), will (1853-).

LIBRARY: Shawnee Library System, 511 Greenbriar Rd., Carterville, IL 62918; Marion Carnegie Library, 206 South Market St., Marion, IL 62959.

GENEALOGICAL SOCIETY: Genealogical Society of Southern IL, John A. Logan College, Box 145, Route 2, Carterville, IL 62918; Frankfort Area Genealogical Society, PO Box 427, West Frankfort, IL 62896.

GENEALOGICAL PUBLICATION: The first society above publishes the Saga of Southern IL, also Newsletter. The second society above publishes Facts and Findings.

101. Winnebago County

Winnebago County, formed 1836 from Jo Daviess and LaSalle Counties, County Seat Rockford (400 West State St., 61101).

CENSUSES: 1840RP, 1850RFMD, 1855S, 1860RFMD, 1865S, 1870RFM, 1880RFMD, 1900R, 1910R, 1920R.

FHL(FHC) RECORDS: atlas (1871/92, 1905), biography (1877/92, 1903/05/16/75/90), Cahokia land (1800-20), cemetery, city directory (1857/59-60, 1902-), early settler, gazetteer (1869), history (1872/92, 1900/03/0516/24/75/90), marriage (1836-66).

IRAD-NIU RECORDS: board of supervisors (1836-40), circuit court (1837-1922), court (1854-1958), deed (1836-91), insanity (1893-1943), jail (1869-1920), land entry (1845-1968), militia (1861-62), mortgage (1845-1918), power of attorney (1887-1909), probate (1854-1922), tax (1851), town plat (1863-88), will (1866-1919).

ILLINET PUBLISHED RECORDS: atlas (1871/86, 1900/05), biography (1877/92, 1905/16), Bible, birth (1877-1916), cemetery, DAR, death (1877-1939), early settlers, genealogical compilations, history (1877/92, 1905/16/75), landowners (1912), map (1859), marriage (1836-

1919), Methodist, mortuary (1878-1921), newspaper abstract (1851-99), obituary (1860-74), veterans' burial.

ISGSQ ARTICLES: 2:83, 4:103, 7:141, 8:198, 9:125, 10:156, 11:18, 11:29, 11:173, 11:219, 12:8, 14:92, 21:153, 25:96.

COUNTY INVENTORY: birth (1877-), board of supervisors (1849-), circuit court (1836-), coroner (1877-1901), county court (1854-), county commissioners (1836-49), death (1878-), deed (1836-), estray (1856-76), guardian (1838-), insanity (1876-), land entry (1836-), marriage (1837-), militia (1861-62), mortgage (1845-), naturalization (1840-1906), physicians (1877-), plat (1866-), probate (1841-), tax (1851-), will (1866-).

LIBRARY: Rockford Public Library, 215 North Wyman St., Rockford, IL 61101.

GENEALOGICAL SOCIETY: Kishwaukee Genealogists, PO Box 5503, Rockford, IL 61104; North Central IL Genealogical Society, PO Box 4635, Rockford, IL 61110; Winnebago/Boone Counties Genealogical Society, Box 10106, Rockford, IL 61131.

GENEALOGICAL PUBLICATION: North Central IL Genealogical Society publishes Twigs and Branches. The other two publish a Newsletter.

102. Woodford County

Woodford County, formed 1841 from McLean and Tazewell Counties, County Seat Eureka (PO Box 38, 61530).

CENSUSES: 1850RFMD, 1855S, 1860RFMD, 1865S, 1870RFM, 1880-RFMD, 1900R, 1910R, 1920R.

FHL(FHC) RECORDS: biography (1878/89, 1900/10), birth (1877-1915), cemetery, death (1877-1915), deed (1832-93), directory (1878), guardian (1845-1963), history (1877/78/89, 1900/10), marriage (1841-1902), military bounty land, naturalization (1855-1906), plat (1893), poor (1868-1957), Presbyterian, probate (1841-1963), soldiers' discharge (1863-1902), will (1869-1925).

IRAD-ISU RECORDS: board of supervisors (1841-1939), court (1841-1912), deed (1833-1928), estray (1841-1921), jail (1880-1914), jury (1857-61), militia (1861-63), physician (1877-1946), poor (1868-1957), probate (1842-47, 1870-1956), soldiers' discharge (1863-65), tax (1846-98), voter (1865-90), will (1869-1964).

ILLINET PUBLISHED RECORDS: atlas (1873/75, 1900/12), biography (1878/89, 1900/04/10), cemetery, genealogical compilations, history (1878/89, 1900/04/10/68), internal revenue assessments (1862-66), marriage (1841-70), plat (1893).

ISGSQ ARTICLES: 3:153, 4:99, 5:168, 8:122, 9:145, 15:250, 19:215, 24:69, 24:162, 24:225, 25:33, 25:38.

COUNTY INVENTORY: birth (1878-), circuit court (1841-), county court (1872-), county commissioners and board of supervisors (1841-), death (1878-), deed (1841-), estray (1842-), guardian (1867-), insanity (1872-), land entry (1841-), marriage (1862-), militia (1861-63), mortgage (1841-), naturalization (1860-1904), physicians (1878-), plat (1879-), poll (1841-), probate (1841-), soldiers discharge (1865-70), survey (1885-), tax (1843-), will (1870-).

LIBRARY: Eureka Public Library District, 202 South Main St., Eureka, IL 61530.

GENEALOGICAL SOCIETY: Peoria Genealogical Society, PO Box 1489, Peoria, IL 61655.

GENEALOGICAL PUBLICATION: Above society publishes Prairie Roots. Also Newsletter.

List of Abbreviations

CCB	=	Cook County Building, Chicago
CCH	=	Chicago City Hall
CH	=	Court House(s)
CHSL	=	Chicago Historical Society Library
CJCLDS	=	Church of Jesus Christ of Latter Day Saints
CPL	=	Chicago Public Library
D	=	Federal mortality censuses
DC	=	Daley Center, Chicago
E	=	Early inhabitant lists
F	=	Federal Farm and Ranch censuses
FHC	=	Family History Center(s), branches of FHL
FHL	=	Family History Library, Salt Lake City, UT
IL	=	Illinois
IRAD	=	IL Regional Archives Repository(ies)
IRAD-EIU	=	IRAD at Eastern IL University, Charleston
IRAD-ISU	=	IRAD at IL State University, Normal
IRAD-NIU	=	IRAD at Northern IL University, DeKalb
IRAD-SIU	=	IRAD at Southern IL University, Carbondale
IRAD-SSU	=	IRAD at Sangamon State University, Springfield
IRAD-UNI	=	IRAD at Northeastern IL University, Chicago
IRAD-WIU	=	IRAD at Western IL University, Macomb
ISA	=	IL State Archives, Springfield
ISGS	=	IL State Genealogical Society, Springfield
ISGSQ	=	IL State Genealogical Society Quarterly
ISHL	=	IL State Historical Library, Springfield
ISHS	=	IL State Historical Society, Springfield
ISL	=	IL State Library, Springfield
LL	=	Local Library(ies)
LR	=	Local Repositories
M	=	Federal Manufactures censuses
NA	=	National Archives, Washington, DC
NAGL	=	National Archives - Great Lakes Region, Chicago
NARC	=	National Archives Regional Centers
NL	=	Newberry Library, Chicago
P	=	1840 Revolutionary War pension census
R	=	Regular federal censuses
RL	=	Regional Library(ies)
S	=	IL State censuses
T	=	IN and IL Territorial censuses

Books by George K. Schweitzer

CIVIL WAR GENEALOGY. A 93-paged book of 316 sources for tracing your Civil War ancestor. Chapters include I: The Civil War, II: The Archives, III: National Publications, IV: State Publications, V: Local Sources, VI: Military Unit Histories, VII: Civil War Events.

GEORGIA GENEALOGICAL RESEARCH. A 238-paged book containing 1303 sources for tracing your GA ancestor along with detailed instructions. Chapters include I: GA Background, II: Types of Records, III: Record Locations, IV: Research Procedure and County Listings (detailed listing of records available for each of the 159 GA counties).

HANDBOOK OF GENEALOGICAL SOURCES. A 252-paged book describing all major and many minor sources (132 in all) of genealogical information with precise and detailed instructions for obtaining data on your ancestors from them. Book contains 132 sections.

ILLINOIS GENEALOGICAL RESEARCH. A 291-paged book containing 1544 sources for tracing your IL ancestor along with detailed instructions. Chapters include I: IL Background, II: Types of Records, III: Record Locations, IV: Research Procedure and Chicago/Cook County Records (detailed listings of records available for Chicago and Cook County), V: Records for Other Counties (detailed listings of records available for each of the 101 other IL counties).

INDIANA GENEALOGICAL RESEARCH. A 189-paged book containing 1044 sources for tracing your IN ancestor along with detailed instructions. Chapters include I: IN Background, II: Types of Records, III: Record Locations, IV: Research Procedure and County Listings (detailed listing of records available for each of the 92 IN counties).

KENTUCKY GENEALOGICAL RESEARCH. A 167-paged book containing 1191 sources for tracing your KY ancestor along with detailed instructions. Chapters include I: KY Background, II: Types of Records, III: Record Locations, IV: Research Procedure and County Listings (detailed listing of records available for each of the 120 KY counties).

MARYLAND GENEALOGICAL RESEARCH. A 208-paged book containing 1176 sources for tracing your MD ancestor along with detailed instructions. Chapters include I: MD Background, II: Types of Records, III: Record Locations, IV: Research Procedure and County Listings (detailed listing of records available for each of the 23 MD counties and for Baltimore City).

MASSACHUSETTS GENEALOGICAL RESEARCH. A 279-paged book containing 1709 sources for tracing your MA ancestor along with detailed instructions. Chapters include I: MA Background, II: Types of Records, III: Record Locations, IV: Research Procedure and County-Town-City Listings (detailed listing of records available for each of the 14 MA counties and the 351 cities-towns).

MISSOURI GENEALOGICAL RESEARCH. Available in November 1997.

NEW YORK GENEALOGICAL RESEARCH. A 252-paged book containing 1426 sources for tracing your NY ancestor along with detailed instructions. Chapters include I: NY Background, II: Types of Records, III: Record Locations, IV: Research Procedure and NY City Record Listings (detailed listing of records available for the 5 counties of NY City), V: Record Listings for Other Counties (detailed listing of records available for each of the other 57 NY counties).

NORTH CAROLINA GENEALOGICAL RESEARCH. A 169-paged book containing 1233 sources for tracing your NC ancestor along with detailed instructions. Chapters include I: NC Background, II: Types of Records, III: Record Locations, IV: Research Procedure and County Listings (detailed listing of records available for each of the 100 NC counties).

OHIO GENEALOGICAL RESEARCH. A 212-paged book containing 1241 sources for tracing your OH ancestor along with detailed instructions. Chapters include I: OH Background, II: Types of Records, III: Record Locations, IV: Research Procedure and County Listings (detailed listing of records available for each of the 100 OH counties).

PENNSYLVANIA GENEALOGICAL RESEARCH. A 201-paged book containing 1309 sources for tracing your PA ancestor along with detailed instructions. Chapters include I: PA Background, II: Types of Records, III: Record Locations, IV: Research Procedure and County Listings (detailed listing of records available for each of the 67 PA counties).

REVOLUTIONARY WAR GENEALOGY. A 110-paged book containing 407 sources for tracing your Revolutionary War ancestor. Chapters include I: Revolutionary War History, II: The Archives, III: National Publications, IV: State Publications, V: Local Sources, VI: Military Unit Histories, VII: Sites and Museums.

SOUTH CAROLINA GENEALOGICAL RESEARCH. A 170-paged book containing 1107 sources for tracing your SC ancestor along with detailed instructions. Chapters include I: SC Background, II: Types of Records, III: Record Locations, IV: Research Procedure and County Listings (detailed listing of records available for each of the 47 SC counties and districts).

TENNESSEE GENEALOGICAL RESEARCH. A 132-paged book containing 1073 sources for tracing your TN ancestor along with detailed instructions. Chapters include I: TN Background, II: Types of Records, III: Record Locations, IV: Research Procedure and County Listings (detailed listing of records available for each of the 96 TN counties).

VIRGINIA GENEALOGICAL RESEARCH. A 216-paged book containing 1273 sources for tracing your VA ancestor along with detailed instructions. Chapters include I: VA Background, II: Types of Records, III: Record Locations, IV: Research Procedure and County Listings (detailed listing of records available for each of the 100 VA counties and 41 major cities).

WAR OF 1812 GENEALOGY. A 75-paged book of 289 sources for tracing your War of 1812 ancestor. Chapters include I: History of the War, II: Service Records, III: Bounty Land and Pension Records, IV: National and State Publications, V: Local Sources, VI: Military Unit Histories, VII: Sites and Events.

All of the above books may be ordered from Dr. George K. Schweitzer at the address given on the title page. Or send a long SASE for a FREE descriptive leaflet on any of the books.